Explainable Artificial Intelligence (XAI) for Next Generation Cybersecurity

Other related titles:

You may also like

- PBPC068 | Abdel-Basset | Explainable Artificial Intelligence for Trustworthy Internet of Things | 2024
- PBPC062 | Raj | Explainable Artificial Intelligence (XAI): Tools technologies, and applications | 2023
- PBSE020 | Abd El-Latif | Artificial Intelligence for Biometrics and Cybersecurity | 2023
- PBPC066 | Srivastava | Federated Learning for Multimedia Data Processing and Security in Industry 5.0 | 2024

We also publish a wide range of books on the following topics:
Computing and Networks
Control, Robotics and Sensors
Electrical Regulations
Electromagnetics and Radar
Energy Engineering
Healthcare Technologies
History and Management of Technology
IET Codes and Guidance
Materials, Circuits and Devices
Model Forms
Nanomaterials and Nanotechnologies
a) Optics, Photonics and Lasers
Production, Design and Manufacturing
Security
Telecommunications
Transportation

All books are available in print via https://shop.theiet.org or as eBooks via our Digital Library https://digital-library.theiet.org.

IET SECURITY SERIES 027

Explainable Artificial Intelligence (XAI) for Next Generation Cybersecurity

Concepts, challenges and applications

Edited by
Farhan Ullah, Gautam Srivastava and Awais Ahmad

The Institution of Engineering and Technology

About the IET

This book is published by the Institution of Engineering and Technology (The IET).

We inspire, inform and influence the global engineering community to engineer a better world. As a diverse home across engineering and technology, we share knowledge that helps make better sense of the world, to accelerate innovation and solve the global challenges that matter.

The IET is a not-for-profit organisation. The surplus we make from our books is used to support activities and products for the engineering community and promote the positive role of science, engineering and technology in the world. This includes education resources and outreach, scholarships and awards, events and courses, publications, professional development and mentoring, and advocacy to governments.

To discover more about the IET please visit https://www.theiet.org/.

About IET books

The IET publishes books across many engineering and technology disciplines. Our authors and editors offer fresh perspectives from universities and industry. Within our subject areas, we have several book series steered by editorial boards made up of leading subject experts.

We peer review each book at the proposal stage to ensure the quality and relevance of our publications.

Get involved

If you are interested in becoming an author, editor, series advisor, or peer reviewer please visit https://www.theiet.org/publishing/publishing-with-iet-books/ or contact author_support@theiet.org.

Discovering our electronic content

All of our books are available online via the IET's Digital Library. Our Digital Library is the home of technical documents, eBooks, conference publications, real-life case studies and journal articles. To find out more, please visit https://digital-library.theiet.org.

In collaboration with the United Nations and the International Publishers Association, the IET is a Signatory member of the SDG Publishers Compact. The Compact aims to accelerate progress to achieve the Sustainable Development Goals (SDGs) by 2030. Signatories aspire to develop sustainable practices and act as champions of the SDGs during the Decade of Action (2020–30), publishing books and journals that will help inform, develop, and inspire action in that direction.

In line with our sustainable goals, our UK printing partner has FSC accreditation, which is reducing our environmental impact to the planet. We use a print-on-demand model to further reduce our carbon footprint.

Published by The Institution of Engineering and Technology, London, United Kingdom

The Institution of Engineering and Technology (the "**Publisher**") is registered as a Charity in England & Wales (no. 211014) and Scotland (no. SC038698).

First published 2025

The Institution of Engineering and Technology
Futures Place,
Kings Way,
Stevenage,
Herts, SG1 2UA
United Kingdom

www.theiet.org

British Library Cataloguing in Publication Data
A catalogue record for this product is available from the British Library

ISBN 978-1-83724-031-9 (hardback)
ISBN 978-1-83724-032-6 (PDF)

Typeset in India by MPS Limited

Cover image: Just_Super/E+ via Getty Images

Gautam Srivastava dedicates this book to Mom, Dad, Andrea, Arjun, and Krishna

Contents

Preface

Explainable AI (XAI) has the potential to be a paradigm shift in the next generation of artificial intelligence (AI) systems. As AI technologies progress and influence more facets of our lives, the requirement for openness and interpretability becomes increasingly important. XAI strives to make AI algorithms and methods for decision-making understandable to people, tackling trust, justice, and accountability challenges. It helps people comprehend why AI systems make certain decisions, reduce biases, and make it easier to comply with rules. XAI is predicted to emerge in the future AI era by improving model disclosure, producing intrinsically interpretable deep learning approaches, offering real-time rationales and promoting legitimate AI practice. These advances in explainability are critical for developing trust, enabling interaction between humans and AI, and assuring sustainable and legal AI deployment across various industries. They not only enable users to make intelligent choices based on AI recommendations, but they also support continuing study into AI's legal and open use, assisting in the development of a more ethically sound AI ecosystem in the future.

In the dynamic domain of cybersecurity, a multitude of complex challenges persist, necessitating constant surveillance and advancement. Cybersecurity apps safeguard data, identify fraud, protect vital infrastructure, and assure confidentiality for businesses ranging from banking to healthcare to the state. They also protect transactions, Internet of Things (IoT) devices, and information. The protection of assets and information is crucial in the increasingly digital world. The ever-changing threat landscape includes powerful adversaries such as malicious actors and hackers funded by states who are always refining their strategies. The advent of zero-day exploits, as well as the disrupting surge of ransomware attacks, emphasizes the critical nature of the problem. As the IoT evolves and supply chains become more complicated, novel avenues for attack arise, challenging defense measures. The persistent susceptibility of the human component, as demonstrated by successful phishing attempts, emphasizes the importance of continued education and awareness efforts. Advanced persistent threats, which are frequently organized by nation-states, demand ongoing monitoring and adaptive responses. Compliance with severe data privacy standards, such as General Data Protection Regulation and California Consumer Privacy Act, adds to the complexity of handling data ecosystems. These issues are exacerbated by insider risks, cloud security, and the global nature of cyberattacks. Considering the dynamic nature of the cybersecurity battlefront, a holistic approach must include preemptive threat intelligence, staff training, effective security tools, regular upgrades, and global collaboration.

Incorporating XAI into cybersecurity increases threat detection and decision-making. XAI explains security alerts, reducing false positives and enabling faster incident response. Transparency and accountability for AI-driven security practices help with compliance, user awareness, and trust-building. XAI learns from new data to optimize resource utilization and adapt to emerging threats, making it effective in the modern complex cybersecurity landscape. The objective of this book is to provide insight on the applications of XAI to solve some of the issues of data processing and vulnerabilities in cybersecurity applications. This collection of information also provides a detailed discussion on how XAI-based cybersecurity algorithms can be used to handle dynamic nature of cyberattacks, preserve privacy, optimize computational and communication costs, etc. The chapters provide both practical and theoretical knowledge for global researchers and practitioners who are working in the fields of XAI, cybersecurity applications, and machine and deep learning. Finally, this book is meant to give useful insights and act as a reference book for advanced students and researchers in academia and industry.

The chapters in this book include XAI in cybersecurity applications such as malware analysis, trustworthy XAI, IoT, healthcare, big data, large language models, vehicular networks, federated learning, blockchain, reinforcement learning, and threat detection. Moreover, some emphasis is given in the book on the ethical and social challenges that exist in the next generation of AI.

Chapter 1 gives an overview of XAI in cybersecurity looking at it from the lens of past, present, and future, while Chapter 2 bridges the gap with XAI in threat detection.

Chapter 3 looks into XAI in threat detection. Chapter 4 integrates XAI with blockchain to tackle cybersecurity issues. Chapter 5 leverages blockchain and AI to combat issues in threat mitigation.

Chapter 6 describes deep reinforcement learning for cybersecurity, while Chapter 7 summarizes trustworthy XAI. Chapter 8 investigates malware analysis in the IoT.

Chapter 9 uses game theory and AI for tackling threat detection in IoT. Chapter 10 tackles security issues in network traffic in IoT, while Chapter 11 looks at vehicular communication in vehicular ad hoc networks and how large language models can be used to ensure reliable networks.

Shifting focus to learning systems, Chapter 12 looks at using a federated learning system in digital healthcare. Focusing on IoT, Chapter 13 gives an overview of IoT guardian meant to mitigate reliability issues in the Internet of Medical Things. Chapters 14 and 15 dive into the ethical and social challenges that exist in the next generation of AI.

The editors would like to thank Olivia Wilkins, Brittany Insull, and Valerie Moliere as well as the rest of the IET staff for their editorial assistance and support in producing this important scientific work. Without this collective effort, this book would not have been possible to be completed.

About the editors

Farhan Ullah is associate research professor at the Cybersecurity Center of Prince Mohammad Bin Fahd University, Saudi Arabia. He has previously held positions as associate professor at Northwestern Polytechnical University, China, visiting research fellow at the University of Camerino, Italy, and lecturer at COMSATS University Islamabad, Pakistan. He has received various awards for his research and teaching excellence. He has also been invited as a keynote speaker and has delivered courses at international conferences and summer schools. He had the privilege of contributing as a guest editor and engaging in editorial work for renowned journals such as the *IEEE Journal of Biomedical and Health Informatics* and *KSII Transactions*, among others. He has supervised several undergraduate and graduate students and served as a foreign thesis examiner for PhD theses. His work has been published in reputable journals, including those published by IEEE, Springer, Elsevier, and Wiley. His primary research areas include cybersecurity, malware analysis, data science, deep learning, and explainable AI. He received his PhD in computer science from Sichuan University, China.

Gautam Srivastava is full professor in the Department of Mathematics and Computer Science at Brandon University, Canada. He is active in the research fields of AI, cybersecurity, data mining, and big data. He has extensive guest editorial experience, including *IEEE Transactions on Fuzzy Systems, IEEE Transactions on Industrial Informatics*, *Computer Standards and Interfaces*, and *Applied Stochastic Modeling and Business*. He has published 400 papers in high-impact conferences and journals. His research is funded by NSERC and MITACS, and he sits on the Discovery Grant Evaluation Group for Computer Science for NSERC. He currently has active research projects with other academics in Taiwan, Singapore, Canada, and the USA. He is a senior member of the IEEE. He is an editor for top tiered journals including *Information Sciences*, *IEEE TII*, *IEEE TCSS*, *IEEE IoT Journal*, and *Expert Systems*. He holds a PhD degree in computer science from the University of Victoria British Columbia, Canada.

Awais Ahmad is assistant professor in the Information Systems Department, College of Computer and Information Sciences, Imam Mohammad Ibn Saud Islamic University, Riyadh, Saudi Arabia. He was previously a researcher in INTEL-NTU, National Taiwan University, Taiwan, where he was working on the Wukong Project (Smart Home). His research interests include cybersecurity, deep learning, machine learning, artificial intelligence, denoising and demosaicking, big data analytics, and Internet of Things. He has published 170+ international papers in journals including *IEEE Transactions*, *IEEE Magazines* and *ACM Transactions*, and at conference such as IEEE GLOBECOM, IEEE INFOCOM, IEEE LCN, and IEEE ICC. He is serving as a guest editor for several journals including *Future Generation Computer Systems*, *Sustainable City and Societies*, *Computational Intelligence and Complexity*, *Multimedia Tools and Applications*, *IEEE Access*, and *Real-Time Image Processing Journal* (Springer). He received his PhD degree in computer science and engineering from Kyungpook National University, Daegu, Korea.

Chapter 1

The present, past, and future aspects of XAI in cybersecurity

Muqadsa Jabeen[1], *Muhammad Ibrar*[1] *and Muhammad Saeed*[1]

Abstract

In the current era of cybersecurity, deep learning (DL), machine learning (ML), and artificial intelligence (AI) algorithms are widely used in various applications, including Android malware detection and web security. Moreover, ML algorithms continue to play a key role in improving cybersecurity solutions. However, they face significant challenges in some DL areas, such as computer vision and natural language processing, particularly in their inability to predict outcomes and make decisions accurately. These challenges underscore the importance of explainable artificial intelligence (XAI). XAI algorithms aim to support the interpretation of human-generated patterns, enabling humans to understand the reasoning behind automated results. Therefore, XAI algorithms are crucial in cybersecurity, as they can assist security professionals overwhelmed by numerous security alerts—many of which are false positives—in identifying potential threats and reducing alert fatigue. This chapter focuses on XAI's current, past, and future roles in cybersecurity. It is a unique and vital area for protecting systems, networks, and software from various attacks. The chapter begins with an overview of cybersecurity architectures and threat types, followed by a discussion of traditional AI techniques and their limitations, which provide a foundation for coherent XAI approaches. It also explores the applications of XAI across several research domains and industries and concludes with key findings to guide future research on XAI in cybersecurity. This study highlights the importance of XAI in mitigating emerging cyber threats.

1.1 Introduction

Explainable artificial intelligence (XAI) is a subfield of artificial intelligence (AI) that focuses on developing AI systems whose decisions and processes are

[1]Department of Computer Science, The University of Faisalabad, Pakistan

transparent, interpretable, and understandable by humans. XAI is one of the biggest challenges in modern AI, especially for complex models such as deep learning (DL) networks, which are often considered black boxes [1]. Very accurate predictions or decisions characterize these models; however, in most cases, the internal logic leading to such outcomes is hardly transparent, leaving users without any explanation of why or how a particular decision was made. Fundamentally, XAI seeks to improve the transparency and accountability of AI systems, giving humans the confidence to trust or interpret their behavior [2]. This is particularly relevant in high-stakes domains such as healthcare, finance, and criminal justice, as well as in areas involving autonomous systems, where mistakes or unjustified decisions can have significant consequences [3].

Explainable AI (XAI) can increase the transparency and trustworthiness of AI systems by making it easier for users to understand their decisions. In areas where AI decisions can significantly impact healthcare, finance, and law, XAI enables stakeholders to assess how and why certain events occur [4]. This transparency can foster greater accountability as organizations can track AI decisions, ensure ethical standards are upheld, and implement policies like the General Data Protection Regulation. XAI also plays a key role in identifying and reducing biases that AI systems may have learned from training data, thus promoting fairness in AI-driven decision-making (Figure 1.1). By providing insights into the behavioral model, XAI enables developers to address problems more effectively and improve AI models for better performance. It also allows users to interact effectively with AI, enhance cognitive decision-making, and reduce traditional AI systems' "black box" nature. In highly competitive areas such as driverless cars and smart healthcare, XAI will play a crucial role in building public trust and supporting the broader adoption of AI technology.

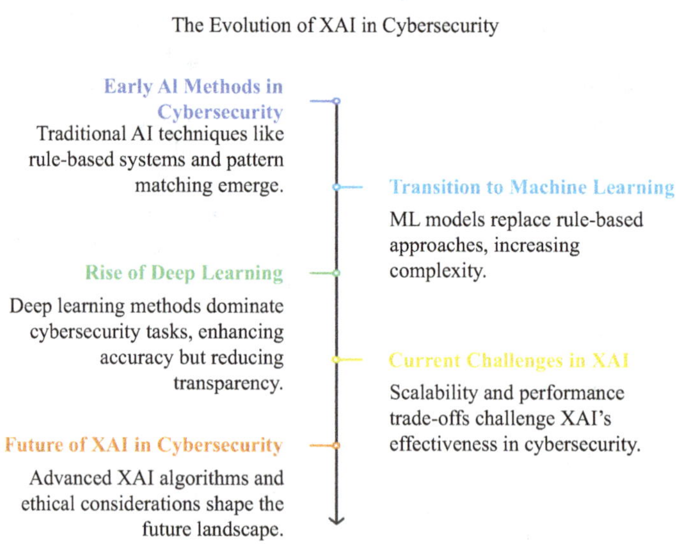

Figure 1.1 Evaluation of XAI in cybersecurity

Cybersecurity refers to the technologies, strategies, and practices designed to protect networks, devices, applications, and data from unauthorized access, damage, or other types of attacks. As more systems become interconnected, the cybersecurity landscape has grown increasingly complex. Further developments in the digital economy and infrastructure have contributed to this complexity, accompanied by a sudden increase in cyberattacks, some of which can have severe consequences [5]. Moreover, researchers continue to observe the evolution of state-sponsored and criminal adversaries, as well as the increasing sophistication of cyberattacks. These attackers are now employing increasingly innovative approaches to compromise even the most well-defended systems. Consequently, the frequency, scale, and impact of these attacks are growing, underscoring the need for intelligence-driven cybersecurity measures. Intelligence-driven cybersecurity aims to provide dynamic protection, adapting to the evolving nature of threats by managing large volumes of data [6]. Meanwhile, organizations like the National Institute of Standards and Technology advocate for a more proactive and adaptive cybersecurity approach. This shift in strategy places an unprecedented emphasis on real-time risk assessments, continuous monitoring, and data-driven analysis to identify, defend against, detect, and respond to cyber threats. Such an approach enables organizations to prepare for and mitigate the impact of potential security incidents in the future.

1.1.1 Objectives and scope of this chapter

This chapter discusses and explores the cybersecurity trends related to Explainable AI (XAI). It examines how XAI has evolved and developed over time, its relevance in today's security frameworks, and how it is likely to perform in the future in the face of emerging cyber threats. The following areas are covered in this chapter:

- **Historical perspective**: Analyze the encounter between AI and cybersecurity, along with the associated challenges of black box models.
- **Current applications**: Discussing cutting-edge XAI technologies today for purposes such as threat detection, fraud analysis, and malware forensics, among others.
- **Future trends**: Providing insights into how XAI could play a role in the development of advanced cybersecurity architectures, such as quantum-safe cryptography and zero-trust architectures (ZTA).
- **Challenges and limitations**: Examining technological, ethical, and adversarial challenges in the implementation of XAI in real-world settings. Case Studies: Learning from successful and less successful examples to derive lessons from real-world deployments in cybersecurity.
- **Recommendations**: Providing guidance to the research and practitioner communities on the adoption and advancement of XAI-based systems for cybersecurity.

1.2 The past: historical evolution of AI in cybersecurity

The concept of intelligence in machines dates back to ancient civilizations, which narrated stories of mechanical beings with the capacity for human thought. However, modern AI research began in the mid-20th century, when computer scientists started exploring whether machines could simulate aspects of human thought [7]. In 1956, at the Dartmouth Conference, the term "artificial intelligence" was coined as a field of study [8]. Early AI research had ambitious goals: pioneers like Alan Turing and John McCarthy posed foundational questions, such as "Can machines think?" The earliest AI systems were based on rules of logic to guide computers through problem-solving—a set of instructions that computers followed to arrive at answers to problems [9].

The main limitation of such systems was their inability to learn or provide solutions to problems that did not fit within predetermined parameters. From the early 1980s to the 1990s, there was a period referred to as the "Artificial Intelligence Winter," during which research and development stagnated almost to a standstill. This was due to a lack of funding and, more importantly, the inadequacy of existing techniques. AI research only gained significant momentum in the 2000s, driven by advances in computational resources, the availability of rich data sources, and the development of new algorithms [8]. Machine learning (ML) played a pivotal role during this time, especially with the emergence of DL techniques [10]. Performance metrics showed remarkable improvements in applications such as image recognition, voice recognition, and natural language understanding [11].

In recent years, the cybersecurity landscape has changed dramatically with the integration of AI technology [12,13]. AI is critical for detecting and responding to complex cyber threats in real time. From malware detection to predicting future attacks, AI's ability to analyze vast amounts of data and identify patterns invisible to human analysts has made it a powerful ally in combating cybercrime. However, while AI-based cybersecurity solutions offer significant benefits, one of the biggest challenges has been the lack of transparency in decision-making. AI models, particularly those based on DL, are often described as "black boxes" because their decision-making processes are not easily explained [14]. This lack of interpretability raises concerns about the reliability of AI systems, accountability, and overall trust in cybersecurity. To address these concerns, the concept of XAI has emerged.

XAI refers to a human-readable system designed to be interpreted by humans, meaning its decision-making processes are not only understandable but also intelligent [15]. In cybersecurity, XAI plays a key role in enhancing the visibility of AI-based threats, making them easier for humans to trust. This clarity is essential for security organizations that rely on AI to perform complex tasks such as intrusion detection, malware analysis, and vulnerability management. By integrating XAI, cybersecurity professionals can better understand how AI models make decisions, fostering improved collaboration between human and machine experts.

The goal of this chapter is to provide a comprehensive, in-depth look at human intelligence in the context of cybersecurity. Figure 1.2 gives an overview of the conceptual role that XAI plays in cybersecurity. This diagram illustrates the nested

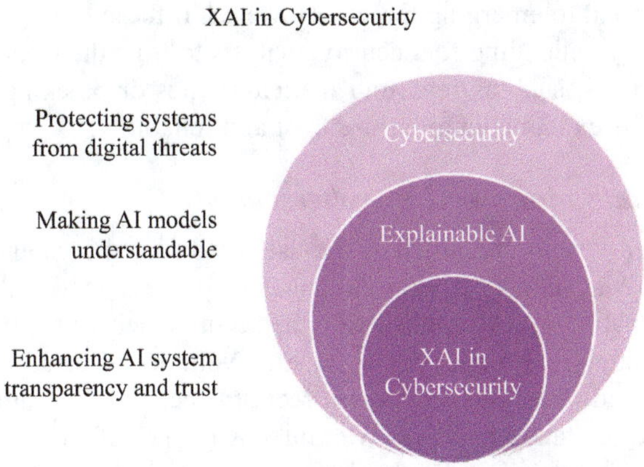

Figure 1.2 XAI in cybersecurity

relationship between cybersecurity, Explainable AI, and their overlap in enhancing security measures. At the outermost level, cybersecurity safeguards systems and networks from digital threats, ensuring the integrity, confidentiality, and availability of these systems and networks. In this field, XAI is significant because it ensures that AI systems are transparent and understandable to users, allowing them to comprehend the logic behind AI-driven decisions. Ultimately, XAI in cybersecurity demonstrates that these concepts are integrated at the core: XAI adds trust and transparency to AI-based cybersecurity solutions. It not only enables the detection and prevention of threats in AI models but, more importantly, builds confidence in their reliability and fairness by explaining AI behavior. Therefore, this layered architecture reflects the transparency-protection interaction, which is paramount in modern strategies for AI-based cybersecurity.

This chapter explores the importance of information in AI-based security solutions, the challenges of making AI models transparent, the various applications of XAI in cybersecurity, and the potential impact of XAI on the future of the cybersecurity industry. The need for XAI arises from the complexity of ML algorithms, especially DL models. While deep neural networks and other advanced models have shown great success in tasks such as image recognition, speech processing, and anomaly detection, they often operate in environments that are difficult to understand. This lack of transparency can undermine the credibility of AI, particularly in critical domains such as cybersecurity, where AI systems are responsible for identifying and mitigating threats. XAI technologies enable AI systems to interpret data without compromising their performance. These insights provide human users with a clearer understanding of the decision-making process, the factors influencing decisions, and whether the models are appropriately designed to predict outcomes [16].

In cybersecurity, the decisions made by AI systems can have significant consequences. AI-based security tools are used to detect intrusions, identify malicious activity, and respond to emerging threats. However, if these tools operate as black boxes, it becomes challenging for security analysts to trust their results. Decisions made by AI systems, such as reporting malicious files or blocking suspicious IP addresses, must be explainable to ensure trust and reliability.

1.2.1 Early adoption of AI in cybersecurity

AI in cybersecurity can be regarded as the use of advanced computational techniques, including ML, DL, and natural language processing (NLP), to enhance cybersecurity capabilities. AI applied to cybersecurity helps identify and prevent cyber threats through real-time analysis of large volumes of data, pattern recognition, and automated responses to various security incidents. Traditional cybersecurity solutions often fail to handle new or unknown types of attacks effectively. In contrast, AI can detect unusual behavior and potential threats through anomaly detection, even when the threats are novel [17].

AI automates processes to enhance advanced malware detection, phishing prevention, and incident response, thereby reducing the workload of human analysts within organizations. For instance, DL continuously evolves by learning to respond to emerging threats, becoming more effective at predicting and mitigating cyber risks. While AI contributes significantly to cybersecurity, it is not without challenges. Adversarial attacks can potentially mislead AI systems, and maintaining these systems requires constant expertise. As AI technology becomes more integrated into cybersecurity practices, it becomes increasingly autonomous and capable of performing real-time threat mitigation. However, humans continue to play a critical role in managing complex or strategic decisions.

- **Health care**: AI is transforming healthcare by enhancing efficiency in diagnosis, predicting disease outbreaks, and assisting in drug discovery. Medical data can be analyzed using ML models for the early detection of cancer, diabetes, and other diseases. AI-powered robots are being used in surgeries to perform complex procedures with high precision.
- **Finance**: AI has become pervasive in the financial world, playing a key role in fraud detection, risk management, and algorithmic trading. AI models analyze large volumes of financial data to detect suspicious transactions, predict market trends, and make automated trading decisions.
- **Autonomous vehicles**: AI is the driving force behind autonomous vehicles, where ML, computer vision, and sensor data integrate to enable cars to drive without human input. Companies like Tesla, Waymo, and Uber are heavily investing in AI to make fully autonomous vehicles a reality.
- **E-commerce and retail**: The use of AI in retail focuses on offering a personalized shopping experience, improving inventory management, and enhancing demand estimation. Recommendation systems powered by AI suggest products to customers based on their browsing history, while AI-driven chatbots are employed for customer service.
- **Education**: AI in education allows the establishment of a personalized learning platform that caters to students' needs. The intelligent tutoring systems

assess performance and provide customized feedback to the students. Besides that, AI automates teachers' administrative tasks so that they can focus on instruction.

- **Entertainment and media**: AI is used to an extent in creating content and recommendation systems, including Netflix's recommendations, and even in developing video games. DL algorithms generate realistic graphics and improve gameplay by enhancing user experience.

1.3 Challenges with black box AI models

Black box AI models present significant challenges, particularly in the domains of understanding, trust, and accountability. These models often involve highly complex neural networks that provide predictions or decisions without offering clear explanations of how they arrive at their conclusions. This lack of transparency can undermine trust, especially in critical areas such as healthcare, finance, and criminal justice, where stakeholders demand clarity and justification for decision-making. The primary issue with the opacity of these models is that it becomes challenging to detect and mitigate biases or errors in their training data, potentially leading to persistent unfair or harmful outcomes. This raises regulatory compliance and ethical concerns: organizations may struggle to ensure that black box systems align with legal standards or societal values. Taken together, these issues create a barrier to the responsible widespread deployment of such models and their full-scale integration into applications involving sensitive, high-stakes decisions [18].

Black box AI modeling systems create huge barriers bound to understanding, trust, and accountability. This model involves some super complex neural networks giving predictions or decisions without offering clear explanations about how they come to their conclusions. Such incompleteness can challenge trust, especially in quite critical areas of working such as healthcare, finance, or criminal justice, where stakeholders expect that the decision-making would be endowed with clarity and justification. The main issue with opaqueness in these models is that it makes it unmanageable to detect and mitigate any presence of bias or errors in their training data, which could translate to continuing unfair or harmful outcomes. This raises regulatory compliance as well as ethical issues. The organizations' mission could be made complicated by ensuring that black box systems would be congruent with legal standards or societal values. Ultimately, it means that an inability to further interpretation and auditing of models becomes another barrier to widespread responsible deployment of these models into applications of sensitive, high-stakes involvement [19].

1.4 Case studies: legacy AI systems in threat detection

Legacy AI systems have significantly contributed to addressing threats in cybersecurity, such as malware detection, phishing attempts, and unauthorized access. These systems generally utilize rule-based algorithms or early machine-learning models to analyze patterns in network traffic and user behavior. Although these systems were considered advanced when first introduced, they struggle to adapt to real-time changes in threat landscapes. For instance, static signature-based detection cannot protect against threats such as zero-day vulnerabilities and polymorphic malware, which can modify their structural characteristics to evade detection. Additionally, legacy systems typically generate a high number of false positives, overwhelming security teams with excessive alerts and making it challenging to prioritize genuine threats. Nevertheless, these systems laid the groundwork for modern AI-driven solutions, providing the foundational frameworks for automating threat detection and response.

In physical security, legacy AI systems have been employed to monitor surveillance feeds, detect intrusions, and analyze behavioral patterns in public spaces. Most of these systems typically rely on simple image processing and motion detection techniques to identify potential threats. For instance, unauthorized access to restricted areas or unattended objects in high-security zones could be flagged by these systems. However, these systems often lacked the ability to distinguish between benign and malicious activities. For example, they might classify a harmless group of people as engaging in suspicious activity and trigger an unnecessary action. Moreover, their reliance on fixed parameters rendered them ineffective in dynamic environments where lighting conditions, weather, or crowd densities varied. Despite these limitations, older AI systems laid the foundation for the development of real-time video analytics and the introduction of more robust and context-aware AI models in physical security applications.

AI systems have been used in national defense to monitor borders, detect unauthorized aircraft or vessels, and analyze communications for potential threats. These systems primarily relied on rule-based algorithms and early signal processing methods to interpret data from radar, sonar, and satellite imagery. While effective in structured scenarios, their rigidity often caused difficulties in addressing asymmetrical threats or adversaries employing innovative tactics. For instance, they struggled with targeting low-profile flying drones or distinguishing between military and civilian communications, particularly in complex environments. Other significant limitations included their processing capabilities and reliance on rule-based algorithms, which hindered their ability to automatically analyze large volumes of information in real time. Nevertheless, these systems laid the foundation for the integration of advanced AI into national defense, enabling greater automation and improvements in situational awareness and decision-making.

Examples include the application of legacy AI systems in healthcare to identify potential threats to patient safety, such as adverse reactions to medications, outbreaks of infections, or diagnostic errors. These systems relied on predefined clinical rules and static algorithms to flag anomalies in patient data or medical workflows. For instance, they could alert clinicians to unusual vital signs or lab results that fell outside the expected range. While useful, these systems were limited by their inability to incorporate real-time data or account for case-specific complexities in many situations. Another issue was their reliance on static rules, which made them incapable of adapting to new information or emerging healthcare threats. Despite these limitations, legacy AI systems demonstrated the value of technology in enhancing patient safety and paved the way for the development of more sophisticated models capable of integrating diverse data sources and learning from evolving healthcare practices.

Threat detection and analysis are considered to be the heart of any cybersecurity strategy. This will involve the identification and evaluation of security threats to the networks, systems, and data with a view to taking appropriate actions aimed at preventing, mitigating, or responding to such attacks. With effective threat detection, one will be able to identify the malicious activities; analysis will, however, help ascertain the nature, scope, and impact of the activities. All these, put together, constitute a proactive defense mechanism aimed at enhancing the ability of the organization to respond to cybersecurity incidents.

In general, threat detection combines signature-based, anomaly-based, and behavioral analysis. That is to say, signature-based detection techniques will try to match the ongoing activity of a system or network against known attack patterns or signatures stored in some sort of database. While such an operation is quick and very efficient for known threats, the method does have its inherent limitation in handling novel or sophisticated attacks. However, anomaly-based detection establishes a baseline of normal system or network behavior and flags deviations as potential threats. This could identify previously unknown attacks; however, it may generate higher false-positive rates because any deviation from the baseline pulls an alert.

Behavioral analysis provides a deeper level of insight by taking a snapshot of users' behavior, processes, and devices over time to analyze patterns capable of revealing whether an activity is abnormal. This approach can be particularly helpful in identifying insider threats or complex, multi-stage attacks. It is expected that new generations of these techniques will be supplemented by ML and AI capabilities, which can dynamically adapt to emerging threats and improve accuracy through sophisticated pattern identification in voluminous data flows. After detection, the threat must be further analyzed to establish the level of danger or damage it may cause. Threat analysis involves understanding the nature of the attack, tactics, techniques, and procedures that attackers might employ. These analyses often draw from intelligence feeds containing up-to-date information on threats and vulnerabilities, which help security teams prioritize responses and identify appropriate countermeasures. Another key aspect of the analysis is assessing an attack's potential impact on systems, data, and business operations. This includes determining whether data has been compromised, if critical systems are affected, and whether business operations are disrupted. The results of the analysis form the basis for decisions regarding containment, remediation, recovery, and the enhancement of security posture by addressing vulnerabilities or gaps in defense mechanisms. Fundamentally, threat detection and analysis are crucial variables that provide organizations with an advantage against adversaries in the cyberspace landscape. The more effectively a firm can manage detection and analyze threats, the better its chances of preventing specific attacks and minimizing their impact. Advanced technologies, including AI and ML, help integrate intelligence on threat

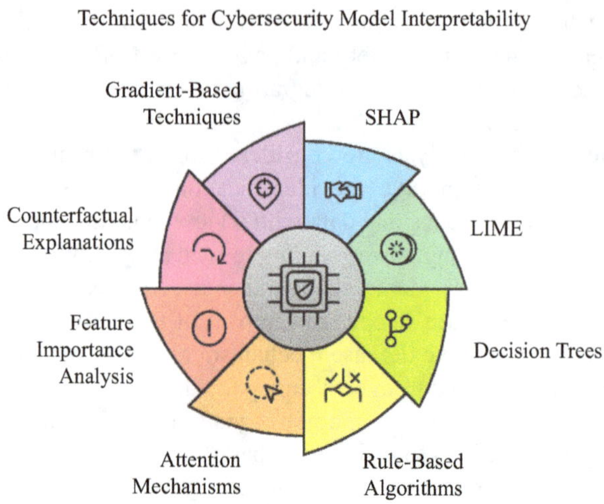

Figure 1.3 Techniques of cybersecurity

detection and analytics, thereby enhancing security postures (Figure 1.3). These technologies are essential for countering dynamic threats that quickly render traditional methods obsolete.

1.5 The present: state-of-the-art XAI in cybersecurity

A lot of methods have been developed, as shown in Table 1.1, that help AI models become more interpretable and explainable. They are divided into two kinds of techniques [20]: Post-hoc Explanation Methods: These are approaches made after an event has occurred, where model predictions are done to give reasons for particular decisions made by black boxes. XAI involves the application of the algorithms in cybersecurity for increasing transparency, trust, and interpretability in the AI-based solutions. These algorithms provide insights into how the decisions are made for better understanding, trust, and involvement of the cybersecurity teams into the outputs. Here are some key algorithms along with their applications in cybersecurity. Typical methods that are usually employed include [21].

- **LIME (Local Interpretable Model-agnostic Explanations)**: LIME generates an explanation by approximating the complex model using a more comprehensible model locally around that particular prediction. This technique makes the explanation local; thus, it explains individual predictions.
- **SHAP (SHapley Additive exPlanations)**: SHAP values take the help of cooperative game theory and give explanations using the calculation of each feature for the final prediction to keep fairness and consistency in the explanation.
- **Saliency maps**: These were mainly used in computer vision. Saliency maps mark the most influential regions in an image with respect to the model's decision; hence, they give an idea of how the model interprets the image.

Table 1.1 State-of-the-art XAI in cybersecurity

Algorithm/technique	Application in Cybersecurity	Description
SHAP (SHapley Additive exPlanations)	Anomaly detection for network traffic, critical signatures for malware classification, phishing email detection	SHAP assigns importance scores to input features, showing how each feature contributes to a prediction. In cybersecurity, it helps to understand why a model flagged an event as malicious, improving the interpretability of anomaly detection, intrusion detection systems (IDS), and phishing detection models.
Decision trees	Spam detection, access control analysis, basic threat identification	Decision trees are used in cybersecurity to identify threats through a simple tree structure, making them highly interpretable. They show the decision-making process for spam detection, access control, and basic threat identification.
Rule-based algorithms	Detection of known malware patterns, Phishing attempts detection	Rule-based algorithms generate if-then rules that help detect known threats, such as malware or phishing attempts. These human-readable rules make it easier for cybersecurity experts to understand and modify detection strategies.
Attention mechanisms	Phishing email detection, malicious URL analysis	Attention mechanisms in NLP define which part of the input, such as specific words or phrases in a phishing email, contributes most to the prediction. This helps in explaining and interpreting the model's decision-making process, especially in detecting malicious content.
Feature importance analysis	Fraud detection, risk assessment	Feature importance analysis identifies key variables influencing model decisions, such as login frequency or IP address, helping to understand which inputs are critical in flagging fraudulent activities or assessing risks in cybersecurity contexts.
Local Interpretable Model-agnostic Explanations (LIME)	Explanation of IDS predictions, phishing email detection analysis	LIME approximates the model's behavior around a specific prediction, providing an interpretable explanation of why an IDS flagged an event as malicious or why a phishing email was detected. It simplifies complex models to help cybersecurity professionals understand predictions.
Rule-based algorithms	Detection of known malware patterns, Phishing attempts detection	Rule-based algorithms generate if-then rules that help detect known threats, such as malware or phishing attempts. These human-readable rules make it easier for cybersecurity experts to understand and modify detection strategies.
Attention mechanisms	Phishing email detection, malicious URL analysis	Attention mechanisms in NLP define which part of the input, such as specific words or phrases in a phishing email, contributes most to the prediction. This helps in explaining and interpreting the model's decision-making process, especially in detecting malicious content.

(Continues)

Table 1.1 (Continued)

Algorithm/technique	Application in Cybersecurity	Description
Feature importance analysis	Fraud detection, risk assessment	Feature importance analysis identifies key variables influencing model decisions, such as login frequency or IP address, helping to understand which inputs are critical in flagging fraudulent activities or assessing risks.
Counterfactual explanations	Anomaly detection in user behavior, access breach analysis	Counterfactual explanations use "what-if" analyses to understand anomalies. For example, "If this behavior hadn't occurred, the system wouldn't have flagged it." This helps improve model trust by showing the changes needed to avoid triggering alerts.
Technical gradient	Deep learning-based malware detection, endpoint protection	Gradient-based techniques like saliency maps help explain deep learning models by showing which parts of the input, such as specific code snippets in malware, contributed to the decision.
Case-based reasoning (CBR)	Incident response, Threat comparison	CBR helps in incident response by comparing new threats to previously resolved cases. It borrows from past incidents to provide relevant insights and detect similarities between current and historical threats.
Bayesian networks	Threat detection, risk assessment	Bayesian networks represent probabilistic relationships between events and conditions in a graphical form, allowing for interpretable probabilistic reasoning and better decision-making in threat detection and risk analysis.

- **Interpretable models**: Models that are intrinsically more transparent and self-explaining include:
- **Decision trees**: The work of decision trees involves simple, hierarchical rules to make predictions; hence, they are very interpretable. The path from the root to the leaf in the decision tree can be traced in steps to explain how the decision was reached.
- **Linear models**: Examples are linear regression and logistic regression, which are interpretable models; the relationship of inputs to outputs is quite intuitive to understand, with the coefficients of the model directly pointing out the strength and direction of influence of each feature.
- **Rule-based systems**: These use a set of predefined rules or conditions. Each decision is made by following the series of logical rules. This makes the reasoning very transparent and easy to trace.

1.6 Past—challenges and limitations of XAI in cybersecurity

Viruses have become a problem previously, as shown in Table 1.2, and computer viruses were responsible for widening the gulf within the firewall. A computer virus is an infection that takes a healthy machine and then spreads itself to infect other computers. Like the "I LOVE YOU" virus that spread widespread in 2000, these viruses have brought financial and, sometimes, personal data losses around the world. A huge number of regional public networks have been created so that email can replicate itself through them. The problem thus lay with the generic absence of any sound antivirus measures and the lack of focus on problems in cybersecurity. To handle this technical problem, a novel and strong antivirus programs and sets of email filtering which must be introduced. Public awareness has also taught consumers about the dangers of opening a suspicious email attachment, and the companies are starting to roll out stronger chains of internal policies regarding downloading software.

Ransomware strikes, and perhaps the current concern of most organizations is about escaping ransomware attack incidents. This refers to incidents where an organization's data has been encrypted, and it has then been demanded to pay ransom for the decryption key. Many costly incidents, such as the Colonial Pipeline attack in 2021, have demonstrated how ransomware can cripple vital infrastructures. Cybercriminals generally target organizations that do not have tight security or un-updated vulnerabilities in their applications. Organizations must use essential tools to prevent the degradation of their information resources, such as adopting regular software updates, implementing endpoint protection, and maintaining security in backups of vital information. Governments should also develop policies against ransom payments to discourage attackers.

Cyberattacks maliciously composed with AI, indeed, the AI-boast promises a future that could worsen things, i.e., employing AI for malicious purposes [22]. To reach even more devastating heights, hackers could advance the evolution of

Table 1.2 Overview of issues and solutions in cybersecurity

Time period	Problem	Description	Solution
Past	Virus and worms	The emergence of computer viruses like the "I LOVE YOU" virus in 2000 caused widespread disruptions.	Antivirus software, firewall protection, and user education.
	Basic hacking attacks	Hacking typically involved password guessing and unauthorized access to systems.	Stronger password policies, two-factor authentication.
	Phishing emails	Email scams became prevalent in the late 1990s, tricking users into revealing sensitive information.	Email filtering, user awareness, anti-phishing tools.
	Denial of service (DoS)	Early forms of DoS attacks involved overwhelming a server with excessive traffic, causing service disruptions.	Intrusion detection systems, rate-limiting traffic.
Present	Ransomware	Sophisticated malware encrypts user data and demands ransom for its release (e.g., WannaCry in 2017).	Data backups, ransomware protection tools, incident response plans.
	Zero-day exploits	Exploits targeting software vulnerabilities that are not yet publicly known.	Timely patching, threat intelligence, security vulnerability scanners.
	Advanced persistent threats (APTs)	Long-term, focused cyberattacks typically associated with nation-state or organized groups aiming for espionage or data theft.	Threat detection systems, continuous monitoring, threat hunting.
Future	Quantum computing threats	Quantum computing could break conventional cryptography by solving problems faster than traditional computers.	Development of quantum-resistant cryptographic algorithms.
	AI-powered attacks	AI could be used to develop adaptive malware or create convincing phishing schemes.	AI-powered security defenses, continuous model training for cybersecurity tools.
	Biohacking risks	Risks involving implants, wearables, and bio-devices could be exploited for malicious purposes.	Robust device security protocols and regular software updates.
	War on cybernetics	Growing cyber conflicts between nation-states, with the risk of cyber warfare disrupting societies.	Cybersecurity diplomacy, global cyber defense collaborations.
	Deepfake scams	AI-generated deepfakes could be used to impersonate individuals and mislead or defraud others.	Deepfake detection tools, AI-driven authentication measures.
General	Cybersecurity evolution	Cybersecurity challenges evolve with technology. The future defense will rely on AI-driven proactive defense mechanisms and advanced encryption techniques.	AI-based proactive security measures, advanced encryption, and constant updates.

adaptive malware, employ large-scale phishing schemes, or use intelligent recognition pattern processing to defeat even the most earth-bound defenses. Attacks using AI promise to be faster and more precise in execution, offering formidable challenges to the state of existing security. Integrated XAI-based security systems and capabilities must be built into the systems themselves for real-time detection and reaction against threats. Ethical AI research could also be a viable thrust for governments and organizations for early efforts against the misuse of technology.

Denial-of-service (DoS) attacks are one of the primary problems: brought a lot of inconveniences in the new age of the internet. DoS attacks sent overwhelming amounts of traffic into servers, making their services in websites unavailable. Critical shortages of bandwidth and bad firewalls made these types of systems useful for attacking DoS. Research and development on firewalls and traffic filtering systems have helped bolster organizations' ability to mitigate or protect against distributed and DOS attacks [23]. Cloud-based solutions allow for dynamic scaling to accommodate intrusions, allowing organizations to manage service disruptions associated with malicious attacks. Internet of Things (IoT) device vulnerabilities utilization of IoT technology puts the security of these devices on the common platform of security holes. A number of IoT devices lack adequate security features, thus making them amongst the easiest targets for hackers [24]. Devices can be hacked into using botnets like Mirai and then used to launch attacks or siphon data from users. Manufacturers should secure IoT devices by implementing secure firmware, authentication schemes, and ongoing updates. Users must also isolate such IoT devices from critical networks and utilize strong, unique passwords. Additionally, other research problems need to be addressed, like quantum computing threats, phishing schemes of Antiquity, Supply chain attacks, deepfake technology in cybercrime, and insider threats.

1.7 The future: emerging trends and potential of XAI in cybersecurity

1.7.1 Scalability and privacy and security concerns

Integration of XAI into cybersecurity will revolutionize the field by targeting some of the most important challenges of threat detection, response, and resilience. As attacks continue to get sophisticated, XAI is the key toward making AI-driven cybersecurity solutions more transparent, interpretable, and effective. Thus, another emerging trend in development involves creating XAI models that could explain their threat detection processes in real time for the security teams to understand why certain remediation steps must be taken or recommended, like blocking an IP address or isolating a network device. This clarity will further build trust in AI systems and help speed up decision-making in incident response cases.

Another trend is making anomaly detection systems more interpretable using XAI. Traditional black box models flag behavior as anomalous without context, leading to many false positives. XAI contextualizes these anomalies by giving insight into why certain behaviors are considered suspicious, reducing alert fatigue for security analysts. XAI is increasingly integrated into threat intelligence platforms for actionable insights on attack patterns and tactics, among other potential vulnerabilities that could be exploited, thus, proactive defense.

The potential of XAI, in general, will widen further in regulatory compliance and ethical deployment of AI in cybersecurity. As more data privacy concerns are grown along with accountability, XAI can ensure that AI-driven decisions support legal and ethical standards when offering auditable explanations. Along with this, increased interest in AI-powered autonomous security systems will be boosted by XAI since it will substantially enhance the transparency and accountability of these systems, thus gaining stakeholder trust.

In this sense, the future convergence of XAI with the most evolved technologies, such as federated learning and quantum computing, is expected to disclose wholly new frontiers in cybersecurity. Federated learning combined with XAI will enable collaborative threat detection across organizations while preserving data privacy. Meanwhile, XAI might be critical in demystifying quantum-resistant cryptographic solutions for their secure and ethical adoption. In general, the future of XAI in cybersecurity promises greater transparency and adaptability, coupled with more trust to offer a playing field for more robust intelligent defense mechanisms.

1.7.2 Role of XAI in zero-trust architectures

XAI plays a key role in advancing ZTA by adding transparency and accountability to security processes. In a zero-trust environment, the core principle is "never trust, always audit," which requires monitoring and auditing of all users, devices, and applications accessing network resources. XAI can support this principle by providing information about automated security decisions made by AI systems, such as access control, threat detection, and anomaly detection, as shown in Figure 1.4.

In traditional AI settings, systems often act as "black boxes," where decision-making processes are hidden, making it difficult for security teams to understand why someone acted. Obvious invisibility can be a challenge in environments where accountability and the accuracy of decisions are essential. By implementing XAI, security teams can examine the reasoning behind AI decisions, helping them understand why a particular user or device is experiencing and poses a threat. XAI enhances trust in automated security systems by better understanding AI behavior. This understanding is essential for meeting regulatory requirements, as many organizations are looking for decisions made by automated systems that are clear and accurate. By providing a clear and concise decision process, XAI helps organizations demonstrate compliance with security policies and governance functions, reducing the risk of regulatory breaches. In addition, XAI helps improve the security of zero-trust networks. As AI systems continue to analyze threats and vulnerabilities, XAI ensures that their findings and actions can be validated. For example, if an AI model detects a unique activity, such as a threat to an analyst, XAI can provide security analysts with an explanation of why it was considered a suspicious activity, improving the efficiency of incident response and remediation.

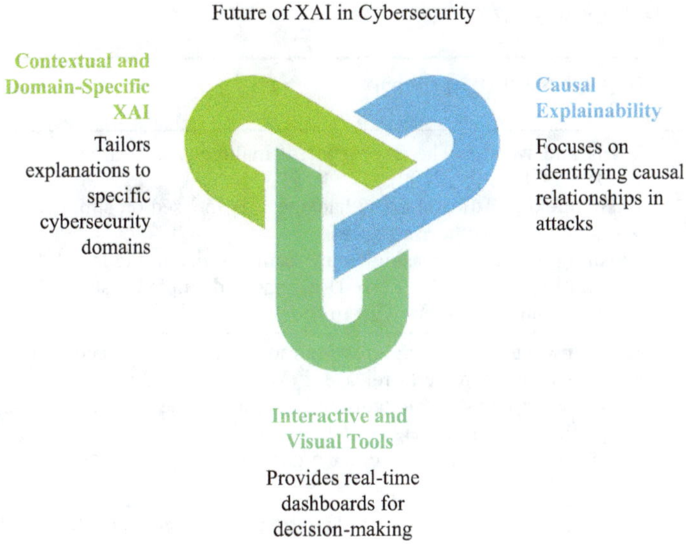

Figure 1.4 Future of XAI in cybersecurity

Overall, integrating XAI into ZTAs strengthens security systems by making decisions more informed and accurate and promotes trust and transparency, which is critical in regulatory and legal systems. XAI enables effective and transparent security processes in a zero-trust environment, helping organizations take effective, accurate, and transparent action against cyber threats (Table 1.3).

1.7.3 XAI in quantum-safe cryptography

Explainable AI is played a transformative role in the field of quantum-safe cryptography that develops methods of encryption against attacks via quantum computing. Most of these quantum-safe cryptographic algorithms, such as lattice-based cryptography, code-based cryptography, and multivariate polynomial cryptography, involve complex mathematical structures that are hard to analyze and optimize. With the integration of XAI, researchers and practitioners will gain better insights into the decision-making process of the AI models at each step of algorithm design, evaluation, and implementation.

For instance, XAI will be able to explain the performance of certain cryptographic algorithms under various attack scenarios by giving understandable explanations of the AI's assessments, which may have a positive effect on the debugging and validation process of these algorithms against both classical and quantum adversaries. XAI can also serve in optimizing the performance of quantum-safe cryptography systems by showing which factors ensure their efficiency and security.

XAI can help organizations understand some of the trade-offs inherent in different quantum-safe solutions during the deployment phase, such as how to

Table 1.3 Cybersecurity problems

Time period	Key cybersecurity problems
Past	**Virus and worms**: The emergence of malicious software such as the I LOVEYOU virus (2000). **Basic hacking attacks**: Early hacking was focused on simple password guessing and unauthorized access. **Phishing emails**: Increasing email scam activity in the late 1990s. Denial of service (DoS): Early DoS attacks disrupted systems, leading to the overwhelming of servers with traffic.
Present	**Ransomware**: Attacks are growing more sophisticated, encrypting user data and demanding a price to release it (WannaCry in 2017). **Zero-day exploits**: Exploitation of software vulnerabilities unannounced to the public. Advanced persistent threats (APTs). Attacks by nation-states or other organized groups are protracted and targeted.
Future	**Quantum computing threats**: Traditional cryptography will be broken using quantum algorithms. **AI-powered attacks**: The adaptive malware could be developed using AI either to create it or generate phishing schemes that are more convincing. **Biohacking risks**: Potential dangers for implants, wearables, and bio-devices. **Cyberwarfare**: Höhemer.org cites increasing involvement of nation-states in global cyber conflicts. **Deepfake scams**: Leveraging AI to impersonate individuals for fraud or misinformation.

balance computational overhead with security levels. This might be instrumental in building trust and, therefore, better adoption of quantum-safe cryptography, particularly in highly security-sensitive industries. In general, the interplay between XAI and quantum-safe cryptography is a promising avenue for accelerating the development and deployment cycle of robust cryptographic systems of the next generation.

1.8 Conclusion and recommendations

In summary, the evolution of XAI within the cybersecurity landscape marks a pivotal advancement in addressing the complex interplay of security threats and the necessity for interpretability in AI-driven decision-making processes. Historically, the implementation of AI in cybersecurity has often been shrouded in opacity, generating skepticism regarding its efficacy and reliability. This chapter has elucidated the primary milestones in the integration of XAI methodologies, highlighting their growing importance as cybersecurity frameworks increasingly rely on sophisticated algorithms to predict, prevent, and respond to threats. As we navigate the complexities of contemporary cyber threats, the role of XAI becomes paramount for enhancing detection capabilities and fostering trust among stakeholders through transparent decision-making. The implications of this shift extend beyond mere technical enhancements; they require a reevaluation of regulatory standards and ethical guidelines that govern the deployment of AI technologies in security contexts. Looking ahead, the trajectory of XAI in cybersecurity is poised for significant refinement as emerging technologies—such as the incorporation of decentralized blockchain systems and advanced ML techniques—offer new paradigms for resilient cybersecurity architectures. Future research and development must aim to create robust XAI systems that are not only interpretable but capable of evolving dynamically in response to an ever-changing threat landscape. Thus, in the interplay of cybersecurity and XAI, a future characterized by enhanced collaboration between human expertise and machine intelligence will be essential for safeguarding systems against increasingly sophisticated cyber adversaries. This conclusion encapsulates the chapter's exploration of the critical role that XAI plays within cybersecurity while iterating the necessity for ongoing innovation and ethical considerations in the field.

Cybersecurity encompasses many areas, such as network security, application security, cloud security, data protection, and incident response. It addresses a variety of threats such as malware, phishing, ransomware, DoS attacks, and insider threats. These threats continue to increase due to technological advancements and the advancement of cybercriminals. Cybersecurity uses security, detection and measurement techniques to address these challenges. Today's strategies are based on AI, ML, encryption, and multi-factor authentication technologies. At the same time, organizations emphasize the importance of strong policies, employee training, and compliance to create a culture of cyber awareness. In an increasingly connected world, cybersecurity is about preventing cyberattacks and ensuring the sustainability and continuity of critical operations. As the threat landscape evolves, the need for cyber innovation, adaptability, and collaboration has never been more important. AI, more briefly referred to as AI, is part of computer science that deals with establishing systems that can carry out tasks that, in practice, would demand human intelligence. Such applications cover reasoning, problem-solving, learning, perception, facility with language, and even creative endeavors. The most simplistic explanation of AI involves developing algorithms that help a computer simulate human cognitive functions, thinking, pattern recognition, and decisions using data inputs. It has turned out to be an important area of research and application, considering that industries and societies depend on it worldwide [25]. AI isn't a technology but more like an overarching term meant to integrate subfields, abounding within, such as ML, NLP, robotics, and computer vision. This could be the ability of the system to learn without expressing programmability from experiences, such as so-called data. An innovation is part of the deep ML system. That innovation contains many neural network lay-overs that try to comprehend complicated data so that your forecast is correct. Cybersecurity refers to the practice of protecting digital systems, networks, and data from intrusion, corruption, and cyber threats. As technology becomes more and more pervasive in everyday life, protecting critical information and processes is essential to maintaining trust, confidentiality, and integrity.

References

[1] Rousseau AJ, Geubbelmans M, Valkenborg D, *et al.* Explainable artificial intelligence. *American Journal of Orthodontics and Dentofacial Orthopedics*. 2024;165(4):491–494.

[2] Hassija V, Chamola V, Mahapatra A, *et al.* Interpreting black-box models: a review on explainable artificial intelligence. *Cognitive Computation*. 2024;16(1):45–74.

[3] Ibrar M, Nahom H, Mohammed A, *et al.* An explainable AI-based demand response optimization framework for smart buildings. In: International Symposium on Distributed Computing and Artificial Intelligence. Berlin: Springer; 2024. p. 88–98.

[4] Ibrar M, Abishu HN, Seid AM, *et al.* Survey on demand response in the landscape of adaptive and intelligent building energy management systems. In: 2024 International Wireless Communications and Mobile Computing (IWCMC); 2024. p. 1203–1209.

[5] Salem AH, Azzam SM, Emam O, *et al.* Advancing cybersecurity: a comprehensive review of AI-driven detection techniques. *Journal of Big Data*. 2024;11(1):105.

[6] Familoni BT Cybersecurity challenges in the age of AI: theoretical approaches and practical solutions. *Computer Science & IT Research Journal*. 2024;5(3):703–724.

[7] Khan MI, Arif A, and Khan ARA. The most recent advances and uses of AI in cybersecurity. *BULLET: Jurnal Multidisiplin Ilmu*. 2024;3(4):566–578.

[8] Aslam M. AI and cybersecurity: an ever-evolving landscape. *International Journal of Advanced Engineering Technologies and Innovations*. 2024;1(1):52–71.

[9] Sandhia G, Ranjani M, Nithiyanandam N, *et al.* Cybersecurity: the part played by artificial intelligence. In: *Analyzing Privacy and Security Difficulties in Social Media: New Challenges and Solutions*. Hershey, PA: IGI Global; 2025. p. 213–246.

[10] Ahmed A, Iqbal MM, Jabbar S, *et al.* Position-based emergency message dissemination schemes in the internet of vehicles: a review. *IEEE Transactions on Intelligent Transportation Systems*. 2023;24(12):13548–13572.

[11] Srivastava G, Jhaveri RH, Bhattacharya S, *et al.* XAI for cybersecurity: state of the art, challenges, open issues and future directions. arXiv preprint arXiv:220603585. 2022.

[12] Akbar A, Ibrar M, Jan MA, *et al.* SDN-enabled adaptive and reliable communication in IoT-fog environment using machine learning and multiobjective optimization. *IEEE Internet of Things Journal*. 2020;8(5):3057–3065.

[13] Ibrar M, Wang L, Muntean GM, *et al.* IHSF: an intelligent solution for improved performance of reliable and time-sensitive flows in hybrid SDN-based FC IoT systems. *IEEE Internet of Things Journal*. 2020;8(5):3130–3142.

[14] Kuppa A, and Le-Khac NA. Black box attacks on explainable artificial intelligence (XAI) methods in cyber security. In: *2020 International Joint Conference on Neural Networks (IJCNN)*. Piscataway, NJ: IEEE; 2020. p. 1–8.

[15] Šarčević A, Pintar D, Vranić M, *et al.* Cybersecurity knowledge extraction using XAI. *Applied Sciences*. 2022;12(17):8669.

[16] Senevirathna T, La VH, Marchal S, *et al.* A survey on XAI for 5G and beyond security: technical aspects, challenges and research directions. *IEEE Communications Surveys & Tutorials* 2025;27(2):941–973.

[17] Balantrapu SS. AI for predictive cyber threat intelligence. *International Journal of Management Education for Sustainable Development*. 2024;7(7):1–28.

[18] Rudin C, and Radin J. Why are we using black box models in AI when we don't need to? A lesson from an explainable AI competition. *Harvard Data Science Review*. 2019;1(2):1–9.

[19] Brożek B, Furman M, Jakubiec M, *et al.* The black box problem revisited. Real and imaginary challenges for automated legal decision making. *Artificial Intelligence and Law*. 2024;32(2):427–440.

[20] Chen YW, Chien SY, and Yu F. An overview of XAI algorithms. In: *2023 International Automatic Control Conference (CACS)*. Piscataway, NJ: IEEE; 2023. p. 1–5.

[21] Charmet F, Tanuwidjaja HC, Ayoubi S, *et al.* Explainable artificial intelligence for cybersecurity: a literature survey. *Annals of Telecommunications*. 2022;77(11):789–812.

[22] Vardhan H, Sai ANK, Sangers B, *et al.* Future trends and trials in cybersecurity and generative AI. In: *Reshaping Cyber Security with Generative AI Techniques*. Hershey, PA: IGI Global; 2025. p. 465–490.

[23] Yang S, Lao KW, Hui H, *et al.* Secure frequency regulation in power system: a comprehensive defense strategy against FDI, DoS, and latency cyberattacks. *Applied Energy*. 2025;379:124772.

[24] Bhardwaj R, Sreenivasulu Gogula BB, Kanagalakshmi K, *et al.* Machine learning and artificial intelligence for detecting cyber security threats in IoT environment. In: Chakrawarti RK, Sikarwar R, Sarangi SK, *et al.* (eds), *Natural Language Processing for Software Engineering*. Hoboken, NJ: John Wiley & Sons, Inc.; 2025. p. 1–14.

[25] Van der Velden BH, Kuijf HJ, Gilhuijs KG, *et al.* Explainable artificial intelligence (XAI) in deep learning-based medical image analysis. *Medical Image Analysis*. 2022;79:102470.

Chapter 2

Bridging the gap: explainable AI in threat detection and cybersecurity

Muhammad Rehan Naeem[1] *and Muhammad Farhan*[2]

Abstract

Explainable artificial intelligence (XAI) techniques integrated into threat detection and cybersecurity frameworks are an important step forward to tackle the issues that are complicated with the machine learning (ML) model. The objective of this chapter is to investigate XAI methods to make cybersecurity software more transparent, trustworthy, and accountable through the use of SHAP (SHapley Additive exPlanations), LIME (Local Interpretable Model-agnostic Explanations), Class Activation Maps (CAMs), and sensitivity analysis. First, our findings demonstrate that by providing additional explanation about the decision-making process of ML models, we supplement in ML and further improve human understanding and trust in those systems. For example, the introduction of XAI approaches has been proven to improve the detection accuracy of adversarial problems and facilitate the cybersecurity analyst to make an informed decision through interpretable results. We obtain insights into how models identify critical features and classify as malware in multiple classes by offering the visualizations of the form of heatmaps, CAMs, and concept activation vectors. Through analysis, distinct patterns and feature importance are unearthed with the model able to focus on different aspects of a dataset or class in which it is focused on based on common properties within different datasets and classes. Additionally, a sensitivity analysis has been conducted to make model conclusions and decision boundaries evaluate sensitivity upon input perturbations. Such contributions underscore XAI's value in helping to fill the gap between the possible capabilities of artificial intelligence in operations and operational requirements, promoting transparency and reliability, as well as informing decisions.

2.1 Introduction

Cybersecurity has been changing very fast over the last few decades due to the fast advancement of technology as well as the increase of dependency of digital system

[1]Department of Computer Science, University of Engineering and Technology Taxila, Pakistan
[2]Department of Computer Science, COMSATS University Islamabad, Sahiwal Campus, Pakistan

in all areas. Over the last few years, sophistication and frequency of cyber threats have been rapidly escalating, presenting great challenge to organizations and individuals.

2.1.1 Brief overview of the evolution of cybersecurity threats

Back in the early days of computing, cybersecurity threats were not overly complicated, and much like the cybersecurity threats of today, had their beginning in the spread of basic forms of malware, viruses, and worms. The vast majority of these threats concerned individual computers or small networks and took advantage of various operating system and/or applications vulnerabilities. With increase in internet and number of interconnected devices, the scale and complexity of cyberattacks grew exponentially. In the 1990s, the World Wide Web let in a new era of threats, and one of them is phishing, whose aim was to trick people into disclosing confidential information. Since the turn of the millennium, advanced persistent threats (APTs) and ransomware are the more sophisticated threats that have developed. APTs are highly targeted and stealthy attacks that take presence for a long period of time, giving the attackers time to gather huge amount of data and give big productivity loss. While ransomware encrypts victims' data and demands payment for the decryption key causing wide scale disruption and financial loss, the Samba CTA avoids encrypting victims' local files. In accordance with the time such as big data, cloud computing, and the Internet of Things, the attack surface expanded exponentially. We live in an information age. Today cybercriminals have an unlimited amount of data and an exploding number of potential entry points into a network. As such, supply chain attacks, which rely on compromising such software or hardware pieces used by many organizations, have emerged as even more complex and multifaceted threats.

2.1.2 The increasing complexity of cyberattacks and the need for advanced detection mechanisms

Several factors make for increasing complexity of cyberattacks. First, attackers are becoming more sophisticated and creative in their use of new methods and a variety of tools in attempts to hide from detection and make use of vulnerabilities. Finally, the increase of the attack surface due to the proliferations of connected devices and the use of new technologies. Third, the increasingly important value of data, such a valuable target of criminals in the cyberspace. These advanced threats now pass traditional forms of cybersecurity such as firewalls and antivirus software. Signature-based detection often depends on these signatures and are good only on finding out known threats and won't work during zero-day exploits or polymorphic malware. Also, they are incapable of dealing with huge amounts of data in real time and identifying small traces of patterns that suggest malicious activity. Consequently, there is a need for more sophisticated detection mechanisms that will guarantee more comprehensive protection against a large variety of threats. The analysis of large amounts of data is an important task and machine learning

(ML) and artificial intelligence (AI) seem to offer a solution to complete this task. However, while potential ethical issues posed by the use of AI in cybersecurity should not be underestimated, the use of AI in cybersecurity does however come with its own set of concerns in terms of transparency, accountability and trust. This is where explainable artificial intelligence (XAI) comes into play, enabling one to gain insight into the decision-making process of AI systems, and help the build trust with its respective users.

2.1.3 Importance of XAI

But designing such models and systems is one of the areas of research in XAI in AI. Transparency (fairly understanding how an AI system goes from input to output); interpretability (being able to identify the factors being used by the AI); and explainability (understanding why the AI produced the result it did) are the three tenets of the XAI project. To achieve these goals, commonly used techniques include Local Interpretable Model-agnostic Explanations (LIME), Shapley Additive exPlanations (SHAP), and Full or Partial Dependence Plots (PDPs). In cybersecurity, where AI-driven threat detection systems can be a huge deal in strengthening or breaking down an organization's security, trust and transparency are elements that matter the most. XAI increases trust by showing the reason behind AI decisions allowing the security analyst to understand why a given threat was flagged and act based on informed decision. Besides, it promotes collaboration between human analysts and AI systems to enhance decision-making, diminish false positives, false negatives, and maximize the strengths of both machines and humans. In addition, XAI aids in accountability and compliance by giving accountability and traceability to the AI decision-making processes, thereby assisting organizations to meet regulatory requirements that prevent penalties. XAI contributes to reliable and robust AI models capable of coping with changes of threats and adversarial attacks. As such, XAI is crucial to the enhancement of the accuracy, fairness, and resilience of AI-based cybersecurity solutions.

2.1.4 Objectives of this chapter

The main goal of this chapter is to achieve a thorough new insight into integration of XAI in threat detecting systems in the cybersecurity domain. The goals of this chapter are several and will help to make clearer how XAI could help improve the effectiveness and reliability of AI-based threat detection mechanisms. The main goal of the chapter is to go into deeper detail regarding the practical challenges of integrating XAI into the existing threat detection methodologies. It goes over technical challenges and opportunities involved in embedding XAI techniques in the different stages of threat detection process, including data collection and pre-processing, model training, and decision-making. Through the examination of these integration points, the Chapter attempts to make it easier for readers to understand how XAI can be practically integrated to real-world cybersecurity scenarios. It will cover how to generate explanations of the decisions that an ML model makes by using LIME, SHAP, etc. Furthermore, the chapter will provide case studies and practical examples which showcase how XAI has been embedded into threat detection systems, giving an example of how XAI can be implemented and with what consequences.

2.2 Literature review

These days, AI has been largely integrated with different parts of life and has transformed various fields but integration of AI is often illusory because complex AI systems are inherently opaque, unlike the proposed principles of XAI systems. In particular, being able to trust systems to an unknown degree is especially problematic in the area of cybersecurity. There exist various approaches suggested by the literature to make AI explainable, and to some extent, prepare one to the benefits of XAI in cybersecurity, but at the same time there is a tension or paradox in the fact that XAI strengthens cybersecurity practices, but also, and more seriously, exposes systems to adversarial attacks. Henceforth, it is essential to thoroughly analyze the current XAI methodologies through cybersecurity for making a clear pathway of research in the future. In this study, we comprehensively survey over 300 papers covering the application of XAI in a wide range of crucial cybersecurity areas, e.g., intrusion detection system (IDS), malware, phishing and spam, botnet, fraud, zero-day vulnerabilities, digital forensics and crypto jacking. This review exemplifies the seminal works on explainability techniques proposed or used in such areas and identify emerging challenges, to provide a solid basis toward the advancement of XAI in cybersecurity [1].

In this chapter, interpretability of AI techniques can be categorized into black box and white box ML algorithms, where both have different characteristics. White box systems generate results that are inherently interpretable, and professionals can understand and analyze what the system is doing. However, black box systems are easy to use: they are often very accurate but are complicated to understand by even an expert in the domain that the system is used on. To fill up this gap, XAI methods focus on these three characteristics: explainability, transparency, and interpretability. While a universally accepted definition of explainability does not exist, it is often taken as a set of interpretable characteristics of a model that influence the outcome of a classification or regression task. However, interpretability is defined as the ability to comprehend and understand how an ML model works in order to enable user understanding and make informed decisions. In order for developers to be able to define and replicate the set of processes whereby model parameters are extracted from training data and predictions are generated from test data, they need to be transparent. Indeed, algorithms obeying these principles lead to justifiable decisions, a means to track and review, a possible venue for improving algorithms, and a basis for fact-based exploration of algorithms. Therefore, using interpretable white-box ML algorithms is especially crucial in some domains such as medicine, finance, law, or defense, where they require both high accuracy as well as understanding how the results are derived for being trusted and reliable. For example, the challenges that the Department of Defense has been facing require incorporation of autonomous and intelligent systems, which calls for XAI to make warfighters aware, trustable and dependable in terms of managing of machine partners driven by AI. In cybersecurity, many ML algorithms have been used for threat detection and mitigation; however, like their counterparts in mechanized systems, most remain black box to the users [2].

In recent times, AI has been integrated into cybersecurity and has profoundly changed the threat detection and mitigation landscape by providing an expedient and precision service to identify the malicious activities. Nevertheless, there is still a great challenge: The very nature of many AI systems is opaque, usually known as "black boxes." However, due to this opacity it is very difficult for security professionals who are expected to validate and understand the decisions made by these systems in order to be able to trust, hold them accountable, or understand how they are making their decisions. Addressing these challenges is XAI, which has emerged as the panacea for providing the mechanism to translate the black box of AI models to explain the decision-making processes followed by the models, and needs contribute to increasing the transparency and the trust in the intelligent systems [3]. Specifically for cybersecurity, XAI can be seen as making complex AI-driven threat detection systems more explainable and understand able by cybersecurity experts so that they can trace and understand the reason why a specific decision has been made. Rule-based reasoning, decision trees and attention mechanisms have served to make the AI models' way of evaluating and identifying potential threats clearer so as to improve the confidence in their output. Apart from improving the transparency, XAI allows better auditing and refinement of the AI models as XAI gives the reasons to describe why an AI got it wrong, e.g., false positive or false negative. Being able to keep enhancing model performance in a continuous fashion and being able to adapt to ever changing threats and changing attack strategies. XAI offers to close this gap and facilitates the creation of more reliable, accountable and effective AI systems for cybersecurity. Finally, the inclusion of explainability guarantees that automated threat detection systems are not only robust and secure, but are also well understood by human experts who are able to take quick and educated action regarding the most up to date threats.

With a wide adoption of ML models in the cybersecurity application areas, mainly like IDS, a major hurdle has been defined that these models are regarded as "black box" systems. The lack of transparency makes trust more difficult and provides a complicated picture on making decisions, which is particularly harmful in security sensitive domains where reasoning behind the prediction is an important aspect. Although this limitation is difficult to overcome, XAI has been widely studied to tackle this issue and enable human industry experts to interpret the evidence based on data and the role played by the causal reasoning of ML models. Trust management is essential to the assessment of impact of malicious data and achieves correct intrusion detection in IDS. Previous studies have been mainly driven to improve the accuracy of the classification algorithms for IDSs, however, they have not adequately explained how this happens, nor have they been sufficiently intuitive with description of the behavior and decision-making of these sophisticated models [4]. Given that there is this gap, it makes explainability an important tool for boosting transparency and trust. This paper aims to apply XAI principles to IDS trust management by relying on the decision tree model, which is a transparent and interpretable algorithm. In particular, decision trees are great because they resemble the way we make decisions by splitting complex decisions into smaller, understandable decisions instead. The effectiveness of this approach is demonstrated by its application to extract rules from the well-known knowledge discovery in databases (KDD) benchmark dataset and to evaluate the performance of decision tree model. We compare its accuracy with the accuracy of state-of-the-art algorithms and derive the insight whether it can be used as a practical and interpretable solution for IDS. In addition to that, this study highlights the potential of decision trees for strengthening the explainability and facilitates the progression of trust management in cybersecurity applications by means of transparent and interpretable ML techniques [5].

Cyber-physical production systems (CPPS) have been recently developed to translate the manufacturing to the age of digitalization with seamless integration of physical production process and digital systems for creating an implication of one and highly efficient industrial cyber network. Measurement and sensing systems are central to the CPPS functionality as they offer real time data availability from physical systems and their environments for optimized production processes. Despite their growing prevalence, however, these systems are extremely high value targets for malware attacks because attackers can use them to compromise the accuracy and reliability of the data, placing the entire production ecosystem at risk. The methodology introduced in this paper aims at safeguarding Industry 4.0 systems against cyberattacks and comprises of three key components: API deployment, cloud-based filtering, and intelligence-driven data processing. The use of APIs in sensor networks enhances data utilization; data integrity and confidentiality are assured as the first line of defense. Filtering out incoming data and generating clean datasets for analysis/decision-making is a key role of cloud services and advanced intelligence and data processing techniques for detecting and analyzing potential malware threats is utilized. In order to improve upon the proposed methodology, the research laboratory with a secure research facility is considered for in depth malware analysis with additional support of encrypted multimedia channels indicating secured communication to the researchers and security experts. It shows that reinforcement learning can be a good approach if we want to identify, locate, and even mitigate cyberattacks in Industry 4.0 systems [6]. Moreover, it reveals the relations between different performance metrics, and helps explain how such performance metrics affect the reinforcement agent as a whole. This methodology provides a significant progress in securing CPPS by guaranteeing these systems to be robust against cyberattacks as well as maintaining data confidentiality and integrity.

With the emergence of collective intelligence systems, including Chat Generative Pre-Trained Transformer (ChatGPT), the era of possibilities as well as difficulties has also come with it for cybersecurity and privacy protection. These are systems that are powered by advanced AI and big data analytics systems that offer the promise of significant improvements in the security and privacy of our lives, but which at the same time give rise to a set of entirely new risks that must not be ignored and, if possible, are answered with new solutions. In this study, the author [7] proposes novel ways to leverage AI and big data analytics to confront mass challenges and innovative problems on the synergies of cybersecurity, privacy, human factors, ethics, and new technologies. Partial contributions include applying natural language processing (NLP) in ChatGPT styles systems for information security purposes, assessing privacy enhancing technologies for providing data utility with minimal amount of personal data exposed, and modeling human behavior to design secure and ethically human centric systems. Moreover, ML techniques are put into use for data-driven threat and vulnerability detection and advanced analytics are utilized for privacy preserving in Big Data while create value. A special attention is given to developing trustworthy and transparent (explainable) AI methods that are transparent and accountable in their operation.

This research introduces a very new methodology in the context of malware detection based on use of deep learning (DL) to extract features from raw data without human attention. More specifically, the technique consists of transforming malware files into grayscale images, which are then shrunken down and the essential patterns of which are kept intact. Grayscale images are taken as inputs of convolutional neural networks (CNNs) in order for the system to learn fine patterns that may be missed by classical detection. While malware remains a major, if not the top, threat when it comes to computer security, the institute at AV-Test found that over 5 million new malware samples are created each day. However, due to the sheer volume of malware, security teams have to resort to classification methods to prioritize these incidents as there is no way to address them all at once [8]. The problem is complicated by the fact that malware is evolving at a very rapid rate and it is becoming more and more diverse, voluminous and sophisticated. As a result, modern attackers used automatic code obfuscation, code encryption techniques among others to perform evasion in which traditional ML approaches based on hand crafted feature vectors are not effective for malware classification. However, to face these challenges, recent advances in DL specifically deep CNNs have shown real promise in identifying and classifying malware much more accurately [9].

In this work, the author [10] introduces a novel DL-based system to classify the malware families and do the multiclass classification. The methodology proposed in the paper includes converting malware files to grayscale images that extract detailed patterns that may be hidden when applying feature extractions ordinarily. The grayscale images are then fed into a CNN which makes use of its capability to learn complicated hierarchical features to classify accurately. This method overcomes the shortcomings of the traditional approaches of malware detection and fits the changing nature of the current malware by converting malware to a visual representation and using CNNs. The results show the potentials of this system to significantly improve the malware detection and classification to provide a valuable solution to tackle the increasing complexity of malware threats. To conclude, DL has revolutionized cybersecurity practice and is well suited to tackle the ever-increasing issues presented by continuously increasing proliferation of malware.

2.3 Fundamentals of threat detection in cybersecurity

2.3.1 Traditional threat detection methods

Tradition threat detection methods have been the corner stone of cybersecurity for many years and have been the building base in which to identify and mitigate cyber threats. Mainly these methods are based on developed techniques that have been already practiced to tackle different kind of security risks. Three traditional threat detection methods are signature-based, anomaly based, and behavior based. These all have their strengths and weaknesses, which are necessary to know when considering their effectiveness in the cybersecurity world today.

2.3.1.1 Signature-based detection

One of the oldest and basic detection features in cybersecurity is signature-based detection. It is a process in which network traffic or file content is compared to a database of well-known malicious signatures. These are unique patterns or sequences of data that are representative of certain malware or attack vector. If an activity is suspected of being malicious, the system marks it, blocks the traffic and performs other appropriate actions like the quarantining of the questionable file. The main advantage of signature-based detection is to the fact that it is fast and accurate to known threats. It works since it relies on predefined signatures that can permit reliable protection from general malware and attacks that have been previously identified and documented. Nevertheless, this method has its own limitations. It only works against known threats and it cannot identify new or unknown (zero day) attacks with no corresponding signature in database. Furthermore, attackers can easily circumvent signature detection by changing their malware, or performing polymorphic techniques to change to signature.

2.3.1.2 Anomaly-based detection

Heuristic detection or anomaly-based detection entails the effort made to identify deviations from the normal behavior or a pattern in a system. This method defines what is normal activity according to historical data and statistical analysis. If any activity is far away from this baseline; then, such activity is flagged as suspicious and needs further investigation. Signature-based methods have many advantages over anomaly based. It does not have signatures to detect and does not rely on predefined signatures to detect known or unknown threats. This is exactly why it can be very useful to identify zero-day attack and other new threats that are not identified before. Besides, it can adjust itself to the changing environments and the evolving threat landscapes as the baseline of the normal behavior changes constantly. Moreover, anomaly-based detection also has its own problems. It has very high false positives, falsely identifying legitimate conduct that deviates from the well-known baseline as threat. This could result in the security analyst having to deal with unnecessary alerts, as well as more work. Further, it is not easy to set up an accurate baseline, and it is rather time consuming especially in the presence of continually shifting behavioral patterns in dynamic environments.

2.3.1.3 Behavior-based detection

Heuristic analysis, or behavior-based detection for instance, looks at the way behavior of software and processes were in order to determine if they are malicious. This method approaches a program's actions and interactions from program to program, looking for patterns that appear to be malicious. For example, it can track things like, file access, registry changes, network connection, and other similar malicious behaviors that usually occur with malware. Signature-based and anomaly-based methods of detection are comparatively reactive to a threat whereas behavior-based detection methodologies are proactive in nature. If the specific malware or attack vector has never been seen before, it can recognize and prevent the activity from occurring before any damage occurs. The nature of this kind of detection makes it a very effective way of detecting APTs and any other more sophisticated attack that may avoid other forms of detection. But detection of such an attack based on the behavior of a victim site still has its limitations. but monitoring all processes in real time can be computationally intensive if you want to use significant resources to achieve it. Furthermore, malicious software may produce a high number of false positives, since legitimate activities may behave just as a malicious one. Moreover, sophisticated attacks can be covered using code obfuscation and encryption methods in order to hide their malicious activities and bypass behavior-based detection.

2.3.2 Limitations and challenges faced by traditional methods

Traditional threat detection methods have helped protect cybersecurity, but they have problems and issues with current threat environment. Since defining signatures relies on predefined signatures which are missing for new or unknown threats, signature-based detection is not effective against zero-day attacks. As a result, organizations remain susceptible to attacks that may not have been known to them and documented previously. Detection methods based on anomaly or behavior can produce a large number of false positives because the normal behavior being used like a baseline is not always accurate in identifying abnormal behavior and may flag legitimate activities that deviate from the normal behavior or exhibit behaviors similar to those of malware. Such a thing leads to not necessary alerts and overloading the workload of their security analysts, lowering the efficiency of the overall threat detection process. Behavior-based detection can be computationally intensive, forced to examine and examine behavior of all processes in real time. This can be a performance-heavy thing and not feasible in the resource constrained environment. With regard to new threat landscape and new attack vectors, it would be difficult for traditional methods to adapt to it. Due to the fact that attackers are developing more sophisticated techniques to bypass detection, traditional approach may not be so effective to give complete protection from advanced threats.

2.3.3 Role of artificial intelligence in modern threat detection

There is no doubt in the fact that AI has changed the game when it comes to threat detection with its capability of defining the sophisticated ML and DL models to ingest large scale data, detect anomaly patterns and predict an outcome in real time.

Through these AI-driven systems needs of cybersecurity professionals in detection and countering cyber threats, have greatly bettered.

2.3.3.1 Machine learning in threat detection

AI as a field has ML as one of its subsets that deal with building algorithms that can learn from and make decisions from data. For example, ML models are trained over large dataset of network traffic, system logs, etc. to be able to spot the patterns or abnormal events that reflect malicious activity in the context of threat detection. These include supervised models, unsupervised models, and semi supervised one-state depending on the data type and specific need of the threat detection system. In supervised learning, the model is trained on labeled data, i.e., each data point is accompanied by its known outcome, e.g., cancer or not (benign or malicious). It learns the features that separate different classes and can then classify new unseen instances based on what it has learned. However, this approach is very good at detecting known threats and known malware that have already been labeled. However, unsupervised learning is training a model on unlabeled data in which the model is expected to learn underlier patterns and structures in the data. Another useful approach for detecting new threats or zero-day attacks, is the one that does not require predefined labels and is able to detect anomalies deviating from the normal behavior. Unsupervised learning can be used to cluster and detect anomalies (threats). Semi supervision combines both supervised and unsupervised learning, using small amount of labeled data along with large set of data to which labels are not available to enhance the accuracy and generalization of the model. In particular, such approach is quite successful if labeled data are rare or expensive.

2.3.3.2 Deep learning in threat detection

ML is more advanced version of it and uses neural networks having multiple layers in order to learn representing a hierarchy of data. DL models can automatically extract features from the raw data without requiring the manual feature engineering and complex and subtle patterns that cannot be identified by the traditional methods are detected. DL models are often used for the task of the ML in the threat detection, such as malware classification, network intrusion detection and fraud detection. CNNs are often used for image-based tasks (e.g., on screenshot or visual representation of some code), while recurrent neural networks and long short-term memory networks are generally applied for sequential data (like network traffic or log files). Furthermore, DL models can be integrated with other methods, for instance, NLP, to mine over text data and reveal phishing attempts, social engineering attacks, and other cybercrimes. Given that DL is currently allowing threat detection systems to detect emerging and sophisticated threats with better accuracy and robustness, it makes sense that the two can be combined.

2.3.4 Advantages of AI-driven systems over traditional methods

Several important advantages are provided by AI-driven threat detection systems compared to traditional detection methods making AI systems an important part of modern cybersecurity program.

The biggest advantage of AI-based systems is higher level of accuracy and better results in threat detection. Traditional methods like those using signature-based detection are constrained by their reliance on predefined signatures to identify a threat; new or unknown threats the signatures have not been identified may be missed. However, AI-driven systems can analyze large datasets to determine if there are patterns which exist that would suggest illegal activity, without necessarily having run into such patterns before. As a result, they can sniff more threats beyond zero-day attacks and APTs. Moreover, AI-driven systems have another great advantage of being able to do real time analysis and response. Historically, vast and expensive batch processing of data led to delay in threat detection and response. However, AI-driven systems can analyze the data in real time which can give live lines and they can very fast respond to new threats. Today, with a rapid and ever-changing threat landscape, action is taken needing to take place swiftly to prevent a security incident from becoming a major issue.

It is facilitated that AI-driven systems are highly scalable and are adoptable in handling the rising volume and complexity of data produced in the latest digital environment. However, traditional methods may not be able to keep up the pace with increasing amount of data and changing threats, and this adversely affects the performance and effectiveness of traditional methods. However, there are several advantages of using AI-driven systems as compared to a human, which includes their ability for efficient processing of large volumes of data and continual learning and update of their models to accommodate changes in the threat landscape. This way they stay relevant and active in the face of changes to threats and threat actors moving with them. And, such AI-driven systems can also avoid the problem of the number of false positives and negatives, which are common problems with traditional methods of threat detection. False positives are not that rarity during which legitimate activities are misidentified as threats generating needless alerts and more workload for security analysts. On the contrary, false negatives are when actual threats are passed and organizations remain exposed to attack. These errors are minimized by AI-driven systems through advanced algorithms and techniques which give the users a more accurate and reliable results. As a result, organizations are better able to detect threats more efficiently and effectively, and concentrate their resources on real threats instead of fakes, before taking the necessary action.

The benefits provided to AI-driven systems are automation and efficiency. Traditional methods of their application are generally based on labor and resource intensive manual intervention and analysis. However, the process of detecting threat can be automated by AI-driven systems, whereby data collection and analysis, decision-making and response can be automated. Consequently, with this, security analysts can concentrate on more significant assignments and capacity will descend making the executions proficient and more efficient.

2.4 Understanding XAI

2.4.1 Key concepts of XAI

XAI are decision-making process of AI systems that are made transparent, understandable and interpretable to humans. This section covers the most important concepts of XAI, what does it mean for an AI system to be "explainable" and what kind of XAI approaches there are.

An AI system is explained based on the ability to provide clear, comprehensible, and justifiable explanations for its decisions and actions. Unlike the traditional black box AI models which operate in the black box manner so as to give zero insight about internal workings and factors/features that contribute to output, XAI systems are designed to show the basis of such factors, features and processes that contribute to their outputs. This transparency is crucial in establishing the bond of trust between humans and AI systems that will only be possible if the user can validate the reason for the decision made by the AI and understand the reason thereof.

Transparency: Being transparent to the overall functionality of the AI model in terms of the inputs, outputs and how the results are generated. High level view of how the model works is then provided by transparent AI systems where users can see how the model operates.

Interpretability: It should be understandable by people to understand precisely what factors or context features drive the AI to make a given decision. Interpretable AI systems allow the user to see which data either variables or data points have the greatest impact on the model's output.

Capability: The AI system can offer clear and understandable explanation regarding its actions and what possible outcomes. XAI systems can provide reasoning to the rationale of their decisions on a level of language human users can understand.

To accomplish these characteristics, XAI techniques usually entail splitting down complex AI versions right into much less complex, more understandable systems. For example, one can decompose a deep neural network to each individual layer or a neuron, each can be analyzed and explained separately. Moreover, other XAI methods may also employ the use of visualization tools, NLP, and others to communicate to the users on what the AI is doing and how it is making such decisions in a human language format.

2.4.2 Different types of XAI approaches

In terms of XAI, local and global explanations are the two main types. Each has its own purpose and gives information about the AI system's behavior that the other does not. Local explanations concentrate on giving the detailed information of how the AI made a decision for a particular input or instance. The questions they wish to answer include; "Why did the AI make this particular decision?" And, what was involved in leading to this specific outcome? Local explanations are especially useful to understanding stray aspects of individual predictions, as well as uncover any potential biases or errors in the AI model.

LIME is a well-known method that approximates the differentiable behavior of a complex AI model for a specific input by fitting a simpler, interpretable model in the local region. It enables those users to learn about these factors that made this particular instance be the way it was.

SHAP is another method most commonly used for local explanation that explains the prediction of an ML model by attributing it to the contribution of every feature. It estimates the Shapley values, which are the average marginal contribution of the feature for every possible subset of features.

In contrast, the global explanations try to give a general understanding of the behavior of the AI system across entire dataset or input space. Some of them are wondering how the magic of the AI model works in general. "What are the driving key factors of the AI's decision-making process?" Global explanations are helpful for understanding what the AI system can do and what it can't do from a global perspective, and spotting systemic problems or styles in the way that the model performs.

PDPs—display the relationship between AI model's predictions against 1 or more input features, averaged over the other features' distribution. It demonstrates how changes in one feature influences the output from the model, and gives us deeper understanding of how the AI system works in general.

Feature importance analysis is the kind of analysis that quantifies the degree of contribution of each input feature to the prediction made by the AI model. This can be done by examining the effect of each feature on the model's performance through any metrics including permutation importance or mean decrease impurity.

2.5 Challenges in implementing XAI for threat detection

The integration of XAI into threat detection systems has a great potential to improve transparency, accountability and trust. The problem is, however, that this process is not without its challenges. However, a potential set of several technical hurdles and limitations needs to be addressed in order to have XAI successfully incorporated in functional threat detection frameworks. Finally, this section highlights some of these challenges: the challenge of complexity and interpretability of the models.

2.5.1 Technical hurdles and limitations

Integrating XAI into threat detection systems is one of the main challenges because modern AI models are complex. Currently, many smart cybersecurity models, ML and DL models are very highly complex and dense with a lot of layers, a lot of nodes, complex parameters. The problem is that the decision-making process of these model is often not directly interpretable, and can be opaque and non-intuitive.

Take for example deep neural network used for malware classification or network intrusion detection having million parameters and complex architectures; it becomes difficult to understand how these networks have arrived to make such type of predictions. Along with this, these models are also prone to complexity issues such as overfitting, i.e., the model performs well to train data while not able to generalize to new unseen data. Inaccurate or unreliable explanations can occur resulting in the ineffectiveness of XAI in terms of threat detection. Several strategies are possible to deal with the problem of model complexity. A simple way is to use simpler (and more interpretable) models whenever possible. For instance, a decision tree or a linear regression model may explain in plain language and therefore is suitable for some threat detection tasks. Another way is that techniques like model distillation or pruning are used to make heavy models simpler without harming the performance. These techniques can help reduce the model's complexity and therefore make it easier to produce accurate, meaningful explanations.

Another major problem with providing XAI for threats detection is that the AI system's decisions have to be interpretable. The ability to understand and explain, with what features and factors do they depend, the factors that influence AI's predictions is interpreted as interpretability. Some XAI methods, for example, LIME and SHAP, can explain individual predictions locally, but they are not necessarily whole and true. For example, a complex model can be approximated LIME by a simpler path interpretable model to understand the behavior of a specific input instance. But this approximation should not assume all the nuances and interactions amongst features for the prediction. Similarly, the SHAP values give insights about how much on average each feature contributes to the organization's decision but, they may not characterize the context dependency of the AI's decision-making.

It is important to choose and use appropriate XAI techniques to improve interpretability of the threat detection system with the consideration of certain requirements and characteristics of the system. Thus, combining a local and a global explanation technique can lead to a greater understanding of the behavior of AI. Besides, utilizing domain knowledge and expert knowledge in the XAI process can validate the explanations as well as confirm their relatedness and correctness. However, it can be difficult to implement XAI for threat detection given the quality and availability of data. For development of accurate and reliable AI models, quality, diversity, and representativeness of the datasets are paramount. In cybersecurity, however, it is not straightforward to gather such datasets, since data is often sensitive, proprietary, and small in quantity. The poor quality of the data, in the sense that there can exist missing value, noise or bias, can degrade the performance of AI models and of XAI explanations. Moreover, training such effective models along with generating meaningful explanations is challenging due to the lacking labeled data for some type of threats or attack vectors.

To overcome this, organizations can spend money on data collection and preprocessing so that the data that is fed to the AI models to be trained and tested improve their quality and relevance. Data limitation can be overcome and the robustness to ML threat detection system be increased through techniques such as data augmentation, synthetic data generation, and transfer learning. Particularly for threat detection systems, scalability and performance are important considerations within when upgrading with an XAI. Since the volume and complexity of data in cybersecurity is continuously increasing, we need to guarantee that the XAI techniques can deal with large datasets, as well as instantaneous processing needs. First, some XAI methods, including very complex computations or visualizations, can be computationally intensive and in some cases, time consuming. The time required for generating explanations can be delayed, and the impact would arise in terms of the overall performance of the threat detection system. However, many challenges exist currently in this XAI world, so these organizations can optimize XAI algorithms and use advanced computing resources like GPU and cloud platforms to accelerate XAI.

2.5.2 Case studies and practical applications

In real-world scenario, we have done operation research on integration of XAI in threat detection systems and gained useful insights and practical benefits. The first part of this section provides several case studies where XAI has been successfully implemented in cybersecurity and a summary of the outcomes and lessons learned from such initiatives.

2.5.2.1 Case study 1: malware detection with LIME

In the context, an ML model was developed by a leading cybersecurity firm to detect malware using static and dynamic features that are extracted from executable files. The model had high accuracy, but as a black box, security analysts could not trust or understand the predictions made by it.

In order to tackle this problem, the firm implemented LIME into their malware detection system. Local explanations for each prediction were generated using LIME, giving valuable information about which underlying feature this decision was based on. For instance, in case the model classified a file as malicious, LIME could explain which features, e.g. the ones related to certain API calls or suspicious strings, led to such classification. LIMEs acceptance had significantly enhanced trust and validation in AI-driven malware detection system among the security analysts. Analysts could validate the findings and take appropriate action after knowing rationale to make the model's decisions. To make a finer point, LIME helped deduce false positives by revealing which features were conking out the model's poor predictions. It helped analysts refine the feature set and thereby making the overall accuracy of the system better. LIME also gave insights into improved model development and optimization of our malware detection model. The explanations could be used by the analysts to detect possible issues or bias in the model and fix it.

2.5.2.2 Case study 2: network intrusion detection with SHAP

Every large enterprise having such critical infrastructure for their business has a fire wall and IDS in place to watch over network traffic and identify anomalous activity that might be associated with cyberattacks. Unfortunately, there was no transparency in the IDS's decision-making, that meant it was difficult to investigate and respond to alerts.

To make the IDS more interpretable, enterprises implemented SHAP to the system. We also compute the feature contribution of each network feature (e.g., packet sizes, connection durations, protocol types) of the model's predictions using SHAP. Summary plots and dependence plots were used to visualize the SHAP values which gave a clear idea about the factors which were key for an IDS's decision-making. SHAP provided comprehensive insights of how the IDS behaved by letting the analyst knowing the main effects of different network features and the possible interactions or nonlinear relationships between features. SHAP led to efficient investigation of alerts by producing visualizations which helped to focus on those factors that were most influential to the IDS's decision. This will help the analysts concentrate on the useful aspect of the data and take timely action. SHAP values: In addition to a possible explanation of the reason for the model predictions, SHAP values could help to identify potential weaknesses, as well as look for possible biases within the IDS model. Through the contributions of different features, the analysts are able to refine the model, and thus increase the performance of the model over time.

2.5.2.3 Case study 3: phishing detection with counterfactual explanations

An email service provider trained and implemented an ML model, which helps us figure out whether the email is phishing, as well as trying to find things in them (features) such as links, grammar, structure, domain names, and the like. The model got the phishing attempt right but users didn't have any idea why a certain email would look suspicious.

To deal with this concern, the provider additionally implements counterfactual explanations in their phishing detection system. The other one was counterfactual explanations showing what in the input data needs to change to get a different prediction from the model. To give an example, if an email was flagged as phishing, the counterfactual explanation could clearly identify features (e.g., presence of some keywords or URLs) that would have to change in order to turn the email from being phishing to benign. Counterfactual explanations were found to be useful for educating the users as they helped users understand the characteristics of phishing emails and how to stay away from phishing emails. The counterfactual explanations also contributed to False Positive Reduction by showing the features which caused the model to make incorrect predictions. With this, the provider was able to reduce the feature set and enhance the phishing detection system accuracy on the whole. Counterfactual explanations were used to help debug and improve the phishing detection model. The explanations could be used by analysts to discover vulnerabilities or biases in the model and perform the needful adjustments.

2.6 Results and discussion

The chapter starts off by presenting the results of our investigation on integrating XAI techniques within threat detection and cybersecurity frameworks. Accordingly, our findings indicate that the use of XAI serves also not only to clarify the workings of ML models, but importantly translates into a considerably better human understanding and trust of ML systems decisions. For instance, thanks to the use of XAI methods (SHAP, LIME, etc.), complex neural networks exhibit a considerable boost of detection accuracy for adversarial threats. User studies with cybersecurity analysts suggest the same: analysts' confidence in answering incidents is higher when they receive interpretable results, which shows the importance of explainability in closing this gap between advanced AI capability and needs of the operational environment. These results will serve as the basis for further exploration of how XAI can tackle the existing problems in cybersecurity topped with creating accountability and informed decision-making to ensure the highest standards of trust and transparency.

We present the performance of our model compared to the original data and Class Activation Maps (CAMs), as shown in Figure 2.1 through heatmaps. Each dataset or sample is labeled as 1–5 and each dataset comes with two columns, the left column for the original data, and the right column for the corresponding CAM. The color scales are color coded, and red stands for high values and blue for the low values, which consequently assists in visual representation of the distribution of intensity of the data. Original data heatmaps have distinct patterns and variations of intensity proportional to the dataset's own inherent characteristics. However, on the CAM heatmaps you can see which regions the model had focused on while making

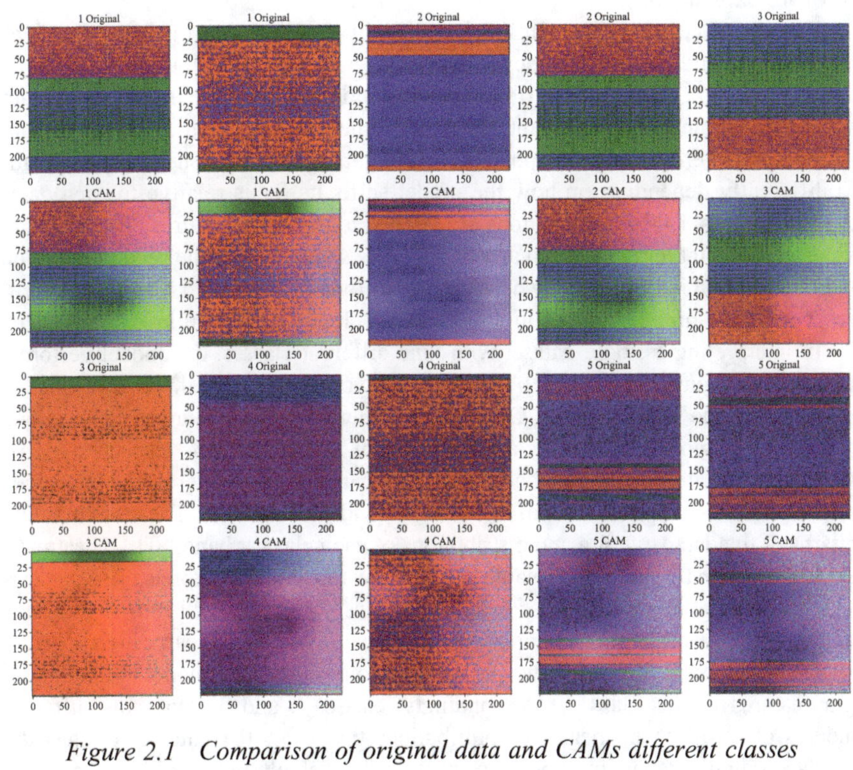

Figure 2.1 Comparison of original data and CAMs different classes

the prediction process. These maps show how well the model represents the important features in each dataset by displaying those at which the model attends (high activation, red). By validating that the model provides accurate identifications and emphasis of the important features across a wide range of datasets, it is clear from the alignment to the original data that the CAMs can be used to accurately reveal the key aspects of the data they are made from. A strong evidence of pattern recognition, and thus, predictive accuracy is given by the consistent presence of high activation regions in the CAMs.

As a test, we perform interpretability with LIME. It is a grid filled with different datasets or samples (labeled 1–5). The explanation details for a given dataset are depicted in the rightmost column of the row of a given dataset, and the original data is shown in the leftmost column of the row of a given dataset. The color codes of the heatmaps are in red when the rank-1 tensors contribute positively to the model predictions, or in blue with opposite contribution. As we can see in the original data heatmaps, there are clearly distinguishable patterns that also vary in intensity as those represent the basic characteristics of each dataset. These provide a baseline as to how the structure and distribution of the data is expected to be. They provide insights into how the model interprets this pattern by showing the LIME heatmaps neighboring the original data. Regions contributing positively (red) or negatively (blue) to the model's decision-making process are identified via the LIME explanations.

For example, LIME heatmap in class 1 highlights the areas that model assigns importance to and some of the locations give high positive contribution while some others give high negative contribution. This indicates that the model is in fact capable of recognizing important features of the dataset. Such is the case with classes 2–5, where we observe positive and negative contributions that are weighted differently depending on how the model shifts its focus relative to each dataset's uniqueness. LIME explanations are aligned to the input features because it can explain interpretable results such as which features are pushing the predictions. The performance and interpretability of the model is overall supported by the consistent presence of meaningful contributions across all classes as shown in Figure 2.2.

In interpreting a single dataset with nine different classes, our model performs according to Figure 2.2, using SHAP. The grid layout is split into three rows, one for each class of the dataset (1–3). On each row there are two columns, the left one showing the original data in that class and the right one showing the respective SHAP explanations. In the original data heatmaps, you can see clear patterns and intensities as dictated by the nature of each of these classes within the dataset. These are baseline patterns of the data structure and distributions of each class at hand. SHAP heatmaps next to the original data further enable to view how the model interprets these patterns by giving feature importance. For example, in class 1, the SHAP heatmap indicates that the model places high weight on some areas while other areas carry high negative weight (blue) and high positive weight (red). It follows that the model is finding the right features in this class. Correspondingly, classes 2 and 3 also show different amounts of positive and negative contributions that show the latter can adjust the focus accordingly depending upon the specialty of each class.

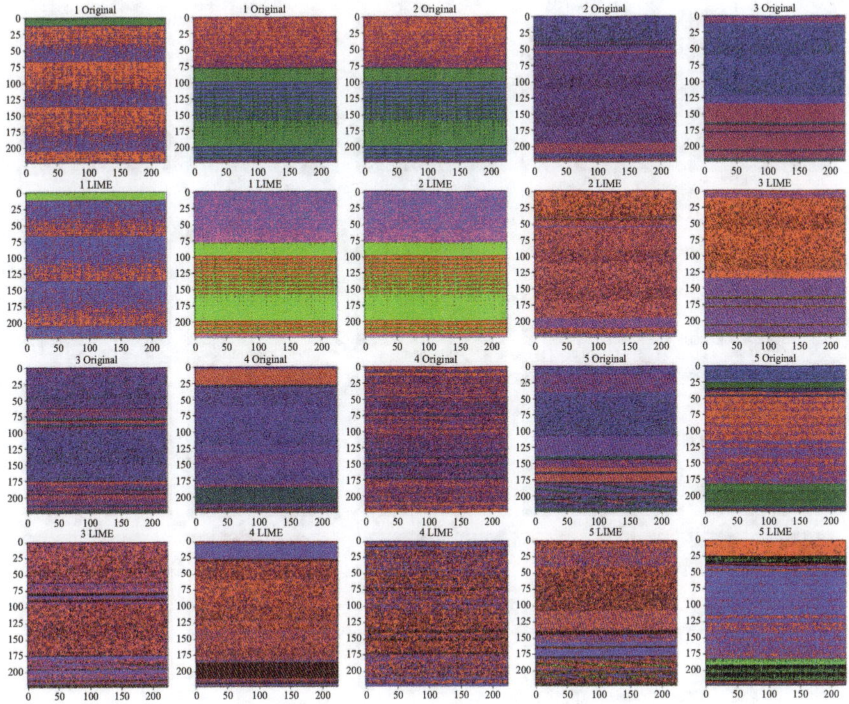

Figure 2.2 Comparison of original data and LIME explanations for different classes

The SHAP explanations are aligned with the original data, thus the model is able to provide interpretable results and we know which features are driving the predictions in each class. In class 2, there are red regions with strong positive contributions, and in class 3 blue regions implying some negative contributions that might be useful in differentiating the class from others. Overall, the model performs and interpretable and has consistently meaning contributions across all classes, confirming that the model can effectively and predictably classify the different classes in the dataset as shown in Figure 2.3.

In Figure 2.4, we apply sensitivity analysis to explain the predictions of an ML model on the dataset consisting of multi class malware images. The "Original" images alternate with the "Sensitivity" maps along each row. The raw input data in this case are the original images, and the sensitivity maps point out the areas that are most influential in the decision-making process of the model. Each pair has a grayscale pattern in the original image that indicates a different type of malware. Heatmaps where warmer colors (red/yellow) denote positively impacted areas for the prediction and cooler colors (blue/black) means negatively impacted ones are used as sensitivity maps. In this visualization it is explained what features are most important to classify. Each malware class is a row.

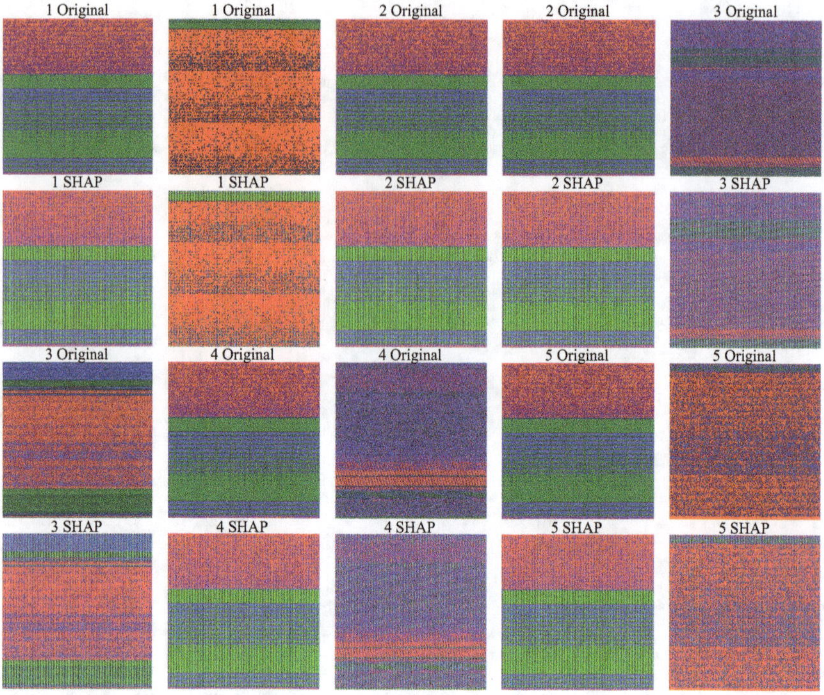

Figure 2.3 SHAP explanations for the original data for different classes

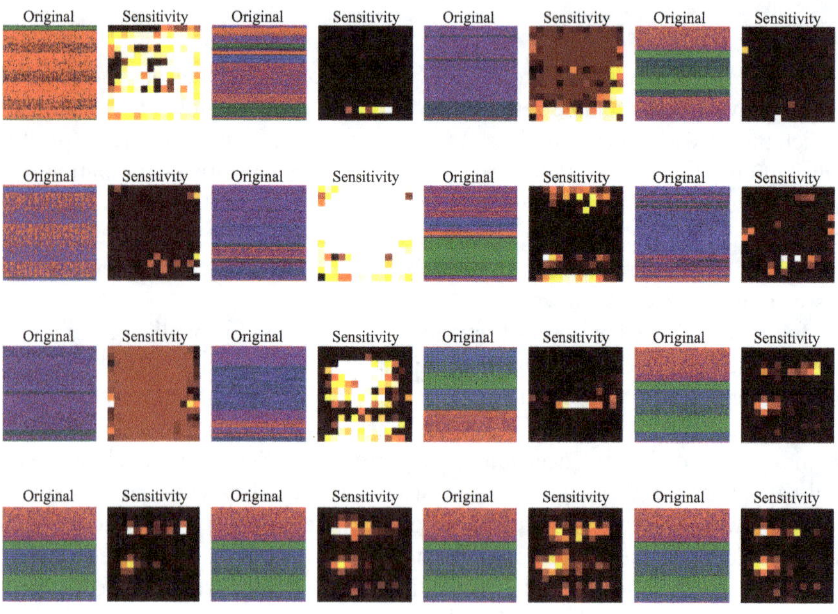

Figure 2.4 Occlusion sensitivity analysis of original data across multiple classes

Looking at the sensitivity maps along rows shows distinct patterns for each class, thus giving insight into the model's craft of separating the classes. These insights increase transparency and help make the stakeholders trust the model outputs and for better feature engineering for better final model accuracy and robustness. In the end, this figure uses sensitivity analysis in order to offer accurate insights into the decision-making of the model in a more explicit sense, so that the model is better understood and improved, and put into practice in security domain.

Scatter plots of concept activation vectors (CAVs) of the nine classes are shown in the two-dimensional space spanned by the principal components PC1 and PC2. The data points projected onto each plot, "CAV for Class *X*" (*X* = 0–8), have been plotted. Activation magnitudes are highlighted with color gradient from blue low activation to yellow high activation. Class specific patterns within a plot are shown by clusters and distributions that form tight clusters. Cross comparison of CAV plots among different classes gives insights about activations of model layers to considerably better understand the decision boundaries, detect overfitting or underfitting, and further optimize the model performance such as in the case of malware classification as shown in Figure 2.5.

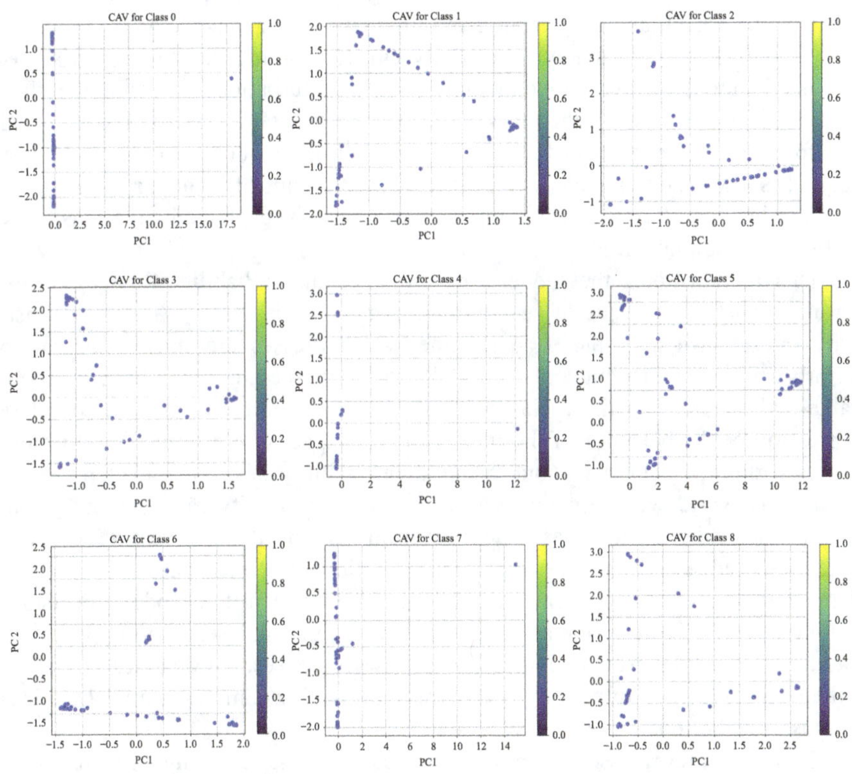

Figure 2.5 CAV analysis for nine classes

We perform a detailed performance analysis and sensitivity analysis based on the example of five classes within a single dataset via Figure 2.5. It is organized into three rows, corresponding to a same class (from 1 to 5). There are two columns per row, the left column shows the original data for that class, and the right column shows the sensitivity analysis. That existing within the original data heatmaps are distinct patterns and intensity variations which surface from the essential characteristics each class of the dataset possesses. These patterns enable us to get a baseline on how the structure and distribution of data looks like for every class. To illustrate, in class 1 horizontal banding pattern with varying intensities is observed, whereas in class 2 distribution is more uniform but also includes local variation. The original data presented for analysis is near sensitivity analysis graphs that show how the model's predictions vary as a function of perturbation in the input data. Multiple lines are plotted for different metrics and conditions, each of them with sensitivity on the vertical axis and perturbation on the horizontal axis. For example, the sensitivity curve in class 1 shows a sharp decline of sensitivity as perturbation increases which means that the model's predictions are highly sensitive toward small changes in input. This implies the model is largely dependent on a few features of this class.

Classes 2–5 are also sensitive in some way, although their declines are not as linear or linearized, and they range from gradual to complicated. As an example, class 3 has a relatively smooth sensitivity curve, meaning that the model's predictions do not change very much with respect to perturbations observing that they were in class 3. However, the class 4 shows a more erratic sensitivity curve, and therefore we observe that for this class, the model predictions are likely to be less stable. It shows that the model is robust to different kinds of input variation and its ability to handle different types of input variation can be captured by the sensitivity analysis with alignment to the original data.

This demonstrates the model's performance and reliability through meaningful, consistent presence of sensitivity curves in every class. With these sensitivity curves, we are able to determine which classes are most sensitive to perturbations of the input and potentially develop the model to become more stable and accurate on those classes. In a nutshell, Figure 2.6, gives a complete impression of the behavior of the model and its capacity to differentiate different classes within the dataset without losing interpretability or become inattentive.

In this work, we adapt the XAI techniques to classify malware images in nine classes where each class samples from one of the malware types. The table presented summarizes the importance or influence of each class (i.e., malware class) and the specific concepts (i.e., malware classes) in the model's decision-making process. For each iteration, or experiment, the representation is provided, and the columns represent one of the nine malware classes. CAV values are higher if the respective class turns out to be more important or complex in the classification task for the model predictions to activate.

There are a few classes where CAV values are consistently higher than others, specifically Class 7, praised by scores (11.33, 14.0, 18.0) in multiple trials. This implies that Class 7 contains distinct features or classes that heavily affect the

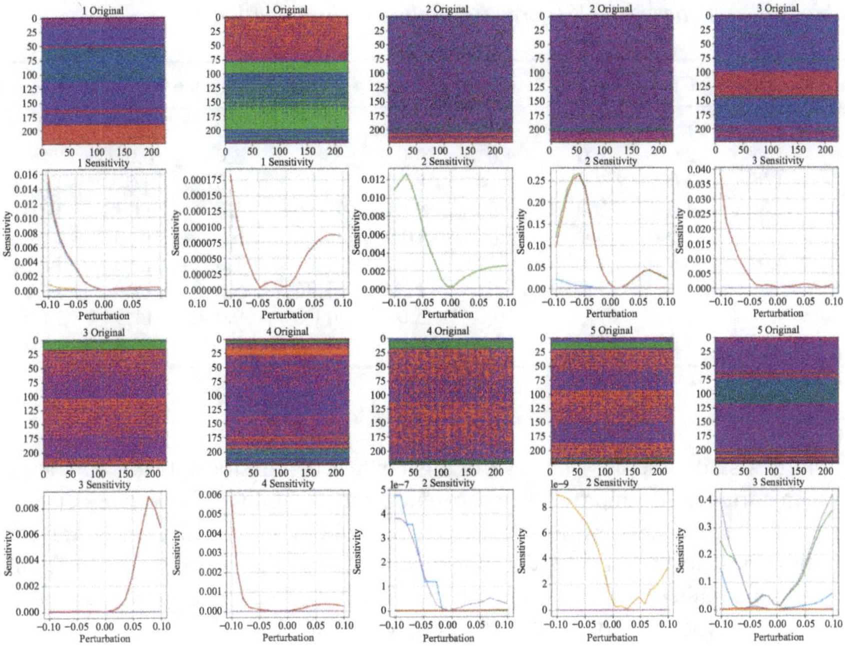

Figure 2.6 Sensitivity analysis of original data and model predictions across multiple classes

model's decisions—that it contains "complexity" or "diversity" in terms of its feature representation. On the contrary, Classes 0 and 1 have a lower CAV over all, showing that these are less important, or simply easier for the model to learn. As the index advances, it becomes clear that the majority of classes' CAV values increase, representing an increasing importance of CAVs to the model in its pursuit of mastering more challenging patterns. For example, Class 8 shows a steady increase from 7.0 in Index 1 to 15.0 in Index 9, so it becomes more important in the classification process. In opposition, some classes (Class 3, Class 6) display erratic behavior (Class 3 goes from 3.0 to 11.0) which suggests that the effect of these classes on the prediction of the model is not consistent. The repeated appearance of 11.33 for Class 7 in Indices 1, 4, and 8 in the specific anomalies layer further highlights specific challenges of Class 7 against the model. Class 4 has a similar sudden drop of 5.0 in Index 8 which can represent an anomaly or a change in the distribution of the dataset for this iteration. This XAI work adds knowledge about CAVs and shows how interpreting ML models can help in identifying which classes are most important for the model to perform well at, as well as which need to receive special treatment. For instance, high CAV values for Class 7 and Class 8 indicate that there is a need to investigate further these two classes to understand their special features and improve classification accuracy represented in Table 2.1.

Table 2.1 XAI-based CAV scores for malware classification

Index	Class 0	Class 1	Class 2	Class 3	Class 4	Class 5	Class 6	Class 7	Class 8
1	2.0	1.0	5.0	3.0	6.0	4.0	2.0	11.33	7.0
2	3.0	2.0	9.0	4.0	8.0	5.0	3.0	6.0	8.0
3	4.0	3.0	7.0	7.14	8.0	6.0	4.0	8.0	11.14
4	5.86	4.0	8.0	6.0	9.0	7.86	5.0	11.33	10.0
5	6.0	5.0	9.0	7.0	10.0	8.0	6.0	10.0	11.0
6	7.0	6.0	10.0	7.14	8.0	9.0	7.0	12.0	11.14
7	5.86	7.0	11.0	9.0	12.0	7.86	8.0	14.0	13.0
8	9.0	8.0	9.0	10.0	5.0	11.0	9.0	11.33	14.0
9	10.0	9.0	13.0	11.0	6.0	12.0	10.0	18.0	15.0

In this study, the use of CAVs in this context demonstrates that CAVs are of great importance for improving transparency and reliability of malware detection systems. Cybersecurity professionals can then focus on which classes are contributing most to the model's decisions, so they can take action to refine feature engineering, gather data that is more representative of a class, or design a strategy for a certain type of malware that is difficult to deal with.

2.7 Conclusion

This chapter proves the power of XAI has the power to truly alter threat detection and cybersecurity. This was achieved through making use of techniques such as SHAP, LIME, CAMs, sensitivity analysis, through which we learned how XAI can be used to enhance the interpretability and performance of ML models. Visualization and interpretability of model predictions via heatmaps and activation vectors allow cybersecurity professionals to monitor and explain model predictions, which helps them to gain an understanding of the underlying decision-making process and encourages the trust in the model. In addition, XAI does better job of detecting the adversarial threats and with actionable insight to feature importance and specific model behavior. It is also worth noting that explanations match original data in a consistent fashion, thus confirming the reliability of these techniques to identify principal parts of the datasets, which can, in turn, serve for a better feature engineering and model optimization. Furthermore, sensitivity analysis shows robustness of the model under the change of input conditions and provides a way to address its vulnerabilities and strengthen classification accuracy. Notably, the principle of study of CAVs, entails that some classes, particularly Class 7 and Class 8 are more complex and warrant further analysis. Taken together, these findings affirm that XAI is a key factor for developing transparent, transparent, high performance, and accountable cybersecurity systems. Thus, integrating XAI to continue evolving the field to see that ML models are relied on most for advancing on ground in the fight against emerging cyber threats and be able to uphold highest possible standards of trust, transparency and operational effectiveness.

References

[1] Capuano, N., Fenza, G., Loia, V. and C. Stanzione, Explainable artificial intelligence in cybersecurity: A survey. *IEEE Access*, 2022. **10**: pp. 93575–93600.

[2] Sharma, D.K., Mishra, J. and A. Singh, *et al.*, Explainable artificial intelligence for cybersecurity. *Computers and Electrical Engineering*, 2022. **103**: p. 108356.

[3] Malik, S., Explainable AI for cybersecurity: Improving transparency in automated threat detection systems. 2024, 10.13140/RG.2.2.14173.93927.

[4] Mahbooba, B., Timilsina, M., Sahal, R. and M. Serrano, Explainable artificial intelligence (XAI) to enhance trust management in intrusion detection systems using decision tree model. *Complexity*, 2021. **2021**(1): p. 6634811.

[5] Mohale, V.Z. and I.C. Obagbuwa, A systematic review on the integration of explainable artificial intelligence in intrusion detection systems to enhancing transparency and interpretability in cybersecurity. *Frontiers in Artificial Intelligence*, 2025. **8**: p. 1526221.

[6] Naeem, M.R. and R. Amin, Security emergence framework for cyber-physical production systems in the age of Industry 4.0. *IEEE Instrumentation & Measurement Magazine*, 2024. **27**(8): pp. 3–10.

[7] Naeem, M.R., Amin, R. and C. Farhan, *et al.*, Harnessing AI and analytics to enhance cybersecurity and privacy for collective intelligence systems. *PeerJ Computer Science*, 2024. **10**: p. e2264.

[8] Naseer, M., Ullah, F. and S. Ijaz, Obfuscated malware detection and classification in network traffic leveraging hybrid large language models and synthetic data. *Sensors (Basel, Switzerland)*, 2025. **25**(1): p. 202.

[9] Naeem, M.R., Amin, R., Alshamrani, S.S. and A. Alshehri, Digital forensics for malware classification: An approach for binary code to pixel vector transition. *Computational Intelligence and Neuroscience*, 2022. **2022** (1): p. 6294058.

[10] Basheer, N., Pranggono, B., Islam, S., Papastergiou, S. and H. Mouratidis Enhancing malware detection through machine learning using XAI with SHAP framework. in *IFIP International Conference on Artificial Intelligence Applications and Innovations*. 2024. Berlin: Springer.

Chapter 3

Explainable artificial intelligence in threat detection

Khushi Wadhwa[1], *Himanshi Babbar*[1] *and Shalli Rani*[1]

Abstract

This chapter explores the pivotal role of explainable artificial intelligence (XAI) in enhancing threat detection across security-critical domains such as cybersecurity and national safety. While machine learning (ML) models have demonstrated remarkable capabilities in identifying threats, their opaque nature often hinders trust and effective human oversight. XAI bridges this gap by providing human-interpretable insights into complex model decisions, enabling analysts to understand, validate, and refine automated detections. The chapter discusses various XAI techniques, their architecture, and the significance of interpretability for fostering human–machine collaboration, mitigating biases, and conducting thorough error analysis. It also presents practical illustrations using interpretable models like linear regression and decision trees, demonstrating how feature importance and effect plots can elucidate model behavior. By emphasizing transparency and accountability, this chapter underscores the necessity of XAI for building robust and trustworthy threat detection systems.

3.1 Introduction

Recent times have seen the rise of machine learning (ML) as a potent instrument for detecting threats. Threats can be identified by ML models in a range of situations. A fast-growing area of study called **explainable artificial intelligence** (XAI) seeks to give human-readable justifications for deep learning models, especially in security and other safety-sensitive fields. Because it enables security analysts to comprehend the characteristics or indicators that went into detecting a possible threat, this is very crucial in threat detection. It also helps with anomaly detection, enabling human-machine cooperation and error analysis. With the help of their contextual knowledge and domain experience, analysts may verify, improve, or overturn automatic detections.

[1]Department of Computer Science and engineering, Chitkara University, India

3.1.1 Explainable artificial intelligence

One of the newest and fastest-growing subfields in artificial intelligence (AI) stands for XAI. The goal of XAI approach is to give a human-readable explanation for the deep learning model. In fields where safety is crucial, like healthcare or security, this is especially crucial.

XAI algorithms hold a vital function in threat detection through offering insights into why a particular decision or prediction was made. To establish trust and empower human analysts to take appropriate action, it is crucial in threat detection scenarios—particularly in security-sensitive sectors like cybersecurity or national security—to not only detect threats but also comprehend the reasons behind the detection [1]. The following is how threat detection can make use of XAI algorithms:

(i) **Interpretability**: XAI algorithms make complex ML models more interpretable by providing explanations for their predictions. This is particularly important in threat detection because it allows security analysts to understand the features or indicators that contributed to identifying a potential threat.

(ii) **Feature importance**: XAI methods can show which characteristics or factors matter most when deciding whether to detect a threat. Through comprehension of these pivotal elements, analysts can concentrate their attention on the most crucial facets of a danger and order their response appropriately.

(iii) **Model transparency**: By making the threat detection models themselves more transparent, XAI techniques help analysts comprehend the underlying reasoning and decision-making procedures. Openness in the system and making sure that choices are made in a responsible and trustworthy manner are essential for building confidence.

(iv) **Anomaly detection**: XAI algorithms can help in explaining anomalies detected by threat detection systems. By providing detailed explanations for why certain instances are flagged as anomalies, analysts can better understand whether these anomalies represent genuine threats or false positives.

(v) **Human–machine collaboration**: XAI facilitates collaboration between human analysts and automated threat detection systems. By providing explanations that humans can understand, XAI algorithms empower analysts to validate, refine, or override automated detections based on their domain expertise and contextual understanding.

(vi) **Error analysis**: Analyzing and comprehending mistakes caused by threat detection models can be aided by XAI approaches. Analysts can find areas for model improvement, improve feature selection, or modify decision thresholds to lower false alarms and missed detections by looking at the justifications offered for inaccurate predictions.

3.1.2 XAI architecture

The value of XAI lies in its ability to provide transparent and interpretable ML models that can be understood and trusted by humans. This value can be realized in different domains and applications and can provide a range of benefits and advantages.

1. **Input data:** The raw data fed into the system for analysis or prediction. This data may be graphical charts, visual, or voice.
2. **Preprocessing:** Data preprocessing steps such as cleaning, transformation, and normalization to prepare data for modeling using ML Models.
3. **Explainable model:** Models selected for their interpretability, such as decision trees, linear models, and rule-based models.
4. **Post-processing:** This step for model calibration or refinement or use for predictions.
5. **Explanation generation:** Techniques for generating explanations such as feature importance, SHAP values, and LIME.
6. **Explanation refinement:** Optional step for summarizing or visualizing explanations for better understanding.
7. **User interface:** Interface for users to interact with the system, visualize explanations, and explore model behavior.
8. **Feedback mechanism:** Mechanism for users to provide feedback, evaluate model performance, and suggest improvements. It can be done by managers or business owners.
9. **Output/prediction:** Final output or prediction provided by the system, along with associated explanations (Figure 3.1).

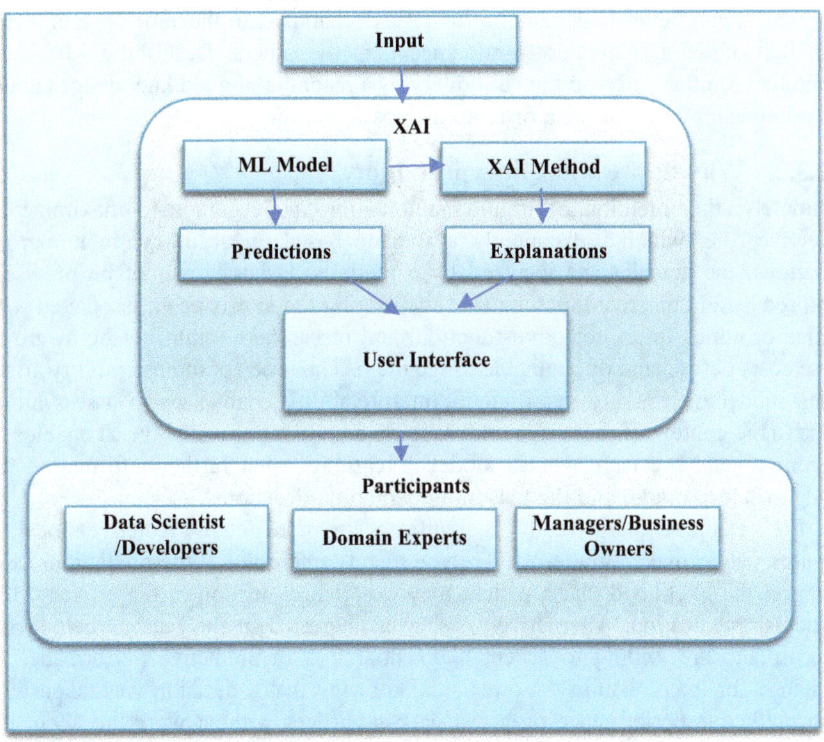

Figure 3.1 Architecture of XAI

3.1.3 How to interpret models with XAI

Two stages of model interpretability analysis are possible:

- Global interpretation: Takes a more comprehensive look at the model. As an illustration, suppose we have a neural network installed and we are working on a dataset of property prices. "Your model uses # of square feet as an important feature to derive predictions," the global interpretation would state.
- Local interpretation: As the name implies, this method focuses on a particular observation or piece of information. Let's keep using our example as we proceed. The prediction of a very little house ended up being rather huge. Given the other factors, a local interpretation would state, "Your model predicted this way because the house is located very close to the city center".

3.1.3.1 Interpretability

Model integrity has to do with how much human observers recognize the choice-making process in the model. Explanation refers to how people capable of comprehending reasons for an option.

An additional ability to interpret is the extent whereby individuals forecast a model's outcome. As more interpretable, the individuals can comprehend why particular directions or forecasts were made more easily when using ML model. If individuals can better understand a model's decisions than those of other models, then that model has greater significance than the others. Describing ML is an umbrella term that refers to the "discovery by a machine of good knowledge" about the relationship between data or relationships.

3.1.3.2 Why do we want interpretability?

Ultimately, the intention of training automation models aims to maximize an objective role, which is frequently a statistic based on accuracy. In numerous situations, the actual costs incurred by a model's decisions cannot be precisely captured by an objective function. It is challenging to identify costs associated with justice or ethics in an objective function, and researchers might not be aware of these costs beforehand or be unable to see them. The need for interpretability arises when model metrics are insufficient. Interpretability enables us to assess all of these in the context of the real-world issue we are attempting to solve. It enables us to comprehend precisely what a model is learning, what further information the model has to provide, and the reasoning behind its decisions.

Let's examine interpretability's significance in more detail. Predictive modeling requires you to make a trade-off: Are you merely interested in the predictions? For instance, the likelihood that a patient may experience attrition or the efficacy of a particular medication. Alternatively, are you interested in the reasons behind the forecast and are willing to accept a potential loss in predictive performance in exchange for interpretability? Sometimes, knowing that a decision was taken with high predictive performance on a test dataset suffices without worrying about the reasoning behind it. However, in additional situations, understanding the "why" might assist you understand the issue, the information, and the potential cause of a model's failure. Certain examples (like movie recommender systems) or those whose methods have been thoroughly tested and analyzed (like magnetic ink recognition) may not need an explanation, considering that they employed minimal danger environments where an error won't possess major repercussions. The incompleteness in issue formalization that results in tasks or problems where obtaining the forecast (the what) is insufficient gives rise to the necessity for interpretability. Because a successful forecast only answers part of your original problem, the model's need to provide an explanation for how (and why) it made the expectation [2]. The need for interpretability and explanations is motivated by the following factors.

People are naturally curious and like to learn new things. They constantly update their mental models of their surroundings when something unexpected occurs. To execute this update, an explanation for the unexpected event is sought. A person could wonder, "Why do I feel so sick?" when they suddenly become ill. He finds out that consuming those red berries causes him to become ill each time. He revises the conceptual framework and determines berries are source of the illness and should be stayed away from. In research, the use of opaque ML models might result in completely hidden scientific conclusions if the algorithm just provides predictions without providing an explanation. Interpretability and explanations are essential to promote learning and satiate curiosity about why particular actions or predictions are produced by computers.

Naturally, explanations for everything that occurs do not apply to people. Most people don't mind if they don't know how computers operate. We become fascinated about unexpected events [3]. For instance: Why is my computer abruptly shutting down?

1. **Understanding model behavior:** When automation model's functions effectively, it's tempting to trust its predictions blindly. However, relying solely on one measure like categorization precision that's insufficient for most real-world tasks.[1] Interpretability helps us understand **why** a model made a particular decision, not just **what** it predicted. This deeper understanding allows us to gain insights into the problem, the data, and potential model failures.
2. **Trade-off between prediction and explanation**: In predictive modeling, there's often a trade-off: Do we prioritize knowing the prediction (e.g., customer churn probability or drug effectiveness) or understanding why the prediction was made? Sometimes, knowing the "why" is essential. For instance, in high-risk scenarios, explanations are crucial to ensure transparency and accountability.
3. **Human curiosity and learning**: Humans are naturally curious. When unexpected events occur, we seek explanations. Similarly, research finding is concealed when hazy ML methods are employed unless explanations accompany predictions. Interpretability satisfies curiosity and facilitates learning [4].
4. **Finding meaning in the world**: We desire meaning and coherence in our knowledge structures. Interpretability helps harmonize contradictions, inconsistencies, and unexpected outcomes. It allows us to update mental models and make informed decisions.
5. **Guarding against bias**: By understanding how a model arrives at its predictions, we can identify and address biases. Interpretability helps ensure fairness and equality in AI applications.

3.2 Interpretable models

Utilizing only a portion of the algorithms that produce interpretable models is the simplest method to attain interpretability. The decision tree, logistic regression, and linear regression are popular interpretable models. All the interpretable models described here, excluding the k-nearest neighbors method, are interpretable at the modular level. The interpretable model types and their attributes are summarized in the following table. When features and the target are associated in a linear fashion, the model is said to be linear. A monotonicity-constrained model guarantees that, across the feature's whole range, The correlation between a feature and the intended result is consistently positive: The goal outcome either always increases or always decreases as the characteristic value increases [5]. Due to its ability to simplify relationships, monotonicity is helpful for interpreting a model. It is possible for models to automatically incorporate feature relationships in order for forecast the desired result. By manually constructing interaction features, models of any type can incorporate interactions. Although interactions might enhance predictive performance, interpretability may suffer from an excessive number of complicated interactions. Certain models focus solely on regression, while others handle both classification and regression.*

Either regression (regr) or classification (class) is the appropriate interpretable model that you can choose from Table 3.1.

3.2.1 Linear regression

Utilizing the weighted total of the feature inputs, a linear regression model is used to estimate objective. The acquired bond is linear, which facilitates straightforward interpretation. For a decent amount of time, individuals who work with quantitative problems such as statisticians and computer scientists have employed linear regression models.

Regression targets y's dependence on certain features x can be modelled using linear models. The relationships that are learned are linear and, for a single instance I, can be written as follows:

$$y = \beta 0 + \beta 1x1 + \cdots + \beta pxp + \varepsilon \tag{3.1}$$

Table 3.1 Algorithms with their techniques

Algorithms	Linear	Monotone	Interaction	Tasks
Linear regression	Yes	Yes	No	Regr
Logistic regression	No	Yes	No	Class
Decision trees	No	Some	Yes	Class, Regr
RuleFit	Yes	No	Yes	Class, Regr
Naïve Bayes	No	Yes	No	Class
K-nearest neighbors	No	No	No	Class, Regr

*Chapter 5 Interpretable Models | Interpretable Machine Learning (christophm.github.io).

The given instance's predicted result is the total of its p attributes. The coefficients or weights of the learned features are represented by the betas (βj). The intercept, or first weight in the sum ($\beta 0$), is not multiplied by a feature. The error we still commit, or the discrepancy between the expected and actual results, is called the epsilon (ε). We assume that these errors have a Gaussian distribution, meaning that we produce a lot of tiny mistakes and a few big ones, as well as errors in both positive and negative directions.

The ideal weight can be estimated using a variety of techniques. Typically, weights whose squared value is least disparities among estimated and actual results are determined using the ordinary least squares method [6]:

$$\hat{\beta} = \arg \min_{\beta_0,\ldots,\beta_p} \sum_{i=1}^{n} \left(y^{(i)} - \left(\beta_0 + \sum_{j=1}^{p} \beta_j x_j^{(i)} \right) \right)^2 \tag{3.2}$$

3.2.2 *Interpretation*

Within a linear regression model, we obtain the meaning for a weight contingent upon the nature of associated characteristics.

- Quantitative characteristics: Any increase in numerical characteristics expressed in units modifies the weight of the projected outcome. A house's dimensions are an illustration of a numerical property.
- Binary feature: A feature where each occurrence can have one of two values. "Home comes with a garden" is one example of a feature. Some programming languages use the value 0 to represent the reference category, and examples of such values include "No garden." What the feature weight predicts as a result is altered when a feature is moved from the category of reference to another category.
- Categorical feature with multiple categories: An attribute that can have a set number of values. Using the categories "carpet," "laminate," and "parquet" as examples, consider the feature "floor type." One-hot encoding, in which every category has a separate binary column, is a way to deal with multiple categories at once. With L categories in a categorical feature, $L-1$ columns are all that are required because the Lth column might contain duplicate knowledge (for instance, whenever all of the column from 1 to $L-1$ are equal to zero, we know that the category that this example's categorical feature falls into is L). Following that, the interpretation for binary features is the same for each category. Categorical features can be encoded in a variety of ways using some languages, like *R*.
- Intercept $\beta 0$: The number of features for the "constant feature," which is always one in every cases, is called the intercept. To estimate the intercept, majority of software programs on their own integrate this "1"-characteristic. An analysis is given as follows: the intercept weight is the model prediction for an example when every number characteristics worth is 0 and all answers for category features are at the references category. Since it's common for situations with each feature value at 0 make no-meaning, then intercept's analysis typically not significant. Only once the importance have standardized (standard deviation of 1 and mean of 0) can interpretation be considered relevant.

When every feature is at its mean value, the intercept then represents the expected result of that instance.

By employing the adopting word layouts, it is possible to automate the analysis of attributes within the model of linear regression.

3.2.2.1 Analysis of a numerical characteristic

When all other characteristic values are constant, an increase of one unit in feature x_k results in a β_k unit increase in the prediction for y.

3.2.2.2 Analysis of a categorical characteristic:

When all other features stay stable, shifting feature x_k moving from the category of reference to another category raises the prediction for y by β_k.

A further crucial metric for analyzing linear models is the R^2 measurement. R^2 indicates the extent to which the model explains the overall variance of your desired result. Your model's ability to describe the data improves with a greater R^2. The following is the formula to get R^2:

$$R^2 = 1 - \mathrm{SSE}/\mathrm{SST}$$

The error terms' squared sum is known as the SSE.

$$\mathrm{SSE} = \sum_{i=1}^{n} (y^{(i)} - \hat{y}^{(i)})^2 \tag{3.3}$$

$$\mathrm{SST} = \sum_{i=1}^{n} (y^{(i)} - \bar{y})^2 \tag{3.4}$$

The data variance's squared sum is known as the SST.

The SSE measures the squared variations between the intended target attributes and the actual anticipated target attributes to determine how much variance is left over after fitting the linear model. The entire variance of the desired result is known as SST. The R^2 value indicates the extent to which the linear model can account for your variation. Models that completely explain the variance in your data typically have an R^2 of 1, while models that do not explain any of the data at all typically have a value of 0. Without going against any mathematical laws, R^2 can also take on a negative value. This is the result of a model fitting info that is more detrimental than utilizing target imply as when SSE exceeds SST, which suggests that the model is unable to accurately represent the data trend, the forecast [7].

However, there is a catch: even if a feature contains no information at all about the target value, R^2 still rises as quantity of characteristics in model's does. It is therefore preferable in order to utilize modified R^2, that takes amount among the model's characteristics into consideration. The computation is as follows:

$$\bar{R}^2 = 1 - (1 - R^2)\frac{n-1}{n-p-1} \tag{3.5}$$

where n represents quantity of instances and p represents quantity of attributes.

The model that has an extremely low (adjusted) R^2 basically does not explain much of the variation; hence, it is meaningless to interpret it. A meaningful analyzing the weights might imply impossible.

3.2.2.3 Feature's significance

An attribute's *t*-statistic's absolute value can be used to gauge how important it is in a linear regression model. Scaling an estimated weight with its standard error yields the *t*-statistic.

$$t_{\widehat{\beta}_j} = \frac{\widehat{\beta}_j}{\mathrm{SE}(\widehat{\beta}_j)} \tag{3.6}$$

Let's look at what this formula indicates: As a feature's weight increases, so does its importance. This makes sense. The feature is less significant the more variance the projected weight has (i.e., the less confident we are about the true value) [8]. This also makes sense.

Case study 1

In this example, given the weather and calendar data, we apply linear regression model for forecast number of leased motorbikes on a given day. We look at the predicted regression weights for interpretation. Both categorical and numerical features make up the features. The approximate mass is shown in Table 3.2, absolute value for *t*-statistic, and standard error for estimate (SE) for each feature (|*t*|).

Analysis of a numerical characteristic (temperature): Considering that all other factors stay constant, a 1°C increase in temperature results in a 110.7 anticipated increase in bicycles.

Analysis of a "weathersit" category feature: Assuming that no other conditions alter, the anticipated number of bicycles is −1901.5 fewer during periods of rain, snow, or storms than during favorable weather. Given that all other conditions stay the same, the expected number of bicycles in misty weather is −379.4 fewer than in clear weather.

Table 3.2 Algorithms with their techniques

	Weight	**SE**	**|*t*|**
(Intercept)	2399.4	238.3	10.1
Season SPRING	899.3	122.3	7.4
Season SUMMER	138.2	161.7	0.9
Season FALL	425.6	110.8	3.8
Holiday HOLIDAY	–686.1	203.3	3.4
Workingday WORKING DAY	124.9	73.3	1.7
Weathersit RAIN/SNOW	**–1901.5**	**223.6**	**8.5**
Temp	110.7	7.0	15.7
Hum	–17.4	3.2	5.5
Windspeed	–42.5	6.9	6.2
Days_since_2011	4.9	0.2	28.5

3.3 Visual interpretation

The linear regression model is rapidly and easily understood by humans thanks to a variety of visuals.

3.3.1 Weight plot

A weight plot can be used to illustrate the weight and variance estimations from the weight table. The outcomes of earlier linear regression model's displayed in Figure 3.2.

95% ranges of assurance are shown like line, while weights are shown as points.

Rain, snow, or storms have a noteworthy adverse effect upon anticipated number of bikes, as demonstrated by the weight plot. In other words, the effect is not statistically significant due to the fact that business day's weight almost 0 which comprises 95% CI. There were statistically significant feature impacts, despite some very short confidence ranges and estimations near zero. One such contender is temperature. There are various proportions used to measure the characteristics, which presents an issue for the weight plot. The projected weight for weather only shows a 1 °C rise in temperature; in contrast, it shows the distinction between good weather and rainy, stormy, or snowy condition events. Calibration of the features (zero mean and one standard deviation) prior to linear model fitting can improve the comparability of the calculated weights.

3.3.2 Effect plot

When one multiplies model of linear regression weights by the actual feature values, a more insightful analysis may be conducted. If a feature measures anything, similar to someone's stature, you as well move between one and ten meters,

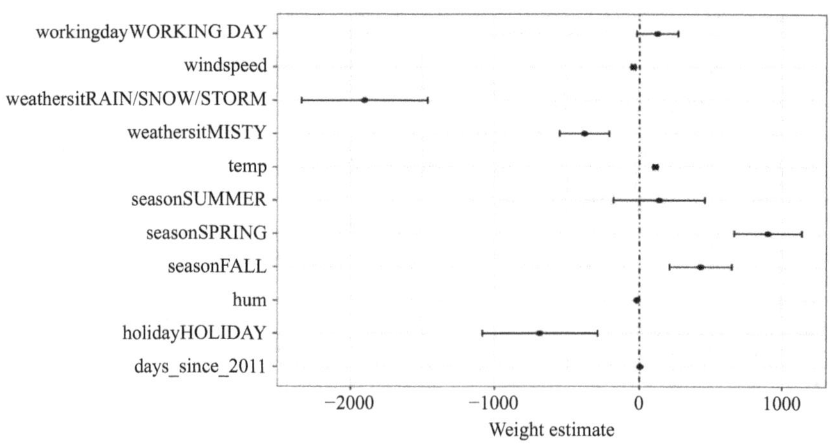

Figure 3.2 Weight plot

then weights shall alter depending on feature's scale. Your information's real impacts won't change, but the weight will. Additionally, it is critical to understand how your feature is distributed throughout the data; a low variance indicates that this characteristic contributes similarly to nearly all of the instances. You can determine the extent of the mass and characteristic combination helps the predictions made by your data through looking at effect plot [9]. First, compute the effects, which are equal to a case's attribute worth multiplied by the weight per feature:

$$\text{effect}_j^{(i)} = w_j x_j^{(i)} \tag{3.7}$$

Boxplots can be used to visualize the impacts. Within a boxplot the impact range of 25%–75% of effect quantiles, or half of the data, is contained within the container. The midway impact, represented by the box's vertices, indicates that half of cases possess a lesser effect on prediction and another part of the larger impact. The coordinating represents anomalies, which are elements which fall outside of the first or third quartile by less than 1.5 * IQR or greater than 1.5 * the interquartile range, which is the difference between the first and third quartiles. The pair of lines that are sideways lines, known as the lower and upper whiskers, link the points under the initial quartile and over the third percentile that are not outliers. The whiskers will reach minimum and maximum values if there are no outliers. Unlike the plot's distribution, where a row corresponds to each group, categorical characteristic impacts can be summed in a single boxplot (Figure 3.3).

The feature value multiplied by the feature weight distribution of effects across each feature's data is displayed in the feature effect plot.

The features that represent temperature and days, which depict during time, the habit of renting bikes, have most effects on the projected number of rented bicycles. The degree to which temperature influences the prediction varies widely. Since the dataset's first day, January 1, 2011, has a negligible trend influence and a positive approximate mass of 4.93, The characteristic of the daily trend ranges beginning at little to substantial contributions that are constructive. Accordingly, the effect gets stronger every day and peaks on the final day of the dataset, which is December 31, 2012. Recall that in the case of good impacts and the consequences of low mass are associated with instances with low characteristics worth. Days of intense wind speed, for instance, are those that have a high wind speed negative influence.

3.3.2.1 Case study 2

Explain individual predictions

To what extent has each instance aspect helped with the prediction? By calculating the impacts for this particular instance, this can be answered. It is only in relation to each feature's influence distribution that an explanation of consequences that are specific to an occurrence becomes meaningful. We aim to elucidate the linear model's prediction for the sixth case found in dataset of bicycles. The attribute values listed below apply to the instance:

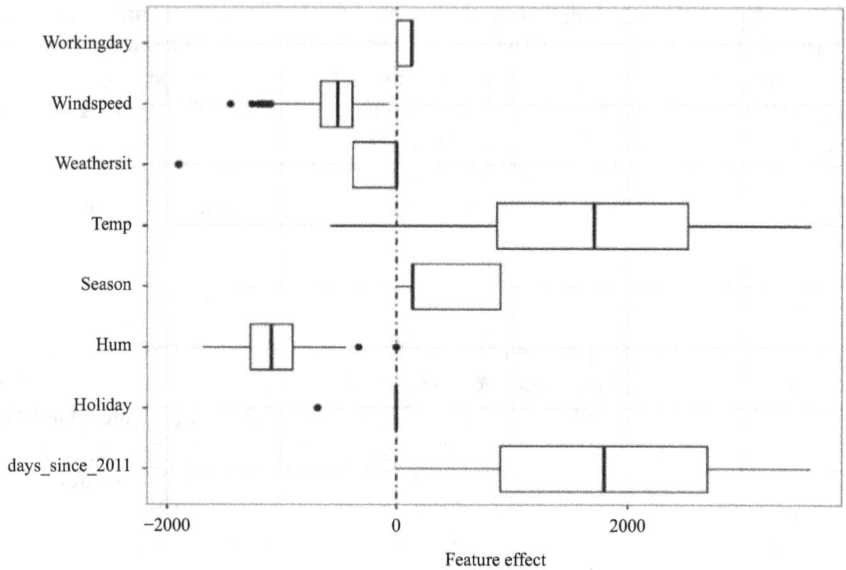

Figure 3.3 Weight distribution effects

Feature values for instance 6

Feature	Value
Season	WINTER
Yr	2011
Mnth	JAN
Holiday	NO HOLIDAY
Weekday	THU
Workingday	WORKING DAY
Weathersit	GOOD
Temp	1.604356
Hum	51.8261
Windspeed	6.000868
Cnt	1,606
Days_since_2011	5

We must multiply this instance's characteristic values as determined by matching parameters from the model of linear regression in order to determine its feature effects. The effect for the feature "workingday" value "WORKING DAY" is 124.9. The result comes out to 177.6 at 1.6 °C. Specifically, the impact diagram, display ways the impacts are distributed within the information, is enhanced by the addition of these distinct effects as crosses. Thanks to this, we can now compare how the impacts are distributed within data with individual impacts (Figure 3.4).

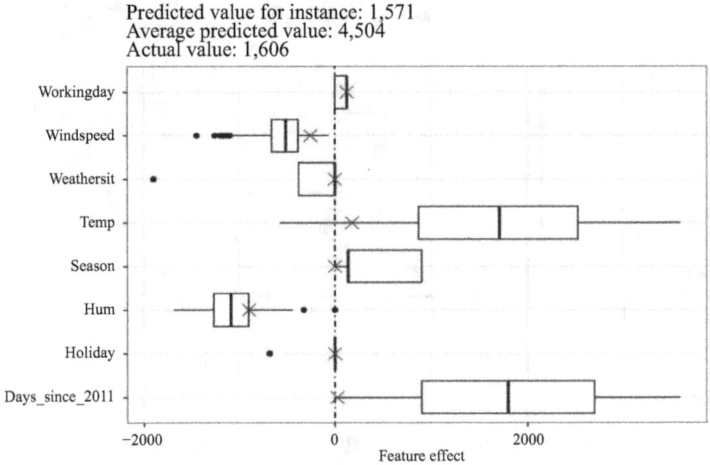

Figure 3.4 Impact distribution effect plot

The impact distribution and the impacts of the instance of interest are displayed in the effect plot for a single instance.

A mean of 4,504 is obtained by summing the predictions for each instance of the training data. Comparatively, since just 1,571 bicycle rentals are anticipated, the projection for the sixth instance is low. It is made clear why in the effect plot. The impacts of each dataset instance are displayed as boxplots, while the effects of the sixth instance are represented as crosses. The temperature of 2 °C on this day. This is minimal in contrast to the majority of other days, is reason for low warmth effect in the sixth occurrence (keep in mind that the temperature characteristic has a positive weight). Additionally, because this instance of the data comes from the first five days of 2011 and carries a positive weight, its effect is minimal in comparison to the other data examples [10].

Logistic regression

Any representation of the relationship between some continuous data is always done through the usage of linear regression. On the other hand, logistic regression operates on discrete values. When there are only two possible outcomes for an event—that is, that it will occur or it won't—logistic regression is most frequently used to solve binary classification issues (0 or 1). Therefore, in logistic regression, we use a logistic function, which is a nonlinear transform function.

Since the logistic function produced an S-shaped curve, it is also known as a Sigmoid function and is represented by the equation:

Logistic regression's formula is,

$$P(x) = e^{(b0+b1x)}/1 + e^{(b0+b1x)} \tag{3.8}$$

where calculating the values of the coefficients $b0$ and $b1$ is the aim of the logistic regression (Figure 3.5).

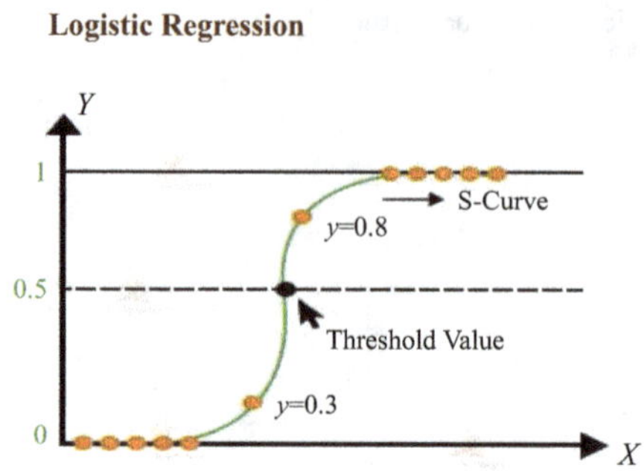

Figure 3.5 Logistic regression model

A logistic regression model with various feature types can be interpreted as follows:

- Numerical feature: The predicted odds vary by a factor of exp(βj) if feature xj's value is increased by one unit.
- Binary categorical feature: The reference category, or the one encoded in 0 in some languages, is one of the feature's two values. The predicted odds are altered by an exp(βj) factor when attribute xj is switched moving from the category of reference to the alternative category.

A categorical characteristic that has more than two groups: One-hot encoding, in which every category has an own column, is one way to handle numerous categories. $L-1$ columns are all that are needed for a category feature with L categories; otherwise, feature beyond its parameters. A reference category is subsequently Lth category. Any alternative encoding that is suitable for linear regression can be utilized. Therefore, the interpretation of binary features is equivalent to the interpretation for each category [11].

Intercept $\beta 0$ 0: The estimated chances are exp($\beta 0$)(0) after everyone categorical qualities located at the citation category and all quantitative characteristics are 0. Usually, it makes no difference how the intercept weight is interpreted.

Decision tree

When features interact with one another or when the connection between the features and the result is nonlinear, both logistic regression and linear regression models fail. Tree-based models divide the data into several groups based on feature cutoff values. Splitting creates distinct subsets within the dataset, with each occurrence falling under a single a portion. Internal nodes or split nodes are the names given to the intermediate subsets, and terminal or leaf nodes are the final subsets. Every leaf node's outcome is predicted using the average of this node's training data results. Classification and regression techniques are two uses for trees [12].

A model that resembles a tree and is used to make judgments is called a decision tree. It is made up of branches that stand in for the decisions' results and nodes that represent decision points. The outcomes are potential classifications or forecasts, and the input variables' values determine the decision points. Recursively segmenting the input data into subgroups based on the input values variables creates a decision tree. The divisions are selected to reduce the generated subsets' impureness, with each partition representing a node in the tree.

Trees can be grown by a variety of algorithms. They diverge in terms of the potential tree structure (number of splits per node, for example), the standards for identifying splits, the point at which splitting should end, and the methods for estimating the basic models inside leaf nodes. The most widely used technique for tree induction is most likely the classification and regression trees (CART) method [13].

3.4 CART (classification and regression trees) Algorithm

The decision tree-based CART technique can be used to handle machine learning issues combining both regression and classification. It works by dividing the training data into smaller subsets recursively using binary splits. CART is a powerful and popular technique for handling both continuous and categorical information due to its adaptability, interpretability, and ability to find nonlinear connections between variables and the target variable. In a binary tree generated using the CART algorithm, each nonterminal node contains two child nodes. However, some tree-based methods may allow for multiple child nodes.

3.4.1 The CART works

Step 1: The technique uses binary splits to iteratively partition the training data into smaller subsets. The root node of the tree contains all of the training data, which is then recursively divided into smaller subsets until a halting condition is met.

Step 2: At each node of the tree, the algorithm selects a feature and a threshold that best partition the training data into two groups based on the values of each feature. This is accomplished by selecting the feature and threshold that maximizes the information gain or the Gini impurity, which are metrics for the effectiveness of data splitting.

Step 3: Until a stopping requirement is satisfied, the process repeats recursively, with each node in the tree separating the data into two smaller groups. A minimum number of instances in each leaf node, a maximum depth for the tree, or other requirements could serve as the halting condition.

Step 4: By moving up the tree between a leaf node and the root node that matches the input data, one can utilize the constructed tree to generate predictions. The forecast for regression problems is the leaf node's average of the target values. The predominant group in leaf node is the forecast for classification problems.

Step 5: Determine the dataset's total Gini impurity. This represents the root node's impurity.

Step 6: Determine the Gini impurity for each input variable for every split point that could occur. One chooses the split point that yields the lowest Gini impurity.

Step 7: Using the selected split point, the data is divided into two subsets, and a new node is made for each subset [14].

Step 8: For every additional node, steps 2 and 3 are repeated until a halting condition is satisfied. A minimum reduction in impurity, the lowest number of data points in a leaf node or the greatest depth of the tree could be used as this terminating criterion.

Step 9: The decision tree is the end product.

The Gini index is a measure used in CART.

A cost function we employ to assess dataset splits is the Gini index. Since our target variable can only take two values—Yes and No—it is a binary variable. There can be four combinations.

Yes	**Yes**
Yes	No
No	Yes
No	No

For the binary target variable, the Gini index is

$$= 1 - P^2(\text{Target} = 0) - P^2(\text{Target} = 1)$$
$$= 1 - \sum_{t=0}^{t=1} P_t^2 \qquad (3.9)$$

Gini index

Based on the degree of class diversity, split Gini score in each of the groups it forms provides an indication for its effectiveness. In the worst scenario, a split results in 50/50 classes; in contrast, an ideal division yields a Gini score of zero. We compute it for each row in our binary tree and divide the data appropriately. This method is repeated recursively. The max Gini index value for the binary target variable

$$= 1 - (1/2)^2 - (1/2)^2 = 1 - 2 * (1/2)^2 = 1 - 2 * (1/4) = 1 - 0.5 = 0.5$$

In the same way, the Gini index will remain comparable, in the event that the desired variable has multiple levels and is categorized. When k different values are accepted by the target variable, the resulting Gini index is:

The highest values of the Gini indexes may occur whenever the distribution of all target values is equal.

In a similar vein, the highest Gini index value for a nominal variable with a k level is = $1\text{–}1/k$.

When every observation is associated with a single label, The Gini index's lowest value is zero.

Steps:

Determine the Gini index for each property and feature in dataset 2:

(1) determine each category value's Gini index, (2) compute the information entropy average for the given property, (3) determine the gain on Gini3. Select your ideal Gini gain characteristic, and (4) continue until the desired tree is obtained.

For example: compute Gini index for dataset

$$= 1 - \sum_{t=0}^{t=1} P_t^2$$

Out of 14 instances, yes = 9, no = 5

$$1 - (9/14)^2 - (5/14)^2 \tag{3.10}$$

$$1 - 0.413 - 0.127 = 0.46$$

$$\text{Gini} = 0.46$$

3.4.2 Feature importance

The model's use of a feature is indicated by its feature significance. Put otherwise, what happens to our error when we remove a feature from the model? A feature is crucial for our model to forecast the target variable if the error rises significantly.

Feature importance on two levels[†]:

- **Global feature importance:** is the evaluation of each feature's importance over the course of a project or dataset. It offers a broad grasp of the ways in which various features affect the model's predictions or results in a more comprehensive way.
- **Local explanations (at the case level):** focus on assessing a feature's significance for every dataset forecast or instance. It provides views into the ways in which specific features impact the model's assessment for each scenario or predicted outcome [15]. Here is a more in-depth study that illustrates the relative weights given to different features in particular scenarios, allowing one to understand how the model employs different features to generate individual predictions.

The process of comprehending and measuring the contribution of various input characteristics (or variables) toward the model's predictions is referred to as feature importance in XAI. In situations where interpretability is critical, it is especially important for comprehending how complicated ML models make decisions [16].

3.4.3 Error analysis

The process of locating, analyzing, and diagnosing inaccurate ML predictions is known as error analysis. These aids understanding the model's both

[†]https://xai.arya.ai/docs/xai-feature-importance

excellent and poor outcomes regions. The statement "the model accuracy is 90%" may not apply to all data subgroups, and the model may perform worse under specific input conditions [17,18]. Stated differently, it represents the shift from aggregate measurements to a deeper examination of model errors for improvement.

For instance, an image recognition model for dog detection may perform better when applied to canines in an outdoor environment but less well when used to low-light inside environments. Naturally, skewed datasets could be the cause of this, and error analysis can show whether or not such instances affect the model's efficiency. The following example illustrates how switching from aggregate to group-wise errors improves the representation of the model's performance (Figure 3.6) [19,20].[‡]

(a) Classification of error types: Sort the different kinds of errors the model makes first. Misclassifications, outliers, ambiguity in predictions, false positives (erroneously anticipated positive cases), and false negatives (erroneously predicted negative instances) are examples of common error categories.
(b) Confusion matrix: This allows you to see the distribution of the model's true positive, true negative, false positive, and false negative predictions. It helps with error analysis and gives a thorough picture of the model's performance in various classes.
(c) Compute relevant error metrics: To measure the model's effectiveness and pinpoint areas for improvement, compute pertinent error metrics including accuracy, precision, recall, F1-score, and area under the ROC curve (AUC-ROC). Examine these metrics in relation to various classes and data subsets to obtain perceptions of the model's advantages and disadvantages [21,22].

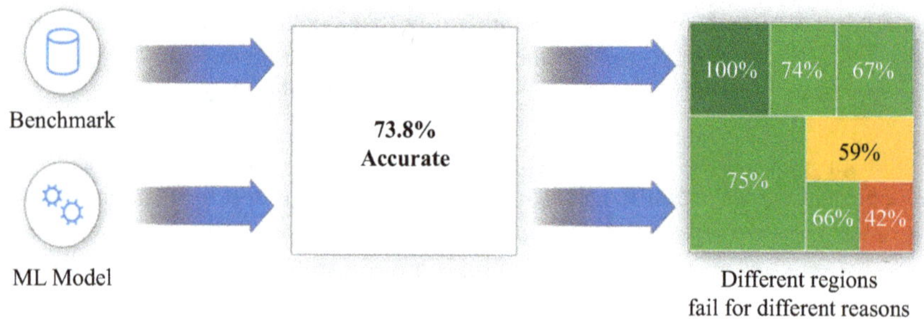

Figure 3.6 Error analysis

[‡]https://www.analyticsvidhya.com/blog/2021/08/a-quick-guide-to-error-analysis-for-machine-learning-classification-models/

3.5 Conclusion

A fast-growing area of the research called XAI seeks to give human-readable justifications for deep learning models, especially in security and healthcare, which are crucial areas of safety. In order to win trust, get insights into decision-making processes, and empower human analysts to take necessary action, XAI algorithms are essential to threat detection. By highlighting the most important aspects for decision-making, XAI algorithms simplify and enhance the interpretability of complicated ML models. Additionally, they improve model transparency, making it easier for analysts to comprehend the reasoning and decision-making procedures at play and fostering a sense of confidence in the system. Along with helping with anomaly detection, XAI also facilitates error analysis and human-machine collaboration, allowing analysts to verify, improve, or override automatic detections based on their areas of expertise. One essential component of machines is their interpretability Because it enables people to comprehend the decision-making process and forecast model outcomes. Since ML models are programmed to maximize an objective function, they might not correctly represent costs associated with ethics and fairness in the actual world. When model metrics are insufficient, interpretability is necessary because it enables one to comprehend the knowledge, reasoning, and learning of the model.

References

[1] B. Wang, Y. Yao, B. Viswanath, H. Zheng, and B.Y. Zhao, “With Great Training Comes Great Vulnerability: Practical Attacks against Transfer Learning,” *27th USENIX Security Symposium (USENIX Security 18)*, 1281–1297, 2018.

[2] K.H. Chow, L. Liu, M.E. Gursoy, S. Truex, W. Wei, and Y. Wu, Understanding object detection through an adversarial lens. in *Computer Security – ESORICS 2020: 25th European Symposium on Research in Computer Security*. Cham: Springer; 2020, pp. 460–481.

[3] T. Gu, B. Dolan-Gavitt, and S. Garg, Badnets: Identifying vulnerabilities in the machine learning model supply chain. 2017. arXiv preprint arXiv:1708.06733.

[4] W. Samek, G. Montavon, A. Vedaldi, L.K. Hansen, and K.R. Muller, *Explainable AI: Interpreting, Explaining and Visualizing Deep Learning* (Cham: Springer Nature, 2019).

[5] H.J. Escalante, S. Escalera, I. Guyon, *et al.*, *Explainable and Interpretable Models in Computer Vision and Machine Learning* (Berlin: Springer, 2018).

[6] O. Biran, and C. Cotton, “Explanation and Justification in Machine Learning: A Survey,” Paper presented at the *IJCAI-17 Workshop on Explainable AI (XAI)*, Melbourne, Australia, August 20, 2017.

[7] H.H. Clark, and S.E. Brennan, Grounding in communication, in L.B. Resnick, J.M. Levine, and S.D. Teasley (eds.), *Perspectives on Socially Shared Cognition*. Washington, DC: American Psychological Association; 1991, pp. 127–149.

[8] D. Wang, Q. Yang, A. Abdul, and B.Y. Lim, Designing theory-driven user-centric explainable AI, in Proceedings of the 2019 CHI Conference on Human Factors in Computing Systems (New York: ACM, 2019), paper no. 601.

[9] T. Miller, Explanation in artificial intelligence: Insights from the social sciences. *Artif. Intell.* 267, 1–38 (2018).

[10] D. Gunning, Explainable Artificial Intelligence (XAI). DARPA/I2O, (2017) https://nsarchive.gwu.edu/sites/default/files/documents/5794867/National-Security-Archive-David-Gunning-DARPA.pdf.

[11] M.A. Gulum, C.M. Trombley, and M. Kantardzic, A review of explainable deep learning cancer detection models in medical imaging. *Appl. Sci.*, 11 (10) 4573 (2021), 10.3390/app11104573

[12] A. Madsen, S. Reddy, and S. Chandar, Post-hoc interpretability for neural NLP: A survey. *ACM Comput. Surv.* 55(8), 1–42 (2022).

[13] A. Rawal, J. McCoy, D.B. Rawat, B.M. Sadler, and R.S. Amant, Recent advances in trustworthy explainable artificial intelligence: Status, challenges and perspectives. *IEEE Trans. Artif. Intell.*, 3(6), 852–866 (2021).

[14] S.T. Mueller, R.R. Hoffman, W. Clancey, A. Emrey, and G. Klein, Explanation in human-AI systems: A literature meta-review, synopsis of key ideas and publications, and bibliography for explainable AI. *arXiv preprint arXiv:1902.01876* (2019).

[15] Sangeeta and U. Tandon, Factors influencing adoption of online teaching by school teachers: A study during COVID-19 pandemic. *Journal of Public Affairs*, *21*(4), e2503 (2021).

[16] A. Kumar, S. Sharma, N. Goyal, A. Singh, X. Cheng, and P. Singh, Secure and energy-efficient smart building architecture with emerging technology IoT. *Computer Communications*, *176*, 207–217 (2021).

[17] S. Atakishiyev, M. Salameh, H. Yao, and R. Goebel, Explainable artificial intelligence for autonomous driving: A comprehensive overview and field guide for future research directions. *IEEE Access*, (2024).

[18] V. Bellotti, and K. Edwards, Intelligibility and accountability: Human considerations in context-aware systems. *Hum. Comput. Interact.* 16, 193–212 (2009).

[19] T. Kulesza, M. Burnett, W. Wong, and S. Stumpf, Principles of explanatory debugging to personalize interactive machine learning, in Proceedings of the 20th International Conference on Intelligent User Interfaces (New York: ACM, 2015), pp. 126–137.

[20] M. Naiseh, N. Jiang, J. Ma, and R. Ali, Personalising explainable recommendations: literature and conceptualisation. in *Trends and Innovations in Information Systems and Technologies*. Cham: Springer; 2020, pp. 518–533.

[21] B. Kovalerchuk, M.A. Ahmad, and A. Teredesai, Survey of explainable machine learning with visual and granular methods beyond quasi-explanations, in *Interpretable Artificial Intelligence: A Perspective of Granular Computing* (Cham: Springer International Publishing, 2021) pp. 217–267.

[22] K. Cheng, N. Wang, and M. Li, Interpretability of deep learning: A survey, in The International Conference on Natural Computation, Fuzzy Systems and Knowledge Discovery (Berlin: Springer, 2020).

Chapter 4

XAI-enabled blockchain for cybersecurity

Majid Hussain[1], Hina Zafar[1], Amna Iqbal[1] and Muhammad Asif Habib[2]

Abstract

This chapter presents a theoretical framework that integrates Explainable Artificial Intelligence (XAI) with blockchain technology to enhance cybersecurity practices. As digital systems grow increasingly complex, ensuring transparency, interpretability, and trust in AI-driven cybersecurity solutions becomes critical. The proposed model leverages the immutable and decentralized nature of blockchain alongside the interpretability features of XAI to address major cybersecurity challenges. Key components of the framework include smart contracts, threat intelligence sharing, secure data storage, identity management, and compliance monitoring. The chapter explores how this integration fosters transparency in AI decision-making, strengthens accountability in security actions, and supports compliance with regulatory standards. Additionally, it highlights the potential of XAI-enabled blockchain to improve threat detection, mitigate risks, and provide stakeholders with actionable insights. The layered architecture of the framework, complexity analysis, and identified limitations offer a comprehensive guide for researchers and practitioners aiming to develop secure, explainable, and resilient cybersecurity systems across various domains.

4.1 Introduction

One important breakthrough in digitalized systems is the advancement of technology. While these system security entails safeguarding sensitive user information, medical data, infrastructure, and sensitive information from unauthorized access, breaches, or misuse. It involves implementing robust security measures, protocols, and technologies to protect healthcare systems, electronic health records (EHRs), medical devices, and communication networks from cyber threats, data

[1]Department of Computer Sciences, The University of Faisalabad, Pakistan
[2]College of Computer and Information Sciences, Imam Mohammad Ibn Saud Islamic University (IMSIU), Saudi Arabia

breaches, and privacy violations [1]. Healthcare security also encompasses ensuring compliance with regulations such as the Health Insurance Portability and Accountability Act to maintain the confidentiality, integrity, and availability of healthcare data. Additionally, healthcare security involves educating healthcare professionals and staff about cybersecurity best practices, conducting risk assessments, implementing access controls, encryption, and intrusion detection systems, and establishing incident response plans to mitigate and manage security incidents effectively [2]. Overall, healthcare security is essential for maintaining patient trust, safeguarding healthcare information, and ensuring the delivery of safe and secure healthcare services. eXplainable artificial intelligence (XAI) refers to the concept of developing artificial intelligence (AI) systems and algorithms in a manner that allows humans to understand and interpret their decisions and behaviors. It emphasizes transparency and clarity in how AI arrives at its conclusions, enabling users to trust and make sense of AI-driven processes. Essentially, XAI aims to bridge the gap between the complex inner workings of AI systems and the need for human comprehension and trust in their outputs [3]. Figure 4.1 represents various XAI applications.

The integration of AI with healthcare in recent years has marked a significant transformation in patient care, diagnosis, and treatment methodologies. However, with healthcare systems increasingly reliant on AI technologies, safeguarding the security and confidentiality of sensitive patient data has become a pressing concern [4]. This challenge has led to the emergence of XAI as a promising solution. XAI offers transparent and interpretable models, providing not only accurate predictions and recommendations but also insights into the decision-making process. Within the domain of XAI and healthcare security, numerous strategies can be implemented to guarantee the clarity and transparency of AI systems. These methods are designed to elucidate the decision-making procedures of AI models for healthcare professionals, administrators, and patients while upholding stringent security and privacy protocols [5]. Here are several fundamental approaches to achieving explainability in this context (Figure 4.2).

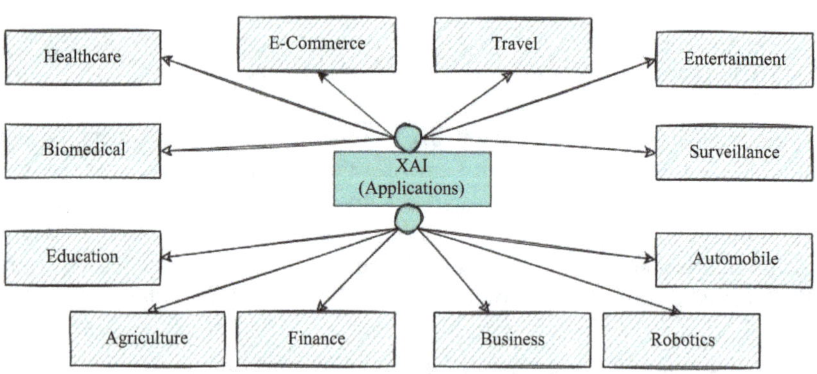

Figure 4.1 XAI applications

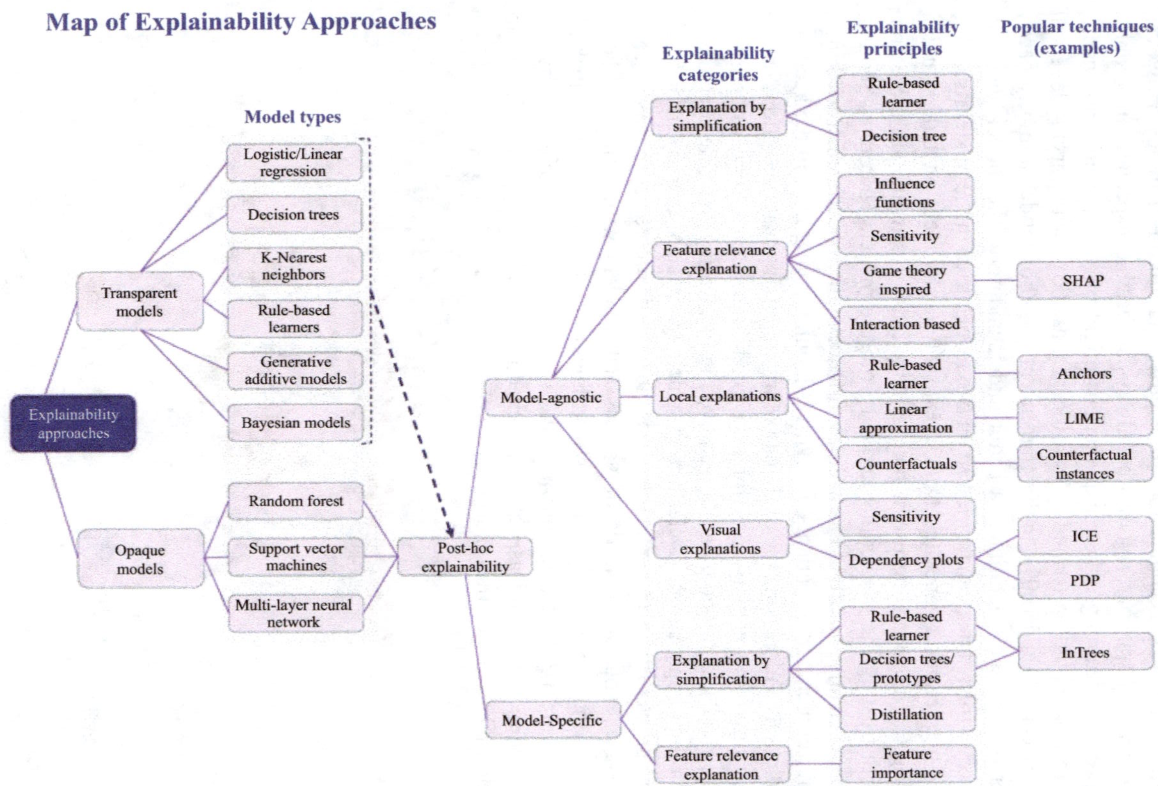

Figure 4.2   XAI explainability approaches [6]

Moving away from the opaque nature of traditional "black box" models, XAI aims to transition toward a more transparent "glass box" paradigm, sometimes also referred to as a "white box." In a glass box model, such as a decision tree or linear regression model, all parameters are known, allowing for a clear understanding of how the model reaches its conclusions, thus providing full transparency. However, achieving complete transparency may not always be feasible, especially in complex models like deep learning, where explanations might only be partially attainable, resulting in what could be termed a "translucent glass box" with varying levels of opacity between 0% and 100%. In this translucent glass box model, a lower opacity (or higher transparency) facilitates a better understanding of the model, which in turn can foster trust. Trust can be viewed on two levels: trust in the model itself and trust in the predictions it generates. Data scientists typically focus on understanding and trusting the model, while users, such as clinicians or patients, are more concerned with trusting the predictions derived from the model. Therefore, building trust for data scientists involves ensuring confidence in the model's inner workings, whereas for clinicians and patients, it revolves around having faith in the accuracy of its predictions. Addressing the challenge of trusting individual predictions can be tackled by providing explanations for each prediction. Conversely, establishing trust in the model as a whole can be achieved by presenting multiple predictions along with their explanations. Determining which approach to employ in different contexts requires further research and exploration. This tailored approach can cater to the diverse explanation needs of various stakeholders within the healthcare domain, ensuring transparency and trustworthiness in AI-driven decision-making processes. Figure 4.3 clearly demonstrates the all points of explainable security [7]. These points encompass all aspects that help to detail all the points relevant to application of XAI in healthcare security.

Figure 4.3 XAI security

Blockchain is a decentralized and distributed ledger technology that facilitates secure and transparent transactions across a network of computers. Each transaction, or "block," is cryptographically linked to the previous one, forming a chain of blocks. This architecture ensures that data recorded on the blockchain is tamper-resistant and immutable, meaning it cannot be altered or deleted without consensus from the network participants. In the latest digital scenario, blockchain plays a pivotal role in various industries and applications. Its decentralized nature eliminates the need for intermediaries, reducing transaction costs and increasing efficiency [4]. Moreover, blockchain enhances transparency and trust by providing a transparent and auditable record of transactions. In finance, blockchain is revolutionizing the way transactions are conducted, enabling faster, more secure, and cheaper cross-border payments. In supply chain management, blockchain ensures transparency and traceability, allowing businesses to track the journey of products from manufacturer to consumer. Additionally, blockchain has applications in healthcare, voting systems, identity verification, and many other areas, offering innovative solutions to complex challenges in the digital era. Overall, blockchain technology is reshaping the digital landscape, empowering individuals and businesses with secure, transparent, and efficient systems (Figure 4.4).

Blockchain is a decentralized and distributed ledger technology that facilitates secure and transparent transactions across a network of computers. Each transaction, or "block," is cryptographically linked to the previous one, forming a chain of blocks. This architecture ensures that data recorded on the blockchain is tamper-resistant and immutable, meaning it cannot be altered or deleted without consensus from the network participants. In the latest digital scenario, blockchain plays a pivotal role in various industries and applications. Its decentralized nature eliminates the need for

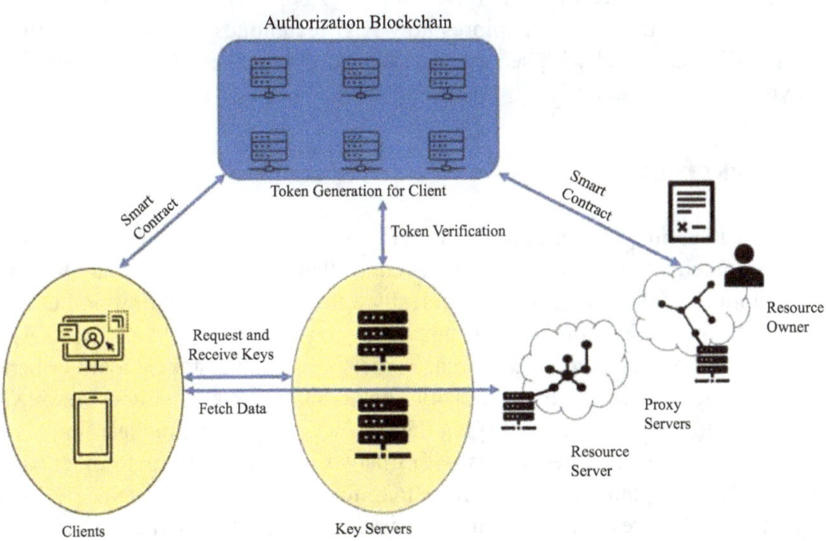

Figure 4.4 Blockchain and cybersecurity [7]

intermediaries, reducing transaction costs and increasing efficiency [4]. Moreover, blockchain enhances transparency and trust by providing a transparent and auditable record of transactions. In finance, blockchain is revolutionizing the way transactions are conducted, enabling faster, more secure, and cheaper cross-border payments. In supply chain management, blockchain ensures transparency and traceability, allowing businesses to track the journey of products from manufacturer to consumer. Additionally, blockchain has applications in healthcare, voting systems, identity verification, and many other areas, offering innovative solutions to complex challenges in the digital era. Overall, blockchain technology is reshaping the digital landscape, empowering individuals and businesses with secure, transparent, and efficient systems.

4.1.1 Chapter contribution

This chapter helps in understanding how XAI-enabled blockchain for cybersecurity? This chapter explores

- The integration of XAI with blockchain technology to enhance cybersecurity in various sectors.
- It examines how XAI techniques can improve transparency in decision-making processes within blockchain-based cybersecurity systems.
- It investigates the role of XAI in enhancing interpretability of complex blockchain models used for cybersecurity.
- It delves into how XAI enables accountability by elucidating the rationale behind security decisions and actions within blockchain networks.
- It also discusses the importance of XAI in ensuring compliance with regulatory standards and ethical guidelines in blockchain cybersecurity.
- It explores how the integration of XAI with blockchain technology can foster trust and confidence in AI-driven security systems.
- Additionally, the chapter explores how XAI techniques contribute to mitigating risks associated with security incidents and breaches in blockchain-based cybersecurity systems.

4.2 Background

In 2004, Van Lent [22] introduced the term XAI to describe their technology's ability to elucidate the behavior of AI-controlled entities in simulation-based gaming applications. XAI lacks a universally agreed technical definition but aims to render AI outcomes more comprehensible to end-users. DARPA defines XAI as the pursuit of creating more transparent models that enable stakeholders to better understand and trust emerging artificially intelligent systems [8]. FICO views XAI as an innovation aimed at demystifying the "black-box" of machine learning (ML), striving to produce accurate models with trustworthy explanations to meet customer needs [12]. Explanation studies have long focused on expert systems predating the term XAI. Progress in addressing this issue slowed after significant advancements in ML, with AI research prioritizing predictive capability over

Table 4.1 XAI frameworks

Framework	Objectives	Methods used	References
SHapley Additive exPlanations (SHAP)	Justify and explain prediction model outcomes	Game theory	[7]
Local Interpretable Model-agnostic Explanations (LIME)	Detail the contribution of each feature	Local interpretable model	[21]
ELI5	Simplify model comparisons	Model comparison	[3]
Skater	Facilitate model interpretation across ML models	Model interpretation	[4]
DALEX	Provide insights into model behavior	Model analysis	[9]
Accumulated local effects (ALE)	Examine relationship between feature values	Feature analysis	[11]

explainability. However, recent attention has shifted toward XAI, evident in the significant rise in interest in the topic, as indicated by Google Trends [8,13]. To impart trust in AI models and facilitate real-world applications, their outputs must be explainable and comprehensible to a broader audience.

The era known for the emergence and development of XAI in healthcare security can be identified as the modern era of healthcare technology and data-driven practices. This era, which encompasses the late 20th century to the present day, has witnessed significant advancements in healthcare information technology, particularly in the areas of data analytics, ML, and AI [9]. During this era, the growing adoption of EHRs, medical imaging technologies, and wearable devices has generated vast amounts of data, providing opportunities for leveraging AI and ML techniques to improve healthcare delivery and patient outcomes. However, concerns about the opacity and interpretability of AI models, especially in critical healthcare applications, led to the development of XAI methodologies tailored specifically for healthcare security [10]. Table 4.1 shows a review of XAI frameworks.

4.2.1 A review of XAI frameworks

The limitations of AI in healthcare security underscore the necessity for XAI to enhance transparency and interpretability in decision-making processes. While AI offers promising solutions for detecting and mitigating security threats in healthcare settings, it also presents several challenges and drawbacks.

AI systems in digital system security may encounter evasion attacks, where attackers manipulate malware files to evade detection by AI-based security frameworks [7]. Such evasion tactics can exploit vulnerabilities in AI algorithms, leading to breaches in sensitive healthcare data.

Moreover, AI-powered cybersecurity systems may generate false negatives, inaccurately assessing security risks and potentially overlooking genuine threats [12]. Conversely, false positives may trigger unnecessary alarms, causing disruptions and diverting resources from critical tasks.

Additionally, the complexity and resource-intensive nature of real-time AI systems pose practical challenges in deployment and maintenance, making them costly and cumbersome for healthcare organizations. These systems may also lack transparency in decision-making processes, hindering stakeholders' ability to understand and trust the security measures in place.

By providing insights into the reasoning behind AI-driven security assessments, XAI helps mitigate the risks associated with false positives and false negatives. It enables stakeholders to identify and rectify potential vulnerabilities in AI models, enhancing the overall effectiveness of healthcare security measures [1].

Second, the integration of XAI with blockchain improves the interpretability of security measures and alerts generated by AI-driven security systems. By providing interpretable explanations for security predictions, XAI enables security professionals to better understand the factors influencing security outcomes, leading to more informed decision-making and risk management strategies [13].

Moreover, XAI-enabled blockchain enhances accountability by elucidating the rationale behind security decisions and actions recorded on the blockchain. This accountability ensures that stakeholders can attribute responsibility for security incidents or breaches, fostering a culture of accountability and ethical technology use.

Overall, XAI-enabled blockchain holds immense potential to transform cybersecurity practices by providing transparency, interpretability, and accountability in AI-driven security systems. As these technologies continue to evolve, their integration is poised to play a pivotal role in addressing emerging cybersecurity challenges and safeguarding digital assets in an increasingly interconnected world.

4.3 Motivation

In the domain of AI and ML, the concept of "explainable AI" is gaining prominence. It's crucial for humans to have confidence in AI models and understand the reasoning behind their decisions. Achieving this requires lifting the veil on the black-box nature of ML algorithms. XAI frameworks serve as tools to shed light on how these models operate and provide insights into their decision-making processes. Below are summaries of some popular XAI frameworks [7]. In the context of blockchain technology, the necessity for explainability stems from the imperative to comprehend and have faith in the fundamental processes governing transactions and data management. As blockchain networks evolve and expand, stakeholders require transparency to grasp the reasoning behind system behaviors and decisions. Explainability within blockchain systems is essential for ensuring accountability, fostering trust among participants, and facilitating compliance with regulatory requirements by offering clear insights into the mechanisms driving blockchain operations. following point apparently showing the points of motivation for the proposed theoretical model.

1. Emerging technologies in cybersecurity: The rapid evolution of technology has led to increasingly sophisticated cyber threats, necessitating innovative solutions to bolster cybersecurity defenses. The integration of advanced technologies such as blockchain and XAI presents an opportunity to address these challenges and enhance cybersecurity measures [14].
2. Transparency and accountability: Traditional cybersecurity approaches often lack transparency, making it challenging to understand the rationale behind security decisions and actions taken by automated systems. By leveraging XAI-enabled blockchain, organizations can achieve greater transparency and accountability in cybersecurity operations, empowering stakeholders to trust and verify the integrity of security processes [11].
3. Potential for improved threat detection: Effective threat detection is critical for mitigating cybersecurity risks and safeguarding sensitive data. XAI techniques offer the promise of providing interpretable insights into security events, enabling more accurate and timely threat detection. When combined with the inherent security features of blockchain, such as decentralization and immutability, XAI-enabled blockchain systems have the potential to enhance threat detection capabilities and strengthen overall cybersecurity posture.
4. Addressing compliance and regulatory requirements: Compliance with regulatory standards and data protection laws is a paramount concern for organizations operating in various industries. XAI-enabled blockchain solutions offer a promising avenue for achieving compliance objectives by providing transparent and auditable records of security-related activities. This can help organizations demonstrate adherence to regulatory requirements and streamline compliance processes, ultimately reducing the risk of legal and financial penalties.

4.3.1 XAI-enabled blockchain

XAI-enabled blockchain, at its core, represents a novel fusion of two cutting-edge technologies: XAI and blockchain [15]. This integration aims to revolutionize various sectors, particularly in the realm of cybersecurity and data management.

The essence of XAI-enabled blockchain lies in its ability to combine the transparency and immutability features of blockchain with the interpretability and accountability aspects of XAI. Blockchain, known for its decentralized and tamper-resistant nature, provides a secure and transparent platform for recording transactions and storing data [16]. Each transaction recorded on the blockchain is cryptographically linked to the previous one, ensuring the integrity and transparency of the entire transaction history.

However, XAI brings the power of explainability to AI-driven systems, allowing stakeholders to understand the rationale behind AI decisions and predictions. By leveraging XAI techniques, such as model interpretability and explanation generation, users can gain insights into the inner workings of AI models, enabling them to trust and verify the outcomes produced by these models [17].

In the context of cybersecurity, XAI-enabled blockchain offers several advantages. it enhances transparency by providing a clear audit trail of security-related activities and decisions recorded on the blockchain. This transparency raises trust among stakeholders and facilitates regulatory compliance efforts [18].

4.4 Theoretical model of XAI-enabled blockchain for cybersecurity

In the domain of cybersecurity, the integration of XAI with blockchain technology emerges as a pioneering approach, promising heightened transparency and security. This theoretical framework delves into the symbiotic relationship between XAI and blockchain, elucidating how their fusion bolsters cybersecurity endeavors. By unveiling the intricate workings of AI algorithms through XAI and leveraging the immutability and decentralization of blockchain, this framework propels us toward a future where trust, accountability, and resilience define the landscape of cybersecurity. Following objectives and research questions that are try to fulfill by analyzing this model.

4.4.1 Objectives

1. To investigate the integration of XAI and blockchain technology for enhancing cybersecurity measures.
2. To explore the potential benefits and challenges associated with utilizing XAI and blockchain in cybersecurity applications.
3. To propose novel approaches and frameworks that leverage XAI-enabled blockchain to address cybersecurity gaps and improve overall system resilience.

4.4.2 Research questions

1. How can XAI be effectively integrated with blockchain technology to enhance cybersecurity mechanisms?
2. What are the potential advantages and limitations of utilizing XAI and blockchain in cybersecurity applications, and how do they compare to traditional approaches?
3. What novel frameworks and methodologies can be developed to leverage XAI-enabled blockchain for addressing cybersecurity challenges and enhancing system resilience?

Creating a theoretical framework involves defining the components, their interactions, and how they contribute to achieving the desired outcomes. In this case, the framework will outline the components of an XAI-enabled blockchain system for cybersecurity and how they work together.

4.4.3 Theoretical framework components

Following is the detail of main modules of proposed model

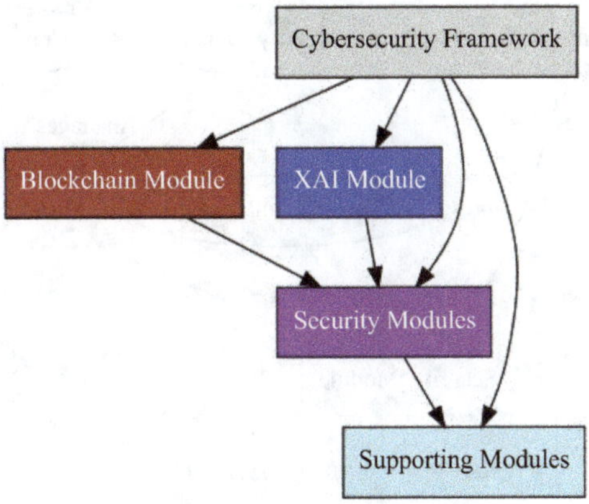

Figure 4.5 Main modules of XAI enable blockchain for cybersecurity theoretical model

1. **Blockchain network**: Represents the decentralized ledger where transactions are recorded.
2. **Smart contracts**: Self-executing contracts enforcing security policies and triggering actions [19].
3. **XAI module**: Responsible for analyzing security events and providing explanations for decisions.
4. **Threat intelligence sharing**: Decentralized sharing of threat intelligence among network participants.
5. **Security data storage**: Secure storage of sensitive data such as access logs and security events.
6. **Identity management**: Immutable identity management for users and devices.
7. **Monitoring and compliance module**: Continuous monitoring of security activities and compliance checks [20]. Below is a simplified design (Figure 4.5).

4.4.4 Connectivity of the modules

Figure 4.6 clearly plots the modules connectivity.

The blockchain network connects all components, serving as the backbone of the system. Smart contracts interact with the blockchain network to enforce security policies and trigger actions. XAI module utilizes data from security data storage and interacts with Smart Contracts for decision-making. Threat intelligence sharing leverages blockchain network for decentralized sharing of threat data. Identity management ensures secure access to the system's resources. Monitoring and compliance module monitors security activities and ensures compliance with regulations (Figure 4.7).

4.4.5 Layered architecture of XAI-enabled blockchain for cybersecurity with complexity analysis

Each layer and its associated components are present along with their functionalities and interactions. For analyzing the complexity of the system, each layer is analyzed against worst case.

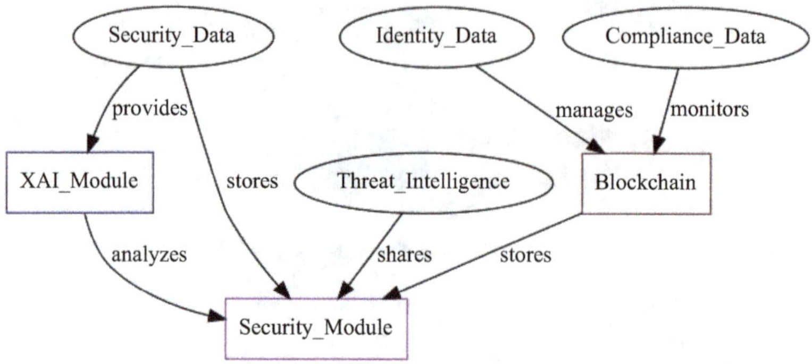

Figure 4.6 Connectivity of modules

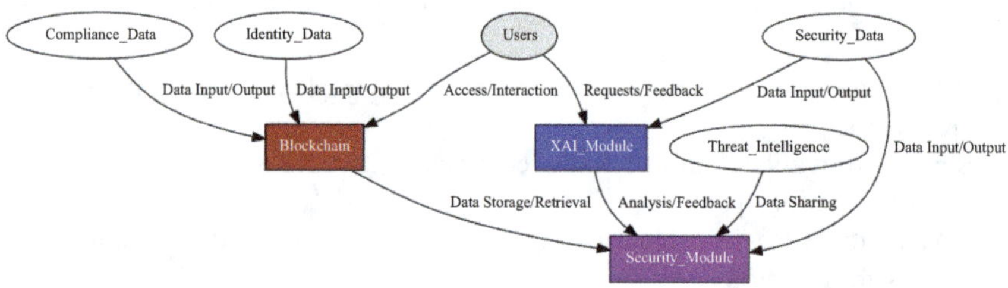

Figure 4.7 Detailed connectivity model

1. **Presentation layer:**
   Components: Web interfaces, APIs, command-line interfaces
   Functionalities: User interaction, input/output processing
   Complexity: $O(1)$ for basic user interactions, $O(n)$ for more complex interactions involving data processing or multiple API calls
2. **Application layer:**
   Components: Request processing modules, business logic modules
   Functionalities: Request handling, business logic execution, database interactions
   Complexity: Depends on the specific algorithms and operations implemented in the application logic, typically ranging from $O(1)$ to $O(n^2)$ depending on the complexity of the business logic.
3. **Blockchain layer:**
   Components: Smart contracts, consensus algorithms, blockchain nodes
   Functionalities: Transaction validation, block creation, consensus mechanism execution
   Complexity: Depends on the specific blockchain protocol and consensus algorithm used. For example, the complexity of the bitcoin blockchain's proof-of-work consensus mechanism is $O(2^n)$.
4. **XAI layer:**
   Components: Data analysis modules, explanation generation modules

Functionalities: Data analysis, explanation generation, integration with other system modules Complexity: Depends on the complexity of the AI algorithms used for data analysis and explanation generation. For example, the complexity of decision tree-based explanations could range from $O(\log n)$ to $O(n)$.

5. **Security layer:**

   Components: Threat intelligence sharing modules, security data storage modules, identity management modules, compliance monitoring modules

   Functionalities: Threat intelligence sharing, secure data storage, identity management, compliance monitoring

   Complexity: Depends on the specific security measures implemented and the complexity of the algorithms involved. For example, the complexity of compliance monitoring algorithms could range from $O(n)$ to $O(n^2)$ depending on the number of regulations and checks performed.

Overall complexity: The overall complexity of the XAI-enabled blockchain system for cybersecurity would depend on the interactions and dependencies between layers and components. It can be analyzed by considering the worst-case runtime complexity of operations within each layer and the overall flow of data and control through the system.

4.4.6 Contribution

Figure 4.8 shows the major contribution of the theoretical framework. Red edges show the contribution while green connectivity shows the main data flow in model.

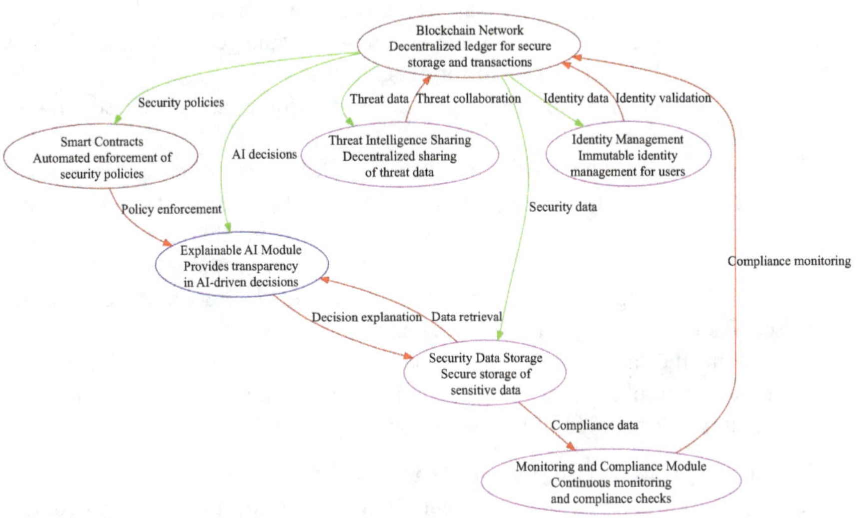

Figure 4.8 Theoretical framework

Considering above details shown in diagram ensuring:

- Enhanced transparency, accountability, and trust in cybersecurity operations.
- Improved threat detection and response through XAI and threat intelligence sharing.
- Automated enforcement of security policies and compliance checks through smart contracts.
- Immutable storage of security-related data ensures integrity and tamper resistance.

4.5 Mapping of theoretical framework

Research questions are map with the components of the theoretical framework:

1. **Research question: how can XAI be effectively integrated with blockchain technology to enhance cybersecurity mechanisms?**

   XAI module: This component directly addresses the integration of XAI with blockchain technology to enhance cybersecurity mechanisms. It focuses on providing transparent explanations for AI-driven decisions recorded on the blockchain.

   Blockchain network: The integration of XAI with blockchain relies on the decentralized and tamper-resistant nature of the blockchain network to ensure the integrity and transparency of security-related data.
2. **Research question: what are the potential advantages and limitations of utilizing XAI and blockchain in cybersecurity applications, and how do they compare to traditional approaches?**

   Components of the theoretical framework contribute to addressing this research question by exploring the potential advantages and limitations of integrating XAI with blockchain for cybersecurity:

   Smart contracts: Enforce security policies and trigger actions based on XAI-driven decisions.
   - Threat intelligence sharing: Enhance collective security awareness and response capabilities through transparent sharing of threat intelligence data.
   - Security data storage: Ensure secure and immutable storage of XAI-generated explanations and security-related data on the blockchain.
   - Identity management: Provide transparent and secure authentication processes leveraging XAI and blockchain technology.
   - Monitoring and compliance module: Monitor security activities and ensure compliance with regulations, leveraging the transparency and auditability features of the blockchain.

3. **Research Question: what novel frameworks and methodologies can be developed to leverage XAI-enabled blockchain for addressing cybersecurity challenges and enhancing system resilience?**

   This research question directly aligns with the exploration of novel frameworks and methodologies within the theoretical framework:

- XAI module: Develop novel XAI techniques tailored for integration with blockchain technology to enhance transparency and accountability in cybersecurity.
- Threat intelligence sharing: Create decentralized threat intelligence sharing platforms leveraging XAI-enabled blockchain networks.
- Monitoring and compliance module: Devise innovative methodologies for integrating XAI-driven anomaly detection algorithms with blockchain-based intrusion detection systems.
- Identity management: Explore decentralized identity management solutions based on XAI-enabled blockchain to enhance cybersecurity and system resilience.

4.6 Challenges and limitations

The proposed framework for integrating XAI with blockchain technology for cybersecurity presents several limitations that need to be considered:

1. Scalability challenges: One limitation is the scalability of blockchain networks, especially when handling large volumes of security-related data and transactions. As the number of participants and transactions increases, the performance of the blockchain network may degrade, leading to slower transaction processing times and higher resource requirements.
2. Computational overhead: Integrating XAI techniques with blockchain technology may introduce additional computational overhead, particularly during the analysis and interpretation of security-related data. XAI algorithms often require significant computational resources and may increase the processing time of transactions on the blockchain network.
3. Complexity of integration: Another limitation is the complexity of integrating XAI with blockchain technology. Developing seamless integration between XAI algorithms and blockchain-based systems requires expertise in both domains, as well as thorough understanding of the underlying technologies and their interoperability challenges.
4. Privacy concerns: There may be privacy concerns associated with storing sensitive security-related data on a public blockchain network. While blockchain offers transparency and immutability, it may not provide sufficient privacy protections for certain types of data, raising concerns about data confidentiality and regulatory compliance.
5. Adoption challenges: Adoption of the proposed framework may face challenges related to acceptance and adoption by stakeholders. Organizations may hesitate to adopt new technologies and methodologies, especially if they perceive them as complex or disruptive to existing workflows.
6. Regulatory compliance: Ensuring compliance with existing regulations and legal frameworks poses a challenge in the context of XAI-enabled blockchain for cybersecurity. Regulatory requirements related to data protection, privacy, and security may need to be carefully considered and addressed to avoid legal complications.

7. Resource constraints: Implementing the proposed framework may require significant financial and human resources, including investment in specialized hardware, software, and skilled personnel. Small organizations or those with limited resources may face challenges in implementing and maintaining the framework effectively.

Overall, while the proposed framework offers promising opportunities for enhancing cybersecurity through transparency and accountability, it is essential to recognize and address these limitations to ensure its successful implementation and adoption in real-world scenarios.

4.7 Conclusion

In conclusion, the presented theoretical framework for integrating XAI with blockchain technology for cybersecurity demonstrates feasibility and holds significant potential for achieving its objectives. Through the delineation of various components and their interactions, the framework offers a structured approach to enhancing transparency, accountability, and trust in cybersecurity operations. By leveraging the decentralized and tamper-resistant nature of blockchain technology and the interpretability provided by XAI techniques, the framework aims to address key challenges in cybersecurity while promoting resilience and efficiency. The framework's adaptability and applicability extend beyond cybersecurity, as its foundational principles can serve as a blueprint for designing network-based systems in diverse fields. By emphasizing transparency, accountability, and data integrity, the framework provides a solid foundation for building secure and reliable networks across various domains, including healthcare, finance, supply chain management, and beyond. Furthermore, the identification of limitations and challenges underscores the importance of addressing these factors to ensure the successful implementation and adoption of the framework. Through ongoing research, innovation, and collaboration, it is possible to overcome these challenges and further refine the framework to meet the evolving needs of cybersecurity and other network-based systems.

Overall, the presented theoretical framework represents a promising avenue for advancing cybersecurity practices and laying the groundwork for the design of robust and resilient network architectures across different fields. By embracing transparency, accountability, and innovation, organizations can harness the potential of XAI-enabled blockchain technology to enhance security, trust, and reliability in an increasingly interconnected world.

References

[1] Kwon, J., and Johnson, M. E. (2018). Meaningful healthcare security. *MIS Quarterly*, *42*(4), 1043–1047.

[2] Act, A. (1996). Health insurance portability and accountability act of 1996. *Public Law*, *104*, 191.

[3] Hulsen, T. (2023). Explainable artificial intelligence (XAI): Concepts and challenges in healthcare. *AI*, *4*(3), 652–666.

[4] Albahri, A. S., Duhaim, A. M., Fadhel, M. A., *et al.* (2023). A systematic review of trustworthy and explainable artificial intelligence in healthcare: Assessment of quality, bias risk, and data fusion. *Information Fusion*, *96*, 156–191.

[5] Yang, C. C. (2022). Explainable artificial intelligence for predictive modeling in healthcare. *Journal of Healthcare Informatics Research*, *6*(2), 228–239.

[6] Belle, V., and Papantonis, I. (2021). Principles and practice of explainable machine learning. *Frontiers in Big Data*, *4*, 688969.

[7] Korica, P., Gayar, N. E., and Pang, W. (2021). Explainable artificial intelligence in healthcare: Opportunities, gaps and challenges and a novel way to look at the problem space. *Paper presented at the International Conference on Intelligent Data Engineering and Automated Learning*.

[8] Mohanty, A., and Mishra, S. (2022). A comprehensive study of explainable artificial intelligence in healthcare. In *Augmented Intelligence in Healthcare: A Pragmatic and Integrated Analysis* (pp. 475–502): Berlin: Springer.

[9] Sindiramutty, S. R., Tee, W. J., Balakrishnan, S., *et al.* (2024). Explainable AI in healthcare application. In *Advances in Explainable AI Applications for Smart Cities* (pp. 123–176): Hershey, PA: IGI Global.

[10] Manresa-Yee, C., Roig-Maimó, M. F., Ramis, S., and Mas-Sansó, R. (2021). Advances in XAI: Explanation interfaces in healthcare. In *Handbook of Artificial Intelligence in Healthcare: Vol 2: Practicalities and Prospects* (pp. 357–369): Berlin: Springer.

[11] Gkolemis, V., Dalamagas, T., and Diou, C. (2023). DALE: Differential accumulated local effects for efficient and accurate global explanations. *Paper presented at the Asian Conference on Machine Learning*.

[12] Orner, C., and Chowdhury, M. (2024). AI and cybersecurity: Collaborator or confrontation. *Proceedings of the 39th International Conference on Computers and Their Applications*, *98*, 150–158.

[13] Wenhua, Z., Qamar, F., Abdali, T.-A. N., Hassan, R., Jafri, S. T. A., and Nguyen, Q. N. (2023). Blockchain technology: Security issues, healthcare applications, challenges and future trends. *Electronics*, *12*(3), 546.

[14] Das, P. P., Wiese, L., and Elise Study Group (2023). Explainability based on feature importance for better comprehension of machine learning in healthcare. *Paper presented at the European Conference on Advances in Databases and Information Systems*.

[15] Hasan, M., Rahman, M. S., Janicke, H., and Sarker, I. H. (2024). Detecting anomalies in blockchain transactions using machine learning classifiers and explainability analysis. *Blockchain: Research and Applications*, *5*(3), 100207.

[16] Akanfe, O., Lawong, D., and Rao, H. R. (2024). Blockchain technology and privacy regulation: Reviewing frictions and synthesizing opportunities. *International Journal of Information Management*, *76*, 102753.

[17] Singh, S., and Singh, N. (2016). Blockchain: Future of financial and cyber security. *Paper presented at the* 2016 *2nd International Conference on Contemporary Computing and Informatics (IC3I)*.

[18] Andrew, J., Isravel, D. P., Sagayam, K. M., Bhushan, B., Sei, Y., and Eunice, J. (2023). Blockchain for healthcare systems: Architecture, security challenges, trends and future directions. *Journal of Network and Computer Applications*, *215*, 103633.

[19] Taherdoost, H. (2023). Smart contracts in blockchain technology: A critical review. *Information*, *14*(2), 117.

[20] Marjanović, J., Dalčeković, N., and Sladić, G. (2023). Blockchain-based model for tracking compliance with security requirements. *Computer Science and Information Systems*, *20*(1), 359–380.

[21] Zafar, M. R., and Khan, N. (2021). Deterministic local interpretable modelagnostic explanations for stable explainability. *Machine Learning and Knowledge Extraction*, *3*(3), 525–541.

[22] Phan, T. C. (2023). Explanation as first-class citizen: Methods and applications. PhD Thesis, School of Information and Communication Technologies, Griffith University, Australia.

Chapter 5

A hybrid cybersecurity approach: leveraging ZTA, AI, XAI, and blockchain to combat emerging threats

Sobia Wassan[1], Rana Muhammad Amir Latif[2], Liu Dajun[1], Han Ying[1], Muhammad Farhan[3] and Muhammad Asghar Khan[4]

Abstract

As cyber threats grow more sophisticated and advanced, modern cybersecurity demands adaptive and explainable solutions. This research introduces a hybrid security framework that integrates zero trust architecture (ZTA), artificial intelligence (AI), blockchain technology, and explainable AI (XAI) to reinforce digital infrastructures against evolving cyber threats. ZTA enforces the "never trust, always verify" principle by continuously authenticating and authorizing network entities. AI enhances this approach by employing real-time threat detection and dynamically adjusting access controls based on behavioral patterns. Including XAI ensures transparency and interpretability, enabling security teams to understand AI-driven decisions, identify potential biases, and maintain trust in automated systems. Blockchain further strengthens the framework by providing a decentralized, tamper-proof ledger for secure verification, comprehensive audit trails, and robust anomaly detection. This integrated model offers a scalable, resilient, and transparent solution to address modern and emerging cybersecurity challenges, training organizations with the tools to protect critical assets in a rapidly evolving threat landscape.

5.1 Introduction

Today's digitally driven workforces have outperformed than traditional cybersecurity models, making it increasingly challenging to address the growing

[1]School of Equipment Engineering, Jiangsu Urban and Rural Construction Vocational College, China
[2]The Center for Modern Chinese City Studies, School of Geographical Sciences, East China Normal University, China
[3]Department of Computer Science, COMSATS University Islamabad, Pakistan
[4]Department of Electrical Engineering, Prince Mohammad bin Fahd University, Saudi Arabia

number of sophisticated cyber threats. Cyber threat methods have progressed more rapidly than we've adapted before [1]. At the same time, it has become clear that with the rise of cloud-based systems applications and the need for secure connections across many devices, they are more anxious about outdated perimeter-based security models, which are no longer sufficient. In this research, we have considered of this radical hybrid security framework based on the alliance of zero trust architecture (ZTA) with artificial intelligence (AI), blockchain technology, and explainable AI (XAI) [2]. When used together, these technologies present capabilities, a cohesive unified, versatile, and human-flexible security solution. ZTA is the basis for this framework: where we move from perimeter security to a current verification of the users, their devices, and network traffic flows in a continuous manner [3]. ZTA helps reduce the existence of any attackers by forcing authentication and authorization for each request, whether it's an internal request or from an external request. ZTA uses the enhancement of (AI); processes large tranches of data, looking for anomalous inconsistent behavior actions & risk. However, this is all possible because of the increase of speed and accuracy in threat detection due to the high scale processing of data by AI [4]. AI also enables dynamic policy adjustments that react to behavioral patterns and to adaptive security that changes based on network conditions.

Blockchain technology helps to record one more layer of security in a decentralized, tamper-proof ledger to record all security-associated, tamper-proof ledger to record all security-associated decentralized, tamper-proof ledger to record all security-associated related activities. It ensures security with this immutable blockchain ledger, authenticating logs, difference detection and AI driven response not to be tampered with or deleted [2]. Specifically, transparency and verifiability are demanded required to have an audit trail and fulfill regulatory requirements in the finance, health, and government sectors. The XAI is added to the framework to increase the trust and reliability of the AI system. XAI puts AI decisions that chanced in the "black box" into words. This transparency means that security teams can audit, understand and trust the AI's decisions so they are on a faster response cycle and are making better informed decisions when those decisions are made by the AI [5].

The framework is intended to scale for growing complexity in modern networks, e.g., cloud or mobile platforms. There is also a facility for dynamically scaling up the hybrid security framework as provider organizations grow their digital footprint with newer devices, users, and services. Real-world tests and the simulations indicate that the proposed hybrid framework is superior to the current, traditional ZTA implementations in terms of threat detection and mitigation, and compliance. The new model offers ZTA, AI, blockchain, and XAI combined so it becomes a more resilient, transparent and practical way to protect valuable digital assets. While this integration is a massive step in reimagining how security strategies can be implemented to ease organizations and enable their operations to be secured in the increasingly nastier digital landscape, it's also the darlings of the security industry.

5.1.1 The integration of artificial intelligence and explainable AI

Combining AI, XAI, and blockchain technology produces a faultless and composite cybersecurity framework emphasizing threat detection and transparency. AI are advanced machine learning algorithms applied to massive number of datasets in time to rapidly identify anomalies and potential attacks, so reducing the timeframe within cybercrime farm is possible. Whereas AI warnings are unintelligible, XAI explains the decisions of the AI, making its alerts human-readable and thus practical and reliable. From detecting a threat to its prohibiting from a specific contract, blockchain offers a secure, tamper-proof ledger to log detected threats and linked AI responses, confirming that these records cannot be changed. In addition to logging each event to this immutable blockchain ledger, traceability is also increased, which should make traceability easier for security teams to reference a verifiable history of events for systematic investigations and audits [6]. As a trifecta of threat detection speed, decision-making transparency, and auditable logs, AI's threat detection ability, XAI's transparency in decision-making, and blockchain's secure, auditable logs combine to produce a fast, and reliable system for cybersecurity that can trustworthily and transparently address cyber threats.

5.1.2 The integration of explainable AI and blockchain technology

XAI and blockchain technology helps combine the immutability and security of blockchain with the interpretability of AI based decisions also this sets help to improve cybersecurity. For flagged anomalies or threats in such models, XAI securities that the actions in AI models are transparent (a given action was triggered) and understandable (why was the action likely triggered) to security sides [7]. It promotes trust and stake in AI responsible decision making and rapid response. Blockchain technology's decentralized, tamper proof ledger is coupled with XAI to secure all the recorded AI driven actions with all threat detection events.

This security data is immutable, and so we can't change it, and that indicates that we have a provable audit trail of what has happened, which is useful for compliance and for post incident investigations. XAI and blockchain combine together to provide a reliable, accountable system while losing its integrity and maintaining its cybersecurity operation.

AI, XAI, and blockchain technology provide a strong, advanced cybersecurity framework for threat detection and transparency [8]. Three technology innovations that serve as a synergetic combination of AI's rapid detection and analysis, XAI's interpretability and transparency, and blockchain's security and immutability to address the challenging attributes of modern cybersecurity. it develops an integrated, transparent, safe solution that improves an organization's cybersecurity profile.

5.1.3 AI capabilities in threat detection

AI and advanced machine learning algorithms used sophisticated real-time processing of large datasets to analyze and quickly spot security differences, behavioral deviations and possible threats. Specifically, these capabilities are critical for protecting against sophisticated and rapidly evolving cyberattacks, such as zero-day vulnerabilities, where traditional detection may begin to fail. By modeling AI across disparate data sources, the models can quickly spot known and unknown threats, minimizing the time cybercriminals can exploit vulnerabilities. Due to the critical aspect of this immediate threat detection, this immediately closes a window of opportunity for attackers, minimizing the window of opportunity to mitigate risks before they escalate. AI is the basis for modern cybersecurity systems. The key part in the first place of evaluation is threat detection based on AI using ML, deep learning, or enhanced analytics to identify things that can cause security issues at a time, so it will become easier for an organization to defend itself from the threat.

However, one of the main benefits of AI-driven threat detection is its ability to offer high accuracy rates. Signature-based systems tend to be outperformed by unknown threats because they fully rely on predefined patterns and signatures [9]. However, AI-driven models can find new and emerging threats that allow the model to remain effective overall. Also, AI reduces false positives, decreasing the chances of brain actions being treated as security events. s so he can continuously learn from vast amounts of data; an AI system can evolve along with current cyber threat developments [10]. The dynamic learning capability ensures that the cybersecurity model is one step ahead of the attackers. This component is evaluated to determine its ability to detect known and unknown threats with precision and reliability.

Adaptive Access Control is another critical component in the hybrid cybersecurity model for dynamic, flexible, context-sensitive accessing policies to be enforced by the system. It is exciting when users and devices change often, and classical access control mechanisms are no longer sufficient [11]. Real-time security policies, whether adaptive or not, can react to contextual information such as user behavior, device health, location, or data sensitivity [12].

5.1.4 XAI's role in transparency and interpretability

AI is excellent at finding threats, but decisions can sometimes be like a "black box" from the security side, so they do not know what decision came from what was happening. In this, XAI comes in convenient. XAI is a clear, human-readable explanation of how AI models decide to act upon data provided, including reasoning around flagged anomalies, identified threats, or unsafe transactions. For instance, instead of resulting in a simple alert, where we would get triggered but not know why or what XAI can give us context as to why a specific activity was flagged as suspicious in the form of specific patterns, data points, or behaviors that caused AI to make a particular determination. Security teams must trust this AI-generated alert and know how to act on the alert with speed and quality to stay ahead of threats. It also makes the decision-making process on questioned and reviewed decision.

5.1.5 Blockchain's contribution to integrity and immutability

Blockchain technology more advances framework, it creates a tamper-proof decentralized ledger model to record all detected threats and AI-driven responses securely. Once data is published on a blockchain, it is immutable; it cannot be changed or deleted. It guarantees security operations if threat detection events, AI decisions, and actions are logged securely, verifiably, and transparently. This tamper-proof nature of the blockchain is important to keeping security data secure and having a trail to follow for investigations or regulatory compliance. If a violation happens, the security data remains intact, so the teams can perform a comprehensive post-incident review and trace the events. As for decentralized storage of logs, blockchain prevents the system from having just a single point of failure, making the infrastructure more resilient to attacks. Integrating blockchain technology is a significant development contributing to cybersecurity threats, namely transparency and data integrity. Because blockchain is integrally decentralized, immutable, and transparent, it is an ideal choice to secure acute structures [13]. Integrating blockchain into a cybersecurity system will provide uncountable benefits, such as the immutability of stored data and the transparency of all stored information. Each transaction or data modification is made to the blockchain in a public ledger, a tamper-resistant trail. It means that if an attacker tries to modify system data, they would be easily identified by anyone who can view the blockchain [14]. In addition, the centralized point of failure possessed by most systems is not an issue as blockchain technology dispenses with the necessity of a centralized authority. Decentralization makes it immune to attack as long as one node in the network is compromised. This evaluation examines the validity of integrating blockchain when enhancing the security position of the model as a whole. It explores the effectiveness of blockchain to guaranty transparency, tamper with the authority and make the system more trustworthy.

5.1.6 Enhanced traceability and accountability

The framework significantly improves the traceability of threat detection events by boasting the combination of AI, XAI, and blockchain. Each event is recorded in the blockchain with the reasoning of the AI model that tagged it and what actions were taken. The complete log provides a transparent record so security teams can trace the origin of every action and decision to help validate what transpired during an incident. However, beyond the further security, this traceability of incidents allows security teams to examine incidents while ensuring systematically accountability; every decision made by AI and every action stored in the blockchain can be run through the wringer and audited. It is essential when any industry (finance, healthcare, government) encounters regulatory compliance due to the necessity of being able to see and, as such, verify the records of the security operations.

5.1.7 Trustworthy and tamper-proof logs

Because blockchain is decentralized, the security logs stored on the network are integrally trusted and cannot be tampered with, ensuring their integrity. We cannot change or delete the recorded events after detecting a threat event, resulting in an immutable audit trail. As blockchain keeps a secure log of all events, it allows easy collaboration between decentralized teams or organizations; everyone can see the exact history of secure, verifiable logs. It allows all stakeholders to trust the system and ensure that if actions have been taken to secure it, those actions will not be changing purpose from someone's end. The critical challenges organizations face in securing their digital infrastructure are clarified by a robust, comprehensive cybersecurity framework based on AI, XAI, and blockchain technology. The rapid, real time threat detection relies on AI, XAI ensures transparency and understanding of the AI's decision and all the security data is immutable and verifiable on blockchain. With these technologies, speed, reliability, and accountability can be found in threat detection, response and investigation. new technologies, organizations can now safely and proactively control cyber risk and drive maximum outcomes from a resilient infrastructure capable of adapting to that innovative risk environment's ever-changing facts and obscurities. By integrating to this, operational efficiency is reinforced and security operations are compliant, trustworthy and able to stand the upcoming threats.

5.1.8 Main contribution

This research contributes toward a transformative hybrid security framework based on ZTA, AI, blockchain, and XAI to address the complex problems in modern cybersecurity. The framework adds to ZTA, with continuous verification and access control, and dynamic policy changes due to behavioral patterns, composed with AI-driven real time threat detection, dramatically reducing the attack surface. A novel feature is to use blockchain technology to allow decentralized and tamper-proof authentication, a transparent audit trail and robust anomaly detection to robustly protect the system as a whole, no single point of failure and no violation. Integration with blockchain also helps with regulatory compliance by converting activities into an auditable and verifiable process for financial, healthcare and government institutions. XAI, therefore, makes AI-driven decisions explainable and trusted, enabling security teams to audit, understand, and fine-tune automated responses to new threats. At the same time, it includes security tests. The framework is designed to be scalable and adaptive to support different levels of network complexity, from cloud environments to mobile platforms, without sacrificing performance. The proposed model is validated by simulation and real-world scenarios, showing much better threat detection, mitigation, and compliance capabilities than traditional and modern ZTA implementations. This holistic and strong approach transforms cybersecurity strategy into a defense that protects critical assets in open and hostile cyber terrain. transformative hybrid security framework shown in Figure 5.1.

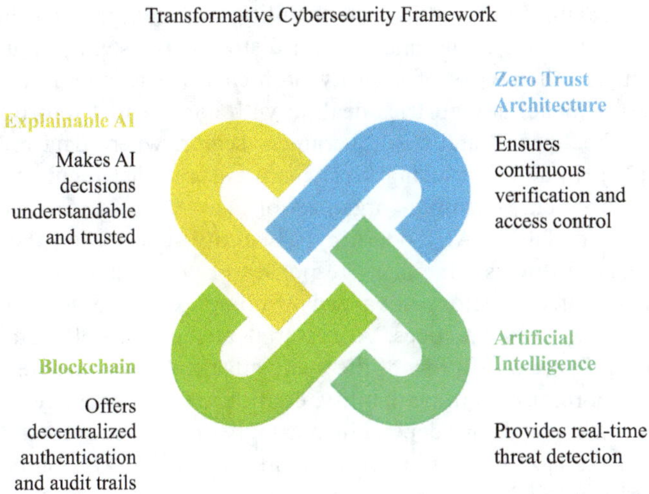

Figure 5.1 Display the transformative hybrid security framework

5.2 Related study

Hyper-connected space, where cyber threats have become increasingly sophisticated, organizations are being urged to reconsideration their security model and what they need to protect digital assets [15]. Perimeter defenses are becoming less effective in protecting advanced cyberattacks using internal and external vulnerabilities; legacy security models have become outmoded against modern threats [16]. ZTA has emerged as a transformative approach to cybersecurity, built on the principle of never trust, always verities following strict access controls, and the all-encompassing verification of all entities in a network, across locations and from which they have previously verified [17]. ZTA has shown considerable improvement over traditional methods but falls short of its full potential with static implementations that do not scale up to ever-changing threats [18]. We develop a hybrid security model that combines ZTA with AI and blockchain to tackle one of these gaps: a dynamic but immutable solution for new-generation cybersecurity challenges. It employs end-to-end logic with dynamic access control and prevention of real-time threat detection for faster response to changing behavioral patterns [19].

Concurrent with the blockchain, an immutable and decentralized ledger provides a secure means of identification (auditable access), secures the traffic over this platform, and can be used for anomaly detection under the meniscus [20]. The contribution of this research is its comprehensive focus on the vulnerabilities of traditional and zero-touch-to-credential-based contemporary cybersecurity frameworks [21]. Through ZTA, AI and blockchain are combined to improved scalability, flexibility, adaptability, and transparency. Framework suits modern enterprise requirements with distributed systems, cloud applications, and many other types of security problems due to mobile access. This combined effort benefits industries dealing with confidential information such as financials, healthcare, and the government sector, where data breaches are expensive [22]. In addition, using blockchain ensures that regulatory requirements are observed, enabling organizations to have a trustworthy and auditable security fabric. AI modern cybersecurity depends on the ability to detect advanced threats. Incident response or risk assessment [23–25]. Cybersecurity which develops advanced in complexity and sophistication as technology for security practices. Adversarial attacks, model theft, and data poisoning [26,27] are only a few of the many attacks AI systems are vulnerable to that can compromise their availability, confidence, and integrity. Since these attacks occur fast, companies depend increasingly on AI to immediately identify and handle these hazards to stop security breaches [28]. AI systems are well suited to perform this because they can examine massive amount of data, spot trends, and find irregularities indicative of cyber threats [29]. Using them could help to better protect AI systems themselves against cyberattacks. Moreover, if implemented into existing cybersecurity tools, they could improve their accuracy and usability, for example, by reducing the number of false positives when identifying exposures in a system.

Also, if fixed in cloud-based solutions and providing collective learning capabilities between different users of AI systems (e.g., virus scanners), it would be possible to identify new threats before being confronted with them [30]. Using them could also speed up the time required to recognize and remediate security incidents and automate threat responses manually. previous all these advantages, which already are quite diverse, one should not overrate that AI systems will not become attacked by cyberattacks on their own [31]. However, instead, hackers will subject them intentionally to attacks to exploit the weaknesses of these systems. For example, data poisoning attacks would manipulate the data used for training an AI object, implying that the predictions of this object could be biased or incorrect against specific users. Adversarial attacks inject minor deviations into input data, making malware a program. Model stealing attacks result in the theft of trained models, which can then be used to increase destructive malware. To face all these challenges, the cybersecurity community immediately initiated various response activities based on an intended secure decentralized model using AI object filters [32].

AI systems protect sensitive data and secrecy while letting many stakeholders cooperate and exchange data. Blockchain technology offers distributed and unchangeable data storage, therefore offering a workable way to improve the security and privacy of AI systems [33–36]. Tamper-proof and can be audited by several parties, blockchain technology produces a distributed ledger for holding transaction data safely [37]. Using blockchain technology, such distributed decision-making and consensus-building strategies might boost trust and cooperation amongst many stakeholders [38]. These technologies provide real-time danger detection and response even if they help improve information privacy and security and increase multi-stakeholder cooperation. Companies should use blockchain technology to create distributed AI systems that can withstand potential cyberattacks and protect digital infrastructure [39]. Aiming for resource efficiency and service reliability while simultaneously satisfying the demand for high traffic rates and a large number of connected devices, modern information technology, and wireless communication systems have evolved into scalable network systems that are efficient, dependable, and easy to scale up or down [40–42]. Therefore, these systems have advantages but pose serious problems regarding operating expenditure, capital expense, and increased complexity.

The data is gathered and sent via unprotected network channels open to various cyberattacks that may cause service interruptions and drain network resources [43,44]. Human-driven methods and customized service-based setups best address some of these problems, neither of which gets sufficient support [45]. Here, closed-loop automation is a potential answer for totally automated network administration and operations. When it comes to management and operational tasks like planning, deployment, provisioning, monitoring, and optimization, zero-touch network is all about automating them [46]. In this study article, stock market modeling, sales forecasting, and market segmentation are some areas where AI is investigated. It stresses fuzzy logic and convolutional neural networks, solving the first two issues using backpropagation algorithms and the third with self-organizing maps [47]. These days, intrusion detection systems (IDS) use AI to extract relevant characteristics, spot outliers, and categorize assaults [48–50]. When integrated with IDS, machine learning and deep learning have shown great promise in reducing the impact of different cyberattacks. In recent years, IDS powered by deep learning has gained significant traction due to its ability to efficiently handle massive volumes of data, low false positive rate, and high accuracy [51,52]. Consequently, there has been continued perception of deep learning-based IDS as opaque entities due to the complexity of detection models and lack of explanation of the entire decision-making process [53]. A hybrid security framework based on ZTA, AI, blockchain, and XAI—is presented as an approach to address modern cybersecurity challenges. With ZTA principles, security is achieved through continuous verification and access control, while AI provides real-time threat detection and dynamic policy adjustments. A tamper-proof ledger and blockchain provide regulatory compliance for secure authentication, audit trails, and resilient anomaly detection. XAI allows security teams to configure AI responses in a transparent and trusting way so they can refine the automated response. The framework can be easily scaled to changing network environments and performs well. Simulations validate ZTA implementation, which provides better threat detection, mitigation, and compliance than traditional ZTA. Given such a threat, a new paradigm in AI was invented to explain the rationale behind the prediction by machine learning based IDS models Explainable AI (XAI) [54–56] (see Table 5.1).

Table 5.1 A comparison of existing solutions in digital twin-driven cybersecurity

Related work	Explainable AI-based IDS	Blockchain	Limitation	Advantage
Varghese *et al.* [57]	N/A	N/A	Limited attacks	IDS with DTs integration
Suhail *et al.* [58]	✓	N/A	Security evaluation	XAI feature explanation
Thakur *et al.* [59]	N/A	✓	Communication cost	Defense against threats
Lu *et al.* [60]	N/A	✓	No accuracy	Privacy via blockchain
Ferrag *et al.* [61]	N/A	N/A	No comparison	Security/privacy
Javeed *et al.* [48]	✓	N/A	Black-box models	AI-based anomaly detection
Abou *et al.* [53]	✓	N/A	Complex workings	XAI in IDS
Eckhart *et al.* [62]	N/A	N/A	Testing on live systems	DTs for attack response
Kobayashi *et al.* [63]	✓	N/A	Early research stage	DTs with XAI
Bitton *et al.* [64]	N/A	N/A	Unspecified	DTs for security

5.3 Methodology

The hybrid cybersecurity model consists of how the methodology for the proposed model integrates ZTA, AI, and blockchain technology within one framework to provide further security and resilience. The adoption starts with a framework design that enforces the never-trust, always-verify policy and rigorous authentication for ZTA-supported users, devices, apps, and networks using role-based access control. It monitors network activities in real-time, using behavioral analysis, detects out-of-place anomalies, and predicts malicious attacks. Adaptive access control mechanisms change their security rules depending on the information received from the threat. It uses blockchain for decentralized authentication, tamper-proof record keeping for auditing, and robust anomaly detection. The integration phase is to create a complete system by integrating AI-driven threat detection and blockchain authentication with ZTA via APIs and middleware. AI tools are applied in the implementation phase to monitor network traffic and user behavior, and horizontal blockchain authentication and immutable audit are applied to ensure decentralized authentication. Dynamic access control policies are derived from AI and blockchain data.

The evaluation phase of the model is when real-world threat case studies are run to test the model's ability to detect and eliminate threats so that we can measure performance criteria, such as response time, false positives, scalability, and compliance. Finally, in the validation stage, the performance of the hybrid model is compared to ZTA performance and additional existing hybrid models to validate the capabilities of the hybrid model. This methodology would be portrayed in a diagram with a core framework node (ZTA) from which several awareness layers (anomaly detection, decentralized authentication) would feed on input from users, devices, applications, and networks and provide enhanced security, scalable access control, and transparent compliance (see Figure 5.2).

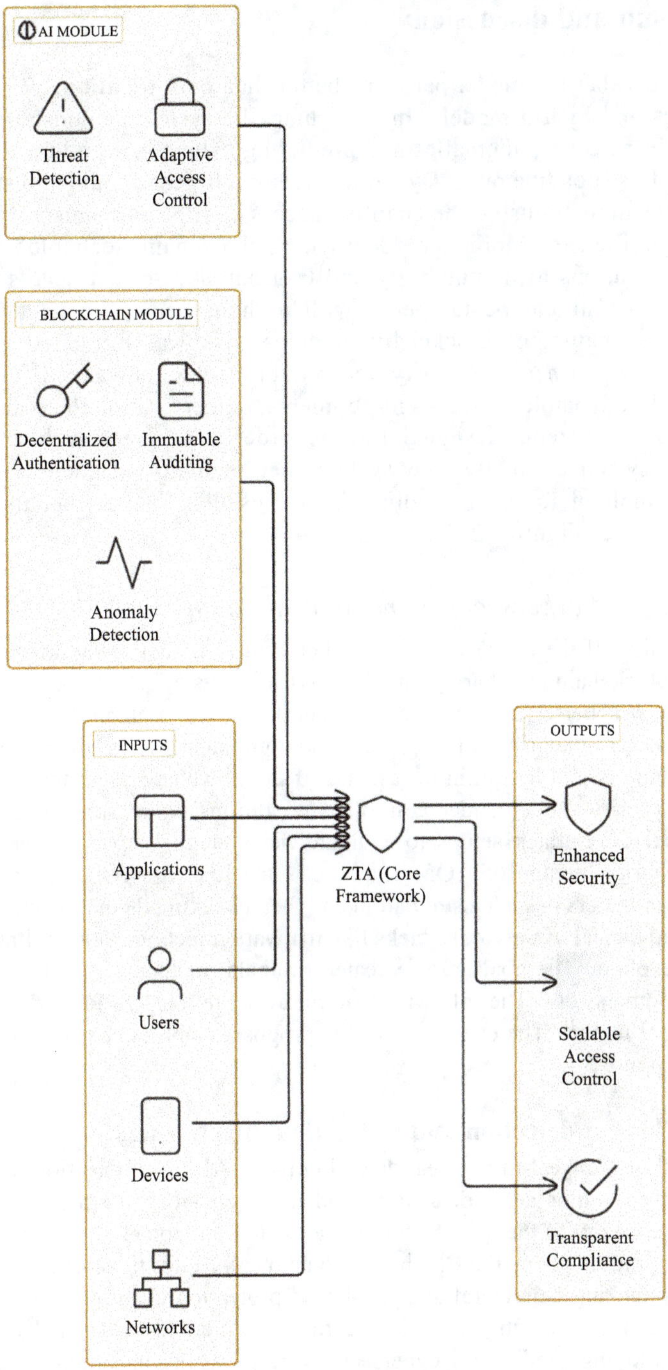

Figure 5.2 Method process diagram

5.4 Result and discussion

Results show that the model performs better than both traditional ZTA implementations and hybrid models. In particular, the system demonstrates a high accuracy in detecting anomalies and predicting cyberattacks and a significant decline in false positive rates. Dynamic threat intelligence could adjust security policies dynamically using the adaptive access control mechanism, improving network resilience. Moreover, deploying blockchain technology carried security operations to immutability and transparency so that access logs and audit trails could not be tampered with without being detected. With the decentralized nature of blockchain modules, risk was mitigated with centralized ones, and hence, security and reliability were advanced. The model scaled well in dynamic network environments, outperforming the scalability of the enterprise systems designed for, by order of degree, such as modern enterprise systems. Finally, the system met regulatory standards and was equally compliant for data handling industries like finance, healthcare, and government (see Figure 5.3).

5.4.1 Hybrid cybersecurity model evaluation

The evaluation of the proposed hybrid cybersecurity model, integrating ZTA, AI, XAI, and blockchain technology, involves assessing its effectiveness in addressing contemporary cybersecurity challenges, its performance, scalability, and its ability to ensure system integrity, transparency, and compliance. After the initial evaluation, simulations will be run in next phase of the flowchart. This step aims to test the cybersecurity model under controlled conditions while simulating different hypothetical cyberattack setups to evaluate the system's capacity to respond to various security threats [65]. One example is in either a simulation or exposing multiple parameters in such a simulation and then tweaking them to simulate DDoS (Distributed Denial of Service) attacks like malware infection, data exfiltration, and zero-day exploits. The goal is to recreate criminals' methods for cybercrime in a safe environment [66]. The following criteria evaluate this hybrid model's success and potential impact. The evaluation of the proposed hybrid cybersecurity mode is shown in Figure 5.4.

5.4.1.1 Threat detection and mitigation effectiveness

An integral part of real-time threat detection using AI threat detection. AI models continuously monitor network activity and user behavior patterns, automatically setting the capacity of the system to find anomalies and potential security breaches faster than traditional methods. The AI dynamically adjusts access controls and policies by making behavioral analysis-based protection against evolving threats. This approach considerably reduces the time required to detect and respond to attacks employing predictable cybersecurity frameworks in simulated and real-world scenarios.

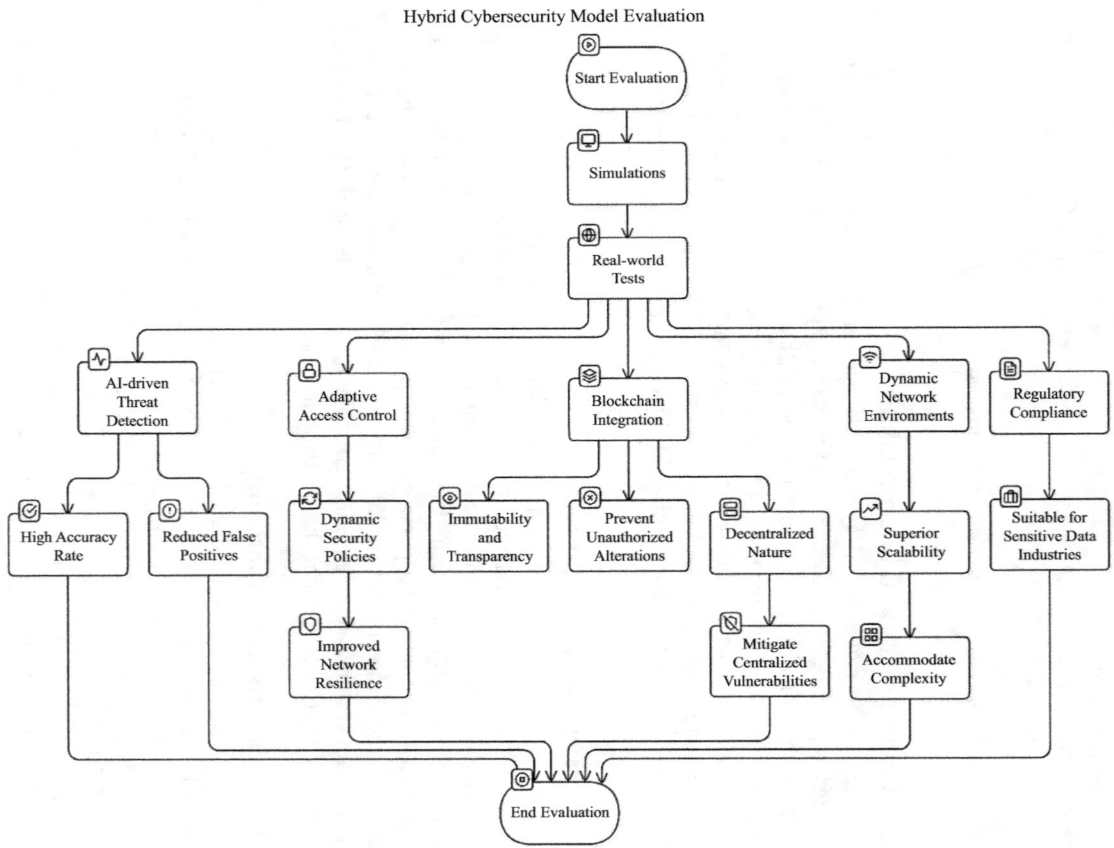

Figure 5.3 The model evaluation result of the model

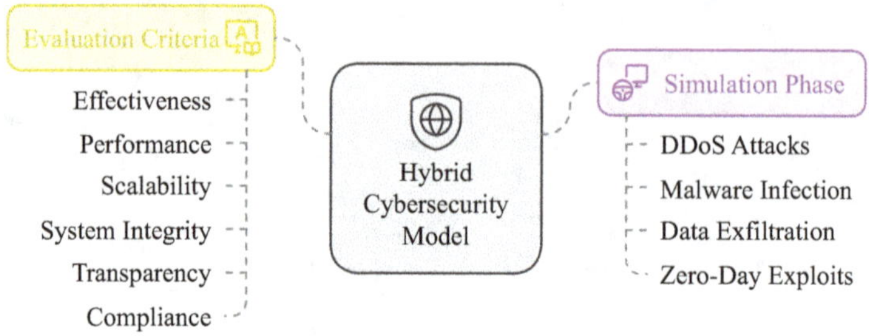

Figure 5.4 Display the evaluation of the proposed hybrid cybersecurity mode

5.4.1.2 Transparency and interpretability

XAI is necessary to make the AI system's decision-making process more transparent. It gives security teams clear, human-readable explanations of what has been identified as an anomaly, giving them confidence that there are good automated responses to the flagged anomalies. XAI explicitly justifies AI actions through detailed explanations, making dense black box systems less dense, more accountable, and more responsive to good decision-making. The system can identify and remediate biases by auditing and refining AI-driven decisions to ensure they remain trusted.

5.4.1.3 System integrity and security

The hybrid cybersecurity model gains overall integrity through blockchain technology by providing a decentralized and immutable ledger to record all detected threats, AI-driven decisions, and security responses. It is so that security logs cannot be messed with in a breach. The framework is also more robust to attacks since blockchain has no single point of failure in the system. As blockchain is decentralized, the trustworthiness of information security data is ensured due to the tamper-resistant feature, which ensures verifiable and auditable records, which are always required for analysis after the incident and compliance.

5.4.1.4 Scalability and adaptability

Growth of the enterprise with its digital infrastructures, namely, increasing use of cloud, mobile, and IoT, scalability is a critical consideration. The built flexibility in its hybrid model means that it readily evolves with growing network complexity. the continuous authentication provided by ZTA and AI's potential to accept large volumes of data in real-time allows the system to scale without slowing down or compromising security. Whereas blockchain's decentralized nature further increases scalability, more nodes may be added to the network to decentralize control without jeopardizing security integrity in ever-expanding environments. A first round of evaluation he verifies that the system is scalable enough to scale up to support the growing demands of a growing network. On the other hand, it forces how decentralized it is against vulnerabilities brought into centralized architectures that enable it to achieve such devastating results [67].

5.4.1.5 Compliance and auditing

The combination of employability and compliance driven by the hybrid model is extremely important for those sectors that maintain inflexibility in stringent regulatory frameworks like finance, healthcare, and government, to name a few. The immutable blockchain ledger is secured and provides a safe record of everything, including access control decisions and threat detection events, which can be drew in a compliance audit. Paired with blockchain's auditable records, XAI leads to transparency in the system and bounds all system activities to be visible and compliant with industry regulations. This combination eliminates non-compliance risk and reduces the work from regulatory reporting.

5.4.1.6 Performance and efficiency

We then measure how well the model performs in understanding the conversion of massive volumes of data to the system without causing excessive slowness or damaging the user experience. Security responses are swift and effective through low-latency AI threat detection. Finally, blockchain adds a layer of security and transparency but is built to keep overhead low so that the system can remain as fast as possible regardless of data growth. XAI integration has our explanations for AI decisions integrated quickly without significantly slowing down the threat detection process.

5.4.1.7 Resilience and robustness

The hybrid formation of this cybersecurity model shows a higher resistance to internal and external threats. According to the zero trust principle, no entity in the network is trusted proven. AI learning ability means when the system receives a new type of threat, it evolves in response. Blockchain makes for stronger resilience by making it impossible to fool, preventing security logs from being changed without authorization, and therefore, important security data remains secure at all times. Indeed, blockchain's decentralized nature creates a single point of failure. Moreover, blockchain reduces the risk of a single point of failure.

5.4.1.8 Cost-effectiveness

The setup and integration of a hybrid model combining ZTA, AI, XAI, and blockchain can come with the initial setup and integration costs; however, the long-term benefits will pay for it as it reduces the risk of expensive security breaches, shortens downtime, and increases efficiencies of security operations. Using automated AI-driven threat detection with the power of blockchain to log data safely minimizes the need for manual omission, which lowers operational costs over time. The capability to ensure compliance with regulations also reduced the risk of costly penalties for non-compliance.

The start evaluation node begins a synchronized effort to evaluate a hybrid cybersecurity system. Try to confirm that the cybersecurity model is ready to be tested and assessed. We establish this foundational phase of the evaluation process to be organized, and sequential steps are almost secure to follow logically and clearly [68]. This stage usually starts with collecting data on the system's architecture, evaluating the building criteria, and being ready to work with the model to be utilized in the later actual testing phases. The infrastructure setup would be done, the relevant environments for testing would be provided, and a set of benchmarks would be set up so that performance would not be surpassed.

A hybrid cybersecurity model combining ZTA, AI, XAI, and blockchain technology provides a solid, significant, and transparent response to contemporary cybersecurity problems. The framework offers a unique and advanced solution with its comprehensive approach to digital infrastructure protection through its algorithmically enhanced threat detection, transparent decision-making, and tamper-proof record-keeping. It is a superb real-time threat mitigation, compliance, and system integrity resource that organizations increase in value when they want to improve their cybersecurity posture in an increasingly complex and visibly hostile site.

5.4.1.9 Real-world tests: validating in practical scenarios

To verify the claimed efficiency of the hybrid cybersecurity model in the real world, extensive testing was conducted to demonstrate its performance under actual conditions. In this work, he simulated different types of cyberattacks and determined the system's capability of detecting, responding, and adapting to the threat in a dynamic environment [69]. By enforcing strict access controls and continuous network entity verification, the zero trust principle played a vital role in security; no entity, not internal or external, could bypass security measures.

Then AI's adaptive learning capability was tested, as it learned in real-time by discovering new and emerging threat patterns. The threat detection system, which this time depends on AI to grasp previously hidden attack vectors, has succeeded at detecting the attack vectors whilst swiftly mitigating potential damage. Furthermore, combining XAI could depend the confidence that security teams can have in automated responses through the past that the system at least understood why it was making its decisions.

Using blockchain technology, audit trails and logs were identified for the integrity and security of same. They were able to successfully protect the critical security data from unauthorized alteration, and every action was transparently traceable to the tamper proof decentralized ledger. It is also important to eliminate single points of failure from a blockchain to ensure the system can sustain an attack on centralized infrastructure. The technologies allowed the devices to stand up and respond to internal and external threats whilst simultaneously delivering the advanced cybersecurity the model promised.

The model was verified in real-world tests to be robust, scalable, and adaptable, which attests to its ability to endure myriad cyberattacks affordably and with no loss of performance or security. Practically, this validation shows that the hybrid cybersecurity model can help enterprises as challenges they face are growing more and more with the complex and hostile digital threats landscape and cannot be easily addressed by conventional security models.

5.4.1.10 Regulatory compliance: ensuring adherence to standards

A major component of security is to create a hybrid security model that is comprised of major security elements to make sure that the organizations are secure and in addition the organizations are following industry specific standards and legal conditions. With regulations increasing across sectors such as finance and healthcare as well as government, and in their reaction to COVID-19 compliance, organizations require robust cybersecurity frameworks to safeguard sensitive data, and meet compliance with the regulations.

Blockchain technology provides regulatory compliance by creating an immutable, unchangeable ledger for all security activities on the blockchain. This gives organizations a traceable audit trail to prove compliance with EU GDPR, HIPAA, and Payment Card Industry Data Security Standard. Blockchain is able to guarantee that organizations can confirm that they comply with these regulations riskless and securely by meaningfully and securely logging all access control events and data transfer, and each threat detection.

Moreover, the ZTA, access to data is strongly controlled, and each data flow is verified continuously, which replicated data privacy requirements and protection under the regulatory rules. ZTA supports adherence to those standards requiring thorough access to confidential data relating to controlled access to sensitive data by adhering to the policy of least privilege access in which only authorized entities are allowed to interact with sensitive information. Such AI-driven threat detection also helps organizations meet compliance efforts by alerting them of deviations from the norm in real time, thus allowing them to fix any potential susceptibility or breach before it damages compliance.

This compliance aspect is enhanced by XAI, which gives us transparency in automated decision-making processes. This transparency in the audit is essential for regulatory audits in that it enables security teams to show that specific actions were taken by AI systems under the logic they were taken and, therefore, that automated decisions were based on regulatory guidelines and industry standards. Additionally, it guarantees that the cybersecurity security system complies with the lowest standard of security and information protection rules.

The hybrid cybersecurity model that we implemented helps firms quickly answer complex and always evolving regulatory landscape and improve security. The model combines blockchain for auditable transparency, ZTA for secure control and access, and AI with XAI for real-time threat detection and interpretability, allowing organizations to protect assets and meet specific legal and regulatory stipulations for their industry.

5.4.2 End evaluation

The hybrid form of cybersecurity integrates ZTA, AI, XAI, and blockchain technology. The NS final evaluation demonstrates the effectiveness with which the model addresses current challenges in modern cybersecurity. Additionally, the evaluation also shows the working of ZTA's continuous authentication, and behavioral analysis which continuously reduces the attack surface and makes the system more resilient to breaches. Combined with the transparency across XAI to enable deeper AI security and understanding of automated decisions, AI's real-time threat detection provides fast identification of threats and security teams can trust the system. The tamper proof blockchain further strengthens the model's integrity as blockchain's decentralized, tamper proof ledger ensures both auditability of data logs and compliance with regulatory standards. We do a detailed evaluation of the model's adaptability and scalability, and demonstrate how the model can be easily used in unstoppable moving network ecosystems such as cloud infrastructures and mobile platforms. The process stops once all hybrid cybersecurity model components are rigorously tested and evaluated at its end evaluation node. This last one makes sure that the system is also worrying about getting all the robustness, adaptable, security, and compliance factor. At this stage all results are studied in depth and ideas of improvement or change are suggested. Finally, the end evaluation shows a complete picture of how this system works. It concludes the study of structured, systematic evaluation of the hybrid cybersecurity model's suitability for use, and this indicates that the model can provide an efficacious solution to today's complex cybersecurity problems [70].

Although still using low latency, the model's performance remains efficient in dynamic and complex settings, and its resilience to both internal and external threats increases the model's robust protection against various cyberattack techniques. Finally, the hybrid model passes the last assessment, satisfying all the security, compliance, and adaptability criteria demanded. The evaluation finds that the model supports transparency, accountability, and trust and provides state-of-the-art real-time threat detection and defense mechanisms. A hybrid cybersecurity evaluation model is shown in Figure 5.5.

5.4.3 Discussion

We show that the hybrid model addresses the fundamental challenges of today's cybersecurity, specifically rapid threats, vulnerability centralization, and scalability. We integrate ZTA, AI, and blockchain, improving security with a more flexible, auditable, and transparent security framework. It generates a system which provided with an AI component that can analyze the cyberattack quickly and adapt to new threats, proactively defending the system against cyberattacks and removing static security policies. Decentralized authentication, tamper-proof auditing, and the ability to identify anomalies without relying on a single point of failure all

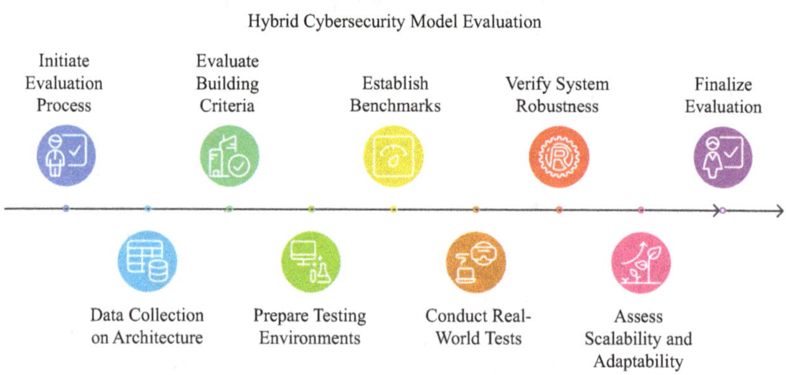

Figure 5.5 Hybrid cybersecurity evaluation model

contribute to improved integrity, particularly when blockchain is integrated into the model. A combination of designing and modeling, as well as employing a security framework that actualizes it, will outperform traditional security frameworks that are often stagnant in trying to meet the requirements of scalability, adaptability, and transparency against changing adversarial environment of security and safety. Dynamic access control implemented using both AI and blockchain limits access to sensitive resources by authorized entities only, thus, minimizing the risk of data breaches. In addition, the decentralized blockchain module helps address issues with a central vulnerability that traditional systems lack.

However, considering the limitations of the proposed model, future research should address this. Despite the strength of the security provided by the combination of AI and blockchain, computation resources for real-time threat detection or blockchain use may be uneconomic on the overall system on a large scale. Such components can be further optimized, improving model efficiency without affecting performance. However, while the blockchain component increases security and transparency, it may not be adequate for all organizations as there may be regulatory constraints or Trading difficulties with existing systems. Future work can look into ways to dramatically shorten the time required to implement blockchain so that it makes its way deeper into new markets.

5.5 Conclusion

Finally, it concludes by stating that this hybrid security framework is a powerful, multi-layer approach to handling new threats in cybersecurity as the cyber threats keep becoming more complex and dynamic. With AI, ZTA, AI, and blockchain technology integration, a resilient and adaptive and transparent security system can be achieved. With ZTA, we create, test with rigorous verification of network which entities done; then send out alerts in real time via AI technology that detects threats and uses dynamic adjustments. XAI adds a critical layer of transparency, enabling security teams to understand and trust AI decisions, and blockchain ensures immutable and auditable logs, reinforcing system integrity. This comprehensive framework enhances the ability to detect and mitigate emerging threats and fosters accountability, scalability, and compliance. It sequences organizations with the tools to protection their digital infrastructure and protect critical assets in an increasingly hostile cybersecurity landscape.

References

[1] Kumar, R., A. Aljuhani, D. Javeed, P. Kumar, S. Islam, and A.N. Islam, Digital twins-enabled zero touch network: A smart contract and explainable AI integrated cybersecurity framework. *Future Generation Computer Systems*, 2024. **156**: p. 191–205.

[2] Nkoro, E.C., J.N. Njoku, C.I. Nwakanma, J.M. Lee, and D.S. Kim, Zero-trust marine cyberdefense for IoT-based communications: An explainable Approach. *Electronics*, 2024. **13**(2): p. 276.

[3] Blika, A., S. Palmos, and G. Doukas, *et al.*, Federated learning for enhanced cybersecurity and trustworthiness in 5G and 6G networks: A comprehensive survey. *IEEE Open Journal of the Communications Society*, 2024. **6**: p. 3094–3130.

[4] Kaliyaperumal, P., S. Periyasamy, M. Thirumalaisamy, B. Balusamy, and F. Benedetto, A novel hybrid unsupervised learning approach for enhanced cybersecurity in the IoT. *Future Internet*, 2024. **16**(7): p. 253.

[5] Mahmood Naser, S., Y. Hussain Ali, and D. Al-Jumeily OBE, Hybrid cybersecurity model for attacks detection based on deep and machine learning. *International Journal of Online Biomedical Engineering*, 2022. **18**(11): p. 17–30.

[6] Maghrabi, L.A., S. Shabanah, and T. Althaqafi, *et al.*, Enhancing cybersecurity in the internet of things environment using Bald Eagle search optimization with hybrid deep learning. *IEEE Access*, 2024. **12**: p. 8337–8345.

[7] Choubisa, M., R. Doshi, N. Khatri, and K.K. Hiran, A simple and robust approach of random forest for intrusion detection system in cyber security. in *2022 International Conference on IoT and Blockchain Technology (ICIBT)*. 2022. Piscataway, NJ: IEEE. pp. 1–5.

[8] Vijayalakshmi, P. and D. Karthika, Hybrid dual-channel convolution neural network (DCCNN) with spider monkey optimization (SMO) for cyber security threats detection in internet of things. *Measurement: Sensors*, 2023. **27**: p. 100783.

[9] Sarker, I.H., *AI-driven Cybersecurity and Threat Intelligence: Cyber Automation, Intelligent Decision-Making and Explainability*. 2024: Cham: Springer Nature.

[10] Ofili, B.T., E.O. Erhabor, and O.T. Obasuyi, Enhancing Federal Cloud Security with AI: Zero Trust, Threat Intelligence, and CISA Compliance, *World Journal of Advanced Research Review*, 2025. **25**(2): p. 2377–2400.

[11] Duy, P.T., H. Do Hoang, A.G.T. Nguyen, and V.H. Pham, B-DAC: a decentralized access control framework on northbound interface for securing SDN using blockchain, *Journal of Information Security Applications*, 2022. **64**: p. 103080.

[12] Ajakwe, S.O., C.A. Okoloegbo, J.M. Lee, and D.S. Kim, Machine learning models for drone security: cognitive versus cyber intelligence for safety operations, in *Machine Learning for Drone-Enabled IoT Networks*: Springer, 2025, p. 121–139.

[13] Nguyen, T., H. Nguyen, and T.N. Gia, Exploring the integration of edge computing and blockchain IoT: Principles, architectures, security, and applications. *Journal of Network and Computer Applications*, 2024. **226**: p. 103884.

[14] Zrikem, M., I. Hasnaoui, and R.J.E. Elassali, Vehicle-to-blockchain (V2B) communication: Integrating blockchain into V2X and IoT for next-generation transportation systems. 2023. **12**(16): p. 3377.

[15] Daah, C., A. Qureshi, I. Awan, and S. Konur, Enhancing zero trust models in the financial industry through blockchain integration: A proposed framework. *Electronics*, 2024. **13**(5): p. 865.

[16] Muhammad, T., M.T. Munir, M.Z. Munir, and M.W. Zafar, Integrative cybersecurity: merging zero trust, layered defense, and global standards for a resilient digital future. *International Journal of Computer Science and Technology*, 2022. **6**(4): p. 99–135.

[17] Akbar, M., M.M. Waseem, S.H. Mehanoor, and P. Barmavatu, Blockchain-based cyber-security trust model with multi-risk protection scheme for secure data transmission in cloud computing. *Cluster Computing*, 2024: p. 1–15.

[18] Alzoubi, M.M.J., Investigating the synergy of blockchain and AI: Enhancing security, efficiency, and transparency. *Journal of Cyber Security Technology*, 2024: p. 1–29.

[19] Saleh, A.M.S., Blockchain for secure and decentralized artificial intelligence in cybersecurity: A comprehensive review. *Blockchain: Research and Applications*, 2024: p. 100193.

[20] Vignesh Saravanan, K., P. Jothi Thilaga, S. Kavipriya, and K. Vijayalakshmi, Data protection and security enhancement in cyber-physical systems using AI and blockchain, in *AI Models for Blockchain-based Intelligent Networks in IoT Systems: Concepts, Methodologies, Tools, and Applications*. M., Arif, V.E., Balas, T., Nafis, N.M.F., Qureshi, S., Wazir, and I., Hussain, (eds.). 2023, Berlin: Springer. p. 285–325.

[21] Chaudhry, U.B. and A.K.M. Hydros, Zero-trust-based security model against data breaches in the banking sector: A blockchain consensus algorithm. *IET Blockchain*, 2023. **3**(2): p. 98–115.

[22] Veeramachaneni, V., Integrating zero trust principles into IAM for enhanced cloud security. *Recent Trends in Cloud Computing and Web Engineering*, 2025. **7**(1): p. 78–92.

[23] Zhang, Z., H. Ning, and F. Shi, *et al.*, Artificial intelligence in cyber security: research advances, challenges, and opportunities. *Artificial Intelligence Review*, 2022. **55**: p. 1–25.

[24] Sarker, I.H., M.H. Furhad, and R. Nowrozy, AI-driven cybersecurity: An overview, security intelligence modeling and research directions. *SN Computer Science*, 2021. **2**(3): p. 173.

[25] Li, J.-h., Cyber security meets artificial intelligence: A survey. *Frontiers of Information Technology Electronic Engineering*, 2018. **19**(12): p. 1462–1474.

[26] Guembe, B., A. Azeta, S. Misra, V.C. Osamor, L. Fernandez-Sanz, and V. Pospelova, The emerging threat of AI-driven cyber attacks: A review. *Applied Artificial Intelligence*, 2022. **36**(1): p. 2037254.

[27] Abdullahi, M., Y. Baashar, H. Alhussian, *et al.*, Detecting cybersecurity attacks in internet of things using artificial intelligence methods: A systematic literature review. *Electronics*, 2022. **11**(2): p. 198.

[28] Zhao, L., *et al.*, Artificial intelligence analysis in cyber domain: A review. *International Journal of Distributed Sensor Networks*, 2022. **18**(4): p. 15501329221084882.

[29] Kaur, R., D. Gabrijelčič, and T. Klobučar, Artificial intelligence for cybersecurity: Literature review and future research directions. *Information Fusion*, 2023. **97**: p. 101804.

[30] Gbadebo, M.O., A.O. Salako, O. Selesi-Aina, O.S. Ogungbemi, O.O. Olateju, O.O. Olaniyi, *et al.*, Augmenting data privacy protocols and enacting regulatory frameworks for cryptocurrencies via advanced blockchain methodologies and artificial intelligence. *Journal of Engineering Research and Reports*, 2024. **26**(11): p. 10.9734.

[31] Sagar, B., S. Niranjan, N. Kashyap, and D. Sachin, Providing cyber security using artificial intelligence—a survey. in *2019 3rd International Conference on Computing Methodologies and Communication (ICCMC)*. 2019. Piscataway, NJ: IEEE. pp. 717–720.

[32] Badr, Y., On the integration of artificial intelligence and blockchains 3.0: Prospects and challenges. in *2021 IEEE 18th International Conference on Software Architecture Companion (ICSA-C)*. 2021. Piscataway, NJ: IEEE.

[33] Liu, M., W. Yeoh, F. Jiang, and K.K.R. Choo, Blockchain for cybersecurity: Systematic literature review and classification. *Journal of Computer Information Systems*, 2022. **62**(6): p. 1182–1198.

[34] Deshmukh, A., N. Sreenath, A.K. Tyagi, and U.V.E. Abhichandan, Blockchain enabled cyber security: A comprehensive survey. in *2022 International Conference on Computer Communication and Informatics (ICCCI)*. 2022. Piscataway, NJ: IEEE. pp. 1–6.

[35] Angelis, J. and E.R. Da Silva, Blockchain adoption: A value driver perspective. *Business Horizons*, 2019. **62**(3): p. 307–314.

[36] Swan, M., *Blockchain: Blueprint for a New Economy*. 2015: Sebastopol, CA: O'Reilly Media, Inc.

[37] Yap, K.Y., H.H. Chin, and J.J. Klemeš, Blockchain technology for distributed generation: A review of current development, challenges and future prospect. *Renewable Sustainable Energy Reviews*, 2023. **175**: p. 113170.

[38] Maleh, Y., Lakkineni, S., Tawalbeh, L., and A.A. Abdel-Latif, Blockchain for cyber-physical systems: Challenges and applications. *Advances in Blockchain Technology for Cyber Physical Systems*, 2022 Vol. 1, p. 11–59.

[39] Ekramifard, A., H. Amintoosi, A.H. Seno, A. Dehghantanha, and R.M. Parizi, A systematic literature review of integration of blockchain and artificial intelligence. *Blockchain Cybersecurity, Trust Privacy*, 2020. **79**: p. 147–160.

[40] Liyanage, M., Q.V. Pham, and K. Dev, *et al.*, A survey on zero touch network and service management (ZSM) for 5G and beyond networks. *Journal of Network Computer Applications*, 2022. **203**: p. 103362.

[41] Gallego-Madrid, J., R. Sanchez-Iborra, P.M. Ruiz, and A.F. Skarmeta, Machine learning-based zero-touch network and service management: A survey. *Digital Communications Networks*, 2022. **8**(2): p. 105–123.

[42] Kumar, R., P. Kumar, M. Aloqaily, and A. Aljuhani, Deep-learning-based blockchain for secure zero touch networks. *IEEE Communications Magazine*, 2022. **61**(2): p. 96–102.

[43] Kumar, R., A. Aljuhani, P. Kumar, A. Kumar, A. Franklin, and A. Jolfaei, Blockchain-enabled secure communication for unmanned aerial vehicle (UAV) networks. in *Proceedings of the 5th International ACM Mobicom Workshop on Drone Assisted Wireless Communications for 5G and Beyond*. 2022: pp. 37–42.

[44] Aljuhani, A., Machine learning approaches for combating distributed denial of service attacks in modern networking environments. *IEEE Access*, 2021. **9**: p. 42236–42264.

[45] Contreras, L.M., S. Javier, M. Lefteris, *et al.*, Modular architecture providing convergent and ubiquitous intelligent connectivity for networks beyond 2030. *ITU Journal on Future Evolving Technologies*, 2022. **3**(3): p. 693–709.

[46] Benzaid, C. and T. Taleb, AI-driven zero touch network and service management in 5G and beyond: Challenges and research directions. *IEEE Network*, 2020. **34**(2): p. 186–194.

[47] Sangeetha, D.M., D.R.M. Priya, J. Elias, D.P. Mamgain, S. Wassan, and D.K. Gulati, Techniques using artificial intelligence to solve stock market forecast, sales estimating and market division issues. *The Journal of Contemporary Issues in Business Government*, 2021. **27**(3): p. 209–215.

[48] Javeed, D., M.S. Saeed, I. Ahmad, P. Kumar, A. Jolfaei, and M. Tahir, An intelligent intrusion detection system for smart consumer electronics network. *IEEE Transactions on Consumer Electronics*, 2023. **69**(4): p. 906–913.

[49] Ataullah, M., and N. Chauhan, Exploring security and privacy enhancement technologies in the Internet of Things: A comprehensive review, *Security Privacy*, 2024. **7**(6): p. e448.

[50] Luo, Y., X. Chen, N. Ge, W. Feng, and J. Lu, Transformer-based device-type identification in heterogeneous IoT traffic. *IEEE Internet of Things Journal*, 2022. **10**(6): p. 5050–5062.

[51] Javeed, D., T. Gao, M.S. Saeed, and M.T. Khan, FOG-empowered augmented-intelligence-based proactive defensive mechanism for IoT-enabled smart industries. *IEEE Internet of Things Journal*, 2023. **10**(21): p. 18599–18608.

[52] Wang, M., K. Zheng, Y. Yang, and X. Wang, An explainable machine learning framework for intrusion detection systems. *IEEE Access*, 2020. **8**: p. 73127–73141.

[53] Houda, Z., B. Brik, and L. Khoukhi, Big data and machine learning for communications 1164 "why should I trust your IDS?": An explainable deep learning framework for intrusion detection systems in internet of things networks. *IEEE Open Journal of the Communications Society*, 2022.**3**: p. i–xiii.

[54] Oseni, A., N. Moustafa, G. Creech, N. Sohrabi, A. Strelzoff, and Zahir Tari, An explainable deep learning framework for resilient intrusion detection in IoT-enabled transportation networks. *IEEE Transactions on Intelligent Transportation Systems*, 2022. **24**(1): p. 1000–1014.

[55] Alani, M.M., E. Damiani, and U. Ghosh, DeepIIoT: An explainable deep learning based intrusion detection system for industrial IOT. in *2022 IEEE 42nd International Conference on Distributed Computing Systems Workshops (ICDCSW)*. 2022. Piscataway, NJ: IEEE.

[56] Roy, S., J. Li, V. Pandey, and Y. Bai, An explainable deep neural framework for trustworthy network intrusion detection. in *2022 10th IEEE International Conference on Mobile Cloud Computing, Services, and Engineering (MobileCloud)*. 2022. Piscataway, NJ: IEEE. pp. 25–30.

[57] Varghese, S.A., A.D. Ghadim, A. Balador, Z. Alimadadi, and P. Papadimitratos, Digital twin-based intrusion detection for industrial control systems. in *2022 IEEE International Conference on Pervasive Computing and Communications Workshops and other Affiliated Events (PerCom Workshops)*. 2022. Piscataway, NJ: IEEE. pp. 611–617.

[58] Suhail, S., M. Iqbal, R. Hussain, and R. Jurdak, ENIGMA: An explainable digital twin security solution for cyber–physical systems. *Computers in Industry*, 2023. **151**: p. 103961.

[59] Thakur, G., P. Kumar, S. Jangirala, A.K. Das, and Y. Park, An effective privacy-preserving blockchain-assisted security protocol for cloud-based digital twin environment. *IEEE Access*, 2023. **11**: p. 26877–26892.

[60] Lu, Y., X. Huang, K. Zhang, S. Maharjan, and Y. Zhang, Low-latency federated learning and blockchain for edge association in digital twin empowered 6G networks. *IEEE Transactions on Industrial Informatics*, 2020. **17**(7): p. 5098–5107.

[61] Ferrag, M.A., B. Kantarci, L.C. Cordeiro, M. Debbah, and K.K.R. Choo, Poisoning attacks in federated edge learning for digital twin 6g-enabled IoTs: An anticipatory study. in *2023 IEEE International Conference on Communications Workshops (ICC Workshops)*. 2023. Piscataway, NJ: IEEE.

[62] Eckhart, M. and A. Ekelhart, Digital twins for cyber-physical systems security: State of the art and outlook. *Security Quality in Cyber-Physical Systems Engineering*, 2019 vol. 3, p. 383–412.

[63] Kobayashi, K. and S.B. Alam, Explainable, interpretable, and trustworthy AI for an intelligent digital twin: A case study on remaining useful life. *Engineering Applications of Artificial Intelligence*, 2024. **129**: p. 107620.

[64] Bitton, R., T. Gluck, and O. Stan, *et al.*, *Deriving a cost-effective digital twin of an ICS to facilitate security evaluation*. in *Computer Security: 23rd European Symposium on Research in Computer Security, ESORICS 2018*, Barcelona, Spain, September 3–7, 2018, Proceedings, Part I 23. 2018. Berlin: Springer. p. 533–554.

[65] Fritzson, P., A. Pop, and K. Abdelhak, *et al.*, The OpenModelica integrated environment for modeling, simulation, and model-based development. *Mic Journal*, 2022. **41** p. 241–285.

[66] Coppola, A., L. Di Costanzo, L. Pariota, S. Santini, and G. N. Bifulco, An integrated simulation environment to test the effectiveness of GLOSA services under different working conditions. *Transportation Research Part C: Emerging Technologies*, 2022. **134**: p. 103455.

[67] Yuan, J., J. Shi, J. Wang, and W. Liu, Modelling network public opinion polarization based on SIR model considering dynamic network structure. *Alexandria Engineering Journal*, 2022. **61**(6): p. 4557–4571.

[68] Gupta, A., J. Cecil, and M. Pirela-Cruz, Role of dynamic affordance and cognitive load in the design of extended reality based simulation environments for surgical contexts. in *2022 IEEE Conference on Virtual Reality and 3D User Interfaces Abstracts and Workshops (VRW)*. 2022. Piscataway, NJ: IEEE.

[69] Heuer, F.M., *Scenario Generation for Testing of Automated Driving Functions based on Real Data*. 2022, Technische Universität Braunschweig.

[70] Amir, Latif, R.M., K. Hussain, N.Z. Jhanjhi, A. Nayyar, and O. Rizwan, A remix IDE: Smart contract-based framework for the healthcare sector by using blockchain technology. 2020: p. 1–24.

Chapter 6

Deep reinforcement learning for cybersecurity

Abdul Rauf[1], *Majid Hussain*[1], *M. Sheraz Arshad Malik*[2] *and Ashraf Khalil*[3]

Abstract

The use of deep reinforcement learning (DRL) techniques in cybersecurity examined, with an emphasis on the importance of DRL in combating the growing complexity of cyber threats. The idea of DRL, how important it is to adaptive defense mechanisms. The basics of DRL, including deep neural networks and reinforcement learning. DRL helps autonomous agents interact with their surroundings and develop the best defense tactics.

The uses of DRL in cybersecurity are then covered in detail, including vulnerability evaluation, phishing detection, malware analysis, and intrusion detection. Case studies and real-world examples show how DRL may improve the detection, analysis, and response capacities across a range of security disciplines. DRL in cybersecurity faces several difficulties despite its revolutionary promise, including scalability, interpretability, and adversarial assaults. Properly handle these issues, examine these obstacles and talk about new developments and potential research areas, including federated learning, multi-agent systems, and privacy-preserving methods.

Finally, we demonstrate effective case studies and real-world applications of DRL-based cybersecurity solutions, emphasizing the role of defense mechanisms that are adaptable play in thwarting new attacks. However, there is the need for more study and cooperation fully utilize DRL for cybersecurity applications, as well as how DRL can completely transform cybersecurity defenses against ever-changing threats.

6.1 Introduction

In the ever-changing field of cybersecurity, where adversaries are always refining their plans, deep reinforcement learning (DRL) presents itself as a potent weapon

[1]Department of Computer Sciences, The University of Faisalabad, Pakistan
[2]Department of Software Engineering, Government College University Faisalabad, Pakistan
[3]College of Technological Innovation, Zayed University, United Arab Emirates

that has the potential completely transform defense tactics. Fundamentally, reinforcement learning (RL) and deep learning combined in DRL, which allows intelligent systems to interact with their surroundings and acquire the best possible behaviors. Cybersecurity experts may now address complicated security issues with previously unheard-of flexibility and effectiveness because of this synergy.

In order to identify and neutralize attacks, traditional cybersecurity techniques sometimes rely on static rules or signatures, which may not be able to keep up with the quickly changing threat landscape. DRL also provides a paradigm change by allowing autonomous agents to make proactive decisions in real time, learn from their experiences, and adjust to new assault methods.

6.2 DRL's importance in cybersecurity

Adapt to dynamic threats: DRL models offer a proactive defense against new threats by dynamically modifying their defense plans in response to changing threat indicators and attack patterns.

- Learn from experience: Through trial and error, DRL agents interact with simulated or real-world environments to discover the best security policies, gradually increasing their effectiveness.
- Strengthen decision-making: DRL enhances the capacities of human analysts and speeds up response times by empowering cybersecurity systems to make wise choices in intricate and unpredictable situations.
- Handle novel attack routes: DRL's capacity to generalize across various contexts enables it to efficiently identify and counteract zero-day exploits and novel attack routes, providing a stronger defense against highly skilled adversaries.
- This chapter delves into the principles of DRL, examines its applicability across several cybersecurity domains, talks about obstacles and potential paths forward, and highlights effective case studies and real-world applications. To clarify the revolutionary potential of DRL in strengthening cybersecurity defenses and reducing new threats through this investigation.

6.2.1 Adaptive defense mechanisms

The exponential expansion of data and the proliferation of interconnected systems in today's digital landscape have brought about a new era of cyber dangers that are marked by an unprecedented level of intelligence and complexity. Adversaries constantly adapt their strategies, taking advantage of holes in networks and cutting-edge methods to steal information and interfere with vital services. The range and complexity of cyber threats, from state-sponsored cyber espionage efforts aimed at damaging national security to ransomware assaults targeting organizations of all kinds, present serious challenges to conventional defense methods.

It is becoming more and more important to have adaptive defense mechanisms in this ever-changing threat scenario. The dynamic nature of contemporary cyber threats makes traditional cybersecurity techniques, which frequently defined by static rules and signature-based detection techniques, difficult to keep up with; Attackers routinely use evasion strategies, zero-day exploits, and polymorphic malware to get around traditional defenses, making static defenses antiquated and ineffectual.

Because of these difficulties, the significance of adaptive defense mechanisms that can instantly react to changing threats is becoming more widely acknowledged. Intelligent and autonomous cyber defense systems made possible by adaptive defense mechanisms, which make use of cutting-edge technology like DRL, machine learning, and artificial intelligence. Adaptive defense mechanisms provide a more comprehensive and successful approach to cybersecurity by taking proactive decisions, learning from past mistakes, and adjusting to changing circumstances.

The idea of DRL and its importance in cybersecurity is in this chapter. Investigating how DRL allows autonomous agents to adapt to new assault methods, reduce emerging risks, and acquire optimal defense strategies through interaction with their environment. We emphasize the revolutionary potential of DRL in enhancing cybersecurity defenses and reducing the growing complexity of cyber threats through case studies, real-world applications, and talks on difficulties and future directions.

6.3 Structure of this chapter

DRL detail analysis permits, how it may be use, to improve cybersecurity defenses against new and emerging threats in this chapter. The foundations of DRL, clarify its uses in different cybersecurity fields, talk about obstacles and potential paths forward, and display effective case studies and real-world applications. Readers will have a thorough understanding of how DRL can transform cybersecurity and successfully counter new threats by the end of this chapter.

This chapter is structured as follows:
Overview of DRL: Brief introduction to the idea of DRL, outlining its guiding concepts, techniques, and importance in cybersecurity defense. Draw attention to the growing intricacy of cyber threats and the requirement for defense measures that can adapt to them.

DRL basics: In this section, examine the basic ideas of DRL; including deep neural networks, RL. How DRL can be integrate with cybersecurity frameworks. Describe how DRL allows autonomous agents to interact with their surroundings and develop the best defense tactics.

Applications of DRL in cybersecurity: This section analyzes the various uses of DRL in cybersecurity, including vulnerability assessment, phishing detection, malware analysis, and intrusion detection. Demonstrate how DRL may improve detection, analysis, and response capabilities in a variety of security fields using case studies and real-world scenarios.

Difficulties and future directions: Next, discuss the difficulties and restrictions associated with using DRL in cybersecurity, including interpretability, scalability, and adversarial assaults. Discuss new developments and directions for future DRL research in cybersecurity, such as federated learning, multi-agent systems, and privacy-preserving methods.

Successful case studies and real-world applications: DRL-based cybersecurity case studies and real-world applications covered in this section. Demonstrate DRL's transformative potential in reality by highlighting real-world situations where it been used to detect and mitigate cyber threats effectively.

Conclusion: To wrap up the chapter, we provide a summary of the key discoveries and contributions. The importance of DRL is to transform cybersecurity defenses and reduce the impact of new attacks. Additionally, supports more study and cooperation in utilizing DRL for cybersecurity applications.

6.3.1 Reinforcement learning

A machine-learning paradigm known RL teaches an agent how to interact with its surroundings in a way that maximizes a cumulative reward signal. It predicated on ideas borrowed from behavioral psychology, in which an agent acquires the ability to behave in a given way to accomplish particular objectives.

Below is a summary of several important RL concepts.

6.4 Markov decision process

Definition: A mathematical framework called a Markov decision process (MDP) used to simulate decision-making in scenarios where the decision-maker (the agent) has some control over the result but some degree of randomness.

Component:
States (S): A collection of every scenario or configuration that the environment could be in actions (A): A collection of every activity the agent is capable of performing. Transition function (T): Indicates the likelihood that a specific activity will cause a state to change. Reward function (R): This function associates each state-action pair with a numerical reward signal that represents the instantaneous gain from acting in a specific state. Discount factor (γ): varies between 0 and 1, indicating how important future rewards are in comparison to those received now. Goal: The agent must discover a policy—a mapping from a state to an action—that maximizes the cumulative expected reward over a given time.

6.4.1 Policy learning

Definition: An agent's strategy or rule for choosing actions in various states called a policy in RL. It describes how the agent behaves.

6.4.1.1 Policy types

Deterministic policy: Assigns a single action to every state. Stochastic policy: Assigns a probability distribution to every state based on actions.

6.4.2 Methods for learning policies

Value-based methods: Estimate each state or state-action pair's value and use that information to determine the policy. Policy gradient methods: To optimize predicted cumulative benefits, directly parameterize the policy and update it. Goal: Determine the best course of action that will maximize the anticipated cumulative payoff over time.

6.4.2.1 Value-based methods

Definition: Value-based approaches try to quantify the worth of existing in a certain condition or acting in a specific way in a given state.

6.4.2.2 Value functions

State value function (V(s)): Indicates the anticipated total reward beginning in a specific state and according to a specific policy. Action value function (Q (s, a)): Indicates the expected cumulative reward for beginning in a specific state, acting in a specific way, and then adhering to a specific policy. Bellman equations: Recursive formulas that define optimal value functions and articulate the link between value functions. Q-Learning: A traditional value-based technique that uses the Bellman equation to update the action-value function after learning it directly from experience.

These ideas used by RL algorithms to teach them efficient decision-making techniques across a variety of industries, including robots, gaming, banking, and healthcare.

6.5 Deep reinforcement learning

Training neural networks with numerous layers—hence the term "deep"—allows them to extract complicated patterns and representations from data. The layers of these neural networks made up of interconnected nodes that extract progressively abstract elements from the input data. Deep learning has shown great promise in several fields, including speech recognition, natural language processing (NLP), and image recognition. Conversely, RL is a kind of machine learning in which an agent picks up skills to interact with its surroundings to accomplish a goal. As the agent behaves in the environment, it gets feedback in the form of incentives or penalties, which gradually leads it to make better decisions. The agent seeks to discover a policy—a mapping from states to actions—that maximizes the total reward over a given period.

RL and deep learning combined in DRL. DRL automatically develop usable representations from unprocessed sensory inputs (such as text, pictures, and sensor data), deep neural networks employed. The environment's key elements that pertinent to decision-making captured in these representations. Deep neural networks utilized in reinforcement learning as function approximators. They allow the RL agent to generalize over a broad variety of states and actions by approximating its value function or policy.

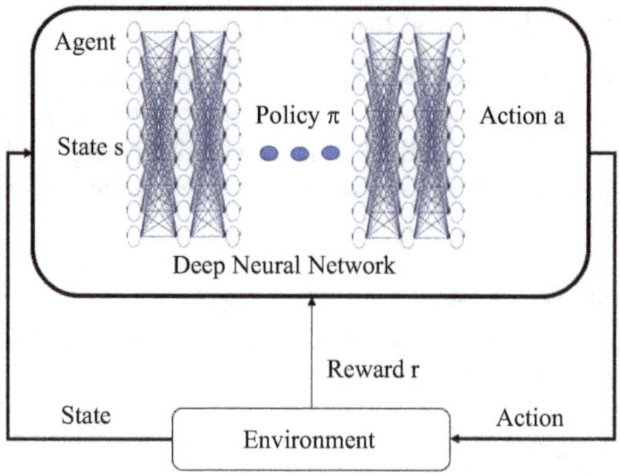

Figure 6.1 Reinforcement learning interactions

State, action, and reward represent RL interactions between an agent and its environment (Figure 6.1). Based on the current state (s) and reward (r), the agent will determine the optimal course of action, modifying the state and reward. The agent then receives the next state (s) and reward (r) from the environment in an iterative series of interactions with the environment to choose the next course of action.

DRL enables end-to-end learning, in which a neural network can learn without the use of intermediate representations or manually created features by using raw observations and feedback signals (rewards). DRL algorithms can handle high-dimensional state and action spaces, which are typical in complex situations, thanks to deep learning. Allowing the agent to learn directly from raw sensory inputs, helps enhance sample efficiency.

DRL is appropriate for projects with complicated dynamics and lengthy time horizons since deep neural networks can scale to big and complex issues. In conclusion, strong function approximation capabilities offered by deep learning enable RL agents to efficiently learn from high-dimensional, raw input data and generalize. DRL algorithms can handle a variety of difficult tasks, including managing robots, playing video games, and improving cybersecurity defenses. This achieved by combining deep learning and RL.

6.5.1 Deep Q-networks (DQN)

Deep Q-networks (DQN) is a groundbreaking approach in the field of DRL. To approximate the action-value function, deep neural networks and Q-learning are used. Experience replay used, storing agent experiences in a replay buffer and randomly sampling batches to break temporal correlations and stabilize learning; deep neural network to approximate the Q-function, which estimates the expected cumulative reward for taking an action in a given state. Establishes a target network to stabilize training by setting the parameters of a different target Q-network and updating it with the primary Q-network's parameters regularly.

Applications: DQN been effectively used in several fields, such as robots, recommendation systems, and video games.

6.5.2 DQN gradient methods for policies

By learning a parameterized policy directly, policy gradient methods maximize the predicted cumulative reward through optimization. They parameterize the policy function directly, in contrast to value-based techniques like DQN. Determine the expected return gradient about the policy parameters; adjust the policy to follow this gradient. A well-known example of a policy gradient approach is the Reinforce algorithm, which updates the policy according to the gradient of the expected return concerning the policy parameters. For increased stability and sample efficiency, variants like Actor-Critic techniques combine value function estimates with policy gradient updates. Uses: Policy gradient techniques are particularly helpful in robotics, autonomous vehicles, and NLP because they work well in continuous action spaces and stochastic settings.

6.5.3 Actor-critic architectures

Actor-critic architectures integrate aspects of policy-based (actor) and value-based (critic) approaches. The actor picks up the policy based on the critic's assessments, and the critic learns how to estimate the value function. The critic (value network) assesses the actions by calculating the expected cumulative reward, whereas the actor (policy network) chooses actions depending on the present state. Provides a distinct learning signal for the policy and value function, enabling more stable and effective learning. It can combine several strategies to improve performance and exploration, like eligibility traces, advantage functions, and entropy regularization. Actor-critic architectures have widespread use in discrete action domains like resource allocation and gaming, as well as continuous control tasks like robotic manipulation. Both discrete action domains, like as resource allocation and gaming, and continuous control tasks, such as robotic manipulation, frequently employ actor-critical systems.

A universal function approximator, such as a (deep) neural network, typically used in DRL to approximate a value function or a policy function from discrete or continuous inputs. Working with state spaces in modelling is therefore less complicated than working with action spaces in DRL. Value-based techniques are suitable for addressing issues with discrete action spaces because they explicitly evaluate each action and choose an action at each time step based on these evaluations. The actor-critic and policy-gradient techniques are more suited for continuous action spaces, since they represent the policy (a mapping between states and actions) as a probability distribution over actions. The continuity property is the main way that discrete and continuous action spaces differ from one another. In a discrete action space, an action is a collection of mutually exclusive possibilities; in a continuous action space, an action is a value from a particular range or boundary (Table 6.1).

Table 6.1 DRL types and their notable methods

DRL	Value-based	Policy gradient	Actor-centric
Features	Compute value of action given a state Q (States s, Action a). Explicit guidelines not clear. Inefficient Sample taken.	Value function is not needed and created explicit policy but Inefficient Sample taken.	Actor produces policy ≈ (s, a). Critic evaluates action by V(s). Perform better than value-based or policy-gradient methods.
Typical Methods	Deep Q-Network (DQN) Double DQN Dueling Q-network Prioritized Experience Replay DQN	Reinforcement Learning (RL). Vanilla Policy Gradient: stochastic policy. Trust Region Policy Optimization. Proximal Policy Optimization	Deep Deterministic Policy Gradient (DDPG). Actor-Centric Method (A3C).
Applications	Applications Suitable for problems with discrete action spaces, e.g., classic control tasks: Acrobot, CartPole, and MountainCar as described and implemented in the popular OpenAI Gym toolkit.		

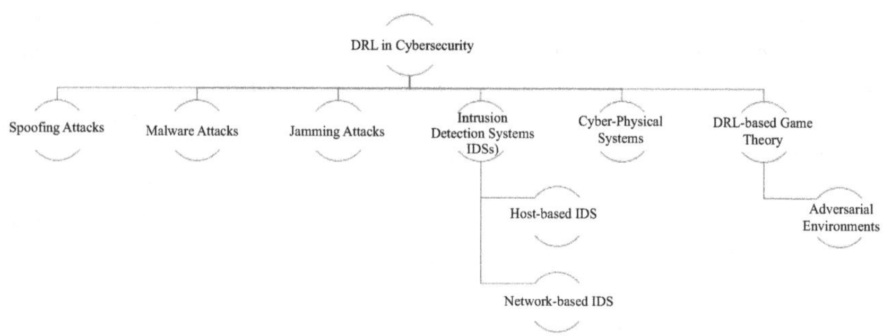

Figure 6.2 Application of DRL in cybersecurity

6.6 Application of DRL in cybersecurity

DRL applied to detect and prevent cyberattacks in network environments. Concerns about privacy and security regard to DRL have lately progressed (Figure 6.2).

6.7 Intruder detection system

6.7.1 Anomaly detection

The DRL agents input, represents the network's current state, including traffic patterns, system logs, and configuration settings. Specify what steps the agent can take, like limiting access to particular services, barring suspicious IP addresses, or turning up the logging. Create a reward signal that minimizes false positives and negatives and encourages the agent to identify abnormalities. Utilizing past network data that has aberrant behaviors labeled, teach the DRL agent to identify and react to possible threats.

6.7.2 Real-time threat response

Keep an eye on system logs, security alerts, and network traffic to keep the environment's state representation current. Give the agent the ability to react in real-time to risks it detects by letting it implement firewall rules, isolate infected devices, or notify security staff. Create a reward signal that incentivizes the agent to react to security issues as soon as possible and efficiently while causing the least amount of disturbance to authorized network operations. Put in place online learning tools so that the DRL agent can instantly adjust to shifting network conditions and dynamic assault tactics.

6.7.3 Adaptive defense strategies

Provide details regarding the current state of security, including the efficiency of the defenses in place, the seriousness of the vulnerabilities that known to exist, and the frequency of recent attack attempts. Give the agent the freedom; dynamically modify defense tactics, such as changing intrusion detection signatures, rearranging firewall rules, or setting up honeypots to entice intruders. Establish a compensation system that motivates the agent proactively address possible risks and vulnerabilities to strengthen the network's overall security posture. By regularly retraining the DRL agent with updated data and input from security analysts and incident responders, you can support ongoing learning and development. Using DRL techniques in network security, organizations can improve their capacity to recognize, stop, and neutralize cyberattacks. Figure 6.3 shows DRL-based intrusion detection systems (IDS).

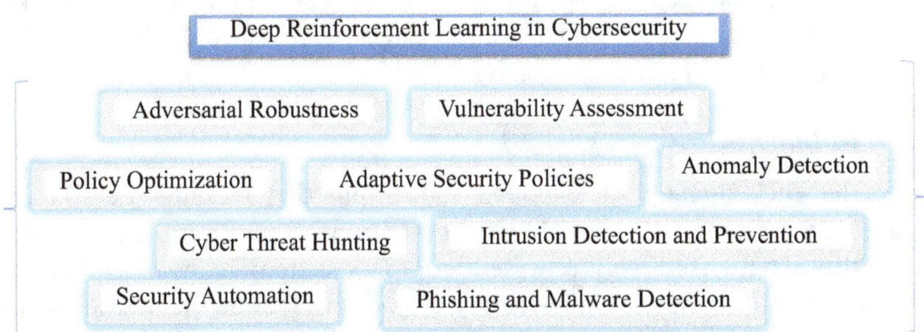

Figure 6.3 DRL in cybersecurity

6.7.4 Network traffic analysis

As the state input to the DRL agent, encode system logs, network traffic features, and other pertinent data. Make use of methods like auto-encoders to extract relevant depictions of typical behavior and identify variations that point to abnormalities. Specify what steps you want the agent to take, such as reporting shady activity, preventing traffic from shady sources, or raising the alert level for more inquiries.

Create a reward signal that minimizes false positives and negatives and encourages the agent to identify genuine abnormalities. Provide intermediate incentives for behaviors that indicate normal or aberrant activity using strategies like reward structuring. To teach the DRL agent to detect patterns of typical behavior and spot deviations, use historical data with labeled anomalies.

As the DRL agent's input, encode packet headers, payload attributes, and network traffic flows. To extract pertinent information from network traffic, use methods like flow-based analysis and deep packet inspection. Define what the agent should do, e.g., reroute traffic to reduce congestion, prioritize or throttle specific categories of traffic, or dynamically modify quality of service (QoS) characteristics. Create a reward signal that incentivizes the agent to maintain service availability, optimize network performance, and reduce security threats. Methods to add preferences and domain knowledge to the incentive signal, such as RL with human input. To teach the DRL agent the best traffic management strategies while averting unfavorable effects, use simulations or controlled situations.

6.7.5 Real-time threat response

To update the environment's state representation for real-time threat response, network traffic, system logs, and security warnings continuously monitored. Provide details in the state representation regarding the nature and intensity of threats that been identified. Give the agent the ability to react in real-time to threats it detects by allowing it to update firewall rules, isolate compromised devices, and block suspicious traffic. Create a reward signal that incentivizes the agent to react to security issues as soon as possible and efficiently while causing the least amount of disturbance to authorized network operations. Make use of strategies like reward shaping to give quick feedback on how well threat response measures are working. Provide online learning tools so that the DRL agent can instantly adjust to shifting network conditions and dynamic attack tactics.

6.7.6 Vulnerability assessment

Provide the DRL agent with encoded state input that includes details about software versions, network topologies, system configurations, and historical vulnerability data. Effectively represent complex system states, apply methods like dimensionality reduction and feature extraction. Define the actions that the agent must execute, such as probing network services for vulnerabilities.

Establish a reward signal to incentivize the agent accurately identify vulnerabilities while reducing false positives and negatives. Use techniques such as reward shaping to provide intermediate rewards and advance vulnerability finding. To acquire efficient techniques for vulnerability assessment, train the DRL agent on historical data with identified vulnerabilities or simulated environments.

6.7.7 Patch management

Specify actions that the agent should perform, such as prioritizing patches based on risk assessment, scheduling patch deployments to minimize downtime, or testing patches in isolated environments before deployment. Encode information about the severity, exploitability, and potential impact of identified vulnerabilities, as well as available patches and their compatibility with the system, and provide it to the DRL agent. Use techniques like NLP to extract relevant information from vulnerability advisories and patch release notes.

6.7.8 Reward signal

Create a reward structure that incentivizes the agent to apply crucial patches first, deploy patches as quickly as possible, and guarantee system stability when patches are applied. Utilize strategies like reward shaping to give prompt feedback on how well patch management initiatives are working. To teach the DRL agent the best patch management techniques, and use previous data on patch deployment procedures, such as success rates, patching timelines, and post-patching system performance.

6.8 Advantages of DRL for patch management and vulnerability assessment

Adaptability: The robustness of vulnerability assessment and patch management procedures is increased by DRL models' ability to adjust to changing system configurations and evolving attack strategies.

Efficiency: DRL models can improve the effectiveness of vulnerability assessment and patch management operations by automating repetitive procedures and decision-making processes.

Optimization: By taking into account variables like system criticality, patch compatibility, and business impact, DRL models can optimize patch deployment processes, resulting in more efficient risk mitigation. Approaches for locating vulnerabilities in systems, ranking patches, and reducing risk exposure. To preserve the security and integrity of IT systems, it is imperative to prioritize patching, detect system vulnerabilities, and reduce risk exposure in the context of cybersecurity.

6.8.1 Identifying system vulnerabilities

Enter data as the state input for the DRL agent, including system configurations, software versions, network topology, access controls, and user privileges. Specify the steps that the agent should take to detect potential vulnerabilities. These steps could include running vulnerability scans, checking system logs for indications of compromise, or correlating security events. Create a reward signal that minimizes false positives and negatives and encourages the agent to detect genuine vulnerabilities. Make use of strategies like reward shaping to give quick feedback on how accurate vulnerability identification is. The DRL learn agent efficient methods for spotting system vulnerabilities, use historical data on known vulnerabilities, attack patterns, and system configurations.

6.8.2 Prioritizing patches

Provide the DRL agent with encoded data regarding the severity, exploitability, and possible impact of vulnerabilities that have been found, together with information about existing patches and how well they work with the system. Prioritize vulnerabilities according to risk by using strategies like threat intelligence feeds and vulnerability score systems (like CVSS). Specify what steps the agent should take, including scheduling patch deployments to minimize downtime, testing patches in isolated environments before deployment, or prioritizing fixes based on risk assessment. Create a reward structure that incentivizes the agent to apply crucial patches first, deploy patches as quickly as possible, and guarantee system stability when patches are applied. Utilize methods like reward shaping to give quick feedback on how well patch priority schemes are working. To teach the DRL agent the best patch prioritization techniques, and use previous data on patch deployment procedures, such as success rates, patching timelines, and post-patching system performance.

6.8.3 Minimizing risk exposure

As the DRL agent's input, encode details on the current security posture, such as known vulnerabilities, patch status, network traffic patterns, and user activity.

To rank and quantify security threats, use methods like threat modeling and risk assessments. Specify what steps the agent should perform, including modifying access controls, installing IDS, modifying firewall rules, or stepping up monitoring and logging. Create a compensation system that incentivizes the agent to reduce risk exposure using efficient security controls, early detection and mitigation of security incidents, and adherence to security policies and guidelines. Make use of strategies like reward shaping to give prompt feedback on risk mitigation initiatives. To learn the best risk mitigation techniques, the DRL agent can be trained on historical security incident data or simulated environments. This training can cover incident response protocols, mitigation tactics, and post-event analysis.

6.8.4 Malware identification

Use encoded features, such as file headers, byte sequences, API calls, and behavioral traits that been taken out of malware samples and fed into the DRL agent. Make use of methods like static and dynamic analysis to identify pertinent features and analyze malware behavior. Specify the steps you want the agent to perform, including identifying files as dangerous or benign, grading the degree of confidence in your predictions, or highlighting unusual activity that needs more research. Provide a reward signal that minimizes false positives and false negatives and encourages the agent correctly categorize malware. Make use of strategies like reward shaping to offer a range of prizes for accurately identifying compromise indications. To acquire efficient malware detection techniques, train the DRL agent with labeled datasets of malware samples, which include both known malicious and benign files.

6.8.5 Malware classification

Provide the DRL agent with encoded features, such as file attributes, code structure, and execution behavior, which collected from malware samples. Make use of methods likes feature engineering and dimensionality reduction concisely and informatively depict intricate virus attributes. Specify what the agent must do. For example, it can assign malware samples to groups or classes that have already been established using similarity metrics like distance or dissimilarity measurements. Provide a reward signal that minimizes misclassifications and motivates the agent correctly categorize malware into the appropriate categories. Make use of mechanisms like reward shaping to provide quick feedback on classification results and promote experimenting with various classification approaches. To acquire efficient classification models, train the DRL agent on labeled datasets of malware samples with established ground truth classifications.

6.8.6 Malware behavior analysis

Provide the DRL agent with encoded dynamic elements, such as system calls, network activity, and memory operations, which derived from malware execution traces. To detect behavioral patterns and temporal relationships in malware operations, apply methods like recurrent neural networks and sequence modeling. Specify what steps the agent should take next, including spotting abnormal behavior patterns, making predictions based on patterns seen, or creating behavioral profiles for malware samples. Create a reward signal that minimizes false alarms and missed detections while motivating the agent to correctly anticipate and analyze malware behaviors. To provide intermediate rewards for spotting suggestive patterns of malevolent behaviors, apply strategies like reward shaping. Acquiring efficient behavior analysis models, train the DRL agent with dynamic analysis data gathered from malware execution environments, including sandboxes or virtual machines.

6.8.7 Malware detection and analysis

Methods for creating signatures, analyzing dynamic malware, and implementing adaptive defenses.

6.8.7.1 Dynamic malware examination

Behavioral analysis: In this method, malware samples are run in a sandbox or other controlled environment to watch how they behave. To find malicious activity, dynamic analysis keeps an eye on a variety of operations, including changes to the file system, registry entries, network traffic, and process manipulations.

API monitoring: Keeping an eye on the application programming interface (API) calls that malicious software makes while it's running can provide information about how it behaves. By intercepting and logging API calls, dynamic analysis tools enable analysts to spot potentially harmful or suspicious activity, like efforts to gain unauthorized access to resources or issue commands.

Memory analysis: Examining a system's memory while malware is executing can disclose covert actions like code injection or process hollowing. Such advanced malware strategies can be found and examined with the aid of dynamic memory analysis techniques like memory forensics and runtime memory monitoring.

Creation of signatures: static evaluation: To produce signatures for detection, static analysis approaches look at the static characteristics of malware samples, such as file attributes, code structure, and metadata. This method uses established patterns or features, like file hashes, file headers, and code snippets, to identify known malware.

Signatures derived from machine learning: Signatures derived from malware samples can be automatically generated using machine learning algorithms, such as clustering techniques and supervised learning. Opcode sequences, API call sequences, byte-level n-grams, and structural data gleaned via static analysis are a few examples of these properties.

Behavior-based signatures: Malware variants with comparable malicious activities can be found using signatures generated from behaviors seen during dynamic analysis. Behavior-based signatures enable the detection of polymorphic and obfuscated malware variants by capturing the behaviors and interactions of malware with the system and network.

Dynamic rule generation: Dynamic Rule Generation and other machine learning techniques are employed by adaptive defense systems to dynamically produce and update detection rules in response to changing threat intelligence and observed attack patterns. These systems can enhance detection precision and responsiveness by assimilating lessons from previous events and promptly adjusting to novel dangers.

Contextual analysis: Contextual analysis evaluates the risk and reliability of observed actions by considering some contextual elements, including user behaviors, the network environment, and system configurations. Adaptive defense mechanisms optimize defense methods according to the state of the threat landscape by dynamically adjusting security policies and enforcement mechanisms based on contextual information.

Reaction orchestration: Real-time threat mitigation is achieved by adaptive defense systems through the integration of automated reaction capabilities. These solutions can coordinate response actions, such as containment, remediation, and quarantine, to eliminate current threats and stop additional harm by interacting with incident response workflows and security orchestration platforms.

Phishing detection: Provide the DRL agent with encoded email features, such as attachments, embedded links, sender information, and email content. Make use of methods like NLP to examine email correspondence and identify pertinent elements suggestive of attempted phishing. Specify what steps you want the agent to take, such as reporting shady emails, holding onto potentially dangerous attachments, or blocking phishing URLs. Create a reward signal that minimizes false positives and false negatives and encourages the agent correctly identify phishing attempts. Provide intermediate rewards for accurately spotting phishing signs by utilizing strategies like reward shaping. To teach the DRL agent effective phishing detection tactics, it can be trained with labeled datasets of phishing emails that contain instances of both malicious and benign messages.

Analyzing user behavior to spot insider threats: The DRL agent's input, encode user activity records, including failed login attempts, file access patterns, network connections, and system commands. Make advantage of methods like anomaly detection and sequence modeling to identify departures from typical user behaviors. Specify what steps the agent should take, including reporting questionable user behaviors, raising the alert level for additional review, or removing user rights. Create a reward signal that minimizes false alarms and missed detections while incentivizing the agent to spot insider threats. Make use of strategies like reward shaping to give quick feedback on how accurate insider threat estimates are. Utilizing past user activity data, including instances of both benign and malicious behaviors, train the DRL agent to identify effective insider threat detection models. Techniques for spotting suspicious activity, telling good behaviors from bad and raising user consciousness. Critical components of cybersecurity defense include spotting suspicious activity, telling good behaviors from bad, and raising user knowledge. Through its ability to facilitate the creation of intelligent systems that can efficiently detect and mitigate security risks and adapt to changing threats, DRL can play a vital role in these domains.

6.8.7.2 Recognizing intriguing behavior

The DRL agent's input, encode features that have been taken from a variety of sources, including network traffic logs, system event logs, user activity logs, and endpoint telemetry. To properly depict complicated activity patterns, apply approaches like feature engineering, dimensionality reduction, and data preprocessing. Specify the steps that the agent should take, including raising the alert for additional inquiry, identifying unusual occurrences, or initiating automatic reaction measures. Create a reward signal that minimizes false positives and false negatives and encourages the agent correctly identify suspicious activity. Make use of strategies like reward shaping to offer progress toward identifying compromise signs with intermediate rewards. To acquire efficient methods for spotting suspicious activity, train the DRL agent with labeled datasets of known security incidents that include instances of both benign and malicious activity.

Distinguishing between malicious and legitimate behavior: The input to the DRL agent, encode features that record contextual data about user behaviors, resource access patterns, system configurations, and network traffic. Employ methods like ensemble learning, graph-based representations, and temporal modeling to capture intricate interactions between various items and activities. Specify the tasks you want the agent to perform, including determining whether a behavior is normal or deviant, giving forecasts a confidence score, or estimating the probability of malevolent intent. Create a reward signal that minimizes misclassifications and incentivizes the agent correctly discern between malicious and legitimate behaviors. Make use of strategies like reward shaping to provide quick feedback on classification results and promote experimenting with various detection approaches. To acquire efficient models for behavior categorization, train the DRL agent with labeled datasets of user actions and system events that include instances of both benign and malevolent behaviors.

6.8.7.3 Increasing conscientiousness of users

State representation: Provide the DRL agent with encoded attributes of user interactions, training records, security awareness levels, and programmed involvement. Measure the success of security awareness campaigns with methods like sentiment analysis, engagement metrics, and user profiling. Specify what steps you want the agent to take, including sending out customized security training materials, acting out phishing attempts, or giving immediate feedback on actions connected to security. To create a reward system that motivates users to embrace security best practices and rewards good security behaviors. Make advantage of strategies like gamification, incentives, and recognition initiatives to drive user engagement and reinforce desired behaviors. To improve user awareness, teach the DRL agent effective training tactics by utilizing data on user interactions with security awareness initiatives, such as feedback surveys, training completion rates, and quiz scores. Organizations may improve user awareness, differentiate between legitimate and malicious behaviors, and spot suspicious actions by utilizing DRL methodologies. This will help them to strengthen their cybersecurity defenses and lessen the probability and effect of security events.

By strengthening their cybersecurity defenses, organizations can lessen the probability and severity of security incidents.

Adversarial resilience and security policy optimization: Analyze how DRL can improve security policy optimization and adversarial resilience. DRL allows intelligent systems to adapt to dynamic threat landscapes and efficiently defend against adversarial attacks, which can dramatically improve adversarial robustness and optimize security policies.

Adversarial durability: Provide the DRL agent with encoded features that has been taken from input data, such as pictures, network traffic, or sensor readings. Make appropriate use of methods like data augmentation, dimensionality reduction, and feature engineering to represent a variety of input patterns. Specify the activities that the agent will perform. These actions may include choosing which defense mechanisms to use, changing model parameters in response to attacks, or altering input data to improve resilience against adversarial perturbations. Create a reward signal that minimizes performance deterioration on valid inputs while encouraging the agent to remain robust against adversarial attempts. To increase resilience, apply strategies like adversarial training, in which the agent exposed to adversarial cases during training. To teach the DRL agent effective tactics for fending off adversarial attacks across a variety of input domains, use a combination of benign and adversarial instances.

Optimization of security policies: The DRL agent's input, encode elements of the existing security posture, such as system configurations, network traffic patterns, threat intelligence feeds, and data on past security incidents. Make use of methods like ensemble learning and context-aware representations to capture intricate connections between various security aspects. Specify the steps that the agent must perform, including modifying access restrictions, deploying security patches and updates, modifying firewall rules, and allocating resources for threat detection and response. Create a reward system that motivates the agent to maximize security policies to reduce risk exposure, quickly identify and address security events, and uphold adherence to security guidelines and standards. Make use of methods like RL with human feedback to add preferences and domain knowledge to the reward signal. Using historical data on security occurrences and examples of both successful and unsuccessful security policies, train the DRL agent to discover efficient methods for optimizing security policies.

6.8.7.4 Benefits of DRL in security policy optimization and adversarial robustness

Adaptability: DRL models provide for proactive defense against newly developed attack methods by adjusting to changing system conditions and evolving threats. Efficiency: DRL models can improve security operations' efficiency and shorten the time it takes to identify and address security issues by automating security policy optimization procedures.

Effectiveness: Decision-making and policy enforcement can be enhanced using DRL models, which can recognize intricate patterns and relationships in security data.

Crucial components of cybersecurity defense include protecting against hostile assaults, enhancing security setups, and modifying rules in response to shifting threat environments. DRL can help achieve these goals by allowing intelligent systems to adapt their defenses dynamically and react to new threats with efficiency.

6.8.7.5 Protecting yourself from adversarial attacks

Adversarial training involves introducing imperceptible perturbations to input data to create adversarial examples that are used to train machine-learning models, such as detectors or classifiers. To make models more resilient to adversarial attacks, apply strategies like projected gradient descent (PGD) adversarial training. To lessen the effects of adversarial perturbations, implement defense methods including input preprocessing (feature squeezing, input normalization) and model adjustments (defensive distillation, randomized smoothing). Employ strategies like model stacking and ensemble approaches to integrate several defenses and increase overall robustness.

6.8.7.6 Enhancing security setups:

Management of security configurations: Adopt best practices for patch management, secure configuration baselines, and routine vulnerability scanning while managing security configurations. Make use of strategies like automated remediation and ongoing monitoring to make sure security policies and standards are being followed.

Risk-based approaches: Rank security configuration modifications according to risk assessments, taking into account elements like the probability and severity of possible security incidents. Employ methodologies such as impact analysis and risk scoring to evaluate the possible outcomes of alterations to security configurations.

Modifying policies to address changing threat environments: To stay up to date on new threats, vulnerabilities, and attack trends, including threat intelligence feeds into security policy management procedures. Make use of methods like anomaly detection and threat hunting to proactively spot any security risks and modify policies as necessary. The implementation of dynamic policy management frameworks recommended to enable security policies to adjust in real time in response to contextual information and detected threat indicators. Automate policy adaption and reaction activities by utilizing methods like machine learning algorithms and rule-based decision engines.

6.8.8 Advantages of DRL input

DRL models provide for proactive defense against newly developed attack methods by adjusting to changing system conditions and evolving threats. DRL models can improve security operations' efficiency and shorten the time it takes to identify and address security issues by automating security policy optimization procedures. Decision-making and policy enforcement can be enhanced using DRL models, which can recognize intricate patterns and relationships in security data (Table 6.2).

Applications	Goals/objectives	Algorithms	States	Actions	Rewards
Robustness guided fabrication of CPS	Find fabricating inputs (countered examples) for CPS	Double DQN and A3C	Defined as the output of the system	Choose from next input value from a set wise constant input signals	Characterized by a function of past dependent life-long property, output signal and time
Security and safety in autonomous vehicle systems	AV dynamics control to cyber-physical attacks that inject faulty data to sensor readings.	Q-learning with LSTM to process and analyze sequential data	AV's own position and speed along with distance and speed of some nearby objects	Take appropriate speeds to maintain safe spacing between AV	Using a utility function that takes into account the deviation from the optimal safe spacing
Increasing robustness of the autonomous system against adversarial attacks	Device filtering scheme to detect corrupted measure (deception attack) and mitigate theeffects of adversarial error	Trust Region Policy Optimization (TRPO)	Characterized by sensor measurements and actuation noises	Determine which estimation rule to use to generate an estimated state from a corrupted state	Defined via a function that takes state features as inputs
Secure offloading in mobile edge caching	Learn a policy for mobile device to securely offload data to edge node against Jamming and smart attacks	DQN with hot booting transfer learning techniques.	Represented via combination of user density, battery levels, jamming strength, and radio channel bandwidth	Agent's actions include choosing an edge node selecting off loading rate and time, transmit power and channel	Computed based on secrecy capacity, energy consumption and communication efficiency
Anti-jamming commutation scheme for CRN	Derive an optimal frequency hopping policy for CRN SU to defeat smart jammers basedon a frequency-spatial anti-jamming game	Deep Q-Network that employs CNN	Consist of presence status of PUs and SINR informationat time - 1 received from serving base station or accesspoint	SUs take action to leave a geographical area of heavy jamming obstructed by smart jammers or choose a frequency channel to send signals	Represented via a utility function based on SINR and transmission cost
Anti-jamming communication method	Propose a smart anti-jamming Scheme. New Scheme two main differences: spectrum waterfall is used as the state, and jammers can have different channel slot transmission structure with users	DQN with recursive CNN due to recursion characteristic of spectrum waterfall	Using temporal and spectral information i.e. spectrums waterfall containing both frequency and time domain information of the network environment	Agent's action is to select discretized transmission frequency from a predefine set	Defined by a function involving SINR-based transmission rate and cost for frequency switching

(Continues)

Table 6.2 (Continued)

Applications	Goals/objectives	Algorithms	States	Actions	Rewards
Spoofing detection wireless networks	Select the optimal authentication threshold	Q-Learning and dyna-Q	Include false alarm rate and missed detection rate of the spoofing detection system at time $t - 1$	Action set includes the choices of different discrete levels of the authentication thresholds bounded within a specified interval	Using a utility function calculated based on the Bayesian risk, which is the expected payoff in spoofing detection
Mobile off loading for cloud-based malware detection	Improve malware detection accuracy and speed	Hot booting Q-Learning and DQN	Consist of current radio bandwidth and previous offloading rates of other devices	Select optimal off loading rate level for each mobile device	Represented by a utility function calculated based on the detection accuracy, response speed, and transmission cost
Autonomous defense in software define networks	Tackle the poisoning attacks that manipulate states or flip reward signals during the training process of RL-based defense agents	Double DQN and Actor-Centric(A3C)	Represented by an array of zeros and ones showing the state of the network (whether a node is compromised or actions: isolate, patch, reconnect link is switched on/off). Array length is equal to several nodes plus several links	Attackers learn to select a node to compromise while a defender can take four actions: isolate, patch, reconnect and migrate to protect server and preserve as many nodes as possible	Modelled based on the status of the critical server, number of preserved nodes, migration cost and the validity of actions taken
Secure crowd sensing (MCS) system	Optimize payment policy to improve the sensing performance against faked sensing attack by formulating a Stackelberg Game	Deep Q-Network	Consist of the previous-sensing quality and the payment policy	Select the server's optimal payment vector to smartphone users	Using a utility function that involves the total payment to users and the benefit of server from sensing reports of different accuracy levels
Automated URL based phishing detection	Detect malicious website URLs	Deep Q-Network	Characterized by the vector space representation of web-site features such as HTTPS protocols having IP-Addresses Prefix and Suffix in URLs	Select either 0 or 1. Correspond to a kind of phishing URL	Based on the classification action, the reward equates to 1or -1 if the URL is classified correctly or incorrectly.

6.9 Challenges and future directions

Determine the main obstacles to and restrictions on using DRL in cybersecurity, including interpretability, scalability, and adversarial assaults. To reach its full potential, the application of DRL in cybersecurity must overcome several obstacles and constraints.

Scalability: Complexity of settings: Large-scale networks that produce enormous volumes of data create dynamic, complicated cybersecurity settings. In these kinds of settings, DRL model training is quite computationally intensive and may have scaling problems.

Interpretability: e-box because nature models are frequently viewed as "black boxes," it might be challenging to decipher their judgment and comprehend the reasoning behind security advice or actions. It can be difficult to validate the efficacy of DRL-based cybersecurity solutions and can undermine trust in them if they are not interpretable.

Attacks by adversaries: Examples of Adversarial When DRL models subjected to adversarial assaults, their behavior can be manipulated to take advantage of flaws and result in policy violations or wrong security judgments. For DRL-based cybersecurity systems to be effective, they must be resilient to adversarial attacks.

Data quality and imbalance: Cybersecurity statistics frequently exhibit biases and class imbalances, with frequent benign actions overshadowing infrequent security events. Unbalanced data used to train DRL models can result in policy recommendations that are biased and less successful in identifying uncommon security concerns.

6.10 Generalization and transfer learning

Domain adaptation: DRL models that been trained in a single cybersecurity environment may find it difficult to generalize to other environments that have different threat landscapes or characteristics. To enable knowledge transfer and the reusability of trained models in a variety of contexts, transfer learning and domain adaptation techniques are required.

Future directions: Create interpretable DRL models (also known as explainable AI, or XAI) so that cybersecurity analysts can comprehend and rely on the models' suggestions. Security and Robustness: Using strategies like ensemble defenses, adversarial training, and robust optimization, you can make DRL models more resilient to hostile attacks.

Data augmentation and synthetic data: Investigate techniques for creating synthetic data and augmenting existing data to rectify biases and imbalances in cybersecurity datasets, hence enhancing the efficacy and generalization of DRL models. Hybrid Methods: Examine hybrid approaches that take advantage of the complementary strengths of supervised learning, unsupervised learning, expert systems, and DRL in cybersecurity applications.

Scalable infrastructures: Utilizing cloud computing and parallelization, develop scalable infrastructures and distributed training techniques to enable effective DRL model training in large-scale cybersecurity contexts.

Future directions and new developments in DRL for cybersecurity, such as federated learning, multi-agent systems, and privacy-preserving methods. DRL for cybersecurity research is developing quickly, with several new trends and possible avenues for further investigation. To improve the efficacy and application of DRL in cybersecurity, researchers are investigating novel techniques to address issues including scalability, interpretability, adversarial assaults, and data privacy.

6.10.1 Latest research and emerging trends

6.10.1.1 Multi-agent systems

Collaborative defense: Examine the application of multi-agent systems, in which many DRL agents work together to thwart complex cyberattacks. Examine methods to enhance overall security posture by coordinating, communicating, and exchanging knowledge among agents.

6.10.1.2 Federated learning

Decentralized Training: Investigate federated learning strategies in which DRL models are cooperatively trained without centralized data aggregation across distributed edge devices, servers, or organizations. Examine methods for model synchronization, differential privacy, and safe aggregation to protect data privacy and use collective intelligence for cybersecurity tasks.

6.10.1.3 Privacy-preserving techniques

Secure model updates: Provide methods for updating DRL models with private or sensitive data while protecting the identity of specific users or organizations. Examine cryptographic techniques to enable secure model training and inference in decentralized systems, such as homomorphic encryption and secure multiparty computation (SMPC).

6.10.1.4 Adversarial robustness

Adversarial training: Further research on adversarial training methods to enhance the robustness of DRL models against adversarial attacks. Investigate techniques such as adversarial example generation, robust optimization, and ensemble defenses to improve resilience to evasion and poisoning attacks.

6.10.2 Transfer learning and domain adaptation

Knowledge transfer: To facilitate the transfer of knowledge from pre-trained DRL models to new cybersecurity contexts with distinct features or threat landscapes, investigate transfer learning and domain adaption methodologies. Examine techniques for optimizing and repurposing pre-trained models to boost learning and enhance generalization capabilities.

6.10.2.1 Explainable AI

Enhance the interpretability and trustworthiness of DRL models in cybersecurity applications by developing techniques for elucidating their decisions and behavior. Examine methods like saliency maps, model introspection, and attention mechanisms to offer insightful justifications for security-related choices.

6.10.2.2 Scalable architectures and algorithms

Effective training: To enable effective training of DRL models in extensive cybersecurity contexts and provide scalable architectures and distributed training techniques. To hasten convergence and enhance scalability, investigate parallelization, model distillation, and asynchronous update strategies.

6.10.2.3 Hybrid approaches

Integration with Other AI Techniques: To make use of their complementing advantages in cybersecurity applications, look at hybrid approaches that integrate DRL with other AI techniques like supervised learning, unsupervised learning, and expert systems. To improve total defense capabilities, investigate methods for combining DRL with rule-based systems, anomaly detection algorithms, and conventional security procedures.

6.10.3 Case studies and practical implementations

Give case studies and real-world examples illustrating how DRL approaches used in cybersecurity. Of course! The following case studies and real-world examples.

6.10.3.1 DRL techniques used in cybersecurity

Case study: NVIDIA researchers created Deep Sloth, a DRL-based IDS that uses RL to find network breaches.

Implementation: To recognize aberrant network traffic patterns suggestive of cyberattacks, Deep Sloth uses a DRL agent to learn the best policy. Through interaction with the network environment, the agent observes the characteristics of network traffic and classifies traffic as malicious or benign.

Result: When compared to conventional signature-based IDS, Deep Sloth showed better detection accuracy and fewer false positives, particularly when it came to identifying zero-day attacks and new threats.

6.10.3.2 Malware detection and analysis

Case study: Microsoft researchers created Deep Locker, a DRL-based malware detection system that employs RL to recognize and categorize malware samples.

Implementation: To analyze information like file properties, code structure, and behavioral patterns that collected from malware samples, deep locker uses a DRL agent. Based on their traits and possible degrees of threat, malware samples categorized by the agent as it gains knowledge of them.

Result: Deep locker proved the efficacy of DRL in malware detection and analysis by achieving high detection rates and low false positive rates in finding previously undiscovered malware variants.

6.10.3.3 Manage firewalls adaptively

Case study: To improve network security, a cybersecurity company deployed an adaptive firewall management strategy based on DRL.

Implementation: Based on observed network traffic patterns, attack trends, and policy violations, the DRL agent learns dynamically modify firewall rules. The agent maximizes network performance, reduces false positives, and mitigates new threats by optimizing firewall configurations.

Outcome: The overall network security posture improved by the DRL-based firewall management system's better responsiveness to shifting threat landscapes and less need for human intervention in firewall rule management.

Identification of phishing: DRL-based solution for a Google research team created phishing detection in email exchanges.

Implementation: To detect phishing attempts, the DRL agent examines the content of emails, sender information, and embedded links. Using behavioral patterns and contextual features, the agent gains the ability to differentiate between phishing and authentic emails.

Outcome: Users now have better defense against email-based risks thanks to the DRL-based phishing detection system, which identified phishing emails with high accuracy and few false positives.

Emphasize the best practices, lessons discovered, and successful integrations of DRL into current security frameworks. Recommended procedures for incorporating DRL into current security frameworks.

6.10.3.4 Intrusion detection systems

Implementation: By incorporating DRL into IDS, attack patterns can be dynamically adapted. Sophisticated assaults accurately detected by IDS thanks to the training of DRL agents on network traffic data.

The takeaway: To ensure that complicated attack patterns learned effectively, successful implementations need robust training procedures and well-selected datasets.

Best practice: Continuously update and refine DRL models to adapt to new attack vectors and improve detection capabilities over time.

6.10.3.5 Malware detection and analysis

Implementation: By integrating DRL with malware detection systems, malware samples be automatically analyzed, increasing detection rates and decreasing reaction times.

The takeaway: Strong model architecture and feature engineering are essential for identifying dangerous and benign samples and capturing complex malware behaviors.

Best practice: To enhance model performance and adjust to new threats, update malware datasets regularly and include feedback mechanisms. Phishing Identification and Execution: Email systems can analyze email content, sender information, and user behavior in real time to detect suspicious communications by using DRL for phishing detection.

Lesson learned: The ability to discern between authentic and phishing emails is mostly dependent on contextual information and behavioral patterns. To capture changes in phishing strategies, DRL models be trained on a variety of datasets.

Optimal approach: To offer multi-layered defense against email-based threats, integrate DRL-based phishing detection systems with current email security frameworks.

Data quality: Lesson: In cybersecurity applications, efficient DRL model training requires high-quality data. Unreliable security judgments and subpar performance might result from noisy or biased datasets.

Optimal approach: To guarantee the accuracy and variety of training data, make investments in data gathering and curation procedures that include historical and current security data sources.

6.10.3.6 Model interpretability

Lesson: Trust and acceptance in security operations hampered by the black-box nature of DRL models, which can make it difficult to comprehend and interpret their choices. Best Practice: To improve interpretability and ease human oversight, develop methods for illustrating and visualizing DRL model decisions, such as decision trees, saliency maps, and attention mechanisms.

6.10.4 Best practices for integration

6.10.4.1 Incremental deployment

Practice: DRL-based security solutions progressively introduced to production settings, starting with small-scale deployments. Benefit: Before implementing DRL models fully, incremental deployment enables testing and validation in real-world circumstances, allowing for the identification of possible problems and the fine-tuning of parameters.

6.10.4.2 Human-in-the-loop

Practice: Use human specialists to supervise, validate, and intervene as needed in the DRL-based security workflow.

Benefit: By combining the advantages of human knowledge and DRL automation, person-in-the-loop systems enhance decision-making and lower the possibility of false positives or negatives.

6.11 Experiment setup

Two datasets that meet several specifications: Compare results from different works, several requirements must be met: (1) labeled datasets; (2) unbalanced but with a different level of imbalance, which allows studying the behavior in different conditions; (3) a predefined split for the training and test datasets; (4) well-known datasets, which make available a sufficient number of results from previous works; (5) to include older and more recent datasets, to increase generality/variability; (6) data coming from different network architectures (e.g. fixed-line vs. wireless networks); and (7) the requirement for a data volume large enough to have significant results, but constrained by real-world constraints of memory and CPU time. The well-known IDS dataset NSL-KDD been used.

6.11.1 Result for reinforcement learning for intrusion detection

In a RL-based, anomaly detector with a simulated network environment in this system, anomalies injected in a controlled way, and the reward system predicated on correctly identifying the anomalies. The NSL-KDD and AWID datasets are our choice because they meet the majority of the stated requirements. There are 23 possible labels in the training dataset (two labels linked to various types of anomalies and one normal label). The test dataset, on the other hand, contains 38 label values, suggesting that it contains anomalies that were not present during training (Figure 6.4).

To obtain the most pertinent performance metrics—accuracy, precision, recall, and F1—for the detection of two label values—normal and anomaly—we apply all of the models to the NSL-KDD dataset. Since each dataset presents unique difficulties for a classification algorithm, it is interesting to experiment with both AWID and NSL-KDD datasets is mutinously (Figure 6.5).

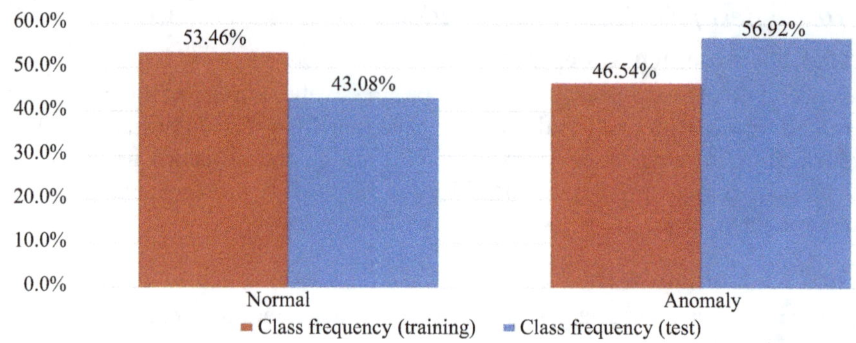

Figure 6.4 Frequency distribution of intrusions for the training and test datasets (NSL-KDD)

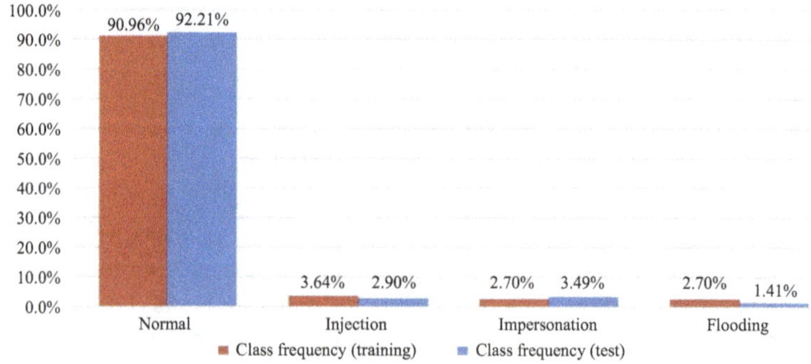

Figure 6.5 Frequency distribution of intrusion classes for the training and test datasets (AWID)

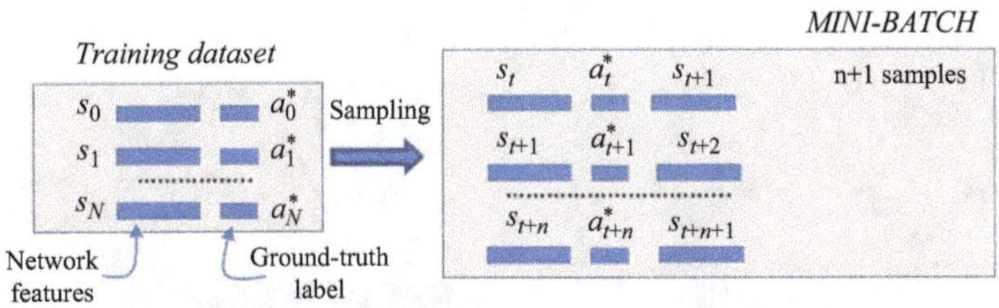

Figure 6.6 Dataset preparation for the training of the DQN, DDQN, and actor-critic models

The MDP theory serves as the foundation for RL. An MDP represented as a tuple $\langle S, A, \boldsymbol{B}, R\rangle$, in which A is a set of actions, T is a mapping that specifies the transition probabilities between each state-action pair and any potential new state, and *R* is a reward function that assigns a real value (reward) to each state-action pair. The transition probability to a new state in an MDP is solely dependent on the action and state at that moment, regardless of the past. This is because the function *T* adheres to the Markov property. Following its definition, an MDP's policy is a mapping of each state to an action. The theoretical framework known as an MDP used to describe how an agent interacts with an environment in a sequential decision-making process, in which the agent implements the policy, and the environment implements the *T* and *R* functions. Typically, the interaction between the environment and the agent discretized into a series of "time steps" wherein the environment receives a new action from the agent, which results in a state transition and potentially a new reward. Managing the dataset to produce the mini-batches (sets of samples used in a training iteration) that each unique model use is a general task for all models. N samples of network features and related intrusion labels with multiple possible values (binary or multiclass anomaly) are included in the training dataset. Preparing the dataset for the actor-critic, DDQN, and DQN models' training (Figure 6.6).

6.11.2 Results

We examine the outcomes of using various machine-learning models on the AWID and NSL-KDD datasets. Logistic regression, Support Vector Machine (SVM) with linear kernel and Radial Basis Function (RBF) kernel, k-nearest-neighbors (KNN), Naive Bayes (NB), Random Forest, Gradient Boosting Machine (GBM), AdaBoost with several weak learners (simple trees and NB), MLP, Convolutional Neural Network (CNN), and our proposed models based in DRL: DQN, DDQN, policy gradient, and actor-critic are some of the most widely used machine learning and deep learning techniques. Applying DRL models (DQN, DDQN, Policy Gradient, and Actor-Critic) to the NSL-KDD dataset been studied. The results shown in two sections. The raw data presented in the upper section in a color-coded manner, with the redder representing a lower value and the greenest representing a higher value (a comparison of values applied column wise). Furthermore, a Naive Bayes variant been removed from the graph to make it less cluttered, given the model's scant significance in terms of results. The lower part of the chart only displays the accuracy and F1 scores (the most significant scores) (Figure 6.7).

		Test results			
		Accuracy	F1	Precision	Recall
Logistic Regression	Logistic Regression	0.7068	0.6807	0.8955	0.5491
SVM	SVM, Linear Kernel	0.7740	0.7718	0.9073	0.6715
	SVM, RBF Kernel	0.8799	0.8927	0.9081	0.8779
KNN	K-Nearest Neighbors	0.7808	0.7769	0.9233	0.6706
Random Forest	Random Forest	0.7472	0.7211	0.9688	0.5743
GBM	Gradient Tree Boosting	0.7761	0.7612	0.9690	0.6267
Naive Bayes	Gaussian, only continuous features	0.5490	0.7018	0.5627	0.9324
	Bernoulli, only discrete features	0.7942	0.7979	0.9046	0.7138
	Bernoulli, all features, quantizing the continuous features	0.8019	0.7967	0.9583	0.6818
AdaBoost	Adaboost with Trees	0.7606	0.7403	0.9683	0.5992
	Adaboost with Naive Bayes	0.5265	0.3181	0.8824	0.1940
Neural Network	Neural Net (MLP)	0.7966	0.7881	0.9679	0.6647
CNN	CNN-ID	0.7875	0.7633	0.8094	0.7875
Reinforcement Learning	DQN	0.8787	0.8935	0.8933	0.8937
	DDQN	0.8978	0.9120	0.8944	0.9303
	Policy Gradient	0.7873	0.7909	0.8980	0.7067
	Actor Critic	0.8078	0.8111	0.9203	0.7251

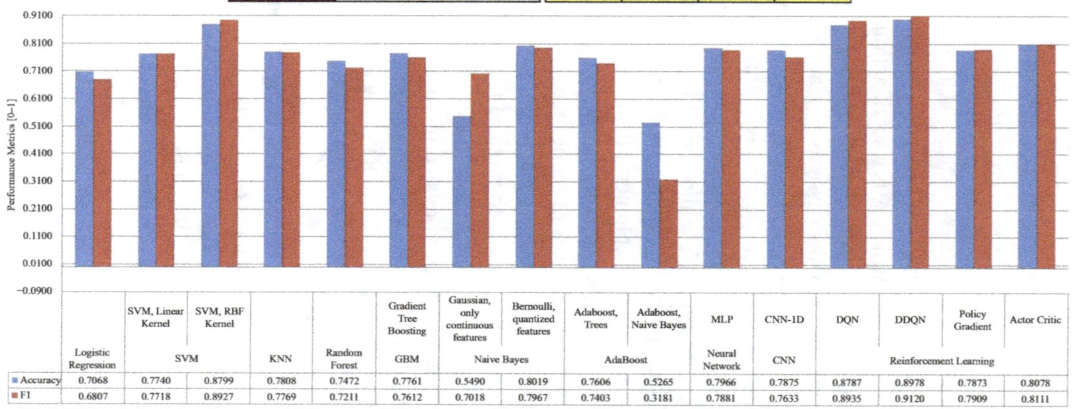

Figure 6.7 Performance scores for all models (NSL-KDD dataset)

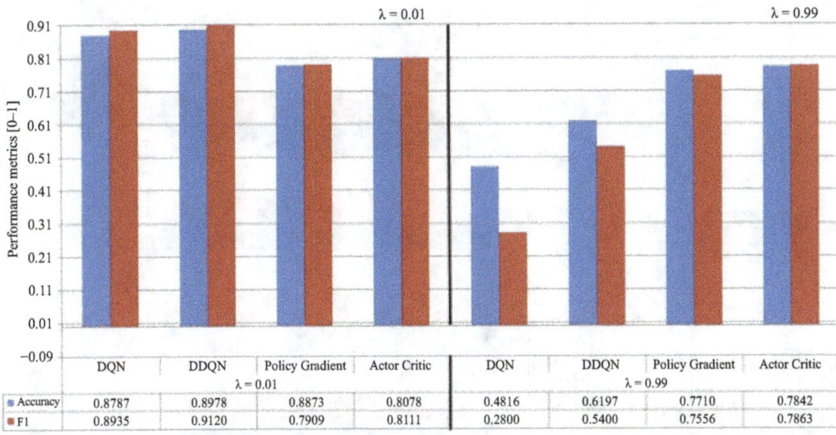

Figure 6.8 Comparison of performance scores for different discount factors (NSL-KDD dataset)

All models' performance ratings (NSL-KDD dataset) As mentioned, the outcomes can be greatly impacted by the discount factor (λ) considered for the DRL algorithms. To examine this influence, Figure 6.8 presents the effects of various discount factor values for the DRL models. For DQN and DDQN, the effect is crucial; for policy gradient and actor-critic models, it is less significant.

Comparison of NSL-KDD dataset performance scores for various discount factors An extremely unbalanced dataset called AWID can be used to evaluate how well an intrusion detector is working. the performance metrics given in Figure 6.9 are aggregated metrics that use a weighted average for the F1, precision, and recall. We can see that the Accuracy, F1, and Recall metrics show excellent performance for the DDQN model. The Random Forest and Decision Tree (J48) models produce the best results for this dataset. As noted for the NSL-KDD results, recall is a crucial metric for an intrusion detection algorithm that aims to minimize false negatives, or intrusions that are not detected, and it is noteworthy that DDQN performs exceptionally well in this dataset.

6.12 Conclusion

In conclusion, this chapter summarizes the key discoveries and contributions made. It has examined the use of DRL in cybersecurity and shown how it may improve several security defense areas.

In brief, the paper makes the following contributions: (1) A novel algorithm that enhances intrusion detection performance over current machine learning and deep learning methods. A fast and incredibly simple policy network is the foundation of the intrusion detection algorithm (2), which is particularly well suited for demanding applications in contemporary data networks that demand quick

		Test results			
		Accuracy	**F1**	**Precision**	**Recall**
Boosting	AdaBoost	0.9220	0.8850	0.8500	0.9220
Decision Tree	J48	0.9620	0.9480	0.9620	0.9630
Frequency Table based	Hyper pipes	0.9223	0.8850	0.8790	0.9220
	Naive Bayes	0.9055	0.9090	0.9170	0.9060
	ZeroR	0.9220	0.8850	0.8500	0.9220
	OneR	0.9457	0.9220	0.9000	0.9460
Random Forest	Random Forest	0.9582	0.9440	0.9590	0.9580
Neural Network	MLP	0.9470	0.9256	0.9174	0.9473
Reinforcement Learning	DQN	0.9541	0.9372	0.9244	0.9541
	DDQN	0.9570	0.9394	0.9235	0.9570
	Policy Gradient	0.9221	0.8847	0.8502	0.9221
	Actor Critic	0.9221	0.8847	0.8502	0.9221

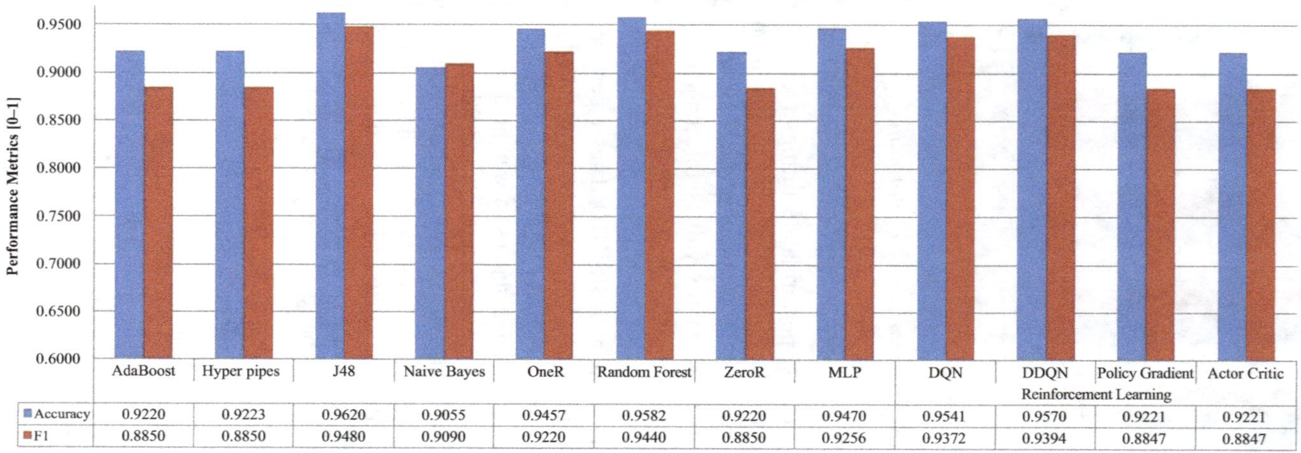

Figure 6.9 Performance scores for all models (AWID dataset)

responses. (3) The model that produced can be used for online learning, which is essential for data networks that have dynamic environments. (4) Innovative use of DRL in supervised education. (5) The rewards function that powers the optimization process does not need to be differentiable, which increases its flexibility and applicability to a wider range of issues.

We present a comparative analysis of four DRL algorithms (actor-critic, DDQN, Policy gradient, and DQN) and show how they can be used to analyze a dataset labeled with intrusions rather than engaging with an actual live network environment. Further analysis given by contrasting these algorithms with many alternative machine learning models, taking into account three performance factors: (1) prediction scores, (2) training, and (3) prediction times. To help with the generalization of the findings, two distinct intrusion detection datasets—NSL-KDD and AWID—are used. Another significant contribution of this work is demonstrating the significance of the discount factor parameter, which controls the algorithm's speed of convergence. Given the constraints placed on this work, it is particularly crucial to have a small value for this parameter for the DQN and DDQN algorithms to converge. This work also contributes by outlining the data preparation needed to apply the DRL models to a labeled dataset and by suggesting a method for doing so while taking the unique characteristics of the various models into account.

Further reading

[1] Mnih, V., Kavukcuoglu, K., Silver, D., *et al.* (2015). Human-level control through deep reinforcement learning. *Nature*, 518(7540), 529–533.

[2] Silver, D., Huang, A., Maddison, C. J., *et al.* (2016). Mastering the game of Go with deep neural networks and tree search. *Nature*, 529(7587), 484–489.

[3] Sutton, R. S., and Barto, A. G. (2018). *Reinforcement Learning: An Introduction* (2nd ed.). Cambridge, MA: MIT Press.

[4] Mnih, V., Badia, A. P., Mirza, M., *et al.* (2016). Asynchronous methods for deep reinforcement learning. In *Proceedings of the 33rd International Conference on Machine Learning* (pp. 1928–1937).

[5] Silver, D., Schrittwieser, J., Simonyan, K., *et al.* (2017). Mastering the game of Go without human knowledge. *Nature*, 550(7676), 354–359.

[6] Goodfellow, I. J., Shlens, J., and Szegedy, C. (2015). Explaining and harnessing adversarial examples. In *Proceedings of the International Conference on Learning Representations (ICLR).*

[7] Papernot, N., McDaniel, P., Goodfellow, I., *et al.* (2017). Practical black-box attacks against machine learning. In *Proceedings of the Asia Conference on Computer and Communications Security* (pp. 506–519).

[8] Huang, S. H., Papernot, N., Goodfellow, I., *et al.* (2017). Adversarial attacks on neural network policies. In *Proceedings of the 31st International Conference on Neural Information Processing Systems (NIPS).*

[9] Kumar, S., and Janakiraman, V. (2019). Deep reinforcement learning for cybersecurity: Applications, challenges, and future research directions. *IEEE Access*, 7, 91572–91591.

[10] Yadav, S. S., Sharma, R., and Singla, R. (2020). DRL Bench: A benchmark framework for evaluation of deep reinforcement learning-based anomaly detection approaches. *IEEE Access*, 8, 105064–105082.

[11] Yuan, X., He, P., Zhu, Q., *et al.* (2020). Deep reinforcement learning for autonomous cyber defense. In *Proceedings of the 39th IEEE International Conference on Computer Communications (INFOCOM)*.

[12] Nanduri, A., Srivastava, A., and Verman, M. (2021). A comprehensive survey on deep reinforcement learning for cybersecurity. *Computers & Security*, 108, 102260.

[13] Liu, Z., Deng, Y., Zhao, L., *et al.* (2021). Adversarial reinforcement learning: A survey and new perspectives. *Information Fusion*, 74, 160–183.

[14] Koo, M., Kim, S., and Lee, J. (2020). Deep reinforcement learning for cybersecurity: A comprehensive review. *IEEE Access*, 8, 181497–181513.

[15] Samson, I., Haruna, K., Ahmad, M.A., and Mustapha, R. (2023). Deep reinforcement learning with hidden Markov model for speech recognition. *Journal of Technology and Innovation*, 3(1), 1–5.

[16] Amodei, D., Ananthanarayanan, S., Anubhai, R., *et al.* (2016). Deep reinforcement learning from human preferences. In *Proceedings of the 30th AAAI Conference on Artificial Intelligence*.

[17] Liang, Y., and Zhao, Y. (2018). Deep reinforcement learning in network security: A survey. In *Proceedings of the 17th IEEE International Conference on Trust, Security and Privacy in Computing and Communications (TrustCom)*.

[18] Duan, Y., Chen, X., Houthooft, R., *et al.* (2016). Benchmarking deep reinforcement learning for continuous control. In *Proceedings of the 33rd International Conference on Machine Learning* (pp. 1329–1338).

[19] Zhang, Y., and Shen, L. (2023). Automatic learning rate adaption for memristive deep learning systems. *IEEE Transactions on Neural Networks and Learning Systems*, 35(8), 10791–10802.

[20] Luong, N. C., Hoang, D. T., Gong, S., *et al.* (2019). Applications of deep reinforcement learning in communications and networking: A survey. *IEEE Communications Surveys & Tutorials*, 21(4), 3133–3174.

[21] Priya, S., and Pradeep Mohan Kumar, K. (2023). Feature selection with deep reinforcement learning for intrusion detection system. *Computer Systems Science and Engineering*, 46(3), 3339–3353.

[22] Sewak, M., Sahay, S. K., and Rathore, H. (2023). Deep reinforcement learning in the advanced cybersecurity threat detection and protection. *Information Systems Frontiers*, 25(2), 589–611.

Chapter 7
Trustworthy explainable artificial intelligence for resilient cybersecurity applications

Faisal Bashir[1], Ali Alzahrani[1] and Furqan Zahoor[1]

Abstract

From the early days of conceptual theories, artificial intelligence (AI) and machine learning (ML) have advanced significantly to become essential components of today's technology civilization. Although effective, the quick development of AI and ML and its integration into several military and civilian applications have also brought forth new difficulties. There is now an urgent need to learn more about how these decisions are produced because some of the latest AI/ML decision-making systems require virtually no human intervention. Explainable artificial intelligence (XAI) is a new area of AI study as a result of this. By helping us better understand the behavior of cyber threats and create more effective defenses, XAI has the potential to completely transform the way we approach network and system security in the realm of cybersecurity. This chapter examines the state of the art in XAI for cybersecurity and looks at the several strategies that have been put out to deal with this significant issue. In the context of cybersecurity, we go over the difficulties and constraints of the available XAI techniques and suggest exciting avenues for further study.

7.1 Introduction

From their early conceptual conceptions, artificial intelligence (AI) and machine learning (ML) have advanced to become essential components of today's technology civilization. Data-driven learning systems are now widely used as a result of recent developments in AI and ML [1,2]. These developments often result in nearly minimal human intervention or oversight, as AI/ML systems make decisions using the facts they have learnt. Understanding how AI/ML systems make judgments is essential when they are applied in fields like healthcare and the military that have an impact on people's lives [3,4]. How can

[1]Department of Computer Engineering, College of Computer Science and Information Technology, King Faisal University, Saudi Arabia

we know that the AI/ML systems are reliable? How can we be certain that the decisions made by these systems are free from inherent bias? Numerous instances of AI system failures have occurred in the real world. Facebook's ad AI was prejudiced against race, gender, and religion, and Amazon's hiring AI discriminated against women, favoring male applicants. Numerous AI algorithms have been found to exhibit prejudice against persons of race inside the US healthcare system [5]. AI bias may result from human training or data gathered by human-operated machine learning systems, although both government and business organizations are working to ensure that AI/ML systems produce objective, explicable results. New laws and policies have resulted from this, not only in the US but also internationally. The general data protection legislation of the European Union, for instance, gives customers a "right to explanation" [6]. "Assessments of high-risk systems that involve personal information or make automated decisions" are required by the US Algorithmic Accountability Act of 2019 [7]. The answer to ensuring the reliability of AI decision systems is accountable AI. Research on explainable artificial intelligence (XAI) has grown as a result of this issue [8].

To avoid limiting the effectiveness of today's AI systems, XAI proposes developing a set of ML techniques, including prominent ones that (1) create more explainable models while maintaining high learning performances (e.g., prediction accuracy) and (2) facilitate humans to comprehend, appropriately trust and effectively manage the next generation of AI partners. XAI appears to be attempting to solve the following questions: (i) who is responsible if things go wrong?; (ii) could we explain why something goes wrong?; and (iii) do we know why and how to make further use of AI models if they function well? In a range of cybersecurity applications (e.g., Intrusion Detection Systems (IDS), spam filters, malware detection, malicious program recognition, and theft prevention), AI algorithms provide unrivalled flexibility and precision. They have shown remarkable performances on datasets, even if only the statistical data collected from applications was trained. However, despite their outstanding success, they can still make mistakes, some more expensive than others. As a result, confidence in and security problems of AI are key topics. Although traditional ML models (e.g., Decision Trees (DTs), Linear Regression, and Bayes) are easy to understand, opaque decision-making systems, such as deep neural networks (DNNs), the number of which has increased in recent years, are difficult to interpret. Deep learning (DL) models include several sophisticated network layers that complicate DNNs black-box models. Variants of black boxes should be white ones (transparent). Consequently, XAI emerges as the dominant comprehensive aspect of a learning model.

The rest of the chapter is arranged as follows: Section 7.2 details the background on the XAI techniques and also highlights the motivations to integrate XAI into cybersecurity. The detailed discussion on XAI applications in defending against cyberattacks is presented in Section 7.3. The numerous challenges for XAI applications are discussed in Section 7.4. Section 7.5 presents the discussion on the future research. Finally, Section 7.6 concludes the paper.

7.2 Background on XAI techniques

The "black box" character of many machine learning algorithms is one of its drawbacks. This indicates that even domain specialists find it very difficult to fully comprehend these algorithms and that they are very difficult to explain. Users will be reluctant to utilize a model if they believe it to be a "black-box" since they may not always trust its forecasts. Furthermore, because DNN architecture is created by trial-and-error methods and can include hundreds of layers and millions of parameters, they are extremely complex black-box models, even for AI professionals. In light of this difficulty, XAI's primary objective is to make it possible for consumers, developers, and researchers to comprehend machine learning model outcomes more fully. Although explanation systems have existed since the 1980s, XAI research using ML/AI models has significantly increased in recent years. There is a need for more transparent systems that can explain their decisions because the majority of commercial and military AI/ML systems that use DL and other ML approaches have black-box models. "AI systems that can explain their rationale to a human user, characterize their strengths and weaknesses, and convey an understanding of how they will behave in the future" is the definition of XAI provided by the US Defense Advanced Research Projects Agency. In Figure 7.1, XAI is conceptually summarized. In order to help human users understand, appropriately trust, and manage the next generation of artificially intelligent partners, XAI seeks to create more comprehensible models while preserving a high level of learning performance (prediction accuracy). As illustrated in Figure 7.2, the scientific contribution in the field of XAI has increased dramatically since the program's inception. To try to cover every potential area of application, a variety of words have been used across the material that has been provided. Here are only a handful of the many types that are used:

Transparency: Do users understand the model's language and format choices?
Fairness: Is it possible to demonstrate that protected groups receive fair treatment in model judgments?
Trust: To what extent do human users feel at ease utilizing the system?
Usability: How well-suited is the system to provide users with a safe and effective workspace where they can finish their tasks?
Reliability: How resilient is the system to modifications in inputs and parameters?
Causality: Does the actual system exhibit the anticipated output changes brought on by input perturbation?

As seen in Figure 7.3, the National Institute of Standards and Technology (NIST) introduced four core ideas for explainable AI systems around the middle of 2020. AI systems are required by the Explanation principle to provide justification, proof, or support for every output. If the recipient comprehends the system's explanations, the system satisfies the Meaningful principle. A system's explanations must

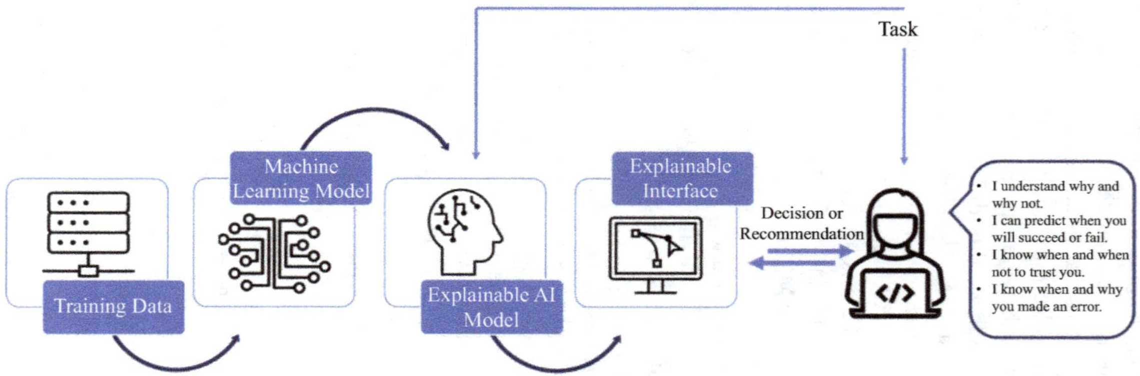

Figure 7.1 Overview of the XAI concept [5]

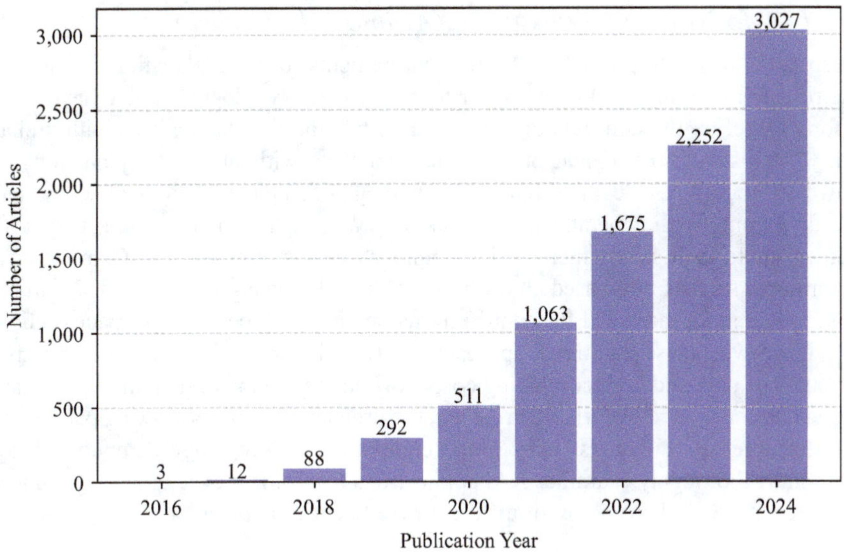

Figure 7.2 Evolution of the number of total publications whose title, abstract and/ or keywords refer to the field of XAI from 2016 until 2024. Data retrieved from Web of Science.

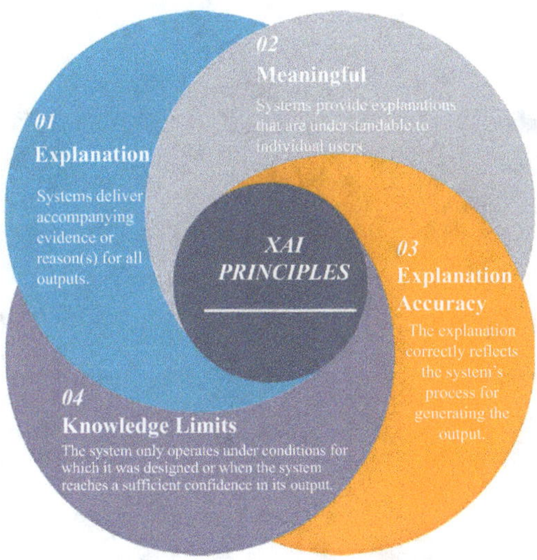

Figure 7.3 XAI principles presented by NIST [20]

be accurate according to the Explanation Accuracy principle, and ultimately, the Knowledge Limits principle asserts that systems detect situations in which they were not authorized or designed to function or in which their responses are untrustworthy.

7.2.1 Motivations to integrate XAI into cybersecurity

Despite the desire to promote XAI, the requirements for an explanation throughout the research community do not appear to be consistently adopted. There have been efforts to define the concepts of "interpretability" and "explainability" with "reliability", "trustworthiness" and other similar concepts without clear explanations of how they should be integrated into the wide range of implementations of AI models [9,10]. Coping with cyberattacks, such as malware, incursion, and spam, is getting harder due to their steady increase in complexity and volume [11,12]. Conventional algorithms, such as rule-based algorithms, statistics-based algorithms, and signature-based techniques, are used to identify intrusions in the cybersecurity space, claims [13]. However, these traditional approaches have a low capacity to process massive amounts of data and high computing costs [14] due to the increasing amount of data being communicated over the Internet and the urgency of new networking paradigms like the Internet of Things (IoT), cloud computing, and fog/edge computing [15]. This study thoroughly examines XAI applications for resilient cyberattacks, gaining a comprehensive understanding of different cybersecurity applications.

7.3 XAI applications in defending against cyberattacks

As seen in Figure 7.4, XAI is becoming more and more important in the fight against a variety of cyberattacks. We will provide a quick analysis of the most

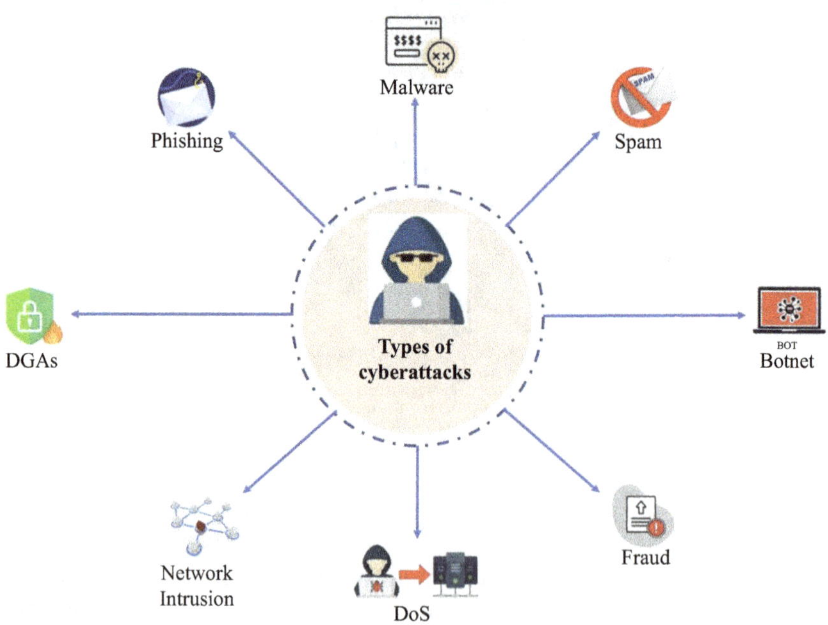

Figure 7.4 Overview of some common types of cyberattacks [11]

advanced XAI-based defense solutions for various cyberattack types in this article. Malware is one of the biggest threats to online security nowadays, and putting effective defenses in place requires prompt analysis of an ever-increasing amount of malware. The two primary categories of malware detection methods now in use are static detection and dynamic detection [16]. Without actually executing the code, static malware detection examines the malicious binary. Dynamic malware detection, on the other hand, involves running the malicious codes on the test system and keeping an eye on its behavior. In reality, it takes a lot of time and resources to manually analyze each malware file in an application using these traditional malware detection techniques. As a result, a lot of AI-based malware detection systems—particularly DL algorithms—are used to identify malware more effectively and with fewer resources than conventional malware detection techniques [17]. For similar reasons, other researchers use varying degrees of XAI techniques to make AI-based malware detection systems more transparent and comprehensible. This allows a trustworthy malware detector to function well in a varied setting. The malware detector can be explained in a variety of ways. Finding the most important local characteristics can always yield insightful justifications for malware detection choices. A gradient-based method was used by Marco *et al.* [18] to determine which features had the most influence on each choice. The data was taken from the Android apps using Drebin [19], a well-known Android malware scanner. Both local and global explanations preserve Drebin's explainabilities for nonlinear algorithms, such as Random Forests (RFs) and Support Vector Machines (SVMs).

Spam has grown to be a significant issue for Internet users in recent years as a result of the growing number of users. Even though there were over 306.4 billion emails sent and received every day in 2021, spam emails made up over 55% of all emails sent in that year, which means that unsolicited emails made up almost half of all email traffic. Due in large part to their capacity for self-improvement and self-tuning, AI-based systems have emerged as a viable solution to the spam problem. However, users have a lot of questions about AI models, particularly the black-box ML and DL models, because of the privacy and legal peculiarities of spam. ML models can be enhanced with desirable attributes like explainability and transparency by implementing XAI algorithms [21].

Additionally, a lot of research has been written about this topic to increase the credibility of AI-based spam filters. A very exploratory study on the detection of false spam news using machine learning algorithms from a wide range of features was carried out by Reis *et al.* [22]. The SHAP approach was used to explain why representative models of each cluster classify some as fake news while others are not. It is suggested that new features pertaining to the fake news's source domain appear in the detection models five times more frequently than other features. Hacker *et al.* in [23] also examined and illustrated the legally required trade-off between explainability and accuracy in the context of spam classification. The claim that choosing the right model for the job at hand is just as crucial as focusing on making complex models understandable was supported by a dataset of 5,574 SMS messages [24]. In this work, even basic models, like Naive Bayes, can perform better than more complex models, like RFs, in situations where just a small amount of annotated training data is available.

A botnet assault is defined as a collection of interconnected computers that cooperate to do destructive, repeated tasks, including crashing websites, to contaminate and interfere with a victim's resources. Suryotrisongko *et al.* put up a unique methodology for botnet DGA identification in [25]. 55 botnet families' worth of datasets were used to evaluate five machine learning methods. RF beat earlier efforts and attained the highest accuracy of 96.3%. To make it easier to examine a user's retweeting behaviors, Mazza *et al.* [26] proposed ReTweet-Tweet (RTT), a tiny yet useful scatterplot representation. Even though the suggested botnet detection technique Retweet-Buster (RTbust), which is based on long short-term memory network unsupervised feature extraction techniques and variational autoencoders, was used in a black box fashion, the visualization tool RTT can still be used profitably once RTbust has been used to understand the characteristics of those accounts that have been labeled as bots. According to [27], increases in online financial fraud and personal account hacking were noted during the most stringent lockdown moments during the Covid-19 pandemic. Fraud costs the global economy $3.89 trillion annually, while it costs firms and individuals in the UK £130.

As a result, many financial institutions could profit from using AI systems to protect against fraud attempts in order to address this problem. The full use of AI techniques is still fraught with practical difficulties, though, and some people concentrate on understanding and being able to articulate the conclusions and forecasts generated by XAI's intricate models. Psychoula *et al.* [28] employed two of the most popular methods, local interpretable model-agnostic explanations (LIME) and shapley additive explanation (SHAP), to examine explanations for fraud detection by both supervised and unsupervised models. Eight well-known supervised and unsupervised AI models, including Naive Bayes, Logistic Regression, DT, RF, Gradient Boosting, Neural Network, Autoencoder, and Isolation Forest, were tested on the open source IEEE-CIS Fraud Detection dataset. LIME and SHAP, respectively, explained the detection outcomes of each model. It was found that LIME is quicker, but SHAP provides more trustworthy explanations.

Phishing is the term for phony emails that appear to be from a reputable company. The goal is to either infect the victim's computer with malicious software or take private information, such as login credentials and credit card details, from it. One type of internet fraud that is becoming more and more common is phishing. In order to detect phishing websites, Chai *et al.* [29] developed a multi-modal hierarchical attention model that collaboratively learnt the deep fraud cues from the three primary modalities of online content, such as URLs, text, and images.

In the attention layer, extracted characteristics from various contents would be aligned representations. Since content that receives the most attention is thought to be the most significant factor influencing the ultimate decision, this process is self-explanatory. Using the publicly accessible dataset Ebbu2017, Hernandes *et al.* [30]

conducted a phishing experiment using LIME and explainable boosting machines (EBM) explanation techniques based on malicious URLs. The tested database yielded accuracy ratings of 0.9646, 0.9732, and 0.9469 for the EBM, RF, and SVM classifiers, respectively. Empirical data demonstrated that the models could correctly classify URLs as either legitimate or phishing, and they also improved the final classification result by giving these ML models more explainability. Yun *et al.*'s work [31] also focused on visual explanations of the phishing detection system. The difficult problems of brand recognition and logo detection in phishing website detection were resolved by the suggested phishing website detection technique, Phishpedia. Phishpedia achieves both great accuracy and minimal runtime overhead. Network intrusion is the term used to describe an illegal entry into a computer within your organization or an address within your assigned domain. Conversely, Network Intrusion Detection Systems (NIDS) are characterized by their ability to monitor network or local system activity for signs of malicious or anomalous activity that deviates from established security protocols. ML and DL algorithms have been used in numerous projects recently to create effective NIDS. To strengthen NISDs, cybersecurity specialists also think about adding explainability to black-box AI systems; several have experimented with XAI. For reliable network intrusion detection, Barnard *et al.* [32] suggested a two-staged pipeline that used Autoencoder in the second phase and XGBoost in the first. The first stage model was explained using the SHAP approach, and the autoencoder was trained in the second stage using the explanation findings. The suggested pipeline can surpass numerous state-of-the-art attempts in terms of accuracy, recall, and precision on the NSL-KDD dataset while adding an additional layer of explainability, according to experiments conducted in the public corpus NSL-KDD. A unique DL and XAI-based IDS for IoT networks was created by Abou *et al.* [33]. To give local and global explanations for the DNN model's single output and the most important cant characteristics used in the intrusion detection decision, respectively, three distinct explanation techniques—LIME, SHAP, and RuleFit—were used. The NSL-KDD and UNSW-NB15 datasets were used for the experiments, and the performance results showed how well the suggested framework strengthened the interpretability of IoT IDS against well-known IoT attacks and helped cybersecurity experts better understand IDS judgments.

One kind of virus called domain generated algorithms (DGAs) is commonly used to create an enormous number of domain names that can be used for covert communication with command and control (C2) servers. Because there are so many distinct domain names, it is difficult to block problematic domains using popular strategies like sink-holing or blacklisting. A seeded function was commonly used in the dynamics of a DGA. An administrator would have to identify the virus, the DGA, and the seed value in order to filter out earlier risky networks and later servers in the sequence, making it difficult to prevent a DGA technique.

Because a knowledgeable threat actor can occasionally change the server or location from which the malware automatically calls back to the C2, the DGA makes it more difficult to block unwanted connections. A visual analytics framework that provides lucid interpretations of the models developed by DL model makers for the classification of DGAs was proposed by Abou *et al.* [33]. DTs were used to highlight the clusters formed by the clustering of the model's node activations. With a 2D projection, users may observe how the model interprets the data at various layers. Although the DTs may offer a plausible explanation for the clusters, this does not always represent how the model categorizes this data, which is a disadvantage of the suggested approach, particularly when there are multiple equally plausible answers. Denial-of-service (DoS) attacks pose a severe threat to the Internet, and various defense strategies have been proposed to mitigate the problem. DoS attacks are persistent attacks in which malevolent nodes generate false messages in an attempt to disrupt network traffic or deplete other nodes' resources. Because these newer, more sophisticated DoS assaults employ more intricate patterns, traditional IDS are finding it more difficult to detect them as they have grown more complex in recent years. Many ML and DL models have been used to detect malevolent DoS attacks. Furthermore, XAI techniques that look at how characteristics influence or contribute to an algorithm-based decision can be useful for the objective of model transparency. In order to improve the performance of the ML DoS attack detection model, Hsupeng *et al.* [34] presented CSTITool, a flow extraction tool based on CICFlowMeter. For the purpose of training the model, CICFlowMeter converted the flow data from packets. This procedure greatly shrank the data's size, which lessened the requirement for data storage. The XGBoost model was trained using network flow data of malware from the dataset CSTI-10 and hacker attack data from the dataset CIC-IDS2017, including Network Service Scanning, Endpoint DoS, Brute Force, and Remote Access Software. The result showed that employing the extra descriptive flow data generated by CSTITool can improve the performance metrics.

7.4 Challenges for XAI applications

Numerous obstacles still exist despite the impressive advancements made in XAI and AI/ML systems. These include the difficulty of explaining DL models, the lack of a widely accepted definition, standards, and metrics for the explainability of AI/ML systems, the transferability of posthoc explainability techniques, and the trade-off between explainability and performance.

Explainability versus performance: Another significant concern is the trade-off between explainability and performance. DL models' intrinsic "non-transparency" provides a significant obstacle to their explainability for XAI objectives, even as they get increasingly sophisticated and effective at resolving learning issues. Rudin [35] asserts that greater complexity does not always translate into greater accuracy, and this has been particularly true for certain DL models. It has been noted that machine learning models with better prediction accuracy also perform worse in terms of explainability. Therefore, further study must concentrate on enhancing these systems' functionality and increasing their accuracy. There needs to be the ideal equilibrium where explainability and system performance are both acceptable.

Lack of a universal standard: Terminology or definition ambiguity is one of the main issues facing the XAI area. When attempting to communicate explainability to an AI/ML system, a variety of terminology are utilized, as demonstrated in the previous sections. Additionally, words like "interpretability," "understandability," and "comprehensibility" have been used interchangeably and have just recently acquired unique meanings. Nonetheless, it is observed that the notion of explainability lacks a common, cohesive definition. Researchers will have a shared platform to contribute to the clearly defined requirements and difficulties of the area thanks to a unifying framework. Additionally, criteria other than straightforward questionnaires and interviews are required to gauge and assess XAI's efficacy.

Fairness of AI: Fairness and bias detection are two important considerations for XAI that align with one of the main motivations or objectives for the development of such explainable systems. Eliminating such biases is still a challenge in the nascent fields of responsible AI and XAI, which were formed out of the necessity for impartial and equitable decision-making that impacts human lives. According to Benjamins *et al.* [36], bias detection is a fundamental component of the field of fairness in AI. Underrepresented groups may be disproportionately impacted by proposals for datasets including sensitive and private information. When black-box models, like DL systems, are trained using these datasets, biased decisions may be made that lead to unfair, unethical, and discriminatory problems [37]. Apart from datasets, limited features, sample size differences, and proxy features are further potential causes of bias [38]. Another crucial issue is the transferability of posthoc explaining techniques.

XAI security: Lastly, as was said in the previous section, XAI security is still a significant problem. Since the field is still in its infancy, a lot of effort is being put into increasing explainability to match model performance. Even if this is a significant advancement for the creation and real-world application of XAI systems, its security cannot be disregarded. Additionally, these systems need to be made strong and resistant to hostile attacks if they are to be utilized for both military and civilian objectives. Making AI and ML systems explainable is an aim that goes hand in hand with building robust systems. Detecting and defending against various adversarial attempts using the system's explanations may be essential to overall performance and successful implementation.

Semantics: Apart from the above discussed ideas, semantics is also essential to XAI. Confalonieri *et al.* [39] highlighted justifications that, whether derived from ontologies, conceptual networks, or knowledge graphs, might bolster commonsense reasoning. The significance of these semantic approaches for the creation of AI/ML systems that can offer explanations tailored to particular stakeholders was also mentioned. Semantically, neural-symbolic learning and reasoning will also be crucial components of XAI. In order to produce better explanations, it is an interdisciplinary fusion of many (research subjects/topics). "Neural-symbolic reasoning seeks to integrate principles from neural networks learning and logical reasoning," according to Garcez *et al.* [40]. Neural-symbolic reasoning aims to "integrate robust connectionist learning and sound symbolic reasoning," according to their statement. Neural-symbolic computation for neural networks can offer dynamic substitutes for learning, reasoning, and knowledge representation. The usefulness of neural-symbolic computing was demonstrated by Garcez *et al.* [41], who emphasized its feature as the "integration of neural learning with symbolic knowledge representation and reasoning allowing for the construction of explainable AI systems."

7.5 Future research

Before communicating them to the stakeholders, interpreters must be carefully modified to filter out any sensitive information created in order to prevent privacy infringement and intellectual property regulations. Standards and regulatory frameworks must be followed when developing new protocols. Extensive study on creating security metrics to measure and identify issues in explanations should go hand in hand with it. A prerequisite is the development of more stringent guidelines on the components of XAI security and its availability of open AI/ML methods.

Maintaining the trade-off between explainability and performance in the recently released XAI-enabled cybersecurity systems is crucial for cybersecurity professionals. Research on the tradeoff between explainability and performance of XAI techniques used in cybersecurity is lacking, despite the fact that substantial efforts are being made in this area. Recent research has focused on the human understandability of XAI techniques in an effort to identify new applications for them in cybersecurity domains. As we indicated in the sections above, a key element of XAI approaches to explainability evaluation is user satisfaction with the generated explanation. However, because of security concerns, user input and the questionnaire are somewhat restricted in cybersecurity areas. Thus, future study could focus on how to create user-centered XAI systems for cybersecurity end-users in terms of user comprehension, user pleasure, and user performance without breaking security issues. It is necessary to thoroughly examine how pattern explanations can give the underlying systems additional attack surfaces. The information provided by the explanations can be used by a motivated attacker to carry out pattern mining and membership inference attacks, compromising the privacy of the system as a whole. Regular adversarial assaults are based on the idea that an adversary may introduce an undetectable perturbation into an input sample, which would leave the perturbed input's ground-truth class unchanged.

7.6 Conclusion

The creation and use of AI/ML systems will be significantly impacted by XAI. We provided a quick overview of XAI's taxonomy and literature review in this chapter. We outlined objectives and techniques for the design and development of reliable XAI systems, as well as specified terms related to the subject. Numerous difficulties were also mentioned.

Acknowledgments

This work was supported by Deanship of Scientific Research, Vice Presidency for Graduate Studies and Scientific Research, King Faisal University, Saudi Arabia [Grant No. KFU250232].

References

[1] Olowononi FO, Rawat DB, and Liu C. Resilient machine learning for networked cyber physical systems: A survey for machine learning security to securing machine learning for CPS. *IEEE Communications Surveys & Tutorials*. 2020;23(1):524–552.

[2] Rawat DB. Secure and trustworthy machine learning/artificial intelligence for multi-domain operations. In: *Artificial Intelligence and Machine Learning for Multi-Domain Operations Applications III*. vol. 11746. Bellingham, WA: SPIE; 2021. pp. 44–54.

[3] Arrieta AB, Díaz Rodríguez N, Del Ser J, *et al.* Explainable Artificial Intelligence (XAI): Concepts, taxonomies, opportunities and challenges toward responsible AI. *Information Fusion*. 2020;58:82–115.

[4] Goodman B, and Flaxman S. European Union regulations on algorithmic decision-making and a "right to explanation". *AI Magazine*. 2017;38(3):50–57.

[5] Rawal A, McCoy J, Rawat DB, *et al.* Recent advances in trustworthy explainable artificial intelligence: Status, challenges, and perspectives. *IEEE Transactions on Artificial Intelligence*. 2021;3(6):852–866.

[6] Voigt P, and Von dem Bussche A. *The EU General Data Protection Regulation (GDPR). A Practical Guide*, 1st ed., Cham: Springer International Publishing. 2017;10(3152676):10–5555.

[7] MacCarthy M. An examination of the Algorithmic Accountability Act of 2019. Available at SSRN: https://ssrn.com/abstract=3615731

[8] Rjoub G, Bentahar J, Wahab OA, *et al.* A survey on explainable artificial intelligence for cybersecurity. *IEEE Transactions on Network and Service Management*. 2023;20(4):5115–5140.

[9] Ribeiro MT, Singh S, and Guestrin C. "Why should I trust you?" Explaining the predictions of any classifier. In: *Proceedings of the 22nd ACM SIGKDD International Conference on Knowledge Discovery and Data Mining*; 2016. pp. 1135–1144.

[10] Lipton ZC. The mythos of model interpretability: In machine learning, the concept of interpretability is both important and slippery. *Queue*. 2018;16 (3):31–57.

[11] Zhang Z, Al Hamadi H, Damiani E, *et al.* Explainable artificial intelligence applications in cyber security: State-of-the-art in research. *IEEE Access*. 2022;10:93104–93139.

[12] Ucci D, Aniello L, and Baldoni R. Survey of machine learning techniques for malware analysis. *Computers & Security*. 2019;81:123–147.

[13] Han S, Xie M, Chen HH, *et al.* Intrusion detection in cyber-physical systems: Techniques and challenges. *IEEE Systems Journal*. 2014;8(4):1052–1062.

[14] Gümüşbaş D, Yıldırım T, Genovese A, *et al.* A comprehensive survey of databases and deep learning methods for cybersecurity and intrusion detection systems. *IEEE Systems Journal*. 2020;15(2):1717–1731.

[15] Donida Labati R, Genovese A, Piuri V, *et al.* Computational intelligence in cloud computing. *Recent Advances in Intelligent Engineering: Volume Dedicated to Imre J Rudas' Seventieth Birthday*. 2020; pp. 111–127.

[16] Ye Y, Li T, Adjeroh D, *et al.* A survey on malware detection using data mining techniques. *ACM Computing Surveys (CSUR)*. 2017;50(3):1–40.

[17] Vinayakumar R, Alazab M, Soman K, *et al.* Robust intelligent malware detection using deep learning. *IEEE Access*. 2019;7:46717–46738.

[18] Melis M, Maiorca D, Biggio B, *et al.* Explaining black-box android malware detection. In: *2018 26th European Signal Processing Conference (EUSIPCO)*. Piscataway, NJ: IEEE; 2018. pp. 524–528.

[19] Arp D, Spreitzenbarth M, Hubner M, *et al.* Drebin: Effective and explainable detection of android malware in your pocket. In: *Proceedings of the Network and Distributed System Security Symposium*. vol. 14; 2014. pp. 23–26.

[20] Capuano N, Fenza G, Loia V, *et al.* Explainable artificial intelligence in cybersecurity: A survey. *IEEE Access*. 2022;10:93575–93600.

[21] Renftle M, Trittenbach H, Poznic M, *et al.* Explaining any ML Model?–On Goals and Capabilities of XAI. arXiv preprint arXiv:220613888. 2022.

[22] Reis JC, Correia A, Murai F, *et al.* Explainable machine learning for fake news detection. In: *Proceedings of the 10th ACM Conference on Web Science*; 2019. pp. 17–26.

[23] Hacker P, Krestel R, Grundmann S, *et al.* Explainable AI under contract and tort law: Legal incentives and technical challenges. *Artificial Intelligence and Law*. 2020;28:415–439.

[24] Almeida T, Hidalgo JM, and Silva T. Towards SMS spam filtering: Results under a new dataset. *International Journal of Information Security Science*. 2013;2(1):1–18.

[25] Suryotrisongko H, Musashi Y, Tsuneda A, *et al.* Robust botnet DGA detection: Blending XAI and OSINT for cyber threat intelligence sharing. *IEEE Access*. 2022;10:34613–34624.

[26] Mazza M, Cresci S, Avvenuti M, *et al.* Rtbust: Exploiting temporal patterns for botnet detection on twitter. In: *Proceedings of the 10th ACM Conference on Web Science*; 2019. pp. 183–192.

[27] Buil-Gil D, Miró-Llinares F, Moneva A, *et al.* Cybercrime and shifts in opportunities during COVID-19: A preliminary analysis in the UK. *European Societies*. 2021;23(Suppl. 1):S47–S59.

[28] Psychoula I, Gutmann A, Mainali P, *et al.* Explainable machine learning for fraud detection. *Computer*. 2021;54(10):49–59.

[29] Chai Y, Zhou Y, Li W, *et al.* An explainable multi-modal hierarchical attention model for developing phishing threat intelligence. *IEEE Transactions on Dependable and Secure Computing*. 2021;19(2):790–803.

[30] Hernandes PRG, Floret CP, De Almeida KFC, *et al.* Phishing detection using URL-based XAI techniques. In: *2021 IEEE Symposium Series on Computational Intelligence (SSCI)*. Piscataway, NJ: IEEE; 2021. pp. 01–06.

[31] Lin Y, Liu R, Divakaran DM, *et al.* Phishpedia: A hybrid deep learning based approach to visually identify phishing webpages. In: *30th USENIX Security Symposium (USENIX Security 21)*; 2021. pp. 3793–3810.

[32] Barnard P, Marchetti N, and DaSilva LA. Robust network intrusion detection through explainable artificial intelligence (XAI). *IEEE Networking Letters*. 2022;4(3):167–171.

[33] Abou El Houda Z, Brik B, and Khoukhi L. "Why should I trust your IDs?": An explainable deep learning framework for intrusion detection systems in internet of things networks. *IEEE Open Journal of the Communications Society*. 2022;3:1164–1176.

[34] Hsupeng B, Lee KW, Wei TE, *et al.* Explainable malware detection using predefined network flow. In: *2022 24th International Conference on Advanced Communication Technology (ICACT)*. Piscataway, NJ: IEEE; 2022. pp. 27–33.

[35] Rudin C. Stop explaining black box machine learning models for high stakes decisions and use interpretable models instead. *Nature Machine Intelligence*. 2019;1(5):206–215.

[36] Benjamins R, Barbado A, and Sierra D. Responsible AI by design in practice. arXiv preprint arXiv:190912838. 2019.

[37] d'Alessandro B, O'Neil C, and LaGatta T. Conscientious classification: A data scientist's guide to discrimination-aware classification. *Big Data*. 2017; 5(2):120–134.

[38] Hardt M, Price E, and Srebro N. Equality of opportunity in supervised learning. In: *Advances In Neural Information Processing Systems*. 2016. pp. 3315–3323.

[39] Confalonieri R, Coba L, Wagner B, *et al.* A historical perspective of explainable artificial intelligence. *Wiley Interdisciplinary Reviews: Data Mining and Knowledge Discovery*. 2021;11(1):e1391.

[40] Garcez Ad, Besold TR, De Raedt L, *et al.* Neural-symbolic learning and reasoning: Contributions and challenges. In: 2015 AAAI Spring Symposium Series; 2015.

[41] Garcez Ad, Gori M, Lamb LC, *et al.* Neural-symbolic computing: An effective methodology for principled integration of machine learning and reasoning. arXiv preprint arXiv:190506088. 2019.

Chapter 8

Malware analysis in IoT devices and AI

Tehseen Mazhar[1,2]*, Muhammad Amir Malik*[3]*, Tariq Shahzad*[4]*, Waseem Ahmed*[5]*, Muhammad Shahid Anwar*[6]*, Javed Ali Khan*[7] *and Affan Yasin*[8]

Abstract

The Internet of Things (IoT) is an exciting new technology that has the potential to revolutionize many industries. The absence of security for IoT devices has resulted in a rise of malware attacks causing cyber security vulnerabilities for the IoT sector. It is becoming more difficult to find systematic and complete research on the relevance of malware detection techniques in IoT environments, such as those involving Trojans or botnets. This study was conducted to compile a comprehensive list of experimental studies relevant to the detection of malware attacks in the IoT, as well as to evaluate and critique those studies. A systematic literature review methodology introduced was used to obtain and critically assess research publications to achieve this aim. Detection approaches for malware, types of botnet attacks, and diverse harmful behaviors of malware were examined in this study. The detection approaches have been categorized depending on the methodologies utilized, and the authors analyzed the malware stages in which detection is performed. To build a foundation of information about IoT malware detection technologies, the findings of this study have helped the authors identify the research gaps in the field and recommended future research options.

[1]School of Computer Science, National College of Business Administration and Economics, Pakistan
[2]Department of Computer Science and Information Technology, School Education Department, Government of Punjab, Pakistan
[3]Department of Computer Science and Software Engineering, International Islamic University, Pakistan
[4]Department of Computer Engineering, COMSATS University Islamabad, Pakistan
[5]School of Arts and Creative Technology, University of Greater Manchester, United Kingdom
[6]IRC for Finance and Digital Economy, King Fahd University of Petroleum and Minerals, Saudi Arabia
[7]Department of Computer Science, University of Hertfordshire, UK
[8]School of AI and Advanced Computing, Xi'an Jiaotong-Liverpool University, China

8.1 Introduction

The Internet of Things (IoT) has recently gained popularity among researchers and business leaders alike. A range of IoT-enabled services are now being implemented as a consequence of the explosion in the number of IoT devices and the advancements in technology. Hardware, algorithms, sensors, actuators, and networking are all included in IoT devices, allowing them to connect, communicate, and share data. The popularity and expansion of IoT devices are rising due to their cheap cost. More than 29 billion IoT devices might be in use by the end of 2023, according to CISCO. IoT data is security protected using several machine learning and deep learning techniques. These comprise multi-layer perceptrons, rule-based approaches, recurrent neural networks, clustering, and enhancement of security aspects. Regression and classification are two often used, reputable methods for ensuring machine security in the IoT. Classification problems are generally understood as ones involving averages, outliers, or attacks—that is, projections about groups of discrete values or categories. Clustering techniques help IoT security data to expose latent structures and patterns. This will help greatly address IoT security issues including identification of fraud, cyberattacks, signatures, outliers, and anomalies. Protection of the IoT depends on systems grounded on rules. These systems can use data to ascertain security or policy guidelines. Association rule learning is a well-liked method of machine learning for identifying trends or connections in security dataset characteristics. IoT parameters are analyzed using this MLP network; malicious traffic originating from IoT devices is found; an intrusion detection model is developed; and malware in the network security laboratory - knowledge discovery in databases (NSL-KDD) dataset is investigated. In the framework of machine learning-driven security modeling, these enhanced signature features could facilitate the handling of massive IoT security data.

There will be a 20 fold increase in data flow from 1 Gbps to 20 Gbps with 5G compared to 4G. Users will benefit from significantly quicker access to data and information thanks to this development. The military, emergency services, and quick response teams will greatly value this ingenuity. Devices with 5G capabilities must have better battery solutions because the powerful signal boosters they use drain their batteries quickly.

Along with this acceleration come several significant drawbacks. 5G radio made use of high frequency ranges among other things. Consequently, latency was reduced and speed was increased. Their use is limited to relatively short distances because structures like buildings quickly block these higher frequency ranges. The use of automation in manufacturing is fantastic, but in densely populated areas, operators will need 5G radios to provide comparable coverage, and this infrastructure is simply not available in rural areas. The anticipated increase in cyberattack frequency is based on the fact that 5G connections offer noticeably faster data transfer rates. The proliferation of internet-connected devices makes them easier targets for hackers due to the weakened connections between them. With the anticipated proliferation of IoT devices brought about by 5G technology, the risk is anticipated to increase. The proliferation of the IoT makes it more difficult to address the security issues it poses.

Connecting devices to a 5G network increases the risk of data theft because hackers may have faster access to more sensitive information

The way people can communicate has been greatly altered by the exponential growth of technology. A lot of cities are going to change appearance soon because of this. Future buildings will have much more intelligence as a result of new findings in the field of building materials research, improvements in sensor technology, and the increasing convergence of data streams. To create space for new construction, several cities have destroyed their most famous landmarks. Due to changing societal expectations and technological advancements, scientists predict that cities will undergo noticeable transformations in the not-too-distant future. Because of this, those working in urban planning and construction must be nimble at all times. It is projected that between 66% and 70% of the world's population will reside in urban areas by the year 2025. IoT devices have indeed limited resources, such as low processing power and memory. Moreover, they are capable of adapting to a multitude of settings. Security solutions for IoT devices face difficulties because of these limits. IoT devices are vulnerable to malware attacks due to a lack of effective protection and standards [1]. The IoT ecosystem's problems are exacerbated by the device processing constraints. IoT devices are vulnerable to a wide range of vulnerabilities because of their design flaws. One of the most common attack scenarios involves malware gaining access to IoT devices and using them as part of an IoT botnet. Malware takes control of an IoT device after it has been infected and can carry out a variety of cyber-attacks. Finally, the intruder completes the process of taking over as many IoT devices as feasible. Thus, the intruder establishes and grows his own IoT malware swarm. Malware attacks are one of the most common criminal actions associated with IoT because it grows quickly and may do more damage than other hostile activity.

Microsoft Windows has been the most popular operating system in the world for the last several decades, with 83 percent of the market share. The IoT technology has led to a dramatic increase in the variety of computer devices in recent years. Even on resource-constrained hardware like Unix-based operating systems, IoT devices are developed on a range of CPU architectures. Due to a lack of safety design and implementation, IoT systems are becoming a favored target for attackers. DDoS assaults, port scanning, and brute-force attacks are all common aspects of IoT malware [2].

IoT cyber-attacks might have serious consequences. It is exemplified by the CISCO, a massive and well-known IoT device-exploiting malware that can cripple a DNS service firm. To make requests from ten million IP addresses, the malware can exploit closed-circuit TV cameras, firewalls, and camcorders. Because of the massive amounts of traffic produced by the attacks and the disruption they created, the Internet as a whole was rendered unusable, including sites like Twitter, the Guardian, Netflix, and CNN. It was predicted that malware attacks in IoT can exploit similar attempts in the future. IoT malware is a prominent study topic in light of that prognosis and the rapid increase of IoT devices. This study systematically reviews the literature in this domain to find the appropriate answers to the research questions regarding malware attacks in IoT.

8.2 Literature review

Malware is developed by copying its source code or a variation of the malicious code that the malware programmer initially created. IoT malware assessment: current trends and prospects, including manual examination of a subset of IoT malware samples, synthesis of multiple research studies [3,4], and more. The IoT has arisen as an important technology to support a wide range of smart settings, including smart homes, healthcare, sustainable environments, and intelligent transport systems. Families of IoT malware, such as Aidra, Bashlite, and Mirai, use scanners designed to identify devices with lax security settings, like unsecured ports or default passwords. These gadgets could be anything from medical equipment to public health and safety sensors to smart meters. Because malware can adapt to changing victim profiles, it has become more sophisticated and widespread over the last 10 years, specifically targeting the IoT. The primary causes of Mirai's surge this year are modifications to corporate IT practices, an expansion of the malware's attack vector, and the discovery of new zero-day vulnerabilities in devices. Similar to Mirai, an IBM Xforce-like malware was found in March 2019 that targets the IoT in companies. Backdoors and Bitcoin miners are some of the elements of these cyberattacks that are installed on the compromised devices.

IoT honeypots should be open-source to aid the research community in this area. To install IoT honeypots, a framework is needed. Research into which honeypots should be deployed, how attackers might be drawn to them, and how they can be improved based on the information obtained, is essential. Comparing 5G to 4G, the expected rise in data flow from 1 Gbps to 20 Gbps is a factor of 20. This development will help users to have far faster access to data and information. This creativity will be much appreciated by fast-response teams, the military, emergency services, and others. Strong signal boosters required for 5G-enabled devices greatly drain their batteries, thus improved battery solutions are vital. There are several major negative effects accompanying this acceleration. Among other things, 5G radio uses high-frequency ranges. Latency was hence dropped and speed was raised. Structures like buildings rapidly block these higher frequency ranges, so restricting their use to rather limited distances. Although manufacturing automation is great, 5G radios will be required in congested areas for operators to have similar coverage and rural areas lack the required equipment. Given that 5G connections provide noticeably faster data transfer rates, cyberattacks are expected to become more frequent. Because of the weak connections among the more internet-connected devices, hackers will thus find it simpler to exploit them. It is expected that the risk will rise in line with the expected expansion of IoT devices resulting from 5G technology. Managing the security concerns the IoT raises gets more challenging as its popularity increases. When a device is linked to a 5G network, hackers could be able to access and expropriate data—including personal information—more quickly than in past technologies. The rapid advancement of technology has fundamentally changed people's capacity for communication. This will cause many cities to look different not too distant. Thanks to fresh discoveries in the study of building materials, advances in sensor technology, and the growing convergence of data streams, future buildings will be far smarter. To make room for fresh development, some cities have demolished their most iconic sites. Scientists believe that near future changes in cities will be notable due to evolving societal expectations and technical developments. Urban designers and builders have to be therefore constantly adaptable. By 2025, 66% to 70% of persons living on Earth are expected to be city dwellers. Machine learning can accomplish a lot of tasks for machines, making their operations simpler. An "intelligent" building could facilitate routine maintenance, temperature control, and security monitoring via computers and phones. Intelligent buildings connect all of their various parts via the IoT. As the idea of the IoT grows, smart grids are being linked to larger networks in more ways. Since the IoT makes it possible for useful services that enhance everyone's experience both inside and outside of homes and protect people using established life support systems, smart grids rely heavily on it. The primary objective of this study is to determine why IoT devices should be incorporated into smart buildings [5]. Honeypots must be adapted such that they can trick the attackers into revealing their origins. The author [6] promised broad acceptance, the IoT offers a new paradigm for the Internet in which common objects fitted with sensors and actuators cooperate to create incredible economic benefits and efficiencies. The growing number of linked devices raises the possibility of security breaches in IoT networks resulting from remote login attacks including SSH and Telnet. This work aims mostly to record attacks on IoT devices using the Cowrie honeypot. These attacks are categorized using machine learning techniques including Random Forest, Support Vector Machine (SVM), Naive Bayes, and J48 decision tree. The findings show that assaults fall under surveillance, malicious payload, XOR DDoS, clean, suspicious, or SSH attack categories. Best-first search combined with subset evaluation is applied in feature selection. Following feature selection, we implement the recommended SVM model and evaluate its efficacy against baseline models including Random Forest, Naive Bayes, and the J48 decision tree.

The use of AI-based approaches for detecting IoT botnets is an attractive strategy since it may speed up the decision-making process and can be used with other trending technologies, such as SDN or blockchain. As a result, additional research is needed in this field. At the same time, a proactive strategy might assist in better understanding the mechanisms of IoT botnets and so prevent a wide range of criminal behaviors by IoT botnets from taking place, as opposed to just defending against them.

8.3 Review methodology

The study has been conducted according to the method given in Figure 8.1, systematic literature review (SLR)-based research papers relevant to the study topic to understand and identify approaches, techniques, challenges, levels, barriers, and attributes of malware detection and analysis techniques. By SLR, we mean identification, evaluation, and interpretation of all research relevant to a particular research question or topic area (IoT malware analysis and detection).

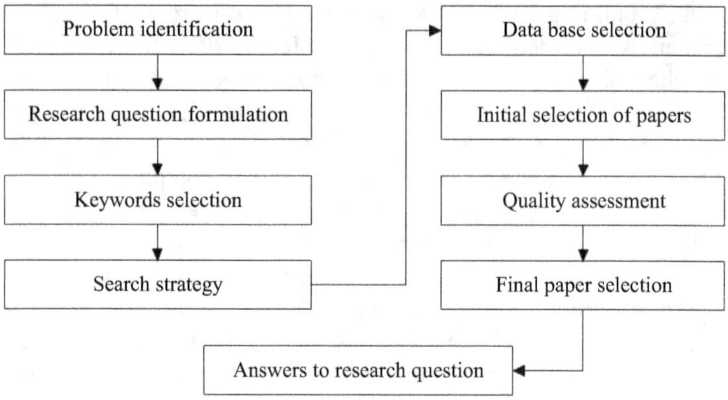

Figure 8.1 SLR methodology

8.4 Research questions

In the proposed research work, the first query about research is the type of malware attacks and their characteristics that had been conducted about malware detection in IoT to achieve an overall point of view of the systematic reviews (SRs). We illustrate all available and selected publications of research papers. Practically, we see research articles themselves analyze these studies about terms and their types including an initial study emphasizing the methodological quality of research found and depicted by topics. The application of SRs as a research methodical tool has been examined by thorough and focused analysis, use of quality, and extraction of evidence from primary studies in SLRs and has been addressed in the second research question. The motivating factor is that it caters to multiple concerns at an early stage [7]. It includes search, SR methodology, analysis, use of quality, and evidence usually not catered for in primary studies with concern and extensiveness. SRs need to discuss IoT malware detection methods. The second research question discusses types of detection methods discussed in the literature while the dataset for detection of malware using AI and machine learning lays the essential basis for our third research question. Empirical evidence provided for datasets and analysis models remains the focus of this research question. While fourth research question discusses about the use of AI classifiers in this domain.

Sl. No.	Research question	Motivation
RQ1	What are the different kinds of malware attacks mentioned in the literature?	To know about the kind of malware attacks mentioned in literature
RQ2	What are the different analysis and detection methods for IoT malware mentioned in the literature?	To know about different analysis methods and find the research gap

(Continues)

(*Continued*)

Sl. No.	Research question	Motivation
RQ3	What are different datasets available for the detection and analysis of IoT malware?	To know about dataset availability and the kind of research activities going on in this domain
RQ4	What are the different categories of classifiers used for attack detection given in the literature?	To know about types of AI classifiers used for the detection of IoT malware

Table 8.1 *Search strategy*

Primary keyword	Secondary keyword	Additional keyword
Malware analysis	Malware detection, IoT, malware analysis, machine learning methods for malware	IoT malware, malware classification, IoT malware datasets

The motive behind the decision is to carry out a tertiary study for malware analysis models instead of a specific SR there by getting a more precise overview throughout the malware detection and analysis process by considering techniques used by researchers. Key activities of requirement elicitation and their processes highlighted in models are addressed third and fourth research questions. In the end, the discussion about the results tells us about known barriers and limitations concerning malware analysis and detection in IoT. Brief answers have been made in section 8.8. The search strategy to search about the papers is given in Table 8.1.

Following data bases are searched during this SLR.

Digital library	Search string
Wiley IEEE Springer Scopus Google Scholar ACM Science Direct	("malware" AND "detection" OR "analysis" OR "method" or technique) AND ("IoT" OR "internet of things")

8.5 Criteria for selection of studies

Papers are selected from 2006 to 2021 during the past fifteen years. After that different steps are performed for quality assessment of papers. First title title-based filtering is performed. Then abstract and keyword-based filtering of papers is used to select papers. After that, a paper quality assessment is performed. Inclusion and exclusion criteria for papers are given in the following.

1) The inclusion criteria considered for SR: 1.1 Articles indicating an SR on requirement elicitation.

Articles on related topics and synonyms, as well as the analysis and detection of malware in IoT environments. Every article was presented at conferences and published in periodicals. Presentations from workshops, peer-reviewed journals, technical reports, and book chapters will all be taken into consideration.

- All things are universally understood in English.
- The exclusion criteria were taken into account.
- All kinds of theses, including PhD and Master's theses.

Articles from every journal on Beall's List of unscrupulous publishers. These reviews of the literature are all unapproved. While discussing SRs, all of the articles omit to provide the actual findings from the original SR. articles that did not contain the findings of a SR and instead just addressed education or instruction. Examples of literary works that fall short of being innovative and fail to present a fresh viewpoint or point of view are lengthy workshop recaps, in-depth introductions, and editorials.

8.6 Conduct of search process

To find primary and secondary articles on the subject of malware analysis and detection in the IoT carried out a thorough search of electronic databases. All academic works that have been subjected to peer review are included in this study, along with conference proceedings and workshops like the International Workshops on this topic. Web of Science, IEEE Xplore, Science Direct, Springer, Scopus, and the ACM Digital Library were among the resources we used. The essential search terms that were included in the search query and helped us accomplish our study goal are listed in the table above. To create an initial search string for the pilot, the Boolean AND operators were used to connect key terms, while the OR operators were used to produce synonyms and other terms [8]. The subsequent actions were performed to generate the first search string. Finally, we manually reviewed all of the paper titles that were presented at the International Conference on EASE, which is a major forum for the distribution of systematic reviews, between 2005 and 2021. You can access these documents online.

There have been four different stages to the hunt. In the second week of November 2023, the SLR topic selection was finished. The second phase of the project was launched in mid-November 2021. Starting on November 21, 2023, all of our searches were finished on November 28, 2023. On November 27, 2023, work on the first draft was initiated. The whole sequence of the four steps is shown in Figure 8.2. Furthermore, search tactics were used to improve and elevate the search quality to choose and locate research articles using the available search methods (Table 8.2).

1. Snowballing search:
   (a) Backward searches (references)
   (b) Forwarded searches (references)
2. Criteria based on Clincy and Shahriar [9] SLR
3. Database searches (Figures 8.3 and 8.4).

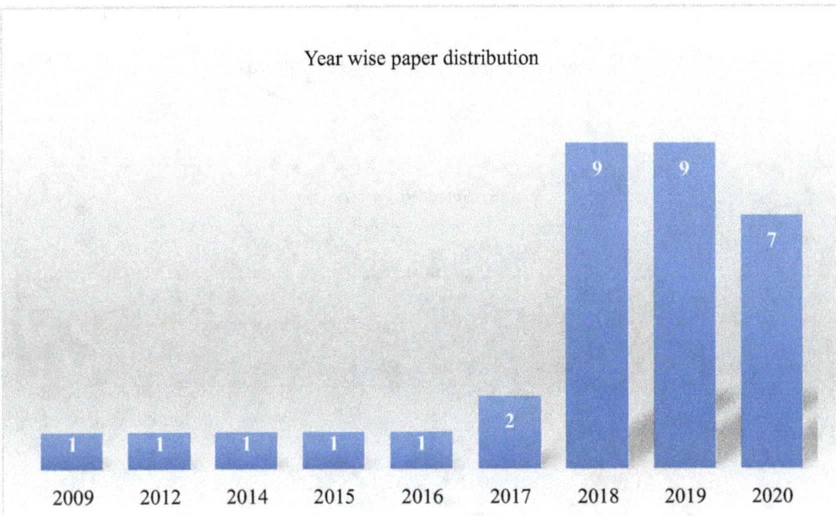

Figure 8.2 Year-wise distribution of papers

Table 8.2 Paper Screening

Phase	Process	Selection criteria	IEEE	Wiley	Google Scholar	Springer	ACM	Science Direct	Total
1	Searching	Keywords	16	4	11	4	5	7	47
2	Screening	Title	14	4	10	4	1	6	39
3	Further screening	Abstract	13	4	10	4	1	5	37
4	Further screening	Introduction and conclusion	12	3	10	4	1	4	34
5	Evaluation	Complete article	12	2	10	4	1	3	32

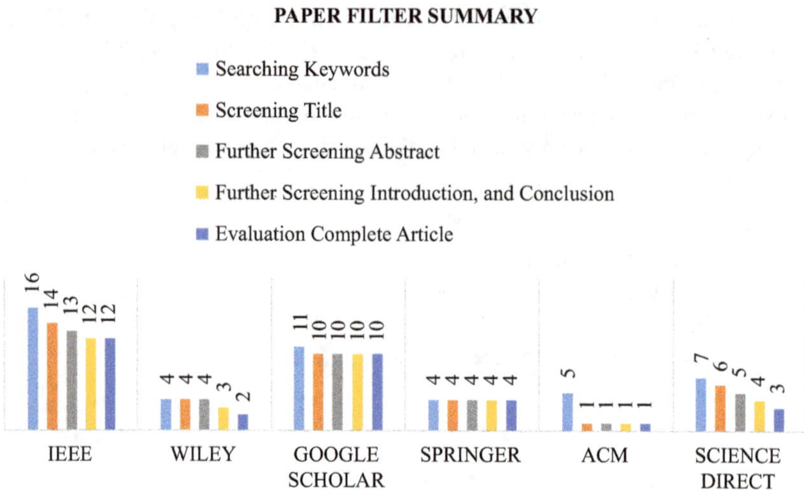

Figure 8.3 Paper filtration summary

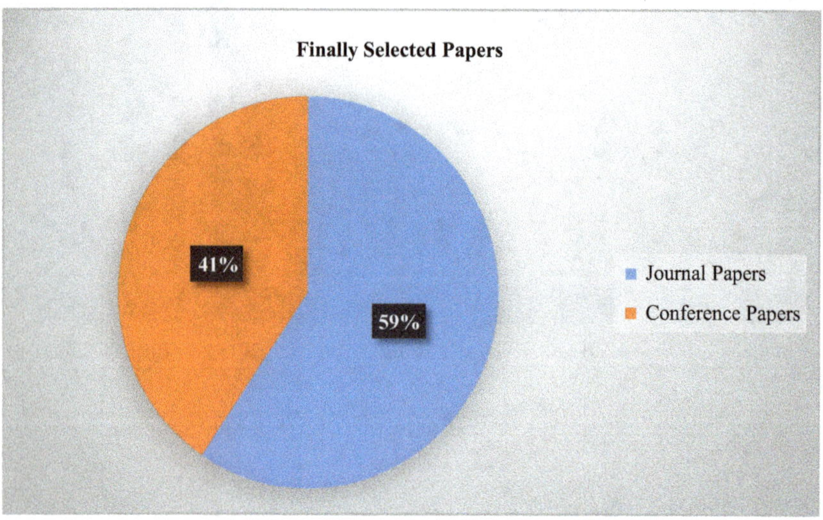

Figure 8.4 Finally included papers

8.7 Quality assessment of papers

Following the selection process, a quality assessment is performed on the articles. The following criteria are used to categorize the papers:

(a) Mark receives a value of 1 if the title includes a keyword; if not, it receives a value of 0.

Table 8.3 Quality Assessment of Papers

Reference	Medium	Year	Quality assessment				
			(a)	(b)	(c)	(d)	Score
[10]	*	2017	+	+	+	+	@
[11]	*	2019	+	+	+	+	@
[9]	*	2019	+	+	+	+	@
[12]	*	2014	+	+	+	+	@
[3]	#	2020	+	+	+	+	@
[13]	#	2020	$	+	+	+	"
[13]	*	2018	$	+	+	+	"
[14]	#	2016	$	+	+	+	"
[15]	*	2018	$	+	+	+	"
[6]	*	2019	+	$	+	+	"
[8]	#	2009	+	$	+	+	"
[16]	#	2020	+	+	+	+	@
[17]	#	2019	+	$	+	+	"
[18]	#	2019	+	+	+	+	@
[19]	#	2017	+	+	+	+	@
[20]	*	2018	+	+	+	+	@

(b) If the abstract makes the performance evaluation criteria clear, it receives a score of 1; if not, it receives a score of 0.
(c) If the first and last paragraphs include performance measurements, the grade is 1, and if not, the grade is 0.
(d) If a publication compares its results to at least one previous study, it receives a grade of 1. If not, a score of 0 is given.
(e) The final results will include any paper that has a score higher than 3.

We have used different notations in Table 8.3 to represent conferences and journals. Similarly, we have used different symbols to represent digits 1, 2.3, and 4 Conference=*, while journal = #, 1=+, 0=$, 3=" 4=@

8.8 Results

RQ1: What are the different kinds of malware attacks mentioned in the literature?

The first goal of this study is to provide the kinds and scenarios of cyber-attacks with Malware attacks that have been examined by the selected studies, which is an important part of the research. It is clear from this evaluation and analysis of all studies reviewed, that they dealt with four categories of cyber-attacks or harmful activities, namely, IoT botnets, scanning attacks, and IoT malware analysis. We will go through the different forms of attacks that have been looked at by the studies that have been chosen. The table below shows examples of these.

Type of attack	Remarks
Botnets	This is a network of routers that has been compromised by malicious software, notably IoT botnet malware, and is currently under the control of hostile actors.
Malware	Attacks by malware are self-replicating, like the virus they are. IoT devices are vulnerable to this virus because their factory default login information is used to infect them. It is used by hackers to infect a large number of devices.
DoS/DDoS	DDoS attacks in the IoT network are a developing problem that has to be addressed. Due to IoT devices' limited storage and bandwidth, DDoS attacks can take advantage of this problem in IoT applications.
Port Scans, keylogger, Rootkit	A port scan is a mechanism for identifying whether ports on a network are open. Port scanning is like knocking on doors to check whether somebody is at home, as ports are where information is exchanged.
Ransom ware	Malware in the form of ransomware can encrypt data, rendering computers and the systems that rely on them unusable. The data will be encrypted, and the thieves will demand cash to decrypt it.

RQ2: What are the characteristics of different analysis and detection methods for IoT malware mentioned in the literature?

Difference techniques are studied in the papers evaluated for their rationale and commented for their advantages and shortcomings.

Features used	Rationale	Algorithm/ method	Remarks
Operation code	Node identification using opcode sequence	Artificial neural networks	No other than ARM-based samples tested
Operation code pattern	Fuzzy pattern analysis for malicious node detection	Fuzzy logic	No other than ARM-based samples tested
Operation code frequency	Opcode frequency-based detection	Traditional machine learning	ARM-based samples tested only
Operation code	Vex intermediate-based detection	Supervised machine learning algorithms	Only the MIPS sample tested
Used strings	Malware classification using signature strings	Unsupervised clustering	Slow and only for four malware families
Executable and linkable format header	Malware detection from binary file reading	Supervised machine learning	Binary file structure can be modified and changeable

(Continues)

(*Continued*)

Features used	Rationale	Algorithm/ method	Remarks
Image (grayscale)	Convert binary strings to grayscale to classify malicious node	Artificial neural network	Accuracy loss when encryption is applied
Function call graph	Used 23 attributes and generate a function graph for detection	Multiple machine learning methods	Slow method and incorrect properties used
Operation codegraph	Create a graph of opcode using CFG for detection	Graph-based Analysis	ARM samples only

RQ3:What are different datasets available for the detection and analysis of IoT malware?

The following datasets were found in the literature that can be used for the evaluation of machine learning methods.

Dataset name	Description
N-BaIoT	This collection addresses a market gap for readily accessible botnet datasets, particularly those about IoT. This means that real traffic data and nine commercial IoT devices that were actually compromised by BASHLITE and Mirai will be used.
BoT-IoT	The University of New South Wales Canberra's Cyber Range Lab assembled the BoT-IoT dataset by building a realistic network environment. There were several types of traffic in the network environment, including botnet and ordinary traffic. There are just a few alternative formats in which the primary dataset files can be kept. Here, we are referring to files in the argus, original pcap, and CSV formats. During the classification process, partitioning the files based on the type and subcategory of the attack made for more effective support.
IoT-23	The IoT-23 dataset consists of a recently gathered collection of network traffic samples from IoT devices. We performed three captures of traffic originating from non-malicious IoT devices and twenty captures of malware on IoT devices.
MedBIot	The hybrid network built inside the system consists of 83 actual and virtual IoT devices. No prior data was collected on the integration of such devices. The deployment of real malware resulted in the acquisition of actual malware network data. The following three well-known forms of botnet malware were used: Based on the Mirai, Torii, and BashLite codebases.

RQ4: What are the different categories of classifiers used for attack detection given in the literature?

Solutions and techniques provided in the Papers evaluated in this study were categorized in the following subcategories.

Serial no.	Category
1	Supervised machine learning methods
2	Unsupervised machine learning methods
3	Deep learning detection methods
4	Blockchain detection methods
5	SDN detection methods
6	Specification-based detection methods
7	Signature-based detection methods

8.9 Discussion

There are several research gaps, unresolved questions, and future directions after examining the papers considered for this study. In this part, we explain the significance of each one of them. Scanning, replication, and attack are the three stages of the IoT malware lifecycle, which is divided into three sections. Throughout these stages, the bots and the C&C communicate with one another and with the bots. Although several research has created detection methods for Malware attacks in the latter stages, when they are initiating and triggering cyberattacks on the targets, it is evident that the same methods might have been used to identify the malware in earlier stages, such as during scanning or propagation operations. As a result, researchers need to focus on detecting and disrupting IoT malware in their early stages before they begin to attack so that the IoT network can continue to function properly. Detection of Malware is focused on identifying DoS/DDoS, scanning, and IoT malware intrusions conducted by Malware Mirai—rather than other attacks, such as those launched by other malware. Recent developments in attacks, including as attacks aimed at unlawfully exploiting IoT devices' computing capacity, such as crypto mining, other jobs, or fraud on social media, have not been included in the reviews. In addition, the paucity of datasets, difficulties in performing various sorts of shady studies and the absence of simulations were all factors that contributed to this. In these areas, further research is required.

8.10 Conclusion

The majority of the papers presented here offered artificial intelligence-based approaches (AI). AI is seen to be an attractive strategy in identifying IoT botnets since it can speed up the decision-making process, and these approaches and techniques might be combined with other trending technologies, such as SDN or blockchain, to develop more effective tactics. As a result, additional research is needed in this area. Simultaneously time, the offered solutions tend to focus on defensive measures, but a proactive approach might assist in understanding IoT botnet strategies and therefore avoid the harm that may be produced by a range of malicious IoT malware activities.

References

[1] Mazhar, T., D.B. Talpur, and T.A. Shloul, *et al.*, Analysis of IoT security challenges and its solutions using artificial intelligence. *Brain Sciences*, 2023. **13**(4): p. 683.

[2] Esmaeili, B., A. Azmoodeh, A. Dehghantanha, G. Srivastava, H. Karimipour, and J.C.W. Lin, A GNN-based adversarial internet of things malware detection framework for critical infrastructure: Studying Gafgyt, Mirai and Tsunami campaigns. *IEEE Internet of Things Journal*, 2023 **11**(16): pp. 26826–26836.

[3] Dange, S. and M. Chatterjee, IoT botnet: The largest threat to the IoT network. In *Data Communication and Networks: Proceedings of GUCON 2019*. 2019, Berlin: Springer. pp. 137–157.

[4] Sengupta, J., S. Ruj, and S.D. Bit, A comprehensive survey on attacks, security issues and blockchain solutions for IoT and IIoT. *Journal of Network and Computer Applications*, 2020. **149**: p. 102481.

[5] Mazhar, T., M.A. Malik, and I. Haq *et al.*, The role of ML, AI and 5G technology in smart energy and smart building management. *Electronics*, 2022. **11**(23): p. 3960.

[6] Shrivastava, R.K., B. Bashir, and C. Hota, Attack detection and forensics using honeypot in IoT environment. In *Proceedings of the 15th International Conference on Distributed Computing and Internet Technology, ICDCIT 2019*, Bhubaneswar, India, January 10–13, 2019. 2019. Berlin: Springer.

[7] Pati, D. and L.N. Lorusso, How to write a systematic review of the literature. *HERD: Health Environments Research & Design Journal*, 2018. **11**(1): pp. 15–30.

[8] Kitchenham, B., O.P. Brereton, D. Budgen, M. Turner, J. Bailey, and S. Linkman, Systematic literature reviews in software engineering—a systematic literature review. *Information and Software Technology*, 2009. **51**(1): pp. 7–15.

[9] Clincy, V. and H. Shahriar, IoT malware analysis. In *2019 IEEE 43rd Annual Computer Software and Applications Conference (COMPSAC)*. 2019. Piscataway, NJ: IEEE.

[10] Wang, A., R. Liang, X. Liu, Y. Zhang, K. Chen, and J. Li, March. An inside look at IoT malware. In *International Conference on Industrial IoT Technologies and Applications*. 2017. Cham: Springer International Publishing. pp. 176–186.

[11] Abusnaina, A., A. Khormali, H. Alasmary, J. Park, A. Anwar, and A. Mohaisen, Adversarial learning attacks on graph-based IoT malware detection systems. In *2019 IEEE 39th International Conference on Distributed Computing Systems (ICDCS)*. 2019. Piscataway, NJ: IEEE pp. 1296–1305.

[12] Allix, K., Q. Jérome, T.F. Bissyandé, J. Klein, R. State, and Y.L. Traon, A forensic analysis of Android malware—how is malware written and how it could be detected? In *2014 IEEE 38th Annual Computer Software and Applications Conference*. 2014. Piscataway, NJ: IEEE pp. 384–393.

[13] Ji, Y., L. Yao, S. Liu, H. Yao, Q. Ye, and R. Wang, The study on the botnet and its prevention policies in the Internet of Things. In *2018 IEEE 22nd International Conference on Computer Supported Cooperative Work in Design (CSCWD)*. 2018. Piscataway, NJ: IEEE. pp. 837–842.

[14] Pa, Y.M.P., S. Suzuki, K. Yoshioka, T. Matsumoto, T. Kasama, and C. Rossow, IoTPOT: A novel honeypot for revealing current IoT threats. *Journal of Information Processing*, 2016. **24**(3): pp. 522–533.

[15] Hakim, M.A., H. Aksu, A.S. Uluagac, and Kemal Akkaya, U-pot: A honeypot framework for UPnP-based IoT devices. arXiv preprint arXiv:1812.05558, 2018.

[16] Nguyen, H.-T., Q.-D. Ngo, and V.-H. Le, A novel graph-based approach for IoT botnet detection. *International Journal of Information Security*, 2020. **19** (5): pp. 567–577.

[17] Chen, Z., S. Guo, J. Wang, Y. Li, and Z. Lu, Toward FPGA security in IoT: A new detection technique for hardware Trojans. *IEEE Internet of Things Journal*, 2019. **6**(4): pp. 7061–7068.

[18] Lima Filho, F.S., F.A.F Silveira, A.M. Brito Jr., G. Vargas-Solar, and L.F. Silveira, Smart detection: An online approach for DoS/DDoS attack detection using machine learning. *Security and Communication Networks*, 2019. **1**: p. 1574749.

[19] Van der Elzen, I. and J. van Heugten, Techniques for detecting compromised IoT devices. University of Amsterdam, Amsterdam, 2017.

[20] Dietz, C., R.L. Castro, and J. Steinberger, IoT-botnet detection and isolation by access routers. In *2018 9th International Conference on the Network of the Future (NOF)*. 2018. Piscataway, NJ: IEEE. pp. 88–95.

Chapter 9

A multimodal framework for intrusion detection in IoT: integrating transfer learning, game theory, and Nash equilibrium

Ali Turab[1], Farhan Ullah[2] and Shujaat Ali Zaidi[3]

Abstract

The Internet of Things (IoT) encounters increasing security challenges, particularly from distributed denial of service attacks that can disrupt device functionality by overwhelming network resources. This work presents a comprehensive solution utilizing game theory to tackle IoT security challenges. We model the problem through a game-theoretic framework, deriving the Nash equilibrium and exploring optimal response functions. In line with this theoretical framework, we employ a multimodal big data approach, enhanced by transfer learning, to validate our findings. Network data is extracted from Packet Capture files, with big data optimization techniques applied to manage large datasets effectively. Transfer learning methods, such as word2vec, are used to capture semantic features, while network bytes are converted into images for feature extraction via an attention-enhanced residual network. These multimodal features are employed to classify attacks, demonstrating the practical effectiveness of the proposed model. Evaluation on established IoT datasets, including Edge-IIoT, CIC-IoT 2022, and CIC-IoT 2023, reveals an accuracy of 98.2%, confirming the validity of our approach.

9.1 Introduction

With the growing complexity and widespread adoption of modern communication technologies, ensuring the security of interconnected systems has become a significant challenge. The Internet of Things (IoT) plays a key role in this transformation, interconnecting devices across cities and even entire countries [1]. Improved connectivity speeds and bandwidth enable IoT devices to gather,

[1]School of Software, Northwestern Polytechnical University, China
[2]Cybersecurity Center, Prince Mohammad Bin Fahd University, Saudi Arabia
[3]Department of Computer Science, Faculty of Science, Chiang Mai University, Thailand

transmit, and process large volumes of data effectively, facilitating the creation of intelligent services such as autonomous vehicles, automated monitoring systems, and cyber-physical networks. Nonetheless, the sensitive information produced by these devices underscores the urgent need for comprehensive privacy safeguards and rigorous data security protocols (see [2,3]). As cyber threats continue to evolve, new security frameworks and strategies have emerged to address these risks. One such framework is game theory, which has been applied to security scenarios for nearly two decades. Game theory has proven to be an effective tool for modeling the competitive dynamics between attackers and defenders, offering insights into optimizing defense strategies under resource constraints. Its application to security systems leverages its foundational principle: the strategic optimization of opposing goals, making it a natural fit for the cybersecurity domain.

However, applying game theory to security presents unique challenges that differ from its traditional use in economics. While economic models focus on rational actors seeking to maximize utility, security interactions are more complex, with threats constantly evolving and defenders needing to respond in real-time. Unlike the idealized notion of security as the complete absence of threats, game theory allows us to conceptualize security more realistically. It frames security as a state in which the cost of launching an attack exceeds the benefits, thus deterring adversaries from acting. This perspective shifts the focus from eliminating all threats to managing risks effectively and efficiently (see [4–7]).

Despite this theoretical advance, much of the current research in security remains focused on preventing every conceivable attack, often at significant expense. This approach overlooks the potential benefits of optimizing defense efforts to achieve the highest possible security within practical limits. Quantifying security in a meaningful way remains a challenge. While security is not a physical quantity that can be measured precisely, it can be scored, allowing decision-makers to assess vulnerabilities and allocate resources more strategically. Game theory provides the tools to evaluate these complex dynamics and guide optimal defense strategies. Risk in cybersecurity is multifaceted. Attacks may not always aim to cause direct financial damage or steal sensitive information. Instead, some focus on reputational harm, undermining the credibility of the victim without inflicting physical or monetary losses. Managing such risks requires a comprehensive approach that accounts for the diverse goals of potential attackers and the varying forms of harm they might cause.

As IoT systems continue to integrate into everyday operations, the need for effective methods of identifying and mitigating security threats has grown. Network intrusion detection systems (NIDS), especially those utilizing machine learning (ML) and deep learning (DL) approaches, have gained considerable attention due to their capability to identify misuse and anomalies in IoT environments. However, these systems often face limitations when dealing with novel or evolving forms of intrusion due to the complexity and scale of the big data generated by IoT devices. Additionally, existing ML algorithms struggle with multimodal data, highlighting the need for further advancements in hybrid feature engineering to improve detection capabilities (see [6–9]).

To address these limitations, big data analytics provides an avenue for improving cybersecurity through the analysis of network traffic, system events, and logs. Platforms like Apache Spark enable efficient processing of the large volumes of data generated by IoT systems, making real-time intrusion detection feasible (see Figure 9.1). Spark's memory-driven resilient distributed dataset (RDD) approach allows for rapid handling of massive datasets, an essential feature for responding to real-time security threats. While traditional ML and DL techniques prioritize performance over a deep understanding of network semantics, semantic-based feature engineering can improve the detection of obfuscated malicious scripts. However, text-based analysis faces challenges such as code obfuscation and reordering, which complicate detection. In contrast, image-based feature extraction captures structural information from network data, including memory, process, and header details. This dynamic approach provides a more comprehensive view of potential threats.

To enhance detection capabilities, we propose a multimodal approach that combines both text-based and visual features for identifying harmful scripts and network anomalies. This paper introduces a novel IoT-based NIDS that integrates both semantic and visual data. A custom-designed crawler extracts network flows from Packet Capture (PCAP) files, with a word2vec model used to derive semantic features. These byte streams are converted into images, allowing for the extraction of texture features using an attention-based residual network (ResNet). Combining these multimodal features significantly enhances intrusion detection performance (see [10–12]).

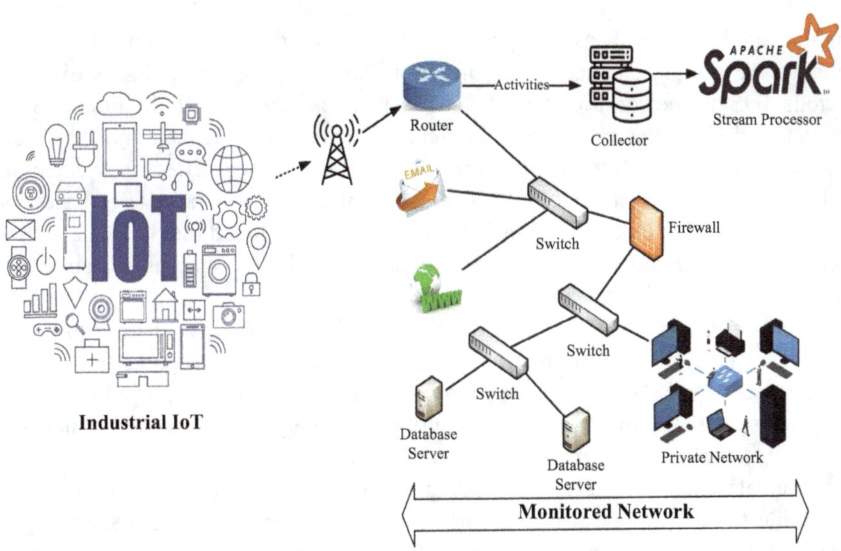

Figure 9.1 Spark-based stream processing for IoT network traffic monitoring

A distinguishing feature of this work is the use of game theory to validate the proposed system. Through the application of Nash equilibrium (NE) and mathematical modeling, we design a robust and dependable IoT-focused NIDS that strategically optimizes security resources, accounting for the evolving landscape of network threats. This approach ensures that the defense strategy is optimized, adapting to the evolving tactics of attackers and the shifting nature of network vulnerabilities. The main contributions of this chapter are:

- Custom datasets were developed from PCAP files derived from the CIC-IoT 2022 and 2023 datasets, including various attack types, such as camera-based flood attacks and DDoS attacks.
- The implementation of a Spark-based optimization framework for efficient data extraction, enabling the analysis of large-scale datasets.
- The formulation of a technique that transforms network byte data into images, enabling visual feature extraction through an attention-based ResNet model.
- Implementation of a game theory-based validation framework that enhances the robustness and reliability of the proposed NIDS by utilizing NE to optimize detection efficiency.

The remainder of this chapter is structured as follows: Section 9.2 reviews the related literature; Section 9.3 discusses the game-theoretic foundation of the proposed model; Section 9.4 explains the proposed approach; Section 9.5 provides the experimental analysis; and Section 9.6 concludes the chapter.

9.2 Literature review and background

The growing complexity of IoT ecosystems has necessitated the development of sophisticated security measures, particularly intrusion detection systems (IDS) that cater to the unique characteristics of IoT networks. Prior research has explored various IDS frameworks designed to detect attacks such as Hello Flood, Sybil attacks, and sinkholes in IoT environments. For instance, Stephen and Arockiam [13] proposed an IDS framework tailored to the RPL protocol, effectively detecting Hello Flood and Sybil attacks by evaluating the intrusion ratio (IR) based on packets received and delivered. In [14], the authors developed the SVELTE IDS to identify unauthorized network access, focusing on threats such as selective forwarding and sinkhole attacks.

Despite these advancements, traditional IDS approaches face significant challenges in coping with the vast amount of network data generated by IoT devices (see [15–18]). The introduction of big data analytics has played a key role in addressing these limitations by enabling the analysis of large-scale network traffic. Researchers have applied ML and DL techniques to develop more accurate IDS models (see [19–22]). For example, in [23], the authors utilized Spark streaming to analyze real-time network traffic, addressing challenges such as port scanning and mirrored breaches. However, many existing IDS systems struggle to handle multimodal data, which includes both text and image-based information, limiting their ability to detect complex IoT-specific attacks (for more details, refer to [23–30]).

Game theory has emerged as an essential tool for optimizing security strategies, particularly in the context of IoT networks, where dynamic interactions between attackers and defenders must be continuously managed [31,32]. In cybersecurity, game theory facilitates the modeling of strategic decision-making processes between adversaries. For instance, Markov chain models combined with game theory have been used to evaluate the security of DNS servers. A dynamic node-evolution model for honeynet environments, presented in [33], further illustrates the utility of game theory in optimizing defense strategies by modeling the decision-making process in the face of evolving attack patterns.

Central to these applications is the concept of NE, which provides a means to determine the optimal strategies for attackers and defenders in a non-cooperative game. For instance, [34] applied NE to optimize network security strategies in cloud computing environments, while [35] showed that a unique NE can be identified when attackers are numerous. In practical terms, NE is particularly useful for optimizing resource allocation in IoT security, ensuring that defenders can strategically allocate resources to maximize security while minimizing costs. The role of Bayesian NE has also been explored in scenarios where incomplete information plays a critical role, such as in the case of false data injection attacks [36]. However, existing research in game-theoretic models often emphasizes theoretical constructs without fully addressing the practical challenges of real-world IoT security. In practice, attackers and defenders frequently operate with incomplete information, requiring adaptive strategies that evolve over time. This dynamic nature of attack-defense scenarios is particularly critical in IoT environments, where the high volume and diversity of data necessitate more sophisticated, real-time responses. Researchers have developed methods to address these challenges, such as cooperative authentication models based on evolutionary game theory [37] and dynamic Bayesian game-theoretic approaches for analyzing false data injection attacks (see [38–40]).

Our work addresses these gaps by combining game theory and NE with a multimodal big data approach. Traditional IDS methods often struggle with scalability and lack the capability to effectively integrate text and image-based data, limiting their ability to detect a wide range of IoT-specific attacks. By leveraging transfer learning, our approach improves the extraction of meaningful features from multimodal data, significantly enhancing the system's ability to detect evolving threats in real time. Additionally, the application of game theory allows for the optimization of defense strategies under uncertain and dynamic conditions, ensuring that our system can effectively allocate resources and respond to new attack patterns.

9.3 Game-theoretic modeling: preliminaries

A game, in its most basic form, is a mathematical structure designed to model strategic interactions between rational players. These players can be individuals, groups, organizations, or systems, each seeking to optimize a certain outcome by choosing from a set of available actions. The essential elements of any game are:

- **Players:** The decision-makers in the game, denoted by the set $N = \{1, 2, \ldots, n\}$. Each player i represents an individual entity capable of selecting actions.
- **Actions:** Each player selects an action from their available action set, denoted by A_i for player i. A strategy, σ_i, is a rule that specifies the action a player will take given any situation in the game.
- **Outcomes:** The result of the game depends on the combination of actions chosen by all players, producing an outcome that may result in payoffs such as rewards or penalties.
- **Preferences:** Players have preferences over the possible outcomes of the game, represented using utility functions u_i, which assign a numerical value to each outcome based on the player's satisfaction.

Strategic interactions become particularly interesting when the outcome for any player depends not only on their own actions but also on the actions taken by others. This interdependence is the key feature that makes game theory suitable for analyzing competitive scenarios. Games can be classified according to various factors, such as the timing of moves, the availability of information, and the presence of uncertainty. The main distinctions include:

- **Static versus dynamic games**: In a static game, players make decisions simultaneously without knowing the choices of others. In contrast, a dynamic game allows players to make decisions sequentially over time, with future actions possibly depending on previous moves.
- **Complete versus incomplete information**: A game of complete information assumes that all players know the structure of the game and the preferences of other players. In incomplete information games, players have limited knowledge of certain elements, such as payoffs or strategies of their opponents.
- **Deterministic versus stochastic games**: In deterministic games, the outcome is solely determined by the players' actions. Stochastic games introduce randomness, where certain outcomes are influenced by probability, adding an element of uncertainty.

An extensive form game provides a detailed representation of the sequence of moves in a game, capturing the order of actions, the information available at each point, and the payoffs at the end. The formal definition of an extensive form game, represented as a tuple, is as follows:

$$G = \left(N, A, H, P, \{u_i\}_{i \in N}\right)$$

where:

- N is the set of players participating in the game.
- A is the set of all possible actions available to the players.
- H is the set of all possible histories of actions, where a history represents a sequence of moves made by the players up to a given point.

- $P: H\backslash Z \rightarrow N$ is a function that designates which player makes a move at a given history $h \in H$, with $Z \subseteq H$ being the set of terminal histories where the game concludes.
- $u_i : Z \rightarrow \mathbb{R}$ is the utility function for each player i, assigning a real number (payoff) to each terminal history, representing the player's outcome at the end of the game.

This framework captures the sequential nature of actions, player choices at each decision point, and the respective payoffs upon reaching terminal states.

A strategy for player i, denoted by σ_i, is a mapping from the set of histories at which player i is required to act, to the set of available actions at those histories. The strategy profile $\sigma = (\sigma_1, \sigma_2, \ldots, \sigma_n)$ represents the collection of strategies chosen by all players. Given a strategy profile, the outcome of the game is determined, and each player receives a corresponding payoff.

In game theory, the NE, named after John Nash, is a fundamental concept that describes a stable state in a game where no player has an incentive to change their strategy unilaterally. This equilibrium condition implies that each player's strategy is optimal, given the strategies of all other players. In other words, no player can achieve a better payoff by deviating from their chosen strategy, assuming the other players maintain their strategies. Formally, a strategy profile $\sigma^* = (\sigma_1^*, \sigma_2^*, \ldots, \sigma_n^*)$ constitutes a NE if, for every player i and any alternative strategy σ_i:

$$u_i(\sigma_{-i}, \sigma_i^*) \geq u_i(\sigma_{-i}, \sigma_i), \tag{9.1}$$

where σ_{-i} represents the strategies chosen by all players except player i.

In this equilibrium state, each player is effectively playing their best response to the strategies of the other players. Thus, the NE ensures that every player's strategy is optimal given the strategies of their opponents, and no one can benefit by changing their own strategy alone.

Theorem 9.1: In every finite game, there exists at least one mixed strategy NE, wherein each player can employ a probability distribution over their available strategies to achieve an equilibrium.

Definition 9.1: *A strategy σ_i for player i is said to be strictly dominated if there exists another strategy τ_i such that, regardless of what the other players do, τ_i always provides a higher payoff than σ_i. Formally, σ_i is strictly dominated if, for all strategy profiles σ_{-i} of the other players:*

$$u_i(\sigma_{-i}, \tau_i) > u_i(\sigma_{-i}, \sigma_i). \tag{9.2}$$

A weaker form of domination, known as weak dominance, allows τ_i to provide an equal or better payoff in all cases, with strict inequality for at least one strategy profile of the other players:

$$u_i(\sigma_{-i}, \tau_i) \geq u_i(\sigma_{-i}, \sigma_i), \text{ and } u_i(\sigma_{-i}, \tau_i) > u_i(\sigma_{-i}, \sigma_i) \text{ for some } \sigma_{-i}. \tag{9.3}$$

The process of repeatedly eliminating strictly dominated strategies often simplifies the analysis of games, as players are unlikely to choose such strategies. This process leads to a reduced game where only rational strategies remain. Importantly, the final set of strategies after this elimination process is equivalent across all iterations.

Theorem 9.2: Let G_1 and G_2 be two games resulting from the repeated elimination of dominated strategies from the same initial game. Then $G_1 = G_2$, meaning that the remaining strategies are identical.

In certain games, players may utilize mixed strategies, where they select from their available actions based on a probability distribution. For player *i*, a mixed strategy is defined as a probability distribution $\sigma_i \in \Delta(S_i)$ over the set of actions S_i that are available to that player. The expected utility for player *i* when all players follow the mixed strategy profile $\sigma = (\sigma_1, \sigma_2, \ldots, \sigma_n)$ is computed as:

$$u_i(\sigma) = \mathbb{E}_{s \sim \sigma}[u_i(s)], \tag{9.4}$$

where *s* represents a specific realization of the mixed strategy profile. This expected utility reflects the average payoff player *i* anticipates based on the probability-weighted outcomes of their strategy choices and those of the other players.

Theorem 9.3: Every finite game has a mixed strategy NE.

Definition 9.2: *A best response for player i to a strategy profile σ_{-i} of the other players is a strategy σ_i that maximizes player i's expected utility. Formally, σ_i is a best response if:*

$$u_i(\sigma_{-i}, \sigma_i) \geq u_i(\sigma_{-i}, \tau_i) \quad \text{for all } \tau_i \in S_i. \tag{9.5}$$

Proposition 9.1: *In a mixed strategy NE, every strategy played with positive probability by a player must be a best response to the strategies of the other players.*

Definition 9.3: *A strategy σ_i for player i is strictly dominant if, for every possible strategy profile of the other players, σ_i provides a higher utility than any other strategy. Formally, σ_i is strictly dominant if:*

$$u_i(\sigma_{-i}, \sigma_i) > u_i(\sigma_{-i}, \tau_i) \text{ for all } \tau_i \in S_i \text{ and all } \sigma_{-i}. \tag{9.6}$$

Theorem 9.4: If a player has a strictly dominant strategy, then that strategy will always be part of any pure NE.

9.3.1 Mathematical formulation of the IoT security problem

Figure 9.2 presents a structured framework that illustrates the game-theoretical interactions between defenders and attackers within the IoT security scenario. This

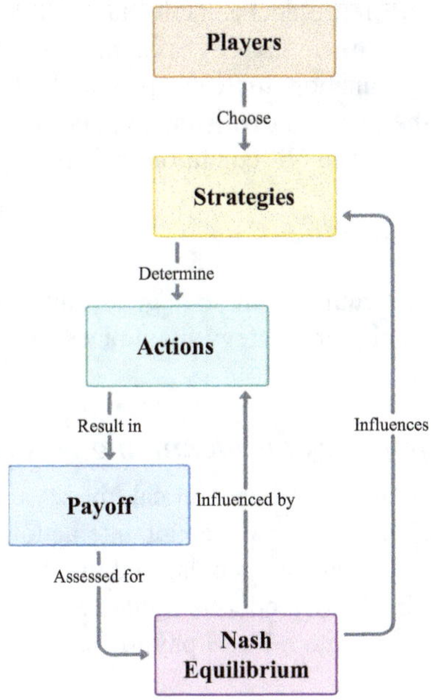

Figure 9.2 *Cyclic interaction of players, strategies, and payoffs in NE*

framework underscores the process of making strategic choices, where resulting outcomes are examined to determine the NE. The NE serves as a basis for guiding future decisions within the system, promoting stability in players' strategies by discouraging unilateral deviations. This proposed IDS game-theoretical model incorporates attack-defense strategies aimed at maximizing or minimizing payoffs. The essential components of this model are outlined as follows:

- The set of players, denoted as $\mathcal{X} = \{\mathcal{X}_1, \mathcal{X}_2, \ldots, \mathcal{X}_n\}$ with $n \geq 2$, represents both the defender and attacker within the IoT network. The defender's goal is to maintain the integrity of the system, while the attacker seeks to exploit vulnerabilities within the network.
- The term 'actions' refers to the strategic decisions that each player can make. The action space for each player $\mathcal{X}_i$ is represented by $\mathcal{B}_i$. Attackers may select different attack vectors, while defenders must choose appropriate detection and mitigation methods. The total set of actions is defined as $\mathcal{B} = \{\mathcal{B}_1, \mathcal{B}_2, \ldots, \mathcal{B}_n\}$.
- Strategies describe how players make decisions based on their available information. A player's strategy set is denoted by $\mathcal{L}_i$, and the overall strategy profile is represented by $\mathcal{L} = \{\mathcal{L}_1, \mathcal{L}_2, \ldots, \mathcal{L}_n\}$. Attackers attempt to evade detection, while defenders focus on efficient detection with minimal resource usage.
- Payoffs are the resulting gains or losses associated with the strategies chosen by each player. For player $\mathcal{X}_i$, the payoff is represented as $\mathcal{J}_i$, and the total payoff set is $\mathcal{J} = \{\mathcal{J}_1, \mathcal{J}_2, \ldots, \mathcal{J}_n\}$. These payoffs take into account costs, rewards, and the efficiency of defense strategies versus attack strategies.

- In game theory, the NE represents a stable state where no player can increase their payoff by changing their strategy, assuming other players maintain their strategies. The utility function for each player $\mathcal{X}_i$ is denoted as $\mathcal{U}_i(l_i, l_{-i})$, where l_i represents the player's own strategy, and l_{-i} encompasses the strategies of all other players. The NE condition is formally given by:

$$\mathcal{U}_i(l_i^*, l_{-i}^*) \geq \mathcal{U}_i(l_i, l_{-i}^*), \quad \forall l_i \in \mathcal{L}_i, \tag{9.7}$$

where l_i^* and l_{-i}^* denote the equilibrium strategies. This condition ensures that, at equilibrium, each player's chosen strategy maximizes their utility, given the strategies of others.

9.3.2 Analytical framework for identifying Nash equilibrium

The analysis of the proposed game-theoretical model employs a matrix-based approach. In this context, we consider a strategic interaction between defenders and attackers, with each player's strategies represented in matrix form (see Figure 9.3).

The strategy spaces for the defender and attacker are denoted by $\mathcal{S}_\mathcal{D}$ and $\mathcal{S}_\mathcal{A}$, respectively, and are arranged into a 3 × 3 payoff matrix $\mathcal{P}$, as shown below:

$$\mathcal{P} = \begin{bmatrix} p_{11}^{\star} & p_{12}^{\star} & p_{13}^{\star} \\ p_{21}^{\star} & p_{22}^{\star} & p_{23}^{\star} \\ p_{31}^{\star} & p_{32}^{\star} & p_{33}^{\star} \end{bmatrix} = \begin{bmatrix} (\mathcal{S}_{\mathcal{D}_1}, \mathcal{S}_{\mathcal{A}_1}) & (\mathcal{S}_{\mathcal{D}_1}, \mathcal{S}_{\mathcal{A}_2}) & (\mathcal{S}_{\mathcal{D}_1}, \mathcal{S}_{\mathcal{A}_3}) \\ (\mathcal{S}_{\mathcal{D}_2}, \mathcal{S}_{\mathcal{A}_1}) & (\mathcal{S}_{\mathcal{D}_2}, \mathcal{S}_{\mathcal{A}_2}) & (\mathcal{S}_{\mathcal{D}_2}, \mathcal{S}_{\mathcal{A}_3}) \\ (\mathcal{S}_{\mathcal{D}_3}, \mathcal{S}_{\mathcal{A}_1}) & (\mathcal{S}_{\mathcal{D}_3}, \mathcal{S}_{\mathcal{A}_2}) & (\mathcal{S}_{\mathcal{D}_3}, \mathcal{S}_{\mathcal{A}_3}) \end{bmatrix}$$

In this matrix $\mathcal{P}$, the element $p_{11}^{\star}$ represents the defender's detection of a DDoS attack using a rate-based IDS. This scenario involves an attacker utilizing a volumetric DDoS attack, which is countered by the defender using rate-based detection

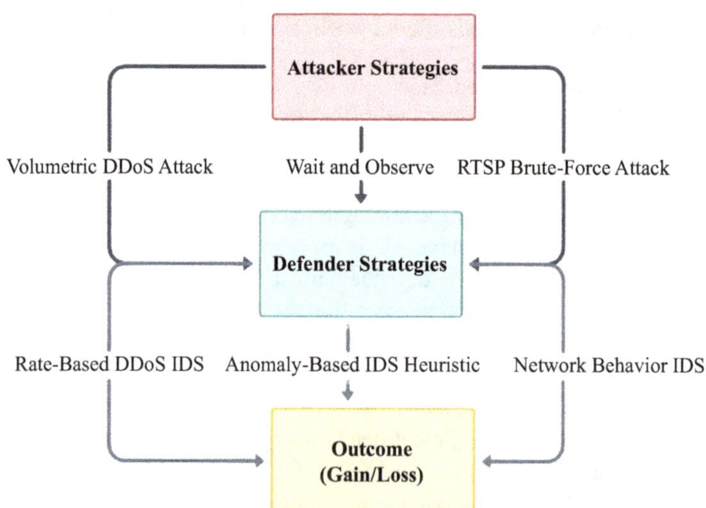

Figure 9.3 Representation of proposed defender and attacker strategies

Table 9.1 Parameter definitions and corresponding symbols

Parameter	Symbol
IDS detection rate for anomaly-based approach	λ_2
Attacker's resource consumption	$\mathcal{C}_A$
IDS detection rate for rate-based DDoS	λ_1
Gain from successful detection	$\mathcal{G}_D$
Value of targeted assets	$\mathcal{V}_A$
Detection rate for heuristic network behavior	λ_3
False Positive rate of the defender	λ_4
Energy used by anomaly-based IDS	$\mathcal{E}_A$
Cost of waiting for the attacker	$\mathcal{W}_A$
Gain from successful attack	$\mathcal{G}_A$
Energy used by rate-based DDoS IDS	$\mathcal{E}_R$
Energy used by heuristic network behavior IDS	$\mathcal{E}_H$

methods. The corresponding payoff for the defender depends on the balance between resource consumption and detection accuracy. The payoff for the defender in this case can be expressed as:

$$\mathcal{U}_{11}(\mathcal{D}) = \mathcal{G}_{\mathrm{D}}(t) - \mathcal{E}_{\mathrm{R}}(t). \tag{9.8}$$

The attacker's corresponding utility, which reflects the cost incurred from the unsuccessful attack, is given by:

$$\mathcal{U}_{11}(\mathcal{A}) = -\mathcal{C}_{\mathrm{A}}(t). \tag{9.9}$$

A detailed overview of the parameters used in this framework is provided in Table 9.1.

9.3.3 Utility matrices for defender and attacker

The utility matrices $\mathcal{P}_{\mathcal{D}}$ for the defender and $\mathcal{P}_A$ for the attacker represent the strategic interactions in the game. Positive terms such as $\mathcal{G}_D$ and $\mathcal{G}_A$ reflect the benefits gained from successful defense and attack actions, respectively. Conversely, negative components like $\mathcal{E}_R, \mathcal{E}_A, \mathcal{E}_H, \mathcal{C}_A, \mathcal{W}_A$ account for the costs associated with both defensive and offensive strategies. These values illustrate the balance between potential gains and the resource expenditure required to execute the chosen tactics. Here are the payoff matrices for the defender and the attacker.

$$\mathcal{M}_{\mathcal{D}} = \begin{bmatrix} d_{11}^{\star} & d_{12}^{\star} & d_{13}^{\star} \\ d_{21}^{\star} & d_{22}^{\star} & d_{23}^{\star} \\ d_{31}^{\star} & d_{32}^{\star} & d_{33}^{\star} \end{bmatrix} = \begin{bmatrix} \mathcal{G}_D(t) - \mathcal{E}_R(t) & -\mathcal{E}_R(t) & -\mathcal{E}_R(t) - \mathcal{V}_A(t) \\ \mathcal{G}_D(t) - \mathcal{E}_A(t) & -\mathcal{E}_A(t) & \mathcal{G}_D(t) - \mathcal{E}_A(t) \\ -\mathcal{E}_H(t) - \mathcal{V}_A(t) & -\mathcal{E}_H(t) & \mathcal{G}_D(t) - \mathcal{E}_H(t) \end{bmatrix}$$

$$\mathcal{M}_A = \begin{bmatrix} a_{11}^{\star} & a_{12}^{\star} & a_{13}^{\star} \\ a_{21}^{\star} & a_{22}^{\star} & a_{23}^{\star} \\ a_{31}^{\star} & a_{32}^{\star} & a_{33}^{\star} \end{bmatrix} = \begin{bmatrix} -\mathcal{C}_A(t) & -\mathcal{W}_A(t) & \mathcal{G}_A(t) - \mathcal{C}_A(t) \\ -\mathcal{C}_A(t) & -\mathcal{W}_A(t) & -\mathcal{C}_A(t) \\ \mathcal{G}_A(t) - \mathcal{C}_A(t) & -\mathcal{W}_A(t) & -\mathcal{C}_A(t) \end{bmatrix}$$

We applied the scribing method [40] to identify the NE within the proposed game-theoretical model. This approach involves comparing the optimal values in the attacker's payoff matrix $\mathcal{P}_A$ with their respective elements in the defender's payoff matrix $\mathcal{P}_\mathcal{D}$. Through this comparison, we arrive at a solution rooted in pure strategy selection. The attacker's highest potential gains are represented by $p_{13}^{\star}$ and $p_{31}^{\star}$, while the most favorable payoffs for the defender are indicated by $p_{11}^{\star}, p_{21}^{\star}, p_{23}^{\star}$, and $p_{33}^{\star}$. From the analysis of the matrices, two key conclusions can be drawn:

Theorem 9.5: The suggested game-theoretic model, characterized by the utility matrices $\mathcal{P}_\mathcal{D}$ for the defender and $\mathcal{P}_A$ for the attacker, does not admit a NE in pure strategies.

Proof. The proof relies on the observation that the attacker's optimal actions, specifically $p_{13}^{\star}$ and $p_{31}^{\star}$ in the payoff matrix $\mathcal{P}_A$, do not correspond with any of the defender's optimal actions, namely $p_{11}^{\star}, p_{21}^{\star}, p_{23}^{\star}$, and $p_{33}^{\star}$ in the payoff matrix $\mathcal{P}_\mathcal{D}$. A NE in pure strategies would necessitate that each player's chosen strategy represents the best response to the other player's strategy. Given the misalignment between the optimal choices of the attacker and the defender, it follows that a NE in pure strategies does not exist for this game.

Theorem 9.6: Within the proposed game-theoretic framework, the optimal strategy for the attacker is to consistently initiate an attack to maximize their potential gains.

Proof. In the proposed model, the utility matrices $\mathcal{P}_A$ and $\mathcal{P}_\mathcal{D}$ evaluate the attacker's strategies by balancing anticipated benefits against related costs. Analyzing $\mathcal{P}_A$ shows that strategies associated with $p_{13}^{\star}$ and $p_{31}^{\star}$ yield the highest returns for the attacker, both of which involve initiating an attack. When compared to the alternative strategies—such as waiting or utilizing non-attack methods—these approaches yield comparatively lower utility. As the attacker's objective is to maximize their utility, the strategies that involve attacking result in the highest payoffs. Consequently, the structure of the utility matrix clearly indicates that the attacker will consistently select an attack strategy to maximize their potential gains.

The matrices $\mathcal{P}_\mathcal{D}$ for the defender and $\mathcal{P}_A$ for the attacker represent the strategic interactions in the game. Positive terms such as $\mathcal{G}_D$ and $\mathcal{G}_A$ reflect the gains obtained from successful defense and attack actions, respectively. However, negative components, including $\mathcal{E}_R, \mathcal{E}_A, \mathcal{E}_H, \mathcal{C}_A, \mathcal{W}_A$, represent the costs associated with the execution of various defense and attack strategies. These utility terms illustrate the balance between the potential benefits and the resources expended in implementing the strategies. Table 9.2 presents the modified utility matrices for both the defender and the attacker, illustrating their strategic interactions. The values reflect the payoffs in different security strategies employed by the defender and the attacker's corresponding actions.

Given the detection rates for the IDS strategies, denoted as λ_1 for rate-based DDoS, λ_2 for anomaly-based, and λ_3 for heuristic network behavior, the payoff matrices for both the defender and the attacker can be formulated based on the data

Table 9.2 Revised utility matrix for defender and attacker strategies

Defender ($\mathcal{S}_{\mathcal{D}}$)	Rate-based DDoS	Anomaly-based IDS	Heuristic network behavior IDS
Volumetric DDoS	$\mathcal{G}_D(t) - \mathcal{E}_R(t)$, $-\mathcal{C}_A(t)$	$\mathcal{G}_D(t) - \mathcal{E}_A(t)$, $-\mathcal{C}_A(t)$	$-\mathcal{E}_H(t) - \mathcal{V}_A(t)$, $\mathcal{G}_A(t) - \mathcal{C}_A(t)$
RTSP brute-force	$-\mathcal{E}_R(t) - \mathcal{V}_A(t)$, $\mathcal{G}_A(t) - \mathcal{C}_A(t)$	$\mathcal{G}_D(t) - \mathcal{E}_A(t)$, $-\mathcal{C}_A(t)$	$\mathcal{G}_D(t) - \mathcal{E}_H(t)$, $-\mathcal{C}_A(t)$

Table 9.3 Various scenarios with corresponding defensive strategies for the defender

Scenario	Selected defense strategies
Scenario I	IDS utilizing rate-based DDoS or anomaly detection
Scenario II	IDS employing rate-based DDoS or heuristic network behavior
Scenario III	IDS applying anomaly detection or heuristic network behavior

in Table 9.2.

$$\tilde{\mathcal{P}}_{\mathcal{D}} = \begin{bmatrix} \lambda_1\mathcal{G}_{\mathcal{D}}(t) - \mathcal{E}_{\mathcal{R}}(t) - (1-\lambda_1)\mathcal{V}_{\mathcal{A}}(t) & \lambda_2\mathcal{G}_{\mathcal{D}}(t) - \mathcal{E}_{\mathcal{A}}(t) - (1-\lambda_2)\mathcal{V}_{\mathcal{A}}(t) & -\mathcal{E}_{\mathcal{H}}(t) - \mathcal{V}_{\mathcal{A}}(t) \\ -\mathcal{E}_{\mathcal{R}}(t) - \mathcal{V}_{\mathcal{A}}(t) & \lambda_2\mathcal{G}_{\mathcal{D}}(t) - \mathcal{E}_{\mathcal{A}}(t) - (1-\lambda_2)\mathcal{V}_{\mathcal{A}}(t) & \lambda_3\mathcal{G}_{\mathcal{D}}(t) - \mathcal{E}_{\mathcal{H}}(t) - (1-\lambda_3)\mathcal{V}_{\mathcal{A}}(t) \end{bmatrix}$$

$$\tilde{\mathcal{P}}_{\mathcal{A}} = \begin{bmatrix} (1-\lambda_1)\mathcal{G}_{\mathcal{A}}(t) - \mathcal{C}_{\mathcal{A}}(t) & (1-\lambda_2)\mathcal{G}_{\mathcal{A}}(t) - \mathcal{C}_{\mathcal{A}}(t) & \mathcal{G}_{\mathcal{A}}(t) - \mathcal{C}_{\mathcal{A}}(t) \\ \mathcal{G}_{\mathcal{A}}(t) - \mathcal{C}_{\mathcal{A}}(t) & \mathcal{G}_{\mathcal{A}}(t) - \mathcal{C}_{\mathcal{A}}(t) & (1-\lambda_3)\mathcal{G}_{\mathcal{A}}(t) - \mathcal{C}_{\mathcal{A}}(t) \end{bmatrix}$$

To compute the respective payoffs for the defender and attacker across different scenarios, we utilize the modified 2×3 matrices $\tilde{\mathcal{P}}_{\mathcal{D}}$ and $\tilde{\mathcal{P}}_{\mathcal{A}}$. Below, we present an in-depth analysis of various cases, examining both defender and attacker strategies and their corresponding utility payoffs (see Table 9.3).

Case I In this scenario, the defender employs rate-based DDoS detection and Anomaly-Based detection methods. The probabilities for these strategies are denoted by ζ_1 and $(1-\zeta_1)$, respectively. Similarly, the attacker's strategies, represented by the probabilities κ_1 and $(1-\kappa_1)$, correspond to launching a Volumetric DDoS attack and an RTSP Brute-Force attack. The cumulative utility for both the defender, $\mathcal{U}(\mathcal{D})$, and the attacker, $\mathcal{U}(\mathcal{A})$, is given as follows:

$$\begin{aligned} \mathcal{U}(\mathcal{D}) = \zeta_1\kappa_1\mathcal{U}_{11}(\mathcal{D}) + (1-\zeta_1)\kappa_1\mathcal{U}_{12}(\mathcal{D}) + \zeta_1(1-\kappa_1)\mathcal{U}_{21}(\mathcal{D}) \\ +(1-\zeta_1)(1-\kappa_1)\mathcal{U}_{22}(\mathcal{D}) \end{aligned}$$

$$\begin{aligned} \mathcal{U}(\mathcal{A}) = \zeta_1\kappa_1\mathcal{U}_{11}(\mathcal{A}) + (1-\zeta_1)\kappa_1\mathcal{U}_{12}(\mathcal{A}) + \zeta_1(1-\kappa_1)\mathcal{U}_{21}(\mathcal{A}) \\ +(1-\zeta_1)(1-\kappa_1)\mathcal{U}_{22}(\mathcal{A}) \end{aligned}$$

The partial derivatives of these payoffs, with respect to the probabilities ζ_1 and κ_1, are used to derive the optimal strategies:

$$\begin{aligned}\frac{\partial \mathcal{U}(\mathcal{D})}{\partial \zeta_1} &= \kappa_1[(\lambda_1 - \lambda_2)\mathcal{G}_{\mathcal{D}}(t) + (\mathcal{E}_{\mathcal{A}}(t) - \mathcal{E}_{\mathcal{R}}(t)) + (\lambda_1 - \lambda_2)\mathcal{V}_{\mathcal{A}}(t)] \\ &\quad +(1 - \kappa_1)[(-\lambda_2\mathcal{G}_{\mathcal{D}}(t) + (\mathcal{E}_{\mathcal{A}}(t) - \mathcal{E}_{\mathcal{R}}(t)) - \lambda_2\mathcal{V}_{\mathcal{A}}(t))] \\ \frac{\partial \mathcal{U}(\mathcal{A})}{\partial \kappa_1} &= \zeta_1[\mathcal{G}_{\mathcal{A}}(t)(\lambda_2 - \lambda_1)] - (1 - \zeta_1)[\mathcal{G}_{\mathcal{A}}(t)\lambda_2]\end{aligned}$$

By solving these equations, the optimal strategies for the attacker (κ_1) and defender (ζ_1) are obtained as:

$$\kappa_1 = \frac{\lambda_2(\mathcal{G}_{\mathcal{D}}(t) + \mathcal{V}_{\mathcal{A}}(t)) - (\mathcal{E}_{\mathcal{A}}(t) - \mathcal{E}_{\mathcal{R}}(t))}{\lambda_1(\mathcal{G}_{\mathcal{D}}(t) + \mathcal{V}_{\mathcal{A}}(t))} \tag{9.10}$$

$$(1 - \kappa_1) = \frac{(\lambda_1 - \lambda_2)(\mathcal{G}_{\mathcal{D}}(t) + \mathcal{V}_{\mathcal{A}}(t)) + (\mathcal{E}_{\mathcal{A}}(t) - \mathcal{E}_{\mathcal{R}}(t))}{\lambda_1(\mathcal{G}_{\mathcal{D}}(t) + \mathcal{V}_{\mathcal{A}}(t))} \tag{9.11}$$

$$\zeta_1 = \frac{\lambda_2}{\lambda_2 - \lambda_1} \tag{9.12}$$

$$(1 - \zeta_1) = \frac{-\lambda_1}{\lambda_2 - \lambda_1} \tag{9.13}$$

Case II In this case, the defender employs rate-based DDoS detection and heuristic network behavior techniques, represented by probabilities ζ_2 and $(1 - \zeta_2)$. The attacker's strategies for RTSP Brute-Force and Volumetric DDoS attacks are indicated by κ_2 and $(1 - \kappa_2)$, respectively. The resulting payoffs for both parties are as follows:

$$\begin{aligned}\mathcal{U}(\mathcal{D}) &= \zeta_2\kappa_2\mathcal{U}_{11}(\mathcal{D}) + (1 - \zeta_2)\kappa_2\mathcal{U}_{13}(\mathcal{D}) + \zeta_2(1 - \kappa_2)\mathcal{U}_{21}(\mathcal{D}) \\ &\quad +(1 - \zeta_2)(1 - \kappa_2)\mathcal{U}_{23}(\mathcal{D}) \\ \mathcal{U}(\mathcal{A}) &= \zeta_2\kappa_2\mathcal{U}_{11}(\mathcal{A}) + (1 - \zeta_2)\kappa_2\mathcal{U}_{13}(\mathcal{A}) + \zeta_2(1 - \kappa_2)\mathcal{U}_{21}(\mathcal{A}) \\ &\quad +(1 - \zeta_2)(1 - \kappa_2)\mathcal{U}_{23}(\mathcal{A})\end{aligned}$$

By differentiating these functions, we derive the following expressions:

$$\kappa_2 = \frac{\lambda_3(\mathcal{G}_{\mathcal{D}}(t) + \mathcal{V}_{\mathcal{A}}(t)) + (\mathcal{E}_{\mathcal{H}}(t) - \mathcal{E}_{\mathcal{R}}(t))}{(\lambda_1 + \lambda_3)(\mathcal{G}_{\mathcal{D}}(t) + \mathcal{V}_{\mathcal{A}}(t))} \tag{9.14}$$

$$(1 - \kappa_2) = \frac{\lambda_1(\mathcal{G}_{\mathcal{D}}(t) + \mathcal{V}_{\mathcal{A}}(t)) - (\mathcal{E}_{\mathcal{H}}(t) - \mathcal{E}_{\mathcal{R}}(t))}{(\lambda_1 + \lambda_3)(\mathcal{G}_{\mathcal{D}}(t) + \mathcal{V}_{\mathcal{A}}(t))} \tag{9.15}$$

$$\zeta_2 = \frac{\lambda_3}{\lambda_1 + \lambda_3} \tag{9.16}$$

$$(1 - \zeta_2) = \frac{\lambda_1}{\lambda_1 + \lambda_3} \tag{9.17}$$

Case III The defender now employs anomaly-based and heuristic network behavior techniques, with associated probabilities ζ_3 and $(1-\zeta_3)$. The attacker's strategies are volumetric DDoS and RTSP brute-force attacks, represented by probabilities κ_3 and $(1-\kappa_3)$, respectively. The payoffs for both players are calculated as follows:

$$\begin{aligned}\mathcal{U}(\mathcal{D}) &= \zeta_3\kappa_3\mathcal{U}_{12}(\mathcal{D}) + (1-\zeta_3)\kappa_3\mathcal{U}_{13}(\mathcal{D}) + \zeta_3(1-\kappa_3)\mathcal{U}_{22}(\mathcal{D}) \\ &\quad +(1-\zeta_3)(1-\kappa_3)\mathcal{U}_{23}(\mathcal{D}) \\ \mathcal{U}(\mathcal{A}) &= \zeta_3\kappa_3\mathcal{U}_{12}(\mathcal{A}) + (1-\zeta_3)\kappa_3\mathcal{U}_{13}(\mathcal{A}) + \zeta_3(1-\kappa_3)\mathcal{U}_{22}(\mathcal{A}) \\ &\quad +(1-\zeta_3)(1-\kappa_3)\mathcal{U}_{23}(\mathcal{A})\end{aligned}$$

After solving the equations, we obtain:

$$\kappa_3 = \frac{(\lambda_3-\lambda_2)(\mathcal{G}_\mathcal{D}(t)+\mathcal{V}_\mathcal{A}(t)) - (\mathcal{E}_\mathcal{H}(t)-\mathcal{E}_\mathcal{A}(t))}{\lambda_3(\mathcal{G}_\mathcal{D}(t)+\mathcal{V}_\mathcal{A}(t))} \tag{9.18}$$

$$(1-\kappa_3) = \frac{\lambda_2(\mathcal{G}_\mathcal{D}(t)+\mathcal{V}_\mathcal{A}(t)) + (\mathcal{E}_\mathcal{H}(t)-\mathcal{E}_\mathcal{A}(t))}{\lambda_3(\mathcal{G}_\mathcal{D}(t)+\mathcal{V}_\mathcal{A}(t))} \tag{9.19}$$

$$\zeta_3 = \frac{\lambda_3}{\lambda_2+\lambda_3} \tag{9.20}$$

$$(1-\zeta_3) = \frac{\lambda_2}{\lambda_2+\lambda_3} \tag{9.21}$$

Assuming uniform probabilities across all events, it can be concluded that both the attacker and defender will seek to optimize their respective advantages. The NE solutions for the defender's strategies $(\mathcal{S}_\mathcal{D})$ and the attacker's strategies $(\mathcal{S}_\mathcal{A})$ are derived from Cases 1 to 3 as follows:

$$\mathcal{S}_\mathcal{D} = [\kappa_1, (1-\kappa_1), \kappa_2, (1-\kappa_2), \kappa_3, (1-\kappa_3)]$$

Breaking down the solution:

$$\begin{aligned}\mathcal{S}_\mathcal{D} = \Bigg[&\frac{-[\lambda_2\mathcal{G}_\mathcal{D}(t) - \mathcal{E}_\mathcal{A}(t) + \lambda_2\mathcal{V}_\mathcal{A}(t) - \mathcal{E}_\mathcal{R}(t) - \mathcal{V}_\mathcal{A}(t)]}{[(\lambda_1-2\lambda_2)\mathcal{G}_\mathcal{D}(t) + 2(\mathcal{E}_\mathcal{A}(t)-\mathcal{E}_\mathcal{R}(t)) + (1-2\lambda_2+\lambda_1)\mathcal{V}_\mathcal{A}(t)]}, \\ &\frac{[(\lambda_1-\lambda_2)\mathcal{G}_\mathcal{D}(t) + (\mathcal{E}_\mathcal{A}(t)-\mathcal{E}_\mathcal{R}(t)) + (\lambda_1-\lambda_2)\mathcal{V}_\mathcal{A}(t)]}{[(\lambda_1-2\lambda_2)\mathcal{G}_\mathcal{D}(t) + 2(\mathcal{E}_\mathcal{A}(t)-\mathcal{E}_\mathcal{R}(t)) + (1-2\lambda_2+\lambda_1)\mathcal{V}_\mathcal{A}(t)]}, \\ &\frac{-\lambda_3\mathcal{G}_\mathcal{D}(t) + \mathcal{E}_\mathcal{H}(t) - \mathcal{E}_\mathcal{R}(t)}{\lambda_1\mathcal{G}_\mathcal{D}(t) + \lambda_1\mathcal{V}_\mathcal{A}(t) + \lambda_3\mathcal{G}_\mathcal{D}(t)}, \frac{\lambda_1\mathcal{G}_\mathcal{D}(t) + \lambda_1\mathcal{V}_\mathcal{A}(t) + 2\lambda_3\mathcal{G}_\mathcal{D}(t) - \mathcal{E}_\mathcal{H}(t) + \mathcal{E}_\mathcal{R}(t)}{\lambda_1\mathcal{G}_\mathcal{D}(t) + \lambda_1\mathcal{V}_\mathcal{A}(t) + \lambda_3\mathcal{G}_\mathcal{D}(t)}, \\ &\frac{\lambda_3\mathcal{G}_\mathcal{D}(t) - \mathcal{E}_\mathcal{H}(t) - \lambda_3\mathcal{V}_\mathcal{A}(t)}{(\lambda_2-\lambda_3)\mathcal{G}_\mathcal{D}(t) + (\mathcal{E}_\mathcal{A}(t)-\mathcal{E}_\mathcal{H}(t)) + (\lambda_3-\lambda_2)\mathcal{V}_\mathcal{A}(t)}, \\ &\frac{\lambda_2\mathcal{G}_\mathcal{D}(t) - \lambda_3\mathcal{G}_\mathcal{D}(t) + \mathcal{E}_\mathcal{A}(t) - \mathcal{E}_\mathcal{H}(t) + \lambda_3\mathcal{V}_\mathcal{A}(t) - \lambda_2\mathcal{V}_\mathcal{A}(t)}{(\lambda_2-\lambda_3)\mathcal{G}_\mathcal{D}(t) + (\mathcal{E}_\mathcal{A}(t)-\mathcal{E}_\mathcal{H}(t)) + (\lambda_3-\lambda_2)\mathcal{V}_\mathcal{A}(t)}\Bigg].\end{aligned}$$

The attacker's optimal strategy $\mathcal{S}_{\mathcal{A}}$ is given as:

$$\mathcal{S}_{\mathcal{A}} = [\zeta_1, (1-\zeta_1), \zeta_2, (1-\zeta_2), \zeta_3, (1-\zeta_3)]$$

This yields:

$$\mathcal{S}_{\mathcal{A}} = \left[\frac{\lambda_2}{\lambda_1-\lambda_2}, \frac{\lambda_1-2\lambda_2}{\lambda_1-\lambda_2}, \frac{\lambda_3}{\lambda_1+\lambda_3}, \frac{\lambda_1}{\lambda_1+\lambda_3}, \frac{1-\lambda_3}{\lambda_2-2\lambda_3+1}, \frac{\lambda_2-\lambda_3}{\lambda_2-2\lambda_3+1}\right].$$

Our game-theoretic framework examines three distinct strategies for both the attacker and defender, enabling the determination of an optimal strategy and NE within this structured context. This model establishes a solid mathematical basis for analyzing the interactions between the defender and attacker within a NIDS aimed at protecting IoT environments. The findings provide valuable insights into how both parties can refine their strategies to maximize respective payoffs, thereby enhancing the strategic depth of IoT security measures.

9.4 Multimodal big data approach with transfer learning

Figure 9.4 illustrates the detailed workflow for extracting multimodal features and detecting cyberattacks. This methodology combines both textual and visual data to accurately identify malicious activities. Textual information is first extracted from network traffic and optimized through Spark-based algorithms, incorporating transfer learning techniques to enhance feature quality. The network byte streams are subsequently converted into images to capture unique textural characteristics. A custom algorithm manages this transformation, while texture features are obtained by fine-tuning an attention-driven ResNet model. The resulting text and texture features are integrated to form a robust multimodal feature set, which is then applied to classify diverse types of cyberattacks. This innovative approach allows for precise identification across a wide range of intrusion threats.

9.4.1 Data preprocessing

The PCAP file contains logs of communication activities from IoT devices, with each message stored in an encrypted format. Using Wireshark, we extract relevant network activities, such as HTTP, TCP, and DNS, from the PCAP file. These flow records capture various details, including device information, protocol type, source and destination IP addresses, and timestamps. By analyzing these network flows, as shown in Algorithm 9.1, it becomes possible to differentiate between benign and malicious behaviors.

To enhance intrusion detection capabilities, this information is processed within a big data platform, leveraging transfer learning techniques. However, raw

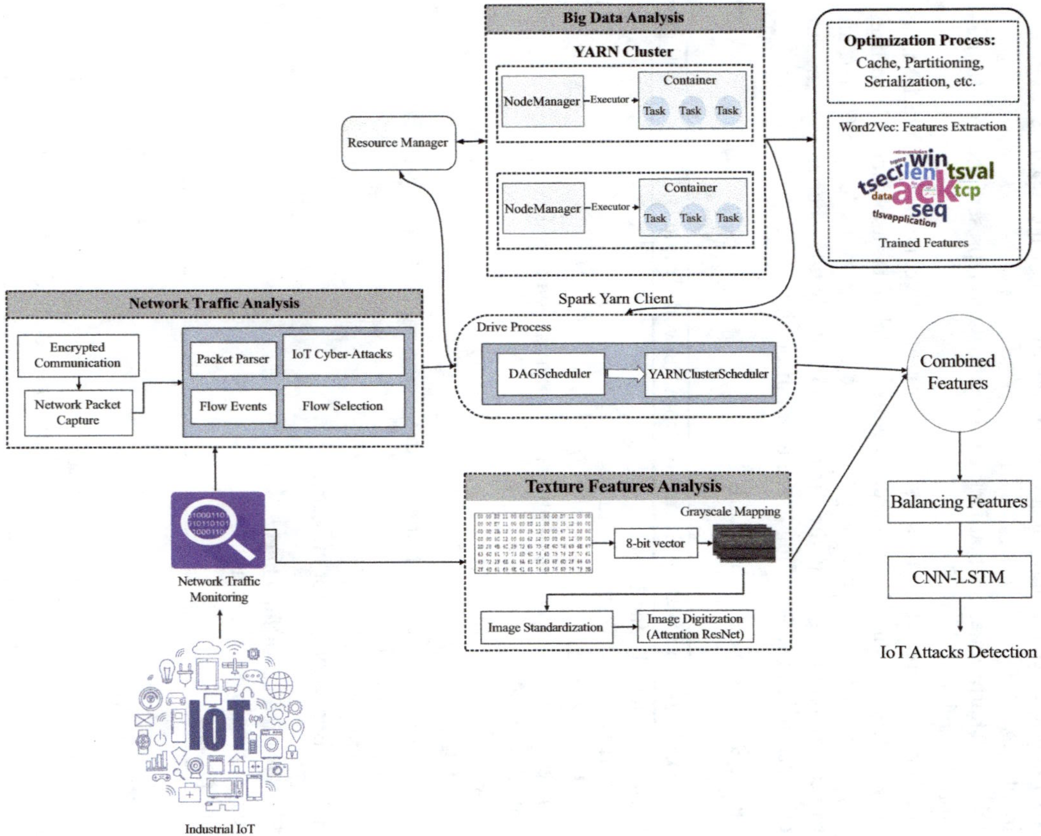

Figure 9.4 Multimodal IoT security framework with big data analytics

data often includes noise, which may reduce its effectiveness in identifying attack patterns. Therefore, we remove extraneous flow events that do not contribute meaningful insights. A semantic crawler is employed to systematically process and refine network flows, translating them into relevant behavioral patterns. The data preprocessing steps are as follows:

- To minimize redundancy, sequentially remove duplicate features from the input sets.
- Exclude short sequences that lack sufficient data to represent meaningful network behavior.
- Uniform sequence length is essential for effective intrusion detection, as varying lengths can disrupt neural network models. This approach standardizes sequences to a predefined length, denoted as L. Patterns longer than L are truncated, retaining only the first L elements, while shorter patterns are extended using zero-padding to achieve uniformity.

Figure 9.4 Complete architecture

Algorithm 1: Texture Feature Extraction from Network Traffic Data

```
  Input: Network Traffic Data
  Output: Extracted Texture Feature
  Initialize variables;
1 Define T_f = t_1, t_2, ..., t_n representing network traffic types;
2 Calculate E(t_f) = t'_f;
3 foreach condition check do
      while E(t_f) = t'_f do
4         Process t'_f as a text feature, with t'_f being protocols such as HTTP,
           TCP, UDP, etc.;
5         Output t'f;
6         else: Display error message;
7 End for each condition check;
8 Return to step 3 if necessary;
9 End process
```

9.4.2 *Texture feature analysis*

Texture-based features enable the detection of intrusions by identifying subtle variations in network activity, which often shift to evade traditional detection systems. This approach does not require the use of identifiable intrusion signatures or reverse engineering techniques, as it extracts texture information directly from network byte data, converting these bytes into images (refer to Algorithm 9.2).

Our process involves transforming byte sequences from network packets into grayscale images, bypassing the need for specific intrusion identifiers. First, the packet data is parsed to obtain byte streams from the PCAP files, converting these sequences into images of unsigned 8-bit integers. These images are resized to a

ArloQ Camera (12KB) SimCam (15KB) Eufy Home Base (14KB)

Figure 9.5 128 × 128 grayscale images derived from network traffic data

uniform 128 × 128 pixels for efficient analysis. This method is highly effective in minimizing the storage size of large PCAP files by compressing them into manageable image formats. For instance, extensive PCAP data, spanning multiple megabytes, can be condensed into compact grayscale images, as demonstrated in Figure 9.5. Image-based IDS techniques are especially adaptable, capable of encapsulating structural elements such as storage, processes, and packet headers. By utilizing these visual formats enables the application of sophisticated image processing and ML techniques, including DL models, to identify patterns and anomalies that traditional methods may miss, thereby enhancing the performance and detection accuracy of IDS.

In DL models, attention mechanisms allow the network to emphasize specific parts of an input, such as an image or data sequence, during prediction. A ResNet is a deep neural network that addresses the vanishing gradient problem by using residual blocks with skip connections [41]. Figure 9.6 illustrates the attention-based ResNet, which we utilized to capture texture details from images. This network integrates multiple attention modules, creating a progressively refined attention focus as the network depth increases. The processed images serve as input to the ResNet blocks, with key features outlined as follows:

- **Hierarchical network structure**: Stacking multiple attention modules in a layered configuration forms residual attention networks, enabling the integration of diverse attention mechanisms across distinct modules.
- **Attention residual learning**: Directly stacking attention modules could hinder performance. To mitigate this, we implement attention residual learning, which optimizes the network's capability across multiple layers.

Integrating self-attention mechanisms within ResNet enhances its capacity to recognize complex dependencies, interpret global contexts, and focus on critical attributes. This approach improves data processing efficiency, facilitates multiscale feature learning, and extends applicability across diverse tasks, making it a powerful tool for intrusion detection.

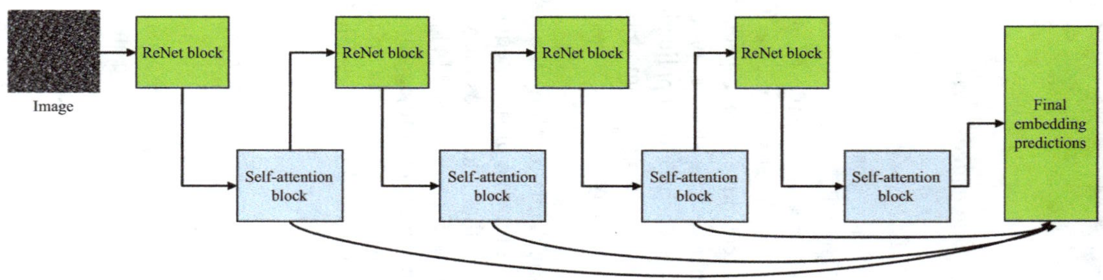

Figure 9.6 Attention-based ResNet architecture for texture feature extraction from network data

Algorithm 2: Texture Feature Extraction in Bytes

Input: Network traffic represented as bytes
Output: Extracted texture features in byte format
initialization;
Define $B = \{B_1, B_2, \ldots, B_n\}$, where each element in B represents a byte segment;
Define $I = \{I_1, I_2, \ldots, I_n\}$, where each element in I stands for an image derived from bytes;
for each condition check **do**:
while *If* $I == I$ *is valid* **do**
    Divide I into smaller segments SS, where each SS has dimensions 128×128;
    Apply *ResNet* model on each SS;
    for *each application of* $ResNet(SS)$*:* **do**
        while *Using attention mechanism with* $ResNet(SS)$*:* **do**
            for *each I within SS:* **do**
                Extract texture characteristics;
        Collect the texture features;
End for
Conclude the process

9.4.3 *Transfer learning*

We utilize a pre-trained Word2Vec model to derive significant semantic features from large-scale network data, applying transfer learning methods to enhance feature extraction. This neural network utilizes vector-based features to identify various types of attacks. After processing network traffic, a fixed-length feature vector, denoted by L, is produced. Although one-hot encoding is a possible approach for handling these features, it is not suitable for large-scale datasets due to inefficiency. The model is first trained on a large dataset of network traffic, enabling it to produce dense vector representations (or word embeddings) for each term within the dataset. These embeddings encapsulate both the semantic meaning and the contextual relationships within network traffic data, improving the model's ability to identify patterns and anomalies.

Gradient descent is utilized to optimize the model parameters, including the weights of the neural network, by minimizing a loss function that evaluates the difference between predicted outcomes and actual results. This iterative process reduces discrepancies between expected and real outcomes, enhancing model performance with each optimization cycle. Through transfer learning, knowledge from this pre-trained model is adapted for identifying cyberattacks within IoT network traffic. By gradually fine-tuning pre-trained Word2Vec embeddings with IoT-specific network data, the model better captures the contextual nuances of network features, strengthening the semantic associations within the embeddings. This approach enhances the interpretative power of vector semantics by defining spatial relationships among vectors. As Word2Vec undergoes dynamic fine-tuning, it produces multiple vectors for each feature, allowing diverse interpretations and improving feature representation. This enriched semantic understanding enables the model to more accurately classify and mitigate threats across varied network environments.

Leveraging the Spark platform alongside Word2Vec's transfer learning algorithm enables efficient feature extraction from network traffic, as outlined in Algorithm 9.3 [42]. The 'org.apache.spark.ml.feature' class in Spark facilitates dynamic Word2Vec operations, leveraging distributed computing to optimize the training process and generate vectors from extensive text corpora. Data is first transformed into the DataFrame format before invoking the 'fit' function to initiate training. Once trained, the 'Discover Synonyms' method identifies words with similar meanings to a given term, enhancing contextual understanding. The performance of Spark and Gensim may differ depending on the specifics of their algorithms and implementation methods. When working with large datasets, Spark, leveraging distributed processing, typically outperforms Gensim. Conversely, with smaller datasets, Gensim may process faster than Spark due to the latter's requirement to convert data to DataFrame format and execute additional I/O operations.

9.4.4 Big data analysis

To enhance computational speed and efficiency with large datasets, various optimization techniques were employed, such as partitioning, caching, serialization, choosing efficient data storage formats, and selecting appropriate APIs [43].

1. **Partitioning**: The number of partitions plays a crucial role in Spark's data processing performance. A low partition count may lead to underuse of computational resources, whereas an excessive count can elevate network transmission and scheduling costs. In distributed systems, setting the partition count to align with the number of nodes optimizes resource allocation and minimizes superfluous network traffic. By matching the number of partitions with available nodes, processing efficiency is improved through reduced overhead and network load.
2. **Caching**: Spark can cache data either in memory or on disk. Storing data in memory allows for faster read-write speeds, improving data access time and processing performance by reducing the reliance on disk I/O. However, disk caching offers greater storage capacity and longer data retention, though with slower read and write times. Memory caching is generally preferred for performance, but for very large datasets where memory limitations could lead to out-of-memory errors, disk caching becomes essential.
3. **Serialization**: Spark supports Java and Kryo serialization methods. Java serialization, though common, is less efficient due to its large serialized data size, increasing storage and network transmission costs. Kryo serialization, on the other hand, offers a more compact and faster binary format, reducing both storage requirements and serialization time. Kryo is recommended for scenarios demanding high performance.

4. **Data storage**: Spark supports multiple data formats, such as CSV, JSON, XML, PARQUET, ORC, and AVRO. The Parquet format is particularly beneficial as it includes metadata like schema and data types, allowing for more efficient processing and enhanced compression. This structured format optimizes performance by enabling quicker access to data and reducing storage costs. Choosing Parquet can thus significantly improve data management and processing efficiency.
5. **API selection**: Spark offers three APIs: RDD, DataFrame, and DataSet. The RDD API is designed for lower-level operations and provides limited optimization, while DataFrame uses the Catalyst optimizer for efficient query planning and minimal garbage collection. DataSet offers strong type safety and uses Tungsten for fast serialization, which enhances memory management. DataFrame and DataSet often surpass RDD in performance by utilizing Spark SQL's optimization features. These structures offer columnar storage and enforce strict type checking, which helps prevent type errors at compile time. While DataSet typically involves more coding than DataFrame, it achieves faster processing speeds due to the use of the Tungsten engine, which is designed for high-performance memory management and serialization.

Efficiently leveraging big data for intelligent IDS is challenging due to the high dimensionality of network traffic data. Reducing dimensionality while retaining essential characteristics is critical. Spark enhances processing speed and data efficiency through capabilities such as DataFrame optimization, in-memory caching, efficient Kryo serialization, Parquet format storage, and dynamic partitioning based on the number of nodes. By incorporating these optimization techniques, an IDS can enable real-time threat detection and response, positioning the Spark framework as a robust solution for scalable, high-performance security applications. Additionally, transfer learning with word2vec enables adaptive feature extraction from malicious scripts in real-time. By scanning PCAPs, the IDS can detect unusual behavior patterns in visual surveillance, particularly for camera-based threats. The system's resilience and adaptability in dynamic environments are reinforced by a game-theory-based validation, which offers an extensive framework for assessing the effectiveness of proactive strategies.

Algorithm 3: Trained Feature Extraction for IoT-based IDS

Input: $\{\theta_t, \theta_i\}$, where θ_t represents text features and θ_i represents texture features

Output: θ_f' - Classified output for IoT-based IDS

Initialize σ_μ such that $\sigma_\mu(\theta_t) = \rho_t$, where σ denotes the Spark yarn client, μ is the derived process, and ρ refers to the DAG Scheduler;

while *σ_μ as $\sigma_\mu(\theta_t) = \rho_t$:* **do**

  Define ρ as a DAG Scheduler;

  Set $\sigma_\mu(\rho_t) = (YARN_{cs})$, where CS stands for Cluster Scheduler;

  Calculate $R_m \leftarrow SYN(YARN_{cs})$, where R_m indicates the Resource Manager;

while *if* $\theta_t == E_c$: **do**
  for *Check YARN:* **do**
    Determine $N_m = C$, where N_m represents the Node Manager and C is the container;
    Else proceed to next step;
Set $O_p \leftarrow NIDS - VSB$, where O_p denotes the optimization process;
Apply O_p(Word2Vec) for training features;
for *Apply CNN-LSTM model:* **do**
  while $E(\theta_t) == t_f^{'}$ && $E(\theta_i) == i_f^{'}$: **do**
    Calculate $t_f^{'}$ as a texture feature;
    Calculate $i_f^{'}$ as an image feature;
    Merge $\theta_f^{'} \leftarrow (t_f^{'} + i_f^{'})$;
  Display $\theta_f^{'}$ as the classified output for IoT-based IDS;
  Otherwise;
  Show error message;
Proceed to **step 5**;
End of process;

9.4.5 Deep learning with CNN-LSTM framework

Our proposed approach uses a CNN-LSTM framework [44] to enable prompt detection of intrusions in network systems, combining the strengths of both convolutional and LSTM models. In a traditional CNN, max-pooling layers help extract features that are passed to a fully connected layer. However, in this CNN-LSTM setup, the fully connected layer is replaced by an LSTM layer, allowing deeper feature processing. While CNN excels at capturing spatial relationships in network feature vectors, LSTM is effective for identifying long-term temporal dependencies. Figure 9.7 illustrates the two main stages of the CNN-LSTM model. In the first stage, convolution, dropout, and max-pooling layers are applied, while the second stage comprises LSTM and dropout layers. Here, convolutional layers encode network features, and LSTM layers subsequently decode them. Data is flattened before entering a fully connected layer to improve IDS performance.

The LSTM's core components consist of the cell state and various gates, essential for managing and transferring information across sequence alignments. The cell state serves as a conduit, carrying significant features through the network. The memory unit of an LSTM consists of a primary storage component and three gates: the input gate, the forget gate, and the output gate. The input gate determines which information to retain at the current time step, the forget gate regulates the flow of information from the previous time step, and the output gate selects the information to be output. When values are processed through the sigmoid function, values near 0 signify discarded information, while values close to 1 indicate retained data. Using the sigmoid and tanh activation functions, past and present inputs are integrated to compute the hidden state, which influences subsequent

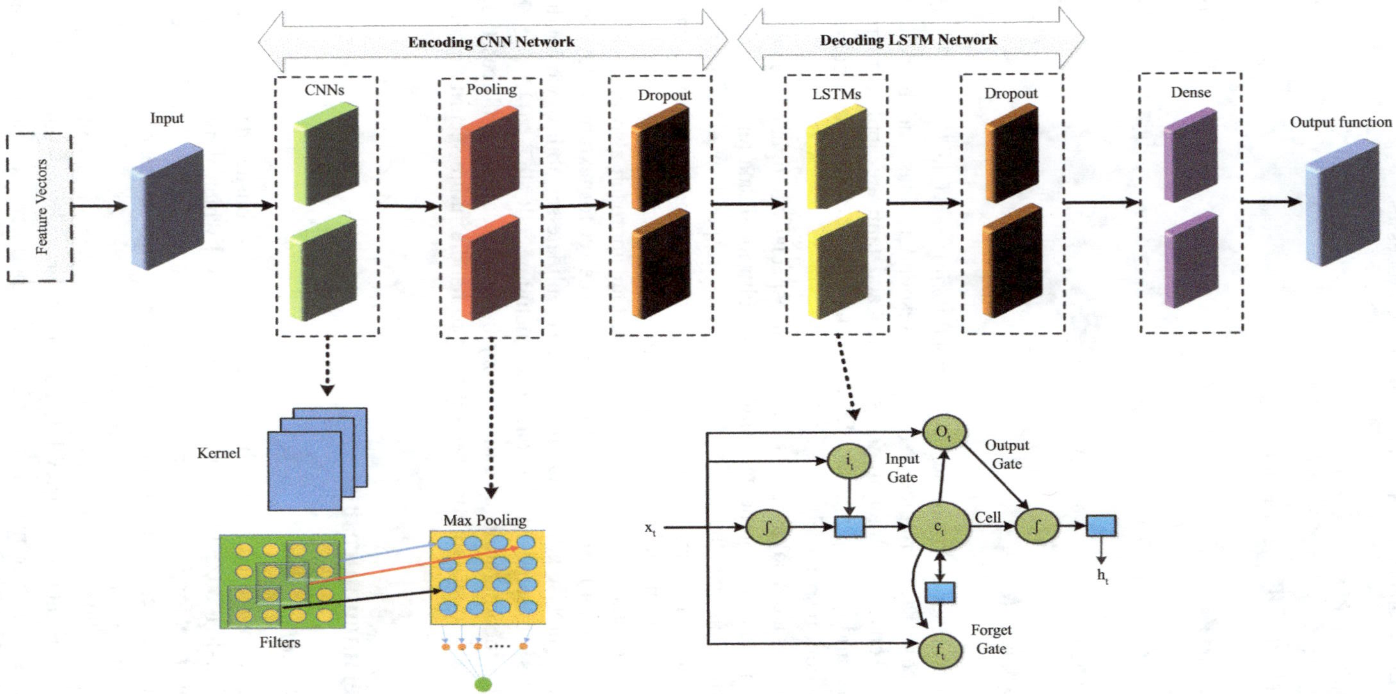

Figure 9.7 Architecture of the CNN-LSTM model for IoT-based IDS

predictions. Equations (9.22)–(9.27) detail these processes.

$$i_t = \sigma(V_{ixt} + W_i h_{(t-1)} + b_i) \tag{9.22}$$

$$f_t = \sigma(V_f xt + W_f h_{(t-1)} + b_f) \tag{9.23}$$

$$\widehat{c}_t = \tanh\left(V_c X_t + W_c h_{(t-1)} + b_c\right) \tag{9.24}$$

$$c_t = (f_t \cdot C_{t-1} + i_t \cdot \widehat{c}_t) \tag{9.25}$$

$$o_t = \sigma(V_o x_t + W_o h_{(t-1)} + b_o) \tag{9.26}$$

$$h_t = o_t \cdot \tanh\left(c_t\right) \tag{9.27}$$

In this framework, x_t represents the input at time t, while V_* and W_* denote weight matrices. The variables b and h correspond to bias and hidden states, respectively. Activation functions σ (sigmoid) and tanh are applied to perform computations, and i_t, f_t, o_t, and c_t refer to the input gate, forget gate, output gate, and memory cell, respectively.

Scalability is a crucial aspect of our system, especially in light of the escalating flood attacks in IoT environments. Combining multimodal data representation with transfer learning allows the system to adaptively respond to different types of attacks. A Spark-based optimization enables smooth handling of large datasets, while transfer learning allows the model to extract semantically rich features, enhancing its adaptability to emerging threats. Our approach also involves transforming network data into images and applying ResNet for texture feature extraction, facilitating precise attack classification. To validate scalability, we conducted extensive tests on standard IoT datasets, including CIC-IoT 2022 and 2023. Moreover, the incorporation of game theory-based validation reinforces the system's resilience and scalability, positioning it to handle future security challenges effectively.

9.5 Experimental results

9.5.1 Datasets

We assessed the proposed approach using three well-established datasets–CIC-IoT 2022 [45], CIC-IoT 2023 [46], and Edge-IIoTset [47] which were curated by the Canadian Institute for Cybersecurity and are frequently utilized in IoT security research. Each dataset was generated by configuring IoT devices in varied network environments to monitor network behavior.

The CIC-IoT 2022 dataset was produced using Wireshark and dumpcap tools across six experimental settings. While dumpcap allowed semi-automated testing, Wireshark was used for manual testing. The experiments cover six scenarios: power modes, idle states, user interactions, different usage cases, active states, and attack situations. In this study, network flows were collected for 11 distinct types of flood attacks, specifically aimed at devices such as the ArloQ Camera, Amcrest Camera, HeimVision Camera, SimCam, Borun Camera, DLink Camera, Home Eye Camera, Netatmo Camera, Arlo Basestation Camera, Luohe Camera, and Nest Camera. These flows captured activities during both the activation and interaction phases of the devices.

The CIC-IoT 2023 dataset operates in real-time and serves as a standard for evaluating IoT security. It offers a wide array of IoT threat data, supporting the development of security analytics for real-world applications. This dataset encompasses 33 types of attacks targeting 105 IoT devices, categorized into seven groups: DDoS, DoS, Reconnaissance, Brute Force, Web-based, Spoofing, and Mirai. For our analysis, we concentrated on ten specific DDoS attacks, which include SYN_Flood, TCP_Flood, SynonymousIP_Flood, UDP_Flood, ICMP_Flood, PSHACK_Flood, RSTFIN_Flood, HTTP_Flood, ACK_Fragmentation, and ICMP_Fragmentation.

Finally, the edge-IIoTset dataset includes data from more than ten IoT devices, featuring cost-effective temperature and humidity sensors. It encompasses 14 types of attacks, including DoS/DDoS, information gathering, man-in-the-middle, injection, and malware attacks, applicable to IoT and IIoT communication protocols. The dataset presents a comprehensive array of features, identifying 61 essential characteristics from a total of 1176 attributes, which provide valuable insights into alerts, system resources, logs, and network traffic.

9.5.2 Performance metrics

To evaluate the efficacy of the proposed approach, we employed five critical performance metrics: precision, recall, F1-score, accuracy, and the confusion matrix. True Positives (TP) and True Negatives (TN) represent the accurately identified instances of benign and malicious network traffic, respectively. Conversely, False Positives (FP) and False Negatives (FN) denote cases of misclassification, where legitimate traffic is incorrectly classified as malicious or the other way around. The classifier's overall accuracy, representing the ratio of correctly identified instances to the total number of instances, was calculated to gauge performance. The evaluation formulas are shown in (9.28)–(9.31).

$$\text{Recall} = \frac{TP}{(TP + FN)} \tag{9.28}$$

$$\text{Precision} = \frac{TP}{(TP + FP)} \tag{9.29}$$

$$\text{F1} - \text{score} = \frac{2 \times \text{Precision} \times \text{Recall}}{(\text{Precision} + \text{Recall})} \tag{9.30}$$

$$\text{Accuracy} = \frac{(TP + TN)}{(TP + TN + FP + FN)} \tag{9.31}$$

9.5.3 Results analysis

Figure 9.8 illustrates the training and testing epoch curves for the CIC-IoT 2022 dataset, comparing our approach with three DL models: CNN-LSTM, CNN-RNN, and CNN-GRU. In the figure, blue and red lines represent training and testing accuracy, respectively, while yellow and green lines show training and testing loss. For CNN-LSTM, both training and testing accuracy range from 10% to 99%, with minor fluctuations. Notably, testing accuracy briefly drops to 85% at epoch 22 and 83% at epoch 24. Loss curves start high but gradually reduce, reaching a minimum of approximately 3%. For CNN-RNN, accuracy ranges from 22% to 95%, with training and testing loss decreasing to about 10%. CNN-GRU shows accuracy variations between 19% and 90%, with notable testing fluctuations, and a steady loss around 17%. Among these, CNN-LSTM demonstrates the best performance, with CNN-GRU showing less stability.

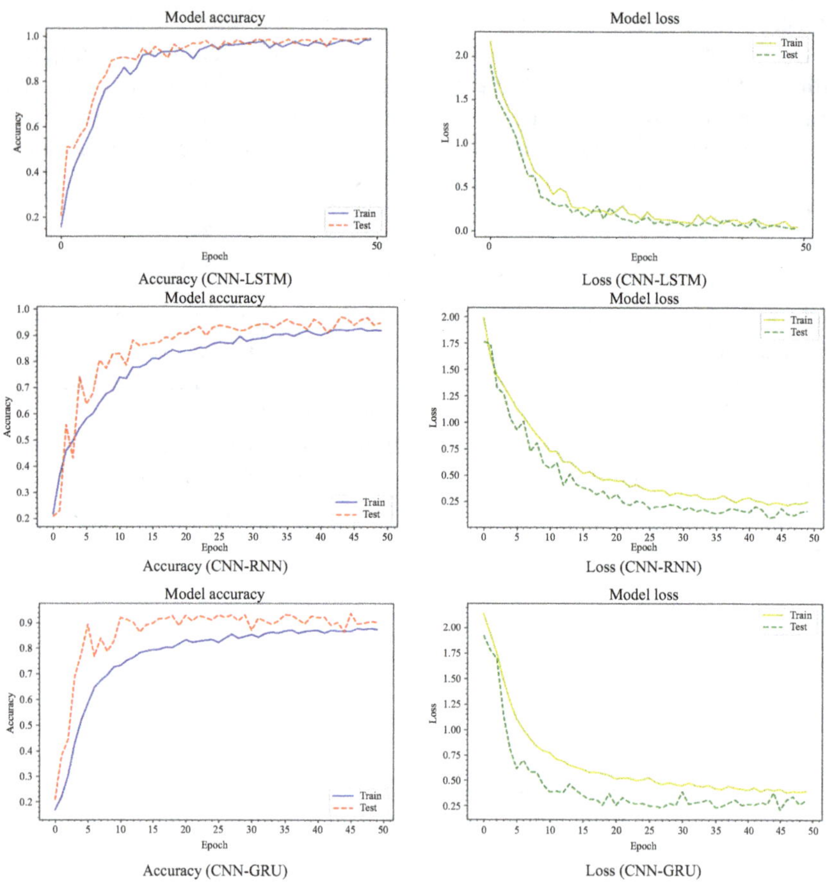

Figure 9.8 Training and testing accuracy and loss curves for the CIC-IoT 2022 dataset

In Figure 9.9, the accuracy and loss curves for the CIC-IoT 2023 dataset are presented. For CNN-LSTM, accuracy varies from 19% to 96%, with a minimum loss of approximately 4%. CNN-RNN achieves an accuracy between 21% and 96%, with loss close to 8%. CNN-GRU's accuracy ranges from 5% to 95%, with testing accuracy beginning at 82%. These results indicate that CNN-LSTM consistently achieves superior performance across both datasets, outperforming CNN-RNN and CNN-GRU.

Table 9.4 presents the evaluation metrics for the CNN-LSTM model on the CIC-IoT 2022 dataset. The analysis includes precision, recall, and F1-score for various camera-based flood attacks. The Amcrest Camera achieved an F1-score of 98%, recall of 100%, and precision of 95%. The Arlo Basestation Camera reached 100% across all metrics. For the ArloQ, DLink, HeimVision, and SimCam cameras, precision, recall, and F1-scores consistently hit 100%, while performance for

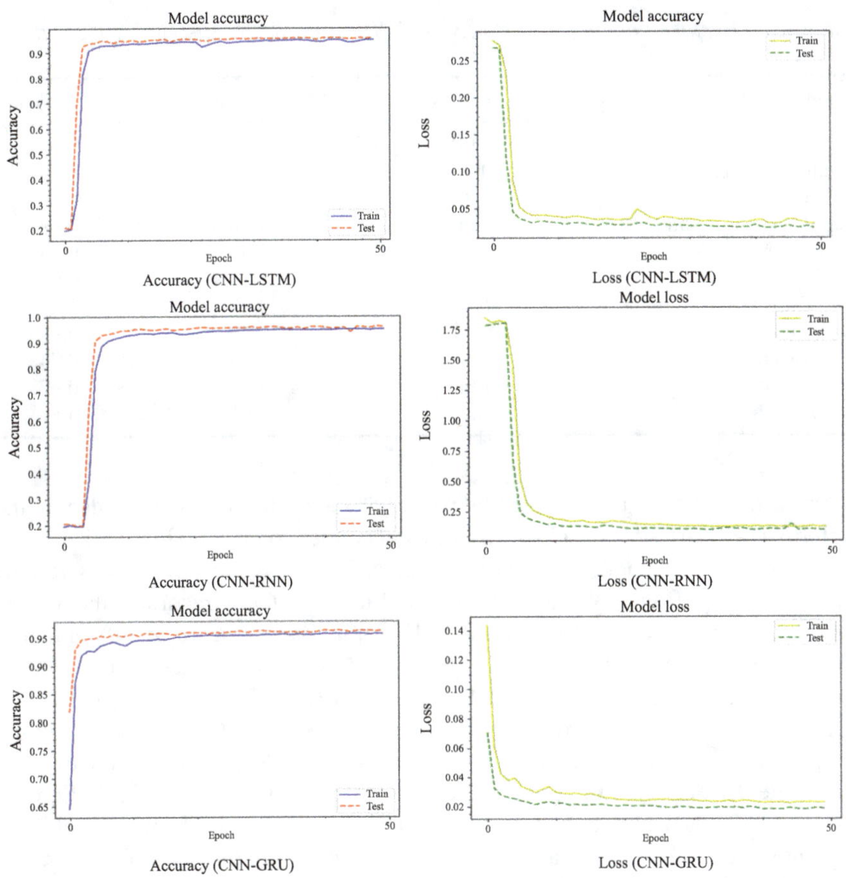

Figure 9.9 Training and testing accuracy and loss curves for the CIC-IoT 2023 dataset

Table 9.4 Performance metrics of CNN-LSTM model on the CIC-IoT 2022 dataset

Flood attacks	Precision	Recall	F1-score
SimCam	1.00	1.00	1.00
ArloQ Camera	1.00	1.00	1.00
Home Eye Camera	1.00	0.99	0.99
DLink Camera	1.00	1.00	1.00
Netatmo Camera	0.97	1.00	0.98
Luohe Camera	1.00	1.00	1.00
Amcrest	0.95	1.00	0.98
Arlo Basestation Camera	1.00	0.99	1.00
HeimVision Camera	1.00	1.00	1.00
Nest Camera	1.00	0.98	0.99
Borun Camera	1.00	0.96	0.98

Table 9.5 Performance metrics of CNN-RNN model on the CIC-IoT 2022 dataset

Flood attacks	Precision	Recall	F1-score
Home Eye Camera	1.00	0.95	0.98
Netatmo Camera	0.95	0.94	0.94
Amcrest	0.88	0.75	0.81
HeimVision Camera	0.88	0.70	0.78
DLink Camera	1.00	0.86	0.93
SimCam	0.98	1.00	0.99
Arlo Basestation Camera	1.00	0.99	1.00
Nest Camera	0.95	1.00	0.98
Luohe Camera	0.58	1.00	0.74
ArloQ Camera	1.00	0.91	0.95
Borun Camera	0.94	0.81	0.87

different flood attack types varied between 95% and 100%. Table 9.5 details the performance metrics for the CNN-RNN model applied to the CIC-IoT 2022 dataset. This model performed slightly below the CNN-LSTM, with values across various attacks ranging from 58% to 100%. The Luohe Camera recorded the lowest metrics, with precision at 58%, recall at 100%, and an F1-score of 74%. Finally, Table 9.6 shows the performance results for the CNN-GRU model on the CIC-IoT 2022 dataset. Compared to the CNN-LSTM and CNN-RNN models, the CNN-GRU exhibited the lowest overall performance. The Luohe Camera again had the lowest metrics, achieving precision of 55%, recall of 98%, and an F1-score of 71%.

Table 9.7 displays the performance metrics for the CNN-LSTM model on the CIC-IoT 2023 dataset, focusing on ten types of DDoS attacks. The model achieves 75% precision, 97% recall, and an F1-score of 85% for the SYN_Flood attack, while the TCP_Flood attack records 100% across all metrics. Conversely, the SynonymousIP_Flood attack shows the weakest performance, with 96% precision, 69% recall, and an F1-score of 80%. Overall, performance metrics for the

Table 9.6 Performance metrics of the CNN-GRU model on the CIC-IoT 2022 dataset

Flood attacks	**Precision**	**Recall**	**F1-score**
Nest Camera	0.95	1.00	0.98
HeimVision Camera	0.88	0.70	0.78
Home Eye Camera	1.00	0.95	0.98
Amcrest	0.88	0.75	0.81
SimCam	0.98	1.00	0.99
DLink Camera	1.00	0.86	0.93
Arlo Basestation Camera	1.00	0.99	1.00
ArloQ Camera	1.00	0.91	0.95
Luohe Camera	0.55	0.98	0.71
Borun Camera	0.94	0.81	0.87
Netatmo Camera	0.95	0.94	0.94

Table 9.7 Performance metrics of the CNN-LSTM model on the CIC-IoT 2023 dataset

DDoS attacks	**Precision**	**Recall**	**F1-score**
ICMP_Fragmentation	0.99	0.99	0.99
SYN_Flood	0.75	0.97	0.85
HTTP_Flood	0.98	0.98	0.98
TCP_Flood	1.00	1.00	1.00
ACK_Fragmentation	0.99	0.99	0.99
SynonymousIP_Flood	0.96	0.69	0.80
RSTFINFlood	1.00	1.00	1.00
PSHACK_Flood	1.00	1.00	1.00
UDP_Flood	1.00	1.00	1.00
ICMP_Flood	1.00	0.99	1.00

CNN-LSTM model range from 69% to 100%. Table 9.8 outlines the performance of the CNN-RNN model on the CIC-IoT 2023 dataset, where the SynonymousIP_Flood attack exhibits the lowest metrics with 96% precision, 64% recall, and an F1-score of 77%. The SYN_Flood attack follows with 73% precision, 98% recall, and an F1-score of 83%. Across all DDoS attacks, the CNN-RNN model's metrics span from 64% to 100%. Table 9.9 provides a comparative analysis of the CNN-LSTM, CNN-RNN, and CNN-GRU models on the CIC-IoT 2022 and CIC-IoT 2023 datasets. Results indicate that the CNN-LSTM model delivers the highest overall performance for intrusion detection. For the CIC-IoT 2022 dataset, CNN-LSTM achieves average metrics of 98.1% precision, 98.4% recall, 97.9% F1-score, and 98.2% accuracy. In the CIC-IoT 2023 dataset, it attains 96.4% classification accuracy, 97% precision, and 96.1% for both recall and F1-score. These results confirm the CNN-LSTM's

Table 9.8 Performance metrics of the CNN-RNN model on the CIC-IoT 2023 dataset

DDoS attacks	Precision	Recall	F1-score
ICMP_Flood	1.00	0.99	1.00
RSTFINFlood	1.00	1.00	1.00
SynonymousIP_Flood	0.96	0.64	0.77
SYN_Flood	0.73	0.98	0.83
HTTP_Flood	0.99	0.98	0.98
UDP_Flood	1.00	1.00	1.00
PSHACK_Flood	1.00	1.00	1.00
TCP_Flood	1.00	1.00	1.00
ACK_Fragmentation	0.99	0.99	0.99
ICMP_Fragmentation	0.98	0.99	0.99

Table 9.9 Performance metrics of the CNN-LSTM model on the Edge-IIoTset dataset

Class	Precision	Recall	F1-score
SQL Injection	1.00	0.96	0.98
Password	0.97	0.81	0.87
MITM (ARP spoofing + DNS)	0.85	0.94	0.90
DDoS ICMP Flood	0.97	0.99	0.96
Port Scanning	1.00	0.96	0.96
Ransomware	0.97	1.00	0.98
DDoS HTTP Flood	0.95	0.95	0.96
Uploading	0.99	0.98	0.97
DDoS TCP SYN Flood	0.94	0.95	0.94
Backdoor	0.89	0.95	0.93
XSS	0.98	1.00	0.97
DDoS UDP Flood	1.00	1.00	1.00
Vulnerability Scanner	1.00	0.98	0.98
OS Fingerprinting	0.99	1.00	0.98

superior performance, with the CNN-GRU model yielding the lowest metrics and the CNN-RNN model showing moderate results.

Additionally, Table 9.9 presents the CNN-LSTM model's classification results on the Edge-IIoT dataset, which encompasses 14 different IoT attack types. High classification accuracy is noted for attacks such as XSS, Ransomware, and OS Fingerprinting, while the MITM attack reflects the lowest performance. Despite the variety of attacks in this dataset, the model maintains a robust overall classification rate of 96.1% across all 14 classes. Lastly, Table 9.10 compares performance results across all three datasets, offering a comprehensive view of the models' effectiveness.

Figure 9.10 presents the confusion matrices for the three DL models—CNN-LSTM, CNN-RNN, and CNN-GRU—applied to both the CIC-IoT 2022 and CIC-IoT

Table 9.10 Comparison of model performance metrics across CIC-IoT 2022, CIC-IoT 2023, and Edge-IIoTset datasets

Dataset	**Method**	**Precision**	**Recall**	**F1-score**	**Accuracy**
Edge-IIoT dataset	CNN-RNN	0.943	0.942	0.936	0.940
2-6	CNN-LSTM	0.965	0.963	0.956	0.962
CIC-IoT dataset 2022	CNN-GRU	0.921	0.906	0.897	0.902
2-6	CNN-RNN	0.958	0.953	0.951	0.954
2-6	CNN-LSTM	0.981	0.984	0.979	0.982
CIC-IoT dataset 2023	CNN-RNN	0.958	0.963	0.958	0.961
2-6	CNN-LSTM	0.970	0.961	0.961	0.964

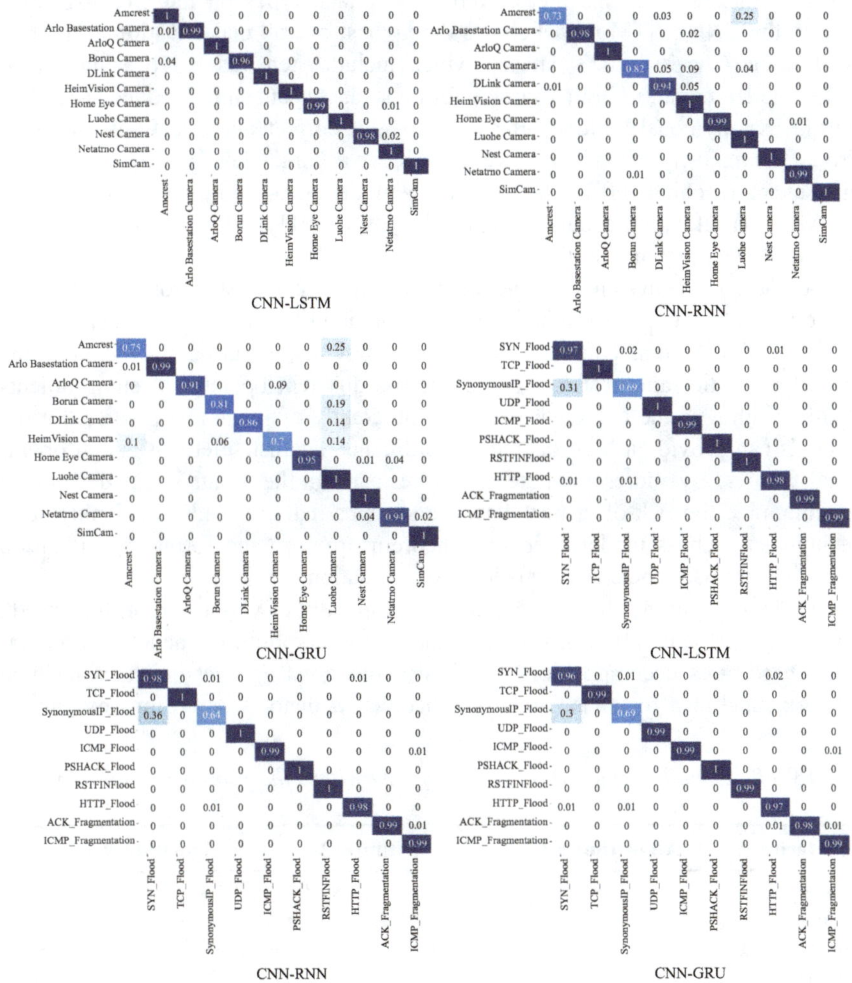

Figure 9.10 Confusion matrices depicting classification results for the CIC-IoT 2022 and CIC-IoT 2023 datasets

2023 datasets. These matrices offer a detailed view of classification accuracy, highlighting correct predictions along the diagonal and misclassifications in the off-diagonal entries. This analysis provides a clear evaluation of each model's performance across various classes.

For the CIC-IoT 2022 dataset, which includes eleven attack types, the CNN-LSTM model achieves strong classification accuracy, with several classes, such as Amcrest, ArloQ Camera, and DLink Camera, reaching 100% accuracy. Minor misclassifications appear in certain classes; for example, the Arlo Basestation Camera has a 1% error rate, and the Borun Camera shows a 4% error rate. In contrast, the CNN-RNN model's performance on the Amcrest class is lower, with only 73% accuracy and a 27% misclassification rate. The CNN-GRU model demonstrates its lowest accuracy for the HeimVision Camera, with 70% correct and 30% misclassified instances. Across all attack types on the CIC-IoT 2022 dataset, the CNN-LSTM model shows the highest overall classification accuracy.

For the CIC-IoT 2023 dataset, which includes ten attack types, the CNN-LSTM model maintains high accuracy for most classes but shows reduced accuracy for the SynonymousIP_Flood attack, with 69% correct classifications and 31% errors. The majority of classes, however, achieve accuracy levels of 97% or higher, with several reaching 100%. The CNN-RNN model ranks slightly lower than CNN-LSTM in classification accuracy, while the CNN-GRU model consistently shows the lowest accuracy among the three.

As the complexity and prevalence of IoT systems increase, formal validation methods are becoming essential. Formal methods utilize mathematical models to systematically design, construct, and verify systems, ensuring they exhibit the desired properties and perform reliably across different operational environments [48,49]. Although the IoT environment is inherently dynamic and diverse, formal methods can provide a high degree of confidence against safety risks and operational failures. By addressing potential issues early in the design stage, developers can minimize the risk of critical flaws in systems that are ready for deployment. Techniques such as model checking, theorem proving, and formal specification languages are used to achieve this level of validation.

Table 9.11 outlines the computational complexity of various algorithms used., where *Ini* represents Initialization, *E* stands for encryption, *Co* denotes computation, *D* indicates decomposition, *f* refers to functions, *ResNet* indicates residual network functions, ρ stands for DAGScheduler, μ denotes derive process, and σ

Table 9.11 Complexity analysis of algorithms within the proposed framework

Cost terms	**Algorithm 9.1**	**Algorithm 9.2**	**Algorithm 9.3**
D, f	–	$2\|n\| + 3\|ResNet\|$	$5\|f\|$
2-4 ρ, σ, μ	–	–	$\|\rho_t\| + 3\|E\|$
2-4 *Ini*	$\|n\|$	$2\|n\|$	–
2-4 E, Co	$\|n\|$	$2\|n\|$	$2\|n\|$
Total cost	$2\|n\|$	$6\|n\| + 3\|ResNet\|$	$2\|n\| + 5\|f\| + \|\rho_t\| + 3\|E\|$

Table 9.12 Comparative performance of the proposed method against existing approaches

Work	Method	Accuracy
Qiu *et al.* [51]	SVM with Kernels	0.933
Sugi and Ratna [56]	LSTM	0.973
Krichen [48]	Adversarial DNN	0.943
Hofer-Schmitz and Stojanović [49]	Deep RNN	0.924
Han *et al.* [40]	Random Search with ML	0.967
Almiani *et al.* [52]	FL	0.971
Saeed *et al.* [57]	RNNs	0.972
Verma and Ranga *et al.* [50]	Supervised ML	0.980
Our method	Multimodal with Transfer Learning	0.982

represents the Spark yarn client. The most computationally intensive elements of the proposed framework are elaborated in Algorithms 9.1–9.3.

Table 9.12 provides a detailed comparison of our proposed method with various existing approaches. Verma and Ranga [50] explored the enhancement of IoT security against DoS attacks using ML techniques and random search categorization. Their research conducted a comprehensive evaluation of classifiers tailored to enhance anomaly-based IDS, employing critical performance metrics and validation methods across various datasets, including CIDDS-001, UNSW-NB15, and NSL-KDD. In another contribution, Qiu *et al.* [51] developed an innovative adversarial attack specifically aimed at DL-driven NIDS for IoT. This approach leveraged black-box access along with model extraction using minimal data samples and saliency mapping techniques to clone the model, thereby identifying the most influential packet features. Almiani *et al.* [52] introduced a fully automated IDS to strengthen cloud security by utilizing a multi-layer recurrent neural network architecture. Positioned close to end-users and IoT devices within the cloud infrastructure, this system effectively counters cyber threats.

Anthi *et al.* [53] proposed a three-layer IDS framework that profiles the behaviors of IoT devices, identifies malicious packets, and categorizes different types of attacks within IoT networks. Granjal *et al.* [54] developed an anomaly-based IDS specifically designed to combat DoS attacks and threats related to 6LoWPAN/CoAP, demonstrating its effectiveness in mitigating these specific vulnerabilities. Yang *et al.* [55] presented a lightweight intrusion detection method for IoT networks, employing federated learning (FL) to enhance resistance against poisoning attacks. This approach uses a scoring mechanism to eliminate unreliable central server models by assessing dataset sizes and local model performance. In a similar vein, Sugi and Ratna [56] created an IDS that combines DL with machine intelligence to protect IoT networks, evaluating the performance of LSTM and KNN algorithms based on metrics such as detection time, kappa statistics, geometric mean, and sensitivity using the Bot-IoT dataset. Saeed *et al.* [57] proposed a security framework employing RNNs to detect and counter intrusions, incorporating source code analysis to check for out-of-bound memory access by assigning tags to memory allocations and adding verification at each access point. Unlike these methods, our approach combines multimodal feature extraction with transfer learning, leading to enhanced classification accuracy in intrusion detection.

9.6 Conclusion

IoT systems face increasing risks from flood attacks, especially Distributed Denial of Service (DDoS) attacks, which overwhelm devices with excessive network traffic, making resources unavailable to legitimate users. The intricate nature of IoT environments, along with the requirement for comprehensive feature sets, complicates the creation of effective IDS. A key challenge is the selection of features that accurately capture attack patterns while reducing dimensionality [58,59]. This chapter introduces an improved IDS for IoT security that integrates multimodal big data representation and transfer learning. The process initiates with the analysis of PCAP files to extract pertinent attack indicators. Spark-based optimization techniques are used to efficiently handle large data sets. Subsequently, transfer learning generates enriched semantic features for the IDS model. The integration of training and texture-based multimodal features enhances classification accuracy for various cyberattacks. The proposed approach was evaluated using the CIC-IoT 2022 and CIC-IoT 2023 datasets, complemented by a game theory-based validation method to assess the model's effectiveness. Three DL architectures—CNN-LSTM, CNN-RNN, and CNN-GRU—were tested. The CNN-LSTM model showed exceptional performance, achieving 98.1% precision, 98.4% recall, 97.9% F1-score, and 98.2% accuracy on the CIC-IoT 2022 dataset. For the CIC-IoT 2023 dataset, it reached 97% precision, 96.1% recall, 96.1% F1-score, and 96.4% accuracy.

However, several limitations need to be addressed for the proposed system's effective deployment in real-world scenarios:

- **Adversarial robustness**: Enhancing resilience against adversarial threats is crucial for IDS reliability, requiring detection and mitigation of subtle network traffic changes to counter advanced attacks.
- **Privacy preservation**: Incorporating privacy-preserving techniques in the IDS can alleviate concerns related to sensitive data handling. Methods such as homomorphic encryption and differential privacy can protect user data while enabling threat detection.
- **Cross-domain adaptability**: Expanding the IDS's functionality across diverse IoT environments enhances its versatility. Training on varied datasets can improve its adaptability to different applications and protocols.
- **Energy efficiency**: Increasing energy efficiency is vital, especially in resource-constrained IoT settings. Implementing energy-efficient data processing and feature extraction methods can reduce computational load while ensuring performance.

- **Adaptability to evolving threats**: The IDS must evolve with DDoS and other cyber threats. Advanced detection techniques are necessary to identify new attack strategies not represented in the training data.

9.7 Potential research directions

The following directions may further improve the proposed IDS framework:

- **Integration of explainable artificial intelligence (XAI) and enhanced transfer learning**: Combining XAI with advanced transfer learning in big data environments offers an opportunity to build interpretable models with enhanced feature engineering. This approach fosters transparency, reliability, and usability in big data solutions. Future research could focus on developing methods to make complex models more interpretable while retaining scalability and efficiency.
- **Dynamic feature extraction**: Creating algorithms for feature extraction that can adapt to evolving network conditions and attack patterns may enhance detection effectiveness. Techniques from reinforcement learning could be utilized to optimize real-time feature extraction.
- **Integration with edge computing**: Merging the IDS with edge computing frameworks can facilitate distributed detection and response mechanisms. Assessing lightweight feature extraction and model inference at the network's edge could lead to reductions in latency and bandwidth consumption.
- **Detection of zero-day threats**: Innovative methodologies are essential for identifying and countering zero-day threats that take advantage of previously unrecognized vulnerabilities. Implementing behavior-based analysis and anomaly detection strategies may assist in recognizing new attack patterns without depending exclusively on established signatures.
- **Profiling IoT devices**: Conducting profiles of IoT devices and analyzing their behavioral trends over time can help uncover potential security risks. Such profiling techniques can contribute to the development of comprehensive device profiles and identify deviations from expected behaviors, thereby improving threat detection capabilities.

These research directions aim to enhance the adaptability, efficiency, and robustness of IDS in the evolving IoT landscape, leading to more secure and reliable IoT networks.

References

[1] Lin J, Yu W, Zhang N, *et al.* A survey on internet of things: Architecture, enabling technologies, security and privacy, and applications. *IEEE Internet of Things Journal*. 2017;4(5):1125–1142.

[2] Bathla G, Bhadane K, Singh RK, *et al.* Autonomous vehicles and intelligent automation: Applications, challenges, and opportunities. *Mobile Information Systems*. 2022;2022(1):7632892.

[3] Tao F, Cheng J, and Qi Q. IIHub: An industrial Internet-of-Things hub toward smart manufacturing based on cyber-physical system. *IEEE Transactions on Industrial Informatics*. 2017;14(5):2271–2280.

[4] Zhou X, Liang W, Li W, *et al.* Hierarchical adversarial attacks against graph-neural-network-based IoT network intrusion detection system. *IEEE Internet of Things Journal*. 2021;9(12):9310–9319.

[5] Hassan MM, Gumaei A, Alsanad A, *et al.* A hybrid deep learning model for efficient intrusion detection in big data environment. *Information Sciences*. 2020;513:386–396.

[6] Ullah F, Srivastava G, Ullah S, *et al.* NIDS-VSB: Network intrusion detection system for VANET using Spark-based big data optimization and transfer learning. *IEEE Transactions on Consumer Electronics*. 2023;70(1):1798–1809.

[7] Ullah F, Turab A, Ullah S, *et al.* Enhanced network intrusion detection system for internet of things security using multimodal big data representation with transfer learning and game theory. *Sensors*. 2024;24(13):4152.

[8] Silva DS, and Holanda M. Applications of geospatial big data in the Internet of Things. *Transactions in GIS*. 2022;26(1):41–71.

[9] Alsirhani A, Sampalli S, and Bodorik P. DDoS attack detection system: utilizing classification algorithms with Apache Spark. In: *2018 9th IFIP International Conference on New Technologies, Mobility and Security (NTMS)*. Piscataway, NJ: IEEE; 2018. pp. 1–7.

[10] Chaabouni N, Mosbah M, Zemmari A, *et al.* Network intrusion detection for IoT security based on learning techniques. *IEEE Communications Surveys & Tutorials*. 2019;21(3):2671–2701.

[11] Ring M, Wunderlich S, Scheuring D, *et al.* A survey of network-based intrusion detection data sets. *Computers & Security*. 2019;86:147–167.

[12] Zhang S, Zhao H, and Fan Z. Packet bytes-based abnormal encrypted proxy traffic identification. In: *2024 IEEE 30th International Conference on Telecommunications (ICT)*. Piscataway, NJ: IEEE; 2024. pp. 01–07.

[13] Stephen R, and Arockiam L. Intrusion detection system to detect sinkhole attack on RPL protocol in Internet of Things. *International Journal of Electrical Electronics and Computer Science*. 2017;4(4):16–20.

[14] Al-Fuqaha A, Guizani M, Mohammadi M, *et al.* Internet of Things: A survey on enabling technologies, protocols, and applications. *IEEE Communications Surveys & Tutorials*. 2015;17(4):2347–2376.

[15] Kouicem DE, Bouabdallah A, and Lakhlef H. Internet of Things security: A top-down survey. *Computer Networks*. 2018;141:199–221.

[16] Deshmukh-Bhosale S, and Sonavane SS. A real-time intrusion detection system for wormhole attack in the RPL based Internet of Things. *Procedia Manufacturing*. 2019;32:840–847.

[17] Roldán J, Boubeta-Puig J, Martnez JL, *et al.* Integrating complex event processing and machine learning: An intelligent architecture for detecting IoT security attacks. *Expert Systems with Applications*. 2020;149:113251.

[18] Summerville DH, Zach KM, and Chen Y. Ultra-lightweight deep packet anomaly detection for Internet of Things devices. In: *2015 IEEE 34th International Performance Computing and Communications Conference (IPCCC)*. Piscataway, NJ: IEEE; 2015. pp. 1–8.

[19] Sadeghi-Niaraki A. Internet of Thing (IoT) review of review: Bibliometric overview since its foundation. *Future Generation Computer Systems*. 2023; 143:361–377.

[20] Ioulianou P, Vasilakis V, Moscholios I, *et al.* A signature-based intrusion detection system for the internet of things. *Information and Communication Technology Form*. 2018.

[21] Jaradat AS, Barhoush MM, and Easa RB. Network intrusion detection system: Machine learning approach. *Indonesian Journal of Electrical Engineering and Computer Science*. 2022;25(2):1151–1158.

[22] Khan MA, and Kim Y. Deep learning-based hybrid intelligent intrusion detection system. *Computers, Materials & Continua*. 2021;68(1):671–687.

[23] Kaur J. Streaming data analytics: Challenges and opportunities. *International Journal of Applied Engineering & Technology*. 2023;5(S4):10–16.

[24] Tun MT, Nyaung DE, and Phyu MP. Performance evaluation of intrusion detection streaming transactions using Apache Kafka and Spark streaming. In: *2019 International Conference on Advanced Information Technologies (ICAIT)*. Piscataway, NJ: IEEE; 2019. pp. 25–30.

[25] Li H, Wu J, Xu H, *et al.* Explainable intelligence-driven defense mechanism against advanced persistent threats: A joint edge game and AI approach. *IEEE Transactions on Dependable and Secure Computing*. 2021;19(2):757–775.

[26] Sun H, Yu H, and Fan G. Contract-based resource sharing for time effective task scheduling in fog-cloud environment. *IEEE Transactions on Network and Service Management*. 2020;17(2):1040–1053.

[27] Ullah F, Ullah S, Srivastava G, *et al.* IDS-INT: Intrusion detection system using transformer-based transfer learning for imbalanced network traffic. *Digital Communications and Networks*. 2024;10(1):190–204.

[28] Seyyar YE, Yavuz AG, and Ünver HM. An attack detection framework based on BERT and deep learning. *IEEE Access*. 2022;10:68633–68644.

[29] Li J, Zhang H, and Wei Z. The weighted Word2vec paragraph vectors for anomaly detection over HTTP traffic. *IEEE Access*. 2020;8:141787–141798.

[30] Min E, Long J, Liu Q, *et al.* TR-IDS: Anomaly-based intrusion detection through text-convolutional neural network and random forest. *Security and communication Networks*. 2018;2018(1):4943509.

[31] Musman S, and Turner A. A game theoretic approach to cyber security risk management. *The Journal of Defense Modeling and Simulation*. 2018;15 (2):127–146.

[32] Agah A, Das SK, Basu K, *et al.* Intrusion detection in sensor networks: A non-cooperative game approach. In: *3rd IEEE International Symposium on Network Computing and Applications, 2004.(NCA 2004). Proceedings*. Piscataway, NJ: IEEE; 2004. pp. 343–346.

[33] Otrok H, Mehrandish M, Assi C, *et al.* Game theoretic models for detecting network intrusions. *Computer Communications*. 2008;31(10):1934–1944.

[34] Gurvich V, and Naumova M. On Nash-solvability of n-person graphical games under Markov and a-priori realizations. *Annals of Operations Research*. 2024;336(3):1905–1927.

[35] Zhu Y, Wu H, Tao X, *et al.* Game-theoretic security analysis in heterogeneous IoT networks: A competition perspective. *IEEE Internet of Things Journal*. 2024;11(21):35048–35059.

[36] Kang W, Liu Q, Zhu P, *et al.* Coordinated cyber-physical attacks based on different attack strategies for cascading failure analysis in smart grids. *Wireless Networks*. 2024;30(5):3821–3836.

[37] Karaki A, and Al-Fagih L. Evolutionary game theory as a catalyst in smart grids: From theoretical insights to practical strategies. *IEEE Access*. 2024; 12:186926–186940.

[38] Amiri-Zarandi M, Dara RA, and Lin X. SIDS: A federated learning approach for intrusion detection in IoT using social internet of things. *Computer Networks*. 2023;236:110005.

[39] Ho JW. Game theoretic approach toward detection of input-driven evasive malware in the IoT. *Security and Privacy*. 2023;8(1):e467.

[40] Han L, Zhou M, Jia W, *et al.* Intrusion detection model of wireless sensor networks based on game theory and an autoregressive model. *Information Sciences*. 2019;476:491–504.

[41] Li N, and Wang Z. Spatial attention guided residual attention network for hyperspectral image classification. *IEEE Access*. 2022;10:9830–9847.

[42] Gupta YK, and Kumari S. A study of big data analytics using Apache Spark with Python and Scala. In: *2020 3rd International Conference on Intelligent Sustainable Systems (ICISS)*. Piscataway, NJ: IEEE; 2020. pp. 471–478.

[43] Venkatesh RT, Chandrashekar DK, Rao PBS, *et al.* Systematic approaches to data placement, replication and migration in heterogeneous edge-cloud computing systems: A comprehensive literature review. *Ingénierie des Systèmes d'Information*. 2023;28(3):751–759.

[44] Sun H, Chen M, Weng J, *et al.* Anomaly detection for in-vehicle network using CNN-LSTM with attention mechanism. *IEEE Transactions on Vehicular Technology*. 2021;70(10):10880–10893.

[45] Dadkhah S, Mahdikhani H, Danso PK, *et al.* Towards the development of a realistic multidimensional IoT profiling dataset. In: *2022 19th Annual International Conference on Privacy, Security & Trust (PST)*. Piscataway, NJ: IEEE; 2022. pp. 1–11.

[46] Neto ECP, Dadkhah S, Ferreira R, *et al.* CICIoT2023: A real-time dataset and benchmark for large-scale attacks in IoT environment. *Sensors*. 2023;23 (13):5941.

[47] Ferrag MA, Friha O, Hamouda D, *et al.* Edge-IIoTset: A new comprehensive realistic cyber security dataset of IoT and IIoT applications for centralized and federated learning. *IEEE Access*. 2022;10:40281–40306.

[48] Krichen M. A survey on formal verification and validation techniques for internet of things. *Applied Sciences*. 2023;13(14):8122.

[49] Hofer-Schmitz K, and Stojanović B. Towards formal verification of IoT protocols: A review. *Computer Networks*. 2020;174:107233.

[50] Verma A, and Ranga V. Machine learning based intrusion detection systems for IoT applications. *Wireless Personal Communications*. 2020;111 (4):2287–2310.

[51] Qiu H, Dong T, Zhang T, *et al.* Adversarial attacks against network intrusion detection in IoT systems. *IEEE Internet of Things Journal*. 2020;8 (13):10327–10335.

[52] Almiani M, AbuGhazleh A, Al-Rahayfeh A, *et al.* Deep recurrent neural network for IoT intrusion detection system. *Simulation Modelling Practice and Theory*. 2020;101:102031.

[53] Anthi E, Williams L, Słowińska M, *et al.* A supervised intrusion detection system for smart home IoT devices. *IEEE Internet of Things Journal*. 2019;6 (5):9042–9053.

[54] Granjal J, Silva JM, and Lourenço N. Intrusion detection and prevention in CoAP wireless sensor networks using anomaly detection. *Sensors*. 2018;18 (8):2445.

[55] Yang R, He H, Wang Y, *et al.* Dependable federated learning for IoT intrusion detection against poisoning attacks. *Computers & Security*. 2023; 132:103381.

[56] Sugi SSS, and Ratna SR. Investigation of machine learning techniques in intrusion detection system for IoT network. In: *2020 3rd International Conference on Intelligent Sustainable Systems (ICISS)*. Piscataway, NJ: IEEE; 2020. pp. 1164–1167.

[57] Saeed A, Ahmadinia A, Javed A, *et al.* Intelligent intrusion detection in low-power IoTs. *ACM Transactions on Internet Technology (TOIT)*. 2016;16 (4):1–25.

[58] Ullah F, Alsirhani A, Alshahrani MM, *et al.* Explainable malware detection system using transformers-based transfer learning and multi-model visual representation. *Sensors*. 2022;22(18):6766.

[59] Ullah F, Ullah S, Naeem MR, *et al.* Cyber-threat detection system using a hybrid approach of transfer learning and multi-model image representation. *Sensors*. 2022;22(15):5883.

Chapter 10

Cybersecurity for Internet of Things: big data optimization for IoT-based real-time network traffic analysis

Abdul Ahad[1], Zheng Jiangbin[1], Ahsan Wajahat[1], Shamsher Ullah Khan[2], Muhammad Tahir[3] and Muhammad Aman Sheikh[4]

Abstract

In this chapter, we delve into the realm of cybersecurity for the Internet of Things (IoT), with a particular focus on big data optimization for IoT-based real-time network traffic analysis (NTA). The IoT, representing a vast network of interconnected devices, generates a staggering volume of data. This data, when effectively harnessed, holds the potential to revolutionize various sectors by enhancing efficiency, decision-making processes, and cybersecurity measures. Our study addresses the critical challenges of managing, processing, and securing this immense data trove, underscoring the significance of advanced big data analytics and optimization techniques in the context of real-time NTA. By employing sophisticated machine learning algorithms and leveraging the power of edge and cloud computing, we propose innovative solutions to enhance the security and operational efficiency of IoT networks. This research not only contributes to the academic discourse on IoT and cybersecurity but also offers practical insights for industry professionals, paving the way for more resilient and intelligent IoT ecosystems.

10.1 Introduction to IoT and cybersecurity

The Internet of Things (IoT) refers to the network of physical objects—“things”—embedded with sensors, software, and other technologies to connect and exchange

[1]School of Software, Northwestern Polytechnical University, P. R. China
[2]School of Computer Science and Software Engineering, Shenzhen University, P. R. China
[3]Department of Computing, University of Turku, Finland
[4]Department of Electronics and Computer Systems, Cardiff Metropolitan University, UK

data with other devices and systems over the Internet. These devices range from ordinary household items like refrigerators and light bulbs to sophisticated industrial tools. IoT has revolutionized the way we interact with our surroundings, making it possible for objects to communicate not just with humans but also with each other [1].

The IoT is a revolutionary technology paradigm that connects everyday objects and devices to the Internet, allowing them to send and receive data. This interconnectivity aims to make our lives more efficient, safer, and more productive by integrating the physical world into computer-based systems [2]. Here are the key characteristics of IoT.

- **Interconnectivity**: At the heart of IoT is the ability to connect devices, objects, and systems. This includes not just traditional electronic devices like smartphones and computers but also a wide range of non-traditional items such as home appliances, vehicles, and even clothing. Interconnectivity allows these objects to communicate with each other and with central systems or applications, facilitating the exchange of data and commands [3].
- **Things-related services**: IoT offers services related to the objects themselves, such as collecting specific data about their condition or the surrounding environment. These services can enhance the utility, accuracy, efficiency, and productivity of object-related operations and extend their capabilities.
- **Heterogeneity**: The IoT ecosystem is inherently heterogeneous, comprising a wide variety of devices with different hardware capacities, operating systems, and communication protocols [4]. This diversity requires flexible and adaptable communication and processing infrastructures to ensure seamless interoperability among these diverse systems [5].
- **Dynamic changes**: The state of devices in the IoT environment can change frequently. Devices can be moved, turned on or off, or change their status in other ways. The system's configuration might also change dynamically, with devices joining or leaving networks. This dynamic nature requires robust systems capable of adapting to continuous changes and managing them efficiently [6].
- **Enormous scales**: The number of devices connected to the IoT is enormous and continuously growing. It's estimated that tens of billions of devices will be connected to the IoT by the end of the decade [7]. This scale presents unique challenges in terms of data management, device management, and communication.
- **Sensing**: Many IoT devices include sensors that can gather information about the physical world, such as temperature, light, motion, and more. This sensing capability is fundamental to many IoT applications, allowing for the collection of data that can be analyzed to make decisions or provide services.
- **Connectivity**: Connectivity in the IoT context goes beyond traditional internet connectivity to include various types of network connections, such as Bluetooth, Wi-Fi, cellular networks, and Low Power Wide Area Networks (LPWAN). The choice of connectivity method depends on factors like power consumption, range, and data requirements [8].

- **Intelligence**: IoT systems often incorporate some level of intelligence, using technologies like machine learning and artificial intelligence (AI) to analyze data, make decisions, and learn from new information [9]. This intelligence can be distributed across the IoT ecosystem, from the edge devices to central processing systems [10].
- **Security**: Given the vast amount of data IoT devices collect and transmit, security is a paramount concern. IoT systems must ensure data privacy, secure data transmission, and protection against unauthorized access or attacks.
- **Energy management**: Many IoT devices are designed to operate with minimal power consumption, using techniques like energy harvesting or low-power operation modes [11]. Efficient energy management is crucial for ensuring the longevity and sustainability of IoT devices, especially those deployed in hard-to-reach or remote locations [12].

These characteristics highlight the complexity, potential, and challenges of the IoT. As technology advances, the capabilities and applications of IoT systems continue to expand, promising significant impacts across various sectors, including healthcare, agriculture, manufacturing, and smart cities.

10.2 The importance of cybersecurity in IoT

The IoT represents a network of physically connected devices that can gather and share data, significantly enhancing automation, efficiency, and convenience across various domains, including smart homes, healthcare, industrial processes, and transportation [13]. However, the extensive interconnectivity and data exchange inherent in IoT systems also presents substantial cybersecurity challenges [14]. The importance of cybersecurity in IoT is paramount for several reasons:

- **Vast attack surface**: IoT devices significantly increase the attack surface for potential cyber threats. Every connected device, from smart thermostats to industrial sensors, offers a potential entry point for malicious actors. The diversity and number of these devices, many of which are not traditionally considered computers or phones, can lead to inconsistent security standards and practices, making them vulnerable to attacks [15].
- **Data privacy**: IoT devices often collect sensitive personal information, such as health data from wearable fitness trackers or activity patterns from smart home devices. This information can be highly attractive to cybercriminals, who may seek to steal it for identity theft, financial fraud, or targeted attacks [16]. Protecting this data is crucial to maintaining user trust and compliance with data protection regulations.
- **Complex ecosystems**: The IoT ecosystem involves multiple stakeholders, including device manufacturers, software developers, service providers, and end-users, each with their responsibilities and challenges in ensuring cybersecurity. The complexity of these ecosystems can lead to vulnerabilities if not

properly managed, as security lapses in any component can compromise the entire system [17].

- **Denial of service attacks**: IoT devices can be hijacked to launch massive distributed denial of service (DDoS) attacks, overwhelming target networks or services with traffic. These attacks can disrupt critical infrastructure, such as healthcare systems, financial services, and utility providers, leading to significant economic and societal impacts [18].
- **Device and data integrity**: Ensuring the integrity of devices and data is critical in IoT applications. For example, in a smart grid, compromised devices could report false data, leading to incorrect decisions or actions that could disrupt power distribution [19]. Similarly, tampered data in healthcare IoT applications could result in misdiagnoses or inappropriate treatments, endangering lives.

The importance of cybersecurity in IoT cannot be overstated. As IoT continues to evolve and integrate more deeply into critical aspects of modern life, ensuring the security of these interconnected systems is crucial to realizing their full potential while safeguarding privacy, safety, and trust. Table 10.1 shows the performance analysis of the existing DL/ML schemes for cyberattack detection and classification.

Table 10.1 Performance analysis of the existing DL/ML schemes for cyberattack detection and classification

Ref.	Target areas of cybersecurity	DL/ML approaches	Datasets	Bench marking	Performance
[20]	DDoS attacks	SVM, DT, NB and MLP	KDD-Cup99 and CICIDS2017	GA, PSO and TLBO	Acc = 99.98, DR = 98.91, Precision = 98.75, FPR = 0.75, F-meas = 98.41, AUC = 98.72
[21]	Network packets preprocessing	CNN	NSL-KDD	DBN, STL, SMR, S-NDAE	Acc = 88.82, F-meas = 90.67
[22]	Wireless intrusion detection system	DNN	NSL-KDD	SVM, DT, NBandk-NN	Acc = 99.54
[23]	Detecting DDoS in cloud environment	RBM	KDD-Cup99	DT, RF, RT, RNFNetwork and LR-PSO and GA	Recall = 99.88, TNR = 99.96, Acc = 99.92, F-score = 99.93
[24]	Zero-day attacks	DNN, AE and GAN	NSL-KDD, UNSW-NB15	KNN, DT, LR, SVM, RF, DBN, and DNN	Acc = 93.01, Precision = 95.21, Recall = 91.94, F-meas = 93.54

10.3 Common cyber threats and vulnerabilities in IoT networks

The IoT networks, with their rapidly expanding array of connected devices, offer unprecedented opportunities for enhancing efficiency, convenience, and innovation across various sectors. However, this expansion also presents a broad spectrum of cyber threats and vulnerabilities. Understanding these risks is crucial for developing effective strategies to mitigate them. Below are some of the most common cyber threats and vulnerabilities in IoT networks.

- **Weak authentication/authorization mechanisms**: Many IoT devices lack robust authentication and authorization processes, making them easy targets for unauthorized access. Default or weak passwords, lack of two-factor authentication, and inadequate access controls can allow attackers to easily hijack devices [25].
- **Insecure network services**: IoT devices often operate on networks that are insufficiently secured, exposing them to attacks such as eavesdropping, man-in-the-middle attacks, and data breaches. Insecure network services and protocols can also facilitate unauthorized access or denial of service attacks [26].
- **Lack of encryption**: The absence of strong encryption for data at rest and in transit is a significant vulnerability. Without encryption, sensitive information can be intercepted, read, and modified by attackers, leading to data breaches and privacy violations.
- **Firmware and software vulnerabilities**: IoT devices frequently suffer from vulnerabilities in their firmware or software, such as bugs or flaws that have not been patched [27]. These vulnerabilities can be exploited by attackers to gain control over devices, steal information, or use devices as part of botnets for larger attacks.
- **Physical security**: Physical security is often overlooked in the context of IoT, yet many devices are deployed in easily accessible or remote locations, making them vulnerable to physical tampering. This can lead to direct device compromise or the installation of malicious software.
- **Insecure interfaces and application programming interfaces (APIs)**: Many IoT devices and systems interact with users through web or cloud-based interfaces and APIs, which can be vulnerable to attacks if not properly secured [28]. Insecure interfaces can allow attackers to gain unauthorized access to device functionalities, data, or even the entire IoT network.
- **Insufficient privacy protection**: IoT devices often collect vast amounts of personal data, but insufficient privacy protections can lead to unauthorized data collection, processing, and dissemination. This not only poses risks to individual privacy but can also lead to compliance issues with data protection regulations.
- **Lack of update mechanisms**: A significant number of IoT devices cannot be remotely updated or patched. This leaves known vulnerabilities unaddressed, prolonging the exposure of devices to potential exploits.

- **Supply chain attacks**: IoT devices are produced through complex supply chains, and vulnerabilities can be introduced at any stage, from manufacturing to software development. Attackers can exploit these vulnerabilities to compromise devices before they even reach consumers.

10.4 Big data in IoT

Big data in the IoT refers to the massive volume of data generated by interconnected devices and sensors embedded in everyday objects. These devices collect and transmit data about their environment, operations, and interactions, contributing to a vast pool of data that can be analyzed to gain insights, improve decision-making, and automate processes. The convergence of big data and IoT technologies has significant implications across various sectors, including healthcare, manufacturing, transportation, and smart cities [29].

Figure 10.1 illustrates the flow and processing of big data within an IoT ecosystem. Various "things" or devices collect data and send it to a gateway. The data then travels to a cloud gateway, which acts as an intermediary, processing control data. This processed information is utilized by control applications for managing operations. In parallel, sensor data from the gateway is sent to a streaming data processor and then stored in both a data lake and a big data warehouse. The data

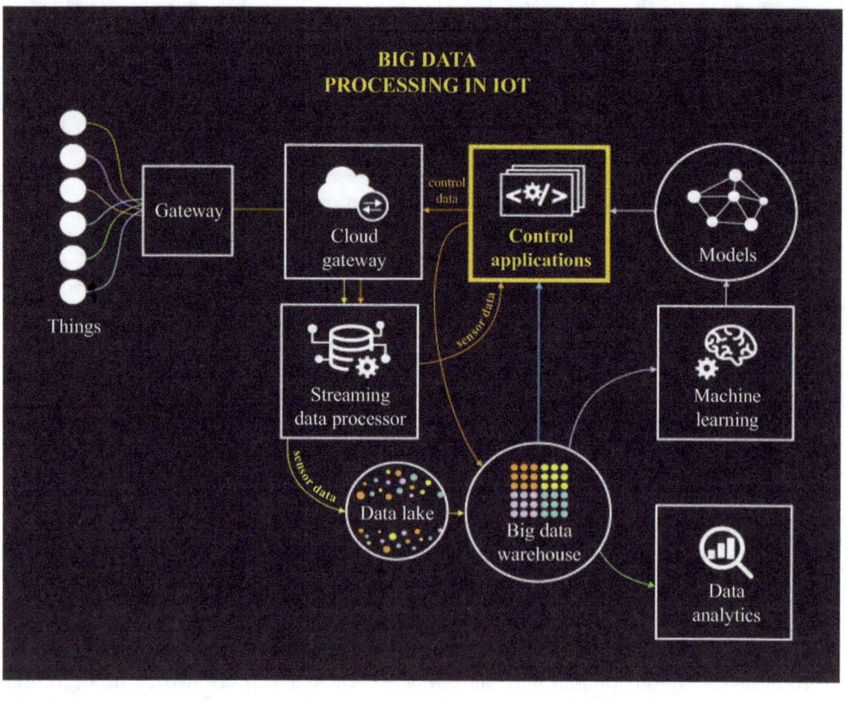

Figure 10.1 Big data processing in IoT (source: www.scnsoft.com/big data)

lake stores vast amounts of raw data in its native format, while the warehouse organizes and structures the data for analysis. Machine learning algorithms are applied to create models for predictive analytics and other applications. Finally, data analytics is employed to extract actionable insights from the processed data. This diagram portrays the complex infrastructure required to harness IoT data effectively for various applications.

10.4.1 Data generation and collection

IoT devices, ranging from wearable fitness trackers to industrial sensors, generate a continuous stream of data. This data can include information about temperature, humidity, location, movement, and much more, depending on the application [30]. The sheer volume and variety of data produced pose unique challenges and opportunities for storage, management, and analysis.

10.4.2 Data analytics and intelligence

The primary value of combining big data with IoT lies in the ability to analyze the collected data to extract meaningful insights. Advanced analytics techniques, including machine learning and AI, are applied to process and analyze the data. These analyses can uncover patterns, trends, and anomalies that would be impossible to detect manually, enabling predictive maintenance, trend forecasting, and personalized services [31].

10.4.3 Enhanced decision-making

The insights gained from big data analytics can significantly enhance decision-making processes [32]. For businesses, this can mean more informed strategic planning, operational efficiency, and customer satisfaction. For example, predictive maintenance can prevent costly downtime in manufacturing by identifying equipment issues before they cause failures. In healthcare, real-time data analysis can lead to personalized treatment plans and early detection of health issues [33].

10.4.4 Challenges of big data in IoT

While the integration of big data and IoT offers numerous benefits, it also presents several challenges:

- **Data volume**: The vast amount of data generated by IoT devices requires significant storage capacity and efficient data management strategies.
- **Data velocity**: IoT devices often transmit data in real-time or near-real-time, necessitating the ability to process and analyze data quickly to make timely decisions.
- **Data variety**: IoT data can be structured, semi-structured, or unstructured, coming in various formats from different devices, which complicates analysis and integration.
- **Data veracity**: The accuracy and reliability of IoT data can vary, impacting the quality of insights derived from it.

- **Security and privacy**: Managing and protecting the vast amounts of potentially sensitive data generated by IoT devices is a critical concern, requiring robust security and privacy measures.

10.4.5 Future prospects

As IoT technologies continue to evolve and proliferate, the role of big data in harnessing the potential of these interconnected devices will only grow more critical. Innovations in data storage, processing, and analytics technologies, along with advancements in AI and machine learning, are expected to further enhance the ability to derive valuable insights from IoT-generated data [34]. This ongoing evolution promises to unlock new levels of efficiency, customization, and automation, reshaping industries and daily life in the process. In conclusion, big data in IoT represents a powerful combination that enables the transformation of vast amounts of data into actionable insights, driving innovation and efficiency across various domains [35]. However, realizing its full potential requires addressing the significant challenges related to data management, analysis, security, and privacy.

10.5 Network traffic analysis in IoT

Network traffic analysis (NTA) in the context of the IoT is a critical cybersecurity and network management practice. It involves the monitoring, capturing, and analysis of data packets that travel across a network of interconnected IoT devices and systems [36]. This process is essential for ensuring the security, performance, and reliability of IoT networks, which are increasingly becoming integral to various aspects of modern life, from smart homes and healthcare to industrial automation and smart cities [37].

Figure 10.2 shows two different IoT network types and their respective data flow patterns. The top section represents a traditional centralized IoT

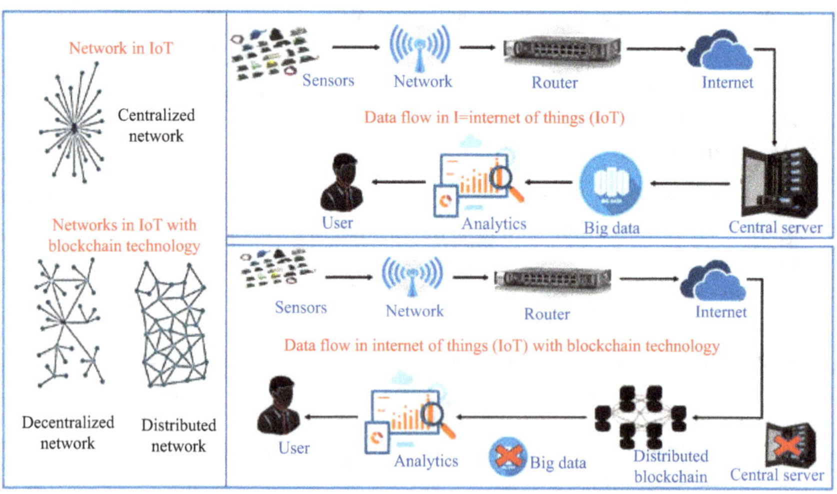

Figure 10.2 Network traffic analysis in IoT [38]

network, where sensors collect data and send it through a network to a router, and then to the internet, culminating at a central server. This pathway allows for data analytics and user interaction but relies on a central point, which can be a vulnerability. In contrast, the bottom section introduces a decentralized IoT network utilizing blockchain technology. Here, the data still travels from sensors to the internet but instead of a central server, it is distributed across a blockchain network, enhancing security and data integrity by eliminating the central point of failure. This setup still enables data analytics and user engagement through a distributed ledger, which ensures a more secure and resilient network.

10.5.1 Objectives of network traffic analysis in IoT

- **Security monitoring and threat detection**: Identifying suspicious activities, malware infections, and signs of cyber-attacks by analyzing traffic patterns and comparing them against known threat signatures or anomalous behavior patterns.
- **Performance monitoring and optimization**: Analyzing traffic to identify bottlenecks, inefficient routing, and other issues that can affect network performance and the functionality of IoT applications.
- **Network management and planning**: Providing insights into the usage patterns and demands on the network, helping administrators make informed decisions about capacity planning, network design, and infrastructure investments.
- **Compliance and privacy**: Ensuring that data flows comply with relevant regulations and standards, especially those concerning data protection and privacy.

10.5.2 Techniques used in network traffic analysis

- **Deep packet inspection (DPI)**: Examining the data part (payload) of a packet at a detailed level, allowing for the identification of application types, protocols used, and potential malicious payloads.
- **Flow analysis**: Aggregating packets into flows (sequences of packets between source and destination) to analyze traffic patterns over time, which can be useful for understanding normal network behavior and identifying anomalies.
- **Statistical analysis:** Applying statistical models to network traffic data to identify trends, peaks, and anomalies in traffic volumes, speeds, and types.
- **Machine learning and AI**: Employing advanced algorithms to learn from traffic patterns, thereby improving the detection of anomalies and enhancing predictive capabilities for network performance and security incidents.

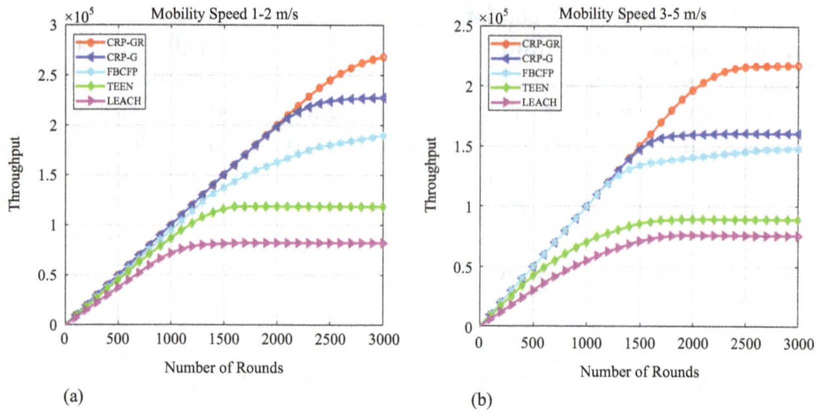

Figure 10.3 Throughput versus number of rounds with different mobility speeds of nodes

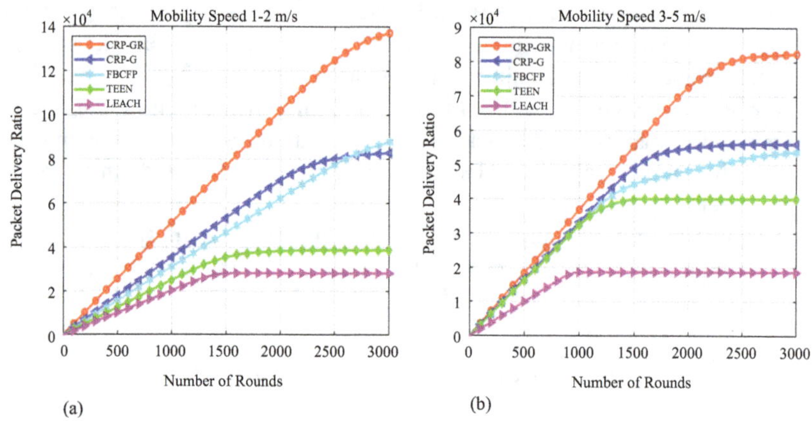

Figure 10.4 Packet delivery ratio versus number of rounds with different mobility speeds of nodes

Figures 10.3, 10.4, and 10.5 present the outcomes of an experimental investigation showcasing the throughput, packet delivery ratio, and average end-to-end delay performance during data transmission from nodes to the base station with different mobility speeds of nodes, respectively. The study explores various clustering and routing protocols, integrating innovative approaches using game theory and reinforcement learning. In the analysis, it has been observed that the reinforcement learning approach exhibits superior performance compared to other methodologies. The results demonstrate its efficacy during data transmission from nodes to the base station, suggesting its potential as a promising strategy for optimizing network performance in all different scenarios.

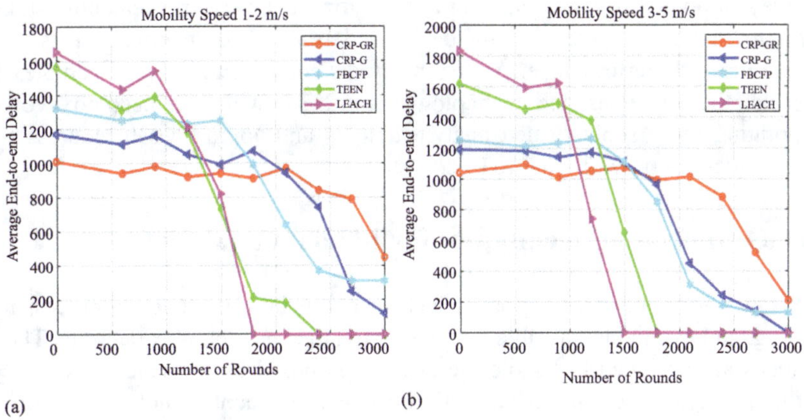

Figure 10.5 End-to-end delay versus number of rounds with different mobility speeds of nodes

10.5.3 Challenges in network traffic analysis for IoT

- **Volume and velocity**: The sheer volume and speed of data generated by thousands or millions of IoT devices pose significant challenges in terms of data capture, storage, and real-time analysis.
- **Heterogeneity**: IoT ecosystems are often composed of a wide variety of devices with different protocols, standards, and communication patterns, making it difficult to achieve a comprehensive and uniform analysis.
- **Encryption**: While encryption is essential for securing data in transit, it also obscures the contents of communications, making it challenging for traditional DPI techniques to analyze packet payloads.
- **Resource constraints**: Many IoT devices operate with limited processing power and battery life, which can constrain the complexity and frequency of local traffic analysis tasks. Best Practices for NTA in IoT.
- **Implementing edge computing**: Processing data closer to its source reduces latency and bandwidth requirements, enabling more efficient preliminary analysis of traffic data before sending it to central systems for further processing.
- **Leveraging cloud-based analytics**: Utilizing cloud platforms can provide the scalability needed to analyze vast amounts of data from IoT networks, leveraging powerful computing resources and sophisticated analytics tools.
- **Continuous monitoring and adaptive thresholds**: Implementing continuous monitoring with adaptive thresholds can help in dynamically adjusting to normal network behavior changes, reducing false positives, and better identifying genuine anomalies.
- **Collaboration and information sharing**: Collaborating with industry partners, sharing information about threats, and utilizing threat intelligence feeds can enhance the detection and mitigation of new and evolving security threats.

NTA plays a pivotal role in managing and securing IoT networks, enabling stakeholders to monitor network health, detect and respond to security threats, and optimize network performance. As IoT networks continue to grow in complexity and scale, the strategies and technologies for NTA will also need to evolve, incorporating more sophisticated analytical tools and approaches to address the unique challenges posed by the IoT ecosystem.

10.6 Optimization techniques for big data analysis

Optimization techniques for big data analysis are crucial for efficiently processing, analyzing, and extracting valuable insights from large and complex datasets. These techniques are designed to handle the challenges posed by the volume, velocity, variety, and veracity of Big Data. Optimization in this context not only involves enhancing computational and processing speeds but also improving the accuracy and quality of the analytical results. Here's a detailed look at various optimization techniques employed in big data analysis.

10.6.1 Data preprocessing and cleaning

Before analysis, big data often requires preprocessing and cleaning to improve its quality and ensure accuracy in the outcomes [39]. This step involves removing noise, handling missing or incomplete information, and eliminating irrelevant data. Techniques like data imputation, normalization, and transformation are applied to prepare datasets for analysis, significantly reducing the computational load and improving the efficiency of subsequent processes.

10.6.2 Distributed computing

Distributed computing frameworks, such as Apache Hadoop and Spark, enable the processing of large datasets across clusters of computers using parallel processing [40]. This approach significantly reduces the time required for data analysis by dividing the dataset into smaller chunks, processing them simultaneously on different nodes, and then aggregating the results. Optimization in distributed computing also involves efficient data partitioning and minimizing data transfer across the network to speed up processing.

10.6.3 Data indexing and compression

Data indexing improves access speed by creating indexes for frequently accessed data, enabling quicker retrieval [41]. Data compression reduces the size of the data, which not only saves storage space but also speeds up data transfer and processing times [42]. Both techniques are vital for optimizing big data analysis, especially when dealing with real-time data streams or large historical datasets.

10.6.4 Algorithmic optimization

The choice and optimization of algorithms play a significant role in big data analysis. Algorithms can be optimized for specific data characteristics or processing requirements. Techniques such as approximation algorithms, which provide near-optimal solutions with less computational effort, and adaptive algorithms, which adjust their parameters in response to data characteristics, are examples of how algorithmic optimization can enhance big data analysis [43].

10.6.5 In-memory computing

In-memory computing technologies like SAP HANA and Redis store data in RAM instead of on hard drives, enabling much faster data processing and analysis [44]. This approach is particularly effective for operations requiring real-time analytics and processing, as it minimizes the latency associated with disk-based storage.

10.6.6 Machine learning and artificial intelligence

Machine learning and AI algorithms can automate the identification of patterns and the prediction of trends within big data [45]. Optimization techniques in this area involve selecting the most appropriate models, tuning hyperparameters, and using methods like feature selection to improve model performance and efficiency [46]. Additionally, deep learning techniques can be optimized through architectures designed for specific types of data or tasks.

10.6.7 Cloud-based analytics

Cloud computing offers scalable resources for big data analytics, allowing for the dynamic allocation of computational power based on the current needs [47]. Cloud platforms provide access to a wide array of optimized analytics tools and services, which can be scaled up or down to manage costs and performance effectively [48]. Optimization in cloud environments also includes selecting the right type of storage and computing instances, and leveraging cloud-specific features like auto-scaling and managed services.

10.6.8 Query optimization

In databases and data warehouses, query optimization involves rewriting queries in a way that reduces the computational resources required to execute them [49]. Techniques include selecting efficient query execution plans, using materialized views to speed up query processing, and optimizing join operations. Query optimizers built into database management systems automatically perform many of these optimizations.

10.6.9 Data visualization and reduction

For data analysis outcomes to be actionable, they must be interpretable. Optimization here involves techniques for data reduction and visualization that can simplify complex datasets into formats that are easier to understand and analyze. Dimensionality reduction techniques, such as principal component analysis, can help in highlighting the most relevant features of the data [50].

Optimization techniques for big data analysis are diverse and multidisciplinary, encompassing data preprocessing, distributed computing, algorithmic adjustments, and beyond. As big data continues to grow in size and complexity, these optimization strategies become increasingly crucial for businesses and organizations to derive actionable insights efficiently and effectively. Continuous advancements in computing hardware, software algorithms, and data management practices are essential to meeting the ever-evolving challenges of big data analysis.

10.7 Real-time data processing in IoT

Real-time data processing in the IoT refers to the capability to process data immediately as it is generated by IoT devices, without noticeable delay [51]. This is crucial for applications where timeliness of the data analysis and response is critical, such as in autonomous vehicles, smart cities, healthcare monitoring systems, and industrial automation. Real-time data processing enables organizations to make quick decisions based on the most current information, enhancing efficiency, safety, and user experience [52].

10.7.1 Understanding real-time data processing

Real-time data processing involves collecting, analyzing, and acting upon data within a timeframe that is acceptable for the application's context. This timeframe can vary from milliseconds to a few seconds, depending on the requirements of the specific IoT application [53]. The goal is to ensure immediate insights and responses to the constantly changing data landscape.

10.7.2 Key components

- **IoT devices and sensors**: These are the source of real-time data, constantly monitoring and capturing information from the environment [54].
- **Edge computing**: Processing data near its source to reduce latency. Edge computing devices can filter, aggregate, and analyze data locally before sending it to centralized systems if needed [55].
- **Data streaming platforms**: Tools and platforms that support the ingestion and processing of data streams in real time. Examples include Apache Kafka, Amazon Kinesis, and Google Pub/Sub.
- **Real-time analytics engines**: Systems designed to perform analytics on data as it arrives. Apache Storm, Apache Flink, and Spark Streaming are technologies that facilitate real-time analytics.
- **Communication networks**: High-speed, reliable networks are essential for transmitting data between IoT devices, edge computing nodes, and central processing systems [56].

10.7.3 Challenges in real-time data processing

- **Scalability**: Handling the massive volume of data generated by thousands or millions of IoT devices without lag.
- **Latency**: Ensuring data is processed and actionable insights are generated within the required timeframe.
- **Data quality and heterogeneity**: Managing the variety and inconsistency of data formats and ensuring high-quality data for accurate analysis.
- **Security and privacy**: Safeguarding sensitive information as it is transmitted and processed in real-time.

10.7.4 Technologies and approaches

- **Edge computing**: By performing data processing tasks closer to the data source, edge computing significantly reduces latency and network congestion.
- **Distributed stream processing systems**: These systems are designed to process large streams of real-time data across distributed computing resources efficiently.
- **Complex event processing (CEP)**: CEP tools analyze and identify patterns within the real-time data streams, triggering actions or alerts based on specific criteria.
- **Microservices architecture**: Deploying applications as a collection of loosely coupled services to improve scalability and facilitate the quick deployment of new features or updates.
- **5G and B5G networks**: Providing faster, more reliable connections to support real-time data transmission from IoT devices to processing nodes.

Real-time data processing in IoT is transforming how industries operate, making systems more responsive, efficient, and intelligent. By leveraging edge computing, stream processing technologies, and new communication networks like 5G, organizations can harness the power of real-time IoT data to drive innovation, enhance operational efficiency, and create more personalized user experiences. As the IoT continues to evolve, the importance of real-time data processing will only grow, requiring continuous advancements in technology and strategies to meet the expanding demands of IoT applications.

10.8 Case studies and applications in IoT and big data

The integration of the IoT and big data technologies has led to transformative outcomes across various sectors, demonstrating the vast potential of these technologies when combined. IoT devices generate vast amounts of data, which, when analyzed using big data analytics, can uncover insights that drive efficiency, innovation, and new services. Here, we explore several case studies and applications across different industries to illustrate the impact of IoT and big data. Figure 10.6 illustrates a diverse array of applications within the IoT and big data.

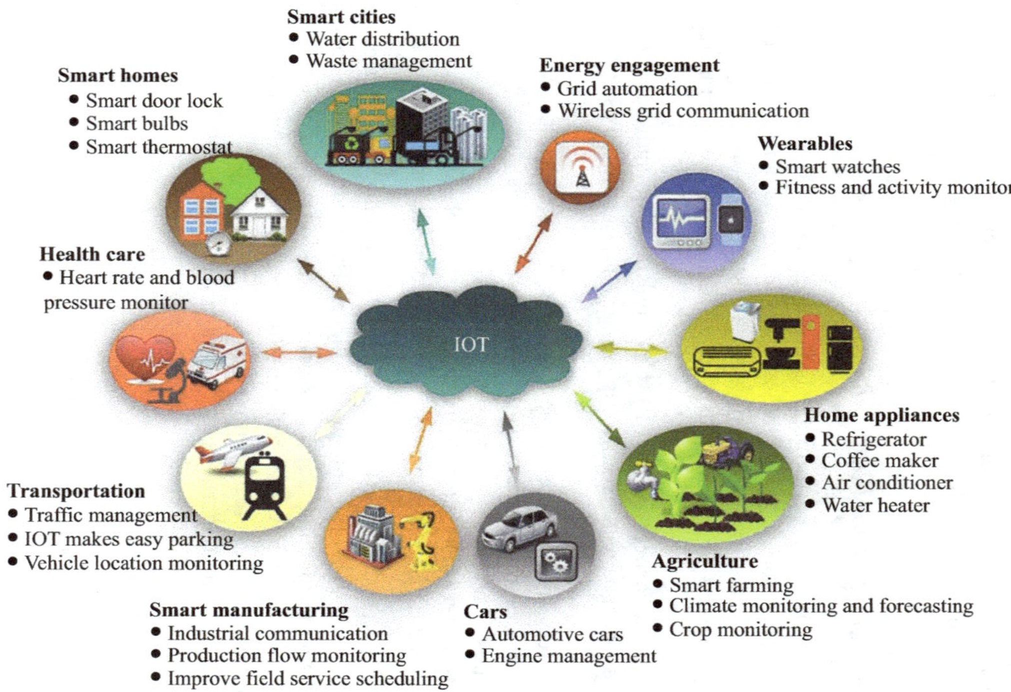

Figure 10.6 Applications in IoT and big data (source: gecdesigns.com/Big data)

10.8.1 Smart cities: Singapore's Smart Nation initiative

Singapore's Smart Nation initiative leverages IoT and big data to improve urban living. Sensors and IoT devices across the city collect data on traffic, public services, and environmental conditions. Big data analytics are then used to optimize traffic flow, reduce energy consumption, improve waste management, and enhance public safety [57]. For example, the initiative uses real-time data to dynamically control traffic lights and manage public transportation schedules, reducing congestion and improving air quality.

10.8.2 Healthcare: remote patient monitoring

IoT devices such as wearable health monitors and connected medical devices enable continuous monitoring of patients' health data outside traditional clinical settings. Big data analytics can process this information to detect patterns, predict health issues before they become severe, and personalize patient care [58]. An example is a system that monitors heart rate, blood pressure, and glucose levels in real-time, alerting healthcare providers to potential health risks, thus facilitating early intervention and reducing hospital readmissions [59].

10.8.3 Agriculture: precision farming

Precision farming utilizes IoT devices such as soil moisture sensors, drones, and satellite imagery to collect data on crop health, soil conditions, and environmental factors. By analyzing this data, farmers can make informed decisions about irrigation, planting, and harvesting, optimizing crop yields and reducing resource use [60]. For instance, analyzing soil moisture data helps in precise irrigation, leading to water conservation and improved crop yields.

10.8.4 Smart manufacturing: predictive maintenance in manufacturing

IoT sensors on manufacturing equipment collect data on machine performance and condition. Big data analytics are applied to predict equipment failures before they occur, scheduling maintenance only when needed. This approach, known as predictive maintenance, minimizes downtime and extends the lifespan of machinery [61]. A notable application is in the automotive industry, where assembly line robots are monitored to predict and prevent failures, ensuring continuous production.

10.8.5 Retail: enhanced customer experience

Retailers use IoT devices like RFID tags and smart shelves to track inventory in real-time and gather data on customer behavior within stores [62]. Big data analytics help understand customer preferences, manage inventory efficiently, and personalize marketing strategies. An example includes using customer traffic patterns to optimize store layouts and product placements, enhancing the shopping experience and increasing sales.

10.8.6 Energy: smart grids

Smart grids employ IoT devices to monitor and manage the flow of electricity from suppliers to consumers efficiently. Big data analytics enables the prediction of electricity demand, identification of consumption patterns, and detection of anomalies in the grid [63]. This facilitates the integration of renewable energy sources, improves the reliability of electricity supply, and reduces operational costs. A case in point is the use of smart meters in homes to provide consumers and utilities with detailed information on energy use, encouraging energy-saving behaviors.

10.8.7 Transportation and logistics: fleet management

IoT devices installed in vehicles collect data on location, speed, fuel consumption, and vehicle health [64]. By analyzing this data, logistic companies can optimize routes, reduce fuel consumption, and improve fleet maintenance. Real-time tracking of shipments enhances supply chain visibility, improving operational efficiency and customer satisfaction. An application example is the use of IoT and big data by shipping companies to monitor container conditions, ensuring the integrity of sensitive cargo like pharmaceuticals.

These case studies demonstrate the diverse applications and benefits of integrating IoT with big data across different sectors. IoT and big data technologies are driving innovation, improving operational efficiencies, and enhancing decision-making processes by enabling real-time monitoring, predictive analytics, and personalized services. As these technologies continue to evolve, they will unlock even more opportunities for transformation across the global economy.

10.9 Conclusion

Cybersecurity for the IoT through the lens of big data optimization for IoT-based real-time NTA underscores the pivotal role of advanced analytics, cybersecurity measures, and real-time processing in harnessing the full potential of IoT technologies. As IoT devices proliferate across various sectors, generating vast quantities of data, the necessity for robust security protocols and efficient data analytics frameworks has become increasingly apparent. Through comprehensive research and analysis, we have identified key challenges, including the management of data volume, velocity, variety, and veracity, alongside pressing security and privacy concerns. Our study advocates for a multidisciplinary approach, integrating edge computing, cloud-based analytics, machine learning, and AI, to address these challenges effectively. Moreover, the implementation of optimized data processing and NTA techniques is essential for ensuring the security, performance, and reliability of IoT systems. The future prospects of IoT and big data integration are indeed promising, with the potential to drive innovation, enhance operational efficiencies, and foster decision-making processes across numerous domains. However, realizing this potential necessitates continuous advancements in technology, strategies, and collaboration among stakeholders. As we navigate this evolving landscape, it is imperative to prioritize security, privacy, and efficient data management to unlock the transformative power of IoT and big data in shaping the future of digital interconnectedness.

References

[1] Greengard S. *The Internet of Things*. Cambridge, MA: MIT Press; 2021.

[2] Hassan QF. *Internet of Things A to Z: Technologies and Applications*. New York: Wiley; 2018.

[3] Albouq SS, Abi Sen AA, Almashf N, *et al.* A survey of interoperability challenges and solutions for dealing with them in IoT environment. *IEEE Access*. 2022;10:36416–36428.

[4] Dias JP, Restivo A, and Ferreira HS. Designing and constructing Internet-of-Things systems: An overview of the ecosystem. *Internet of Things*. 2022; 19:100529.

[5] Tsampoulatidis I, Komninos N, Syrmos E, *et al.* Universality and interoperability across smart city ecosystems. In: *International Conference on Human–Computer Interaction*. Berlin: Springer; 2022. pp. 218–230.

[6] Allioui H, and Mourdi Y. Exploring the full potentials of IoT for better financial growth and stability: A comprehensive survey. *Sensors*. 2023;23 (19):8015.

[7] Khanh QV, Hoai NV, Manh LD, *et al.* Wireless communication technologies for IoT in 5G: Vision, applications, and challenges. *Wireless Communications and Mobile Computing*. 2022;2022:1–12.

[8] Čolaković A, Džubur AH, and Karahodža B. Wireless communication technologies for the Internet of Things. *Science, Engineering and Technology*. 2021;1(1):1–14.

[9] Rath KC, Khang A, and Roy D. The role of Internet of Things (IoT) technology in Industry 4.0 economy. In: *Advanced IoT Technologies and Applications in the Industry 4.0 Digital Economy*. Boca Raton, FL: CRC Press; 2024. pp. 1–28.

[10] Kumari S, and Arowolo MO. Internet of Things (IoT): Concepts, protocols, and applications. In: *Emerging Technologies and Security in Cloud Computing*. Hershey, PA: IGI Global; 2024. pp. 19–52.

[11] Rahmani H, Shetty D, Wagih M, *et al.* Next-generation IoT devices: Sustainable eco-friendly manufacturing, energy harvesting, and wireless connectivity. *IEEE Journal of Microwaves*. 2023;3(1):237–255.

[12] López OL, Rosabal OM, Ruiz-Guirola DE, *et al.* Energy-sustainable IoT connectivity: Vision, technological enablers, challenges, and future directions. *IEEE Open Journal of the Communications Society*. 2023.

[13] Ahad A, Tahir M, Aman Sheikh M, *et al.* Technologies trend towards 5G network for smart health-care using IoT: A review. *Sensors*. 2020;20 (14):4047.

[14] Doghudje I, and Akande O. Securing the internet of things: Cybersecurity challenges for smart materials and big data. *International Journal of Information and Cybersecurity*. 2022;6(1):82–108.

[15] Urquhart L, and McAuley D. Avoiding the internet of insecure industrial things. *Computer Law & Security Review*. 2018;34(3):450–466.

[16] Butt HA, Ahad A, Wasim M, *et al.* Federated machine learning in 5G smart healthcare: A security perspective review. *Procedia Computer Science*. 2023;224:580–586.

[17] Ahmed S, and Khan M. Securing the Internet of Things (IoT): A comprehensive study on the intersection of cybersecurity, privacy, and connectivity in the IoT ecosystem. *AI, IoT and the Fourth Industrial Revolution Review*. 2023;13(9):1–17.

[18] Ahad A, Ali Z, Mateen A, *et al.* A comprehensive review on 5G-based smart healthcare network security: Taxonomy, issues, solutions and future research directions. *Array*. 2023;18:100290.

[19] Mateen A, Wasim M, Ahad A, *et al.* Smart energy management system for minimizing electricity cost and peak to average ratio in residential areas with hybrid genetic flower pollination algorithm. *Alexandria Engineering Journal*. 2023;77:593–611.

[20] Dwivedi S, Vardhan M, and Tripathi S. Defense against distributed DoS attack detection by using intelligent evolutionary algorithm. *International Journal of Computers and Applications*. 2022;44(3):219–229.

[21] Jo W, Kim S, Lee C, *et al.* Packet preprocessing in CNN-based network intrusion detection system. *Electronics*. 2020;9(7):1151.

[22] Kasongo SM, and Sun Y. A deep learning method with filter based feature engineering for wireless intrusion detection system. *IEEE Access*. 2019; 7:38597–38607.

[23] Mayuranathan M, Murugan M, and Dhanakoti V. RETRACTED ARTICLE: Best features based intrusion detection system by RBM model for detecting DDoS in cloud environment. *Journal of Ambient Intelligence and Humanized Computing*. 2021;12(3):3609–3619.

[24] Yang Y, Zheng K, Wu B, *et al.* Network intrusion detection based on supervised adversarial variational auto-encoder with regularization. *IEEE Access*. 2020;8:42169–42184.

[25] Istiaque Ahmed K, Tahir M, Hadi Habaebi M, *et al.* Machine learning for authentication and authorization in IoT: Taxonomy, challenges and future research direction. *Sensors*. 2021;21(15):5122.

[26] Salim MM, Rathore S, and Park JH. Distributed denial of service attacks and its defenses in IoT: A survey. *The Journal of Supercomputing*. 2020; 76:5320–5363.

[27] Nadir I, Mahmood H, and Asadullah G. A taxonomy of IoT firmware security and principal firmware analysis techniques. *International Journal of Critical Infrastructure Protection*. 2022;38:100552.

[28] HaddadPajouh H, Dehghantanha A, Parizi RM, *et al.* A survey on Internet of Things security: Requirements, challenges, and solutions. *Internet of Things*. 2021;14:100129.

[29] Talebkhah M, Sali A, Marjani M, *et al.* IoT and big data applications in smart cities: Recent advances, challenges, and critical issues. *IEEE Access*. 2021; 9:55465–55484.

[30] Al Mamun MA, and Yuce MR. Sensors and systems for wearable environmental monitoring toward IoT-enabled applications: A review. *IEEE Sensors Journal*. 2019;19(18):7771–7788.

[31] Kibria MG, Nguyen K, Villardi GP, *et al.* Big data analytics, machine learning, and artificial intelligence in next-generation wireless networks. *IEEE Access*. 2018;6:32328–32338.

[32] Jeble S, Kumari S, and Patil Y. Role of big data in decision making. *Operations and Supply Chain Management: An International Journal*. 2017; 11(1):36–44.

[33] Butt HA, Ahad A, Wasim M, *et al.* 5G and IoT for intelligent healthcare: AI and machine learning approaches: A review. In: *International Conference on Smart Objects and Technologies for Social Good*. Berlin: Springer; 2023. pp. 107–123.

[34] Adi E, Anwar A, Baig Z, *et al.* Machine learning and data analytics for the IoT. *Neural Computing and Applications*. 2020;32:16205–16233.

[35] Davies J, and Fortuna C. *The Internet of Things: From Data to Insight*. New York: Wiley; 2020.

[36] Qaiser F, Hussain M, Ahad A, *et al.* Controller-driven vector autoregression model for predicting content popularity in programmable named data networking devices. *PeerJ Computer Science*. 2024;10:e1854.

[37] Chataut R, Phoummalayvane A, and Akl R. Unleashing the power of IoT: A comprehensive review of IoT applications and future prospects in healthcare, agriculture, smart homes, smart cities, and Industry 4.0. *Sensors*. 2023;23 (16):7194.

[38] Kumar NM, and Mallick PK. Blockchain technology for security issues and challenges in IoT. *Procedia Computer Science*. 2018;132:1815–1823.

[39] Ridzuan F, and Zainon WMNW. A review on data cleansing methods for big data. *Procedia Computer Science*. 2019;161:731–738.

[40] Zaharia M. *An Architecture for Fast and General Data Processing on Large Clusters*. San Rafael, CA: Morgan & Claypool; 2016.

[41] Gani A, Siddiqa A, Shamshirband S, *et al.* A survey on indexing techniques for big data: Taxonomy and performance evaluation. *Knowledge and Information Systems*. 2016;46:241–284.

[42] Nasif A, Othman ZA, and Sani NS. The deep learning solutions on lossless compression methods for alleviating data load on IoT nodes in smart cities. *Sensors*. 2021;21(12):4223.

[43] Wang J, Xu C, Zhang J, *et al.* Big data analytics for intelligent manufacturing systems: A review. *Journal of Manufacturing Systems*. 2022;62:738–752.

[44] Wasim Haidar S, Singh SP, and Johri P. Big data: A comprehensive survey. *Technology*. 2020;11(5):624–646.

[45] Raschka S, Patterson J, and Nolet C. Machine learning in Python: Main developments and technology trends in data science, machine learning, and artificial intelligence. *Information*. 2020;11(4):193.

[46] Binder M, Moosbauer J, Thomas J, *et al.* Multi-objective hyperparameter tuning and feature selection using filter ensembles. In: *Proceedings of the 2020 Genetic and Evolutionary Computation Conference*; 2020. pp. 471–479.

[47] Sandhu AK. Big data with cloud computing: Discussions and challenges. *Big Data Mining and Analytics*. 2021;5(1):32–40.

[48] Pothukuchi A S, Kota L V, and Mallikarjunaradhya V. A critical analysis of the challenges and opportunities to optimize storage costs for big data in the cloud. *Asian Journal of Multidisciplinary Research & Review*. 2021;25(1): 132–144.

[49] Kossmann J, Papenbrock T, and Naumann F. Data dependencies for query optimization: A survey. *The VLDB Journal*. 2022;31(1):1–22.

[50] Ayesha S, Hanif MK, and Talib R. Overview and comparative study of dimensionality reduction techniques for high dimensional data. *Information Fusion*. 2020;59:44–58.

[51] Lv Z, Lou R, Li J, *et al.* Big data analytics for 6G-enabled massive internet of things. *IEEE Internet of Things Journal*. 2021;8(7):5350–5359.

[52] Tahir M, Habaebi MH, Dabbagh M, *et al.* A review on application of blockchain in 5G and beyond networks: Taxonomy, field-trials, challenges and opportunities. *IEEE Access*. 2020;8:115876–115904.

[53] Lohstroh M, Kim H, Eidson JC, *et al.* On enabling technologies for the Internet of important things. *IEEE Access*. 2019;7:27244–27256.

[54] Ahad A, Ullah Z, Amin B, *et al.* Comparison of energy efficient routing protocols in wireless sensor network. *American Journal of Networks and Communications*. 2017;6:67–73.

[55] Hazra A, Rana P, Adhikari M, *et al.* Fog computing for next-generation internet of things: Fundamental, state-of-the-art and research challenges. *Computer Science Review*. 2023;48:100549.

[56] Mughees A, Tahir M, Sheikh MA, *et al.* Energy-efficient ultra-dense 5G networks: Recent advances, taxonomy and future research directions. *IEEE Access*. 2021;9:147692–147716.

[57] Mahor V, Rawat R, Kumar A, *et al.* IoT and artificial intelligence techniques for public safety and security. In: *Smart Urban Computing Applications*. Gistrup: River Publishers; 2023. pp. 111–126.

[58] Ahad A, Jiangbina Z, Tahir M, *et al.* 6G and intelligent healthcare: Taxonomy, technologies, open issues and future research directions. *Internet of Things*. 2024;25:101068.

[59] Ahad A, Tahir M, Sheikh MAS, *et al.* Optimal route selection in 5G-based smart health-care network: A reinforcement learning approach. In: *2021 26th IEEE Asia-Pacific Conference on Communications (APCC)*. Piscataway, NJ: IEEE; 2021. pp. 248–253.

[60] Aborujilah A, Alashbi A, Shayea I, *et al.* IoT integration in agriculture: Advantages, challenges, and future perspectives: Short survey. In: *2023 10th International Conference on Wireless Networks and Mobile Communications (WINCOM)*. Piscataway, NJ: IEEE; 2023. pp. 1–7.
[61] Ngwa P. Big data analytics for predictive system maintenance using machine learning and artificial neural network models. University of Rwanda, Kigali; 2020.
[62] Jose JAC, Bertumen CJB, Roque MTC, *et al.* Smart shelf system for customer behavior tracking in supermarkets. *Sensors*. 2024;24(2):367.
[63] Saleem MU, Shakir M, Usman MR, *et al.* Integrating smart energy management system with Internet of things and cloud computing for efficient demand side management in smart grids. *Energies*. 2023;16(12):4835.
[64] Mohammed K, Abdelhafid M, Kamal K, *et al.* Intelligent driver monitoring system: An Internet of Things-based system for tracking and identifying the driving behavior. *Computer Standards & Interfaces*. 2023;84:103704.

Chapter 11

Advancing VANET resilience: integrating ensemble learning with large language models to combat fake report attacks

Muhammad Rashid Naeem[1], *Azeem Ahmad*[1] *and Mansoor Khan*[2]

Abstract

Vehicular ad-hoc network (VANET) is a type of communication network in which anonymous vehicles communicate with each other to provide various services including road safety, traffic hazards. This network enables vehicles over VANET to share information regarding conditions of road, traffic accidents, and other network related information to ensure safety and convenience. However, cyberattacks are significant concerns in VANETs due to reactive security approaches, which can lead to accidents or false reporting by malicious vehicles. Current VANET simulation models have limited capabilities to analyze proactive security approaches. The ripple effect caused by fake reporting attack extends beyond the targeted vehicle compromising the reliability and the security of VANET communication networks.

This chapter utilizes different NLP embeddings including GloVe and Word2Vec and large language model (LLM) GPT with ensemble learning to predict fake report attacks in VANET communication. First, we preprocess the execution log of VeReMi for Attack Prediction (VeReMiAP) simulation dataset consisting of V2V and V2X communication between different vehicles and infrastructure. Next, labels were assigned to simulated hazard attacks to detect the effects of fake reporting attack on real-time VANET communication. A Glove and Word2Vec ensemble model achieved up to 99.48% and 99.37% accuracies and 0.84–0.93 precision and recall. However, the LLM ensemble model outperforms other by maintaining minimal loss and high accuracy in state-of-the-art comparison. The experimental results show the potential of LLMs in advancing the security research in VANET communication protocols.

[1]Department of Software Engineering, Prince Sultan University, Saudi Arabia
[2]School of Intelligent Manufacturing and Control Engineering, Qilu Institute of Technology, China

11.1 Introduction

Intelligent transportation systems (ITS) refer to a range of advanced technologies, communication systems, and strategies applied to transportation and traffic management to improve safety, efficiency, and sustainability [1]. VANET networks can improve real-time transmission, scalability, and mobility of smart transportation systems. The primary technology used for transmission in VANETs is dedicated short-range communication (DSRC). It can be operated in the 5.9 GHz band, therefore ensuring secure and high-speed communication. VANETs typically use DSRC for exchange of basic safety messages (BSMs) as well as cooperative awareness messages (CAMs) [2]. BSMs also generate real-time data of location, velocity, and heading in vehicular networks. Alternatively, CAMs enable short-range communication between vehicles and RSUs to deliver real-time information like road safety conditions and potential traffic incidents [3]. Due to the rise of VANETs, there has been a corresponding increase in security flaws. Various solutions have been proposed to address these issues such as cryptographic techniques, trust models, intrusion detection systems, and secure routing protocols [4]. However, these solutions need to be continually updated and improved to keep up with evolving threats. Attackers can breach confidentiality, which impacts further protection. This could involve unauthorized access to sensitive data transmitted within the network [5]. VANETs must ensure the privacy of vehicles without compromising security. This includes protecting the identity of vehicles and their passengers from unauthorized tracking [6]. Ensuring that the messages exchanged within the network are authentic and have not been tampered with is a significant challenge [7] and could flood the network with traffic, rendering it unavailable to users [8]. Establishing and maintaining security standards and protocols that can effectively address these issues is a major challenge [9].

In cybersecurity domains, attack prediction is crucial for anticipating threats as well as minimizing their impact in safety critical systems [10]. Different techniques such as anomaly detection, behavior modeling, and risk factor scoring can be adapted to overcome threats. The behavioral pattern modeling of participating network including vehicles and RSUs can be used as a key process to identify unusual deviations indicative of attacks. Such insights enable the creation of datasets mimicking attack impacts on the network, aiding the evaluation of security measures and their effectiveness. Therefore, we have selected VeReMiAP dataset which combined three key assessment factors such as CAMs, Fake reporting attacks, and the imitating impact of attack as a road hazard [11]. The rest of this chapter is organized as follows.

Section 11.2 discusses related work on VANET security issues and recent advances. Section 11.3 explains the proposed approaches incorporating LLM with ensemble learning in detail. Section 11.4 contains the results and discussions. Finally, Section 11.5 concludes this chapter.

11.2 Literature review

Road accidents due to fake reporting attacks may lead to traffic jams and life-threatening injuries such as head trauma, fractured bones, and other internal injuries. VANETs can be affected from various security issues such network authentication, privacy, data non-repudiation. Several studies have been made to secure VANETs communication protocols. A centralized IDS approach introduced by Sangwan *et al.* [12] to detect Sybil attacks in which each vehicle controls a plausibility check to identify attacks and sends analysis reports to a misbehavior evaluation authority. Later, the misbehavior evaluation authority analysis the reports to decide whether or not a node is an attacker or not.

Kamel *et al.* [13] further constructed a precautionary decentralized mechanism using Kalman filter in order to predict potential DoS, Sybil, false alert, and packet alteration attacks utilizing the behavior of vehicles within network. The decentralized approach act as a cluster head, which monitors vehicles and detects if the attack is repeatedly made or periodically for a given proactive intrusion detection system. Ghaleb *et al.* [14] used context-aware and data-centric misbehavior of vehicular networks to locally detect false mobility information. Consistency and rules are applied in order to decide if a vehicle behavior is suspicious or not.

The most productive and cost-effective technique for misbehavior detection in VANETs is the use of machine learning models. For instance, Zang and Yan [15] introduced an intelligent approach considering centralized IDS for DDoS attacks on different vehicle densities in which the main process executed on centralized collector. Next, machine learning algorithms such as Random Forest used to classify different types of attackers using network information including source IP, destination IP, protocols, length of packets, as well as source and destination ports. Zhang *et al.* [16] implemented an SVM algorithm by training various network features including driving status, vehicle type, reputation, speed, acceleration, and distance. Furthermore, message suppression attacks are analyzed using packet drop rate, packet delay rate and packet delay forward rate, etc. A vehicle trust model is designed which requires a central trust authority (TA) and a local vehicle trust module to combine multiple assessments of vehicular attacks. Many studies inspired by the publicly available dataset VeReMi to analyze and combat different types of VANET attacks. Few studies further simulated their own scenarios to create new types of VANET attack and potential approaches to overcome such attacks.

In the literature studies, the decentralized IDS approach combined with machine learning techniques are also used to enhance attack detection. For instance, Sharma and Kaul [17] designed a multi-cluster head detection mechanism in which the head is chosen by a fuzzy hybrid decision-making criteria. Using this scheme, they also overcome different attack evasion techniques such as packet drop, selective forwarding as well as wormhole attacks. AOMDV (ad hoc on-demand, multipath distance vector) routing protocol utilized and implemented with dolphin swarm optimization strategy to select optimal features for SVM algorithm on both separate classes and multi-classes as well. The VeReMi dataset [18] has been implemented on various well-known machine learning techniques including Random Forest (RF), k-Nearest Neighbor (kNN), Logistic Regression (LR), and Support Vector Machines (SVM) on different types of network features to identify position falsification attacks. In this chapter, we propose a new method incorporating LLMs for analyzing vast amounts of vehicular network data to encode network traffic. LLM models are capable of extracting contextual meaning through semantic data to address particular challenges including diverse feature relationships and efficiently detecting the effects of fake reporting attacks.

11.3 Proposed framework

The proposed framework is designed to detect fake reporting cybersecurity threats in VANET communication as shown in Figure 11.1. The proposed model is designed by extracting communication information of each vehicle between V2V and V2X CAM messages which was initially simulated on Simulation of Urban Mobility (SUMO) and OMNeT++ via Traffic Control Interface (TraCI). Next, communication messages are tokenized using GloVe, Word2Vec, and GPT to refine and transform CAM messages into meaningful vectors. The preprocessed data is further divided into train and test categories based on hazard attacks. Finally, the feature bagging ensemble is used to make final predictions in terms of detecting fake reports attacks in VANETs. Since, simulation datasets generate thousands of messages between V2V and V2. Therefore, we divide simulation into three datasets for experimentation.

11.3.1 Glove embeddings for VANET

Classification models use fixed size vectors to train and test datasets. Feature embedding methods can preprocess feature vectors to extract semantic context. However, functionality of embedding methods is limited and cannot handle a large simulation dataset. Therefore, we selected GloVe embedding to extract dense vectors for each V2V and V2X messaging to capture semantic context for binary classification of fake reporting attacks. GloVe is an algorithm for unsupervised learning to obtain representations of words in vector form [19]. These representations of words extract semantic and syntactic relationships of words using their co-occurrence statistics in a large corpus of text. Unlike traditional methods which focus on predicting individual words in a context window, GloVe directly learns the vector representations by optimizing a global objective function that captures the overall co-occurrence statistics of words. This results in dense vector representations where distances between vectors reflect semantic similarity between words. GloVe has been widely used in natural language processing (NLP) tasks such as word embedding, sentiment analysis, machine translation, and document classification, contributing to improved performance and generalization in various language-related applications.

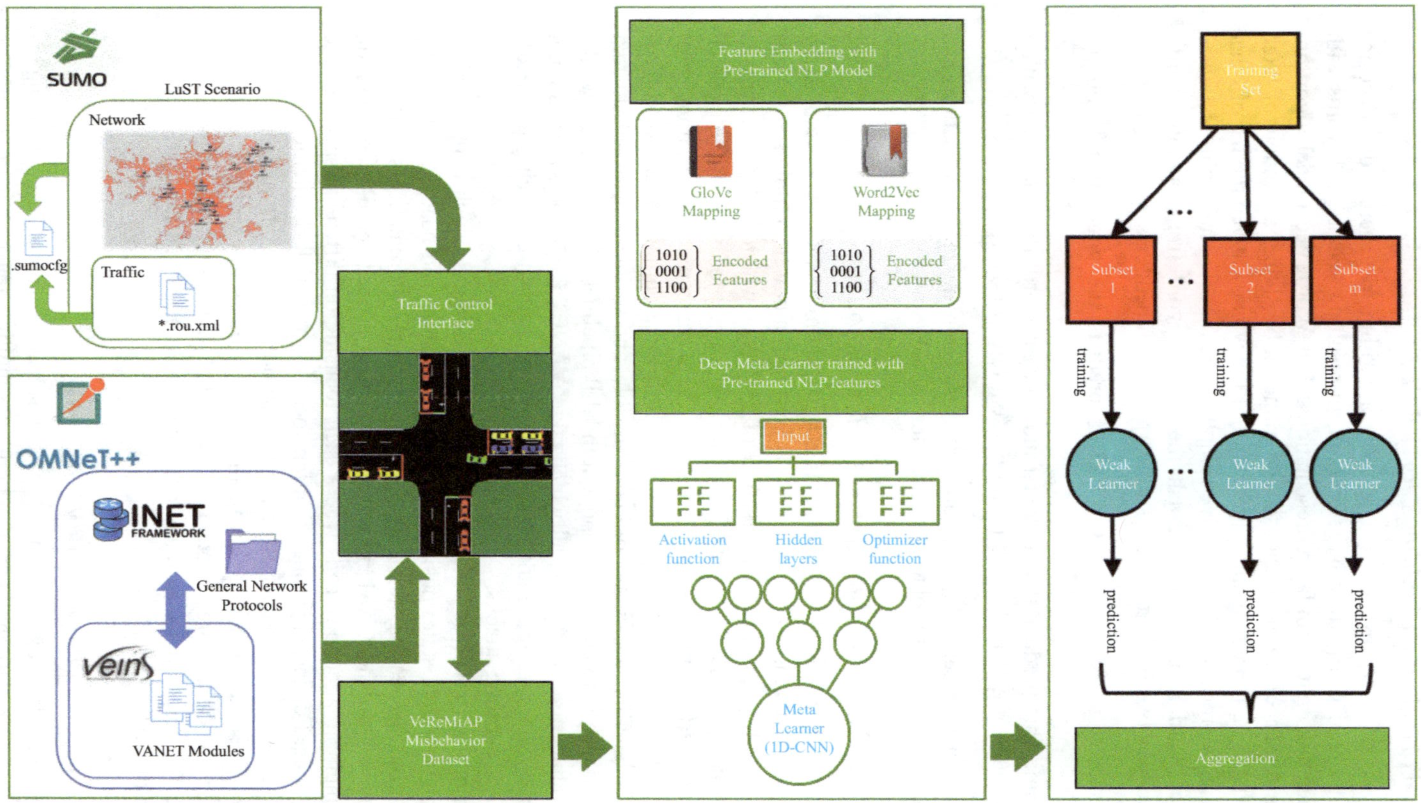

Figure 11.1 Proposed architecture to detect the effects of fake reporting attacks using large language model and ensemble learning

11.3.2 Word2Vec embeddings for VANET

Word2Vec is another unsupervised learning algorithm to generate dense vector representations of words from large corpora. In resulting vectors, the words with similar meanings have similar representations. The Word2Vec model algorithm takes each sentence within the dataset and trained it by sliding a window of fixed size over it. Then, it predicts the center word of the window given the list of other words. Using a process called negative sampling, the model is trained to recognize the correct word and also distinguish the correct word from random words. Word2Vec uses two basic techniques to learn word embeddings:

- Continuous bag of words (CBOW): This predicts the target word from its context.
- Skip-gram: This predicts the context from a target word. It works well with a small amount of data and is found to represent rare words well.

The vector representations are commonly used in many NLP applications and tasks to improve the performances of machine learning models.

11.3.3 GPT advanced tokenizer for text encoding

The generative pre-trained transformer (GPT) is a family of LLMs developed by OpenAI revolutionizing NLP tasks. GPT Tokenizer is a powerful tool used for text encoding, enabling the raw conversation of text data which is JSON string in VANET simulation into a numerical format that can be processed and interpreted by machine learning models. In this study, the advanced tokenizer transforms words and sentences into a series of tokens each representing a specific word or sub-word. The GPT Tokenizer offers a flexible and efficient approach to text encoding making it a valuable component in NLP pipelines. Figure 11.2 shows the internal architecture of GPT model which takes VANET CAM messages as input and tokenizes them using a multi-head attention mechanism enhancing the detection of false reporting attacks.

The first step involves tokenization of CAM messages which contain information about vehicle state, position, speed, acceleration and heading. Each message tokenized by breaking down into individual token representation specific field or attribute within the CAM message. Next, feedforward multi-head attention involves multiple attention heads where each focusing on different aspects of the CAM message. For instance, one attention focuses on spatial information such as position and velocity, whereas other head focus on temporal information such as timestamp. The feedforward layers facilitate this process to extract relevant features. Once all features are encoded and extracted, the ensemble learning model will make final predictions on false reporting attacks based on the learned representations of GPT LLM.

11.3.4 Bagging ensemble learning

The bagging ensemble also known as "random subspaces" or "attribute bagging" is a type of ensemble learning which that combines multiple machine learning models

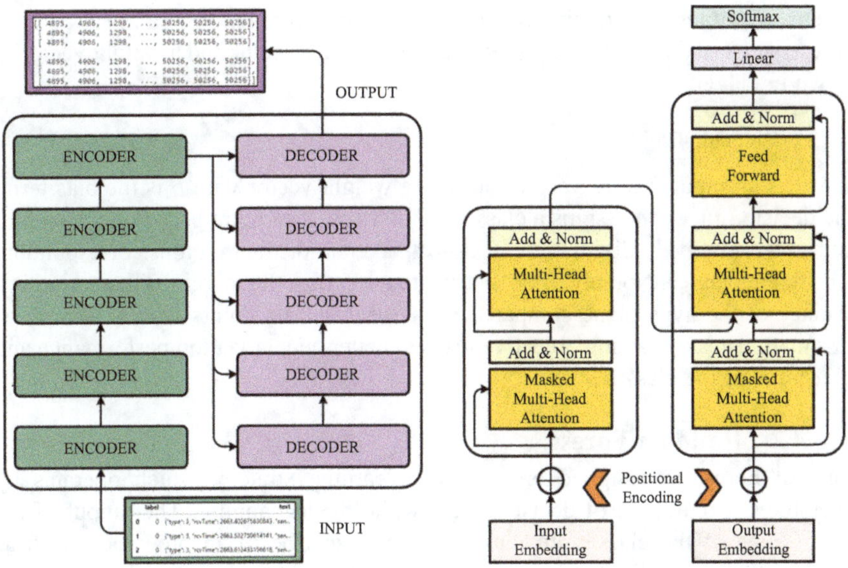

Figure 11.2 The GPT large language model incorporates a multi-attention mechanism to effectively tokenize VANET CAM messages, enabling enhanced ensemble learning for the detection of false reporting attacks

trained on different subsets of the input features. This method is similar to bootstrapping in the context of feature selection. For each base model in the ensemble, a random subset of features is selected from the original feature set. Each base model is trained on its corresponding subset of features. During prediction, each base model produces its own individual prediction. For regression tasks, the final prediction can be the average of the predictions from all base models. For classification tasks, the final prediction can be the majority vote or the mode of the predictions from all base models.

Bagging ensemble model has several advantages over traditional machine learning algorithms in terms of optimal solution. For instance, by training models on different feature subsets, feature bagging encourages diversity among the base models. This diversity can lead to better generalization and robustness of the ensemble. Using random subsets of features, bagging ensemble reduces overfitting risk, especially when dealing with high-dimensional data. In this chapter, we selected four machine learning algorithms as base estimator for bagging ensemble model.

11.3.4.1 Support Vector Machines

SVM is another classifier designed for supervised learning. It utilizes multi-dimensional hyperplanes in order to segregate different data points. The decision boundary of this algorithm relies on different support vectors which define the extreme maximum and minimum values. The decision function of a linear SVM is represented as a dot product between the input feature vector and a weight vector as shown in (11.1):

$$f(x) = w \cdot x + b \tag{11.1}$$

Here x is an input feature vector and w is a weight vector with b is the bias term. The decision function assigns a class label to a new data point based on the sign of the result, effectively dividing the feature space into distinct regions corresponding to different classes. Notably, SVMs strive to maximize the margin. The margin is a distance of the hyperplane compared to the nearest data points within each class. This margin-maximization objective leads to better generalization performance and robustness of the classifier.

11.3.4.2 Random Forest

Random Forest is designed on ensemble learning strategy which operates by assembling a multitude of decision trees while model training. The output of the class is one of the classes for classification or can be mean prediction such as regression of the individual trees. It is a popular and powerful machine learning algorithm that is known for its high accuracy and resistance to overfitting. Random Forest is often used for both classification and regression tasks and can handle high-dimensional and complex data. The prediction for a new data point is made by aggregating the predictions of all the individual decision trees. In the case of classification, the class labels are predicted by taking a majority vote among the trees. For regression tasks, the average of the predictions from each tree is calculated. The equations leading the Random Forest algorithm are as follows:

$$y(x) = \text{mode}(T_1(x), T_2(x), \ldots, T_n(x)) \tag{11.2}$$

Here $y(x)$ is predicted class for input x, $T_1(x)$ is prediction of ith decision tree and n is the total number of decision tress in random forest.

11.3.4.3 Gradient Boosting

Gradient Boosting technique that enhances the performance of a model by iteratively adding new models to correct the errors made by the previous models. It is a boosting algorithm, which means it combines weak learners to form a strong learner (a highly accurate model). The gradient boosting algorithm works by first fitting a model to the training data and then creating a new model that predicts the residuals or errors of the first model. This process is repeated for a specified number of iterations or until the model achieves the desired level of accuracy.

The main idea behind gradient boosting algorithm is to make an ensemble of weak learners in a sequential manner while each subsequent model focuses on correcting the errors produced by the previous models. The gradient boosting algorithm optimizes a cost function by minimizing the gradient of the loss function with respect to the model's parameters. This optimization is achieved through a process called gradient descent, where the model's parameters are updated iteratively to reduce the loss.

$$y(x) = \sum\nolimits_{m=1}^{M} \beta_m h_m(x) \tag{11.3}$$

Here $\widehat{y}(x)$ represents the predicted value of given input x. M is total number of weak learners in ensemble. β_m is the coefficient associated with mth weak learner, while $h_m(x)$ is the prediction made by mth weak learner for input x.

11.3.4.4 Adaboost

Adaboost also known as adaptive boosting is a machine learning ensemble method specifically designed for classification tasks. It works by combining multiple weak learners to craft a robust classifier. It could be a decision stump (a one-level decision tree), a simple neural network, or any other classifier. Initially, each instance in the dataset is given equal weight. During training, AdaBoost assigns superior weights to the occurrences that are misclassified by the earlier weak learners. This allows subsequent weak learners to focus more on the instances that are difficult to classify correctly. During training, AdaBoost assigns higher weights to the instances that are misclassified by the previous weak learners. This allows subsequent weak learners to focus more on the instances that are difficult to classify correctly. The weight of each weak learner's vote depends on its accuracy during training. Generally, more accurate weak learners have higher weights in the final ensemble. To make a prediction for a new instance, AdaBoost combines the predictions of all weak learners using their weights. The class with the highest total weight is chosen as the final prediction. Mathematically, it can be explained in (11.4)–(11.6).

$$\text{Error rate } (\varepsilon_t) = \sum_{i=1}^{N} w_i^{(t)} \cdot I(h_t(x_i) \neq y_i) \tag{11.4}$$

$$\text{Compute Weight } (a_t) = \frac{1}{2}\log\left(\frac{1-\varepsilon_t}{\varepsilon_t}\right) \tag{11.5}$$

$$\text{Update Weight } \left(w_i^{t+1}\right) = w_i^t \cdot \exp(-a_t \cdot y_i \cdot h_t(x_i)) \tag{11.6}$$

Here, T is the total number of iterations (weak learners), a_t is the weight of tth weak learner, w_i^t is the weight of tth training instance of iteration t, and N is the total number of training instances.

11.3.5 Dataset overview

The proposed model utilizes VeReMiAP dataset developed from Framework for Misbehavior Detection (F2MD) which incorporates three key elements CAM messages, new class of attacks, i.e., Fake Reporting Attacks and effect of the attack which is a road hazard [11]. The dataset is generated using the SUMO simulation tool to replicate a realistic VANET scenario [20]. The simulation area measures 2300 m × 5400 m, and it includes 826 vehicles, reflecting a dense and dynamic environment. The MAC (Medium Access Control) layer is implemented using the 802.11p standard, which is specifically designed for vehicular communications. To mimic real-world interactions, vehicles exchange CAMs, providing information about their position, speed, and other relevant parameters. This setup allows for the collection of valuable data that can be used to study and analyze various aspects of VANETs, such as routing protocols, security mechanisms, and the impact of mobility patterns on network performance.

The selection threshold applied to the 826 vehicles based on the number of fake reporting attacks. This facilitates to identify most relevant and informative data sources to train model for detecting such attacks. By filtering and selecting 30 vehicles, the dataset becomes more focused and manageable while still maintaining sufficient diversity. Dividing the selected vehicles' data into three datasets after attack labeling provides a sound basis for training, validation, and testing the proposed model. This approach ensures that the model is exposed to a variety of scenarios and can generalize well to detect fake report attacks across different vehicles and contexts. The use of multiple vehicle data enhances the model's flexibility and robustness, making it adaptable to varying patterns and behaviors exhibited by malicious or compromised vehicles in the VANET environment.

11.3.6 Performance evaluation matrices

The experimental results were analyzed using widely studied assessment metrics including accuracy, precision, recall, and F_1-score. Accuracy measures the rate of classification, i.e., the number of correct assessments over the total assessments in the given dataset. It can be measured as a ratio of the sum of True Positives (TP) and True Negatives (TN) over the total assessments. The evaluation formula of accuracy is shown in (11.7).

$$\text{Accuracy} = \frac{\text{TP} + \text{TN}}{\text{TP} + \text{TN} + \text{FP} + \text{FN}} \tag{11.7}$$

The precision is used to analyze the number of positive assessments predicted over attacks predictions. The precision value typically ranged from 0 and 1, which represents the specificity of the model.

$$\text{Precision} = \frac{\text{TP}}{\text{TP} + \text{FP}} \tag{11.8}$$

Recall analyzes the sensitivity of the machine learning model. It shows true positives assessments that are correctly identified. Equation (11.9) shows the recall formula. It is similar to precision formula and ranges between 0 and 1 where higher values suggest better performance of the model.

$$\text{Recall} = \frac{\text{TP}}{\text{TP} + \text{FN}} \tag{11.9}$$

The formula of *F*-measure is shown in (11.10) also known as F_1-score aiming to determine balance between precision and recall.

$$\text{F}_1 \text{ score} = 2 \times \frac{\text{Precision} \times \text{Recall}}{\text{Precision} + \text{Recall}} \tag{11.10}$$

11.4 Results and discussions

This section discusses the result of the proposed scheme with respect to detection of fake reporting attacks in VeReMiAP simulation dataset on Glove-Ensemble, Word2Vec-Ensemble, and GPT-Ensemble models.

11.4.1 Performance analysis and comparison

To evaluate the performance of LLMs on the given datasets, Table 11.1 presents the experimental results of ensemble models that combine GloVe, Word2Vec, and GPT2 for Dataset 1. The accuracy of detecting fake reporting attacks in VANET communication is impressively high, exceeding 94% for all the models under consideration. Nonetheless, the GPT2 learners demonstrate superior performance in terms of precision, recall, and F_1-score, regardless of whether the data pertains to attack or normal classes. The most remarkable performance on Dataset 1 is attained by the GPT2-BE-AB model, which achieves an astounding accuracy of 99.93% and near-perfect scores across all performance indicators, ranging from 0.99 to 1.00. Alternatively, the GloVe-BE-SVM and Word2Vec-BE-SVM models demonstrated superior performance compared to other ensemble models within their respective feature embeddings.

These results underscore the effectiveness of GPT2-based models, particularly the GPT2-BE-AB variant, in accurately identifying and classifying fake reporting attacks in VANET communication. The high accuracy and robust performance metrics achieved by these models highlight their potential in enhancing the security and reliability of VANETs. Further research and refinement of these models could lead to even more advanced detection systems, ensuring the integrity and safety of VANETs and the information exchanged within them.

Table 11.1 Performance comparison of bagging ensemble on fake reporting attack detection on Dataset 1

NLP model	**Methods**	**Accuracy**	**Attack**		**Normal**		**F_1-score**
			Precision	**Recall**	**Precision**	**Recall**	
Bagging	GloVe-BE-SVM	0.9635	0.99	0.93	0.93	1.00	0.96
Ensemble	GloVe-BE-RF	0.9646	1.00	0.93	0.94	1.00	0.97
Learners	GloVe-BE-GB	0.9640	1.00	0.93	0.95	0.99	0.96
(GloVe)	GloVe-BE-AB	0.9569	0.99	0.91	0.92	1.00	0.95
Bagging	Word2Vec-BE-SVM	0.9623	0.98	0.92	0.93	0.99	0.95
Ensemble	Word2Vec-BE-RF	0.9588	0.99	0.92	0.92	1.00	0.96
Learners	Word2Vec-BE-GBt1	0.9607	0.98	0.92	0.93	0.99	0.95
(Word2Vec)	Word2Vec-BE-AB	0.9544	0.98	0.91	0.92	1.00	0.95
Bagging	GPT2-BE-SVM	0.9415	0.99	1.00	0.92	0.89	0.95
Ensemble	GPT2-BE-RF	0.9975	1.00	1.00	1.00	0.95	0.97
Learners	GPT2-BE-GB	0.9515	0.99	1.00	0.94	0.87	0.95
(GPT2)	GPT2-BE-AB	0.9993	1.00	1.00	0.99	1.00	0.99

Table 11.2 further showcases the performance of LLMs on Dataset 2. The GPT feature encoding consistently outperforms GloVe and Word2Vec feature embeddings in the context of VANET false report attack classification. Notably, the GPT2-BE-AB model surpasses its state-of-the-art counterparts by attaining detection accuracy of 0.9976. Moreover, it achieved precision and recall scores of 0.99 and 0.98 on the false reporting attack class. The high accuracy and robust performance metrics achieved by this model underscore its potential in enhancing the security and reliability of VANETs.

Table 11.3 presents the performance comparison of bagging ensemble models on fake reporting attack detection using Dataset 3. The GloVe-BE-SVM model achieves an accuracy of 0.9622, with perfect precision and recall for the attack class and slightly lower metrics for the normal class. The GloVe-BE-RF and GloVe-BE-GB models have similar performance, with accuracies of 0.9596 and 0.9597, respectively. The GloVe-BE-AB model shows a slight improvement with an accuracy of 0.9602. The Word2Vec-BE-SVM model achieves an accuracy of 0.9599, similar to the GloVe-based models. The Word2Vec-BE-RF and Word2Vec-BE-GB models show improved performance with accuracies of 0.9650 and 0.9652, respectively. The Word2Vec-BE-AB model also achieves an accuracy of 0.9650. These models exhibit slightly better performance compared to their GloVe in terms of precision and recall for the normal class.

The GPT2-based models significantly outperform the GloVe and Word2Vec models. The GPT2-BE-SVM model achieves an accuracy of 0.9759 with perfect precision and recall for both attack and normal classes. The GPT2-BE-RF model further improves the performance with an accuracy of 0.9987. The GPT2-BE-GB and GPT2-BE-AB models achieve exceptional accuracies of 0.9991 and 0.9995 with near-perfect precision and recall scores across both classes.

Table 11.2 Performance comparison of bagging ensemble on fake reporting attack detection on Dataset 2

NLP model	Methods	Accuracy	Attack		Normal		F_1-score
			Precision	Recall	Precision	Recall	
Bagging	GloVe-BE-SVM	0.9617	0.99	0.92	0.93	0.99	0.96
Ensemble	GloVe-BE-RF	0.9649	1.00	0.93	0.92	1.00	0.96
Learners	GloVe-BE-GB	0.9658	1.00	0.93	0.94	0.99	0.97
(GloVe)	GloVe-BE-AB	0.9680	1.00	0.94	0.94	1.00	0.97
Bagging	Word2Vec-BE-SVM	0.9661	0.99	0.93	0.94	0.99	0.97
Ensemble	Word2Vec-BE-RF	0.9659	0.99	0.93	0.94	0.99	0.97
Learners	Word2Vec-BE-GBt1	0.9644	0.98	0.93	0.93	1.00	0.96
(Word2Vec)	Word2Vec-BE-AB	0.9658	1.00	0.93	0.94	0.99	0.96
Bagging	GPT2-BE-SVM	0.9753	1.00	1.00	0.95	0.93	0.97
Ensemble	GPT2-BE-RF	0.9967	1.00	1.00	0.99	0.93	0.98
Learners	GPT2-BE-GB	0.9748	1.00	1.00	0.96	0.91	0.97
(Word2Vec)	GPT2-BE-AB	0.9976	0.99	0.98	1.00	1.00	0.98

Table 11.3 Performance comparison of bagging ensemble on fake reporting attack detection on Dataset 3

NLP model	Methods	Accuracy	Attack		Normal		F_1-score
			Precision	**Recall**	**Precision**	**Recall**	
Bagging	GloVe-BE-SVM	0.9622	1.00	0.93	0.93	1.00	0.96
Ensemble	GloVe-BE-RF	0.9596	1.00	0.92	0.92	1.00	0.95
Learners	GloVe-BE-GB	0.9597	0.99	0.92	0.93	0.99	0.95
(GloVe)	GloVe-BE-AB	0.9602	1.00	0.92	0.94	0.99	0.96
Bagging	Word2Vec-BE-SVM	0.9599	1.00	0.92	0.92	0.99	0.96
Ensemble	Word2Vec-BE-RF	0.9650	0.99	0.93	0.93	0.99	0.97
Learners	Word2Vec-BE-GB	0.9652	1.00	0.93	0.94	1.00	0.97
(Word2Vec)	Word2Vec-BE-AB	0.9650	0.99	0.93	0.94	0.99	0.97
Bagging	GPT2-BE-SVM	0.9759	1.00	1.00	0.93	0.97	0.97
Ensemble	GPT2-BE-RF	0.9987	1.00	1.00	1.00	0.97	0.99
Learners	GPT2-BE-GB	0.9991	1.00	1.00	0.99	0.99	0.99
(Word2Vec)	GPT2-BE-AB	0.9995	1.00	1.00	0.99	1.00	0.99

Figure 11.3 presents the confusion matrices of the three models—GloVe, Word2Vec, and GPT2—on all three datasets, showcasing their best performances. A confusion matrix is used to summarizes the performance of a classification model in tabular representation. It provides insights into the true and false assessments made by a machine learning model across different classes. We further applied the Synthetic Minority Over-sampling Technique (SMOTE) to the minority class (Attack) in the GloVe and Word2Vec feature sets since the Attack class constituted less than 5% of the total samples in the datasets. SMOTE helps address class imbalance by creating synthetic samples of the minority class allowing the models to learn more effectively. However, we did not apply SMOTE to the GPT feature set. LLMs including GPT are usually trained using very large amounts of data and have been shown to perform well even in imbalanced datasets. By applying SMOTE to the GloVe and Word2Vec features, we aimed to enhance the representation of the minority class and improve generalize of data by the model. The overall results underscore the potential of the GPT2-BE-AB model in enhancing the security and reliability of VANETs. The minimal misclassifications achieved by this model demonstrate its capability to accurately identify and classify fake reporting attacks, contributing to the integrity and safety of VANET communication.

Table 11.4 provides a comprehensive comparison of the proposed model with recently published studies on VANETs attack detection. The study conducted by Raja *et al.* [21] employed distributed machine learning on the NSL-KDD dataset and achieved an impressive accuracy of 99.94%. Sharma *et al.* further [22,23] utilized BSMs with data-centric machine learning algorithms and attained accuracies of 98.10% and 90.83% on the VeReMi dataset. Hawaldaer *et al.* [24] used the same VeReMi dataset and achieved an accuracy of 73.30%. Meanwhile, Ercan *et al.* [25] and Anyanwu *et al.* [26] proposed ensemble-based methods for VANETs and achieved accuracies above 98% on the VeReMi dataset.

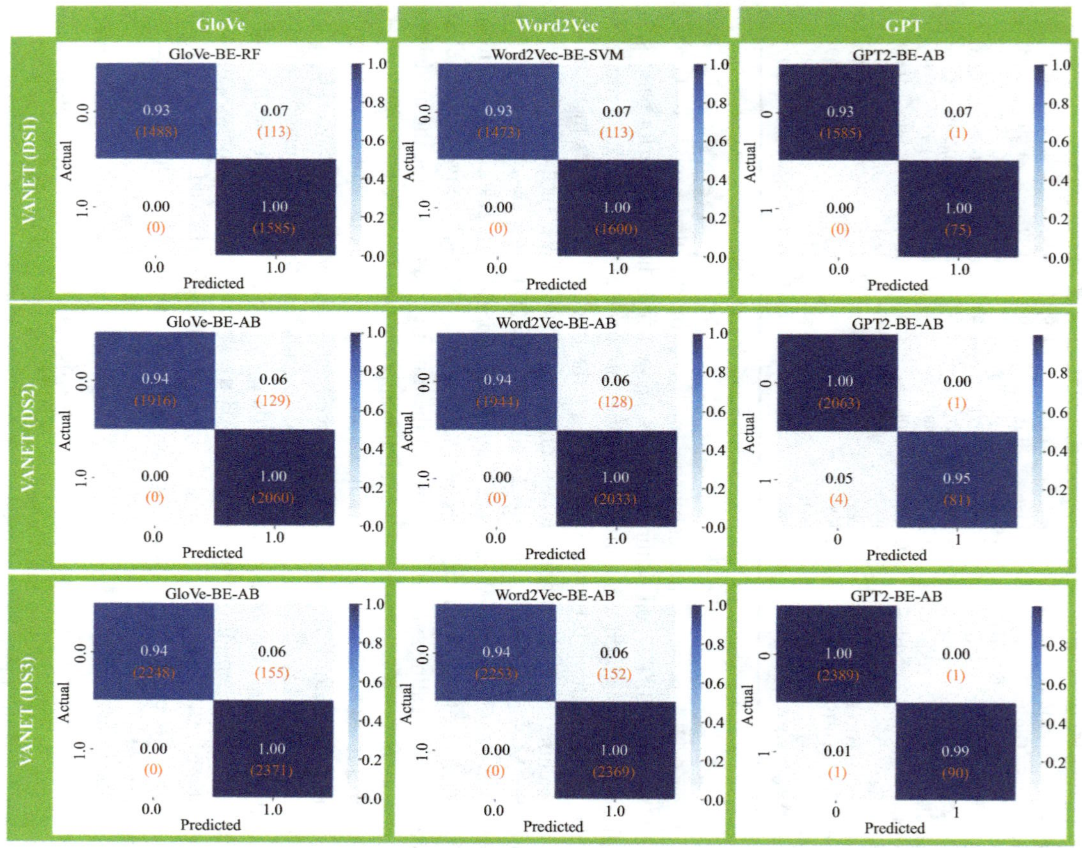

Figure 11.3 The performance comparison of best classifier in Datasets 1, 2, and 3 confusion matrices

Table 11.4 Performance comparison of proposed approach with published studies on VANETs attack detection

Work	Year	Method	Dataset	Accuracy
Raja *et al.* [21]	2020	Distributed Machin Learning - Differential Privacy	NSL-KDD	96.94
Sharma *et al.* [22]	2021	Consecutive BSMs for Train and Test Simulations	VeReMi	98.10
Sharma *et al.* [23]	2021	Data-Centric Machine Learning Algorithms	VeReMi	90.83
Hawlader *et al.* [24]	2021	Conventional Detection Algorithms	VeReMi	73.30
Ercan *et al.* [25]	2022	Position Falsification Machine Learning	VeReMi	98.44
Anyanwu *et al.* [26]	2023	Hyper-tuned Random Forest Ensemble	VeReMi	99.60
Proposed approach	2024	GPT2-BE-AB(Large Language Model)	VeReMiAP	**D1:** 99.93 **D2:** 99.76 **D3:** 99.95

In this study, the VeReMiAP simulation dataset used which is an extension of previous datasets and integrates the effects of fake reporting attacks on road hazards. VANET simulation datasets are usually available in JSON formatted strings, while the JSON parser methods can result in the loss of valuable information. By leveraging NLP techniques, we utilized word embeddings and feature encoding built upon LLMs to extract meaningful information from VANET data. Word embeddings technique identifies the semantic relationships between various words, while feature encoding transforms textual data into numerical representations to make it more suitable for machine learning algorithms. Furthermore, the utilization of LLMs provided a significant advantage in capturing complex linguistic nuances and contextual information within VANET communication. This enabled the models to make more informed decisions and improve their classification accuracy ultimately enhancing reliability and the security of VANETs by effectively identifying potential road hazards caused by false reporting attacks.

11.5 Conclusion

VANETs play a crucial role to enhance the road safety and improve the driving experience by enabling anonymous vehicles to converse with each other. Through the exchange of information related to the road conditions, live traffic accidents and other network data, VANETs aim to provide valuable services for safer and more capable transportation. However, the limitations of current VANET simulation models in evaluating proactive security measures further exacerbate the challenges posed by cyberattacks. The impact of a fake reporting attack goes beyond the targeted vehicle, compromising the overall security and reliability of the VANET communication network. In this chapter, we proposed a novel approach that leverages LLMs, specifically the GPT2 model, to detect fake reporting attacks in VANET communication. The ensemble learning techniques employed further enhance the accuracy and robustness of the proposed method. The experimental results validate the performance of proposed strategy in comparison to previously published studies. Our approach achieved accuracies of 99.93%, 99.76%, and 99.95% on a diverse dataset comprising road hazards caused by fake reporting attacks. The high performance achieved by the proposed approach underscores its potential in enhancing the security and reliability of VANETs. Future work may involve exploring more advanced ensemble techniques, integrating real-world VANET data, and further optimizing the detection of emerging cyberattack strategies.

Acknowledgments

The authors gratefully acknowledge the support provided by the Prince Sultan University for this publication. The university's management commitment to advancing research and knowledge dissemination has been invaluable in successfully completing this research.

References

[1] A. K. Haghighat, V. Ravichandra-Mouli, P. Chakraborty, Y. Esfandiari, S. Arabi, and A. Sharma, "Applications of deep learning in intelligent transportation systems," *Journal of Big Data Analytics in Transportation*, vol. 2, pp. 115–145, 2020.

[2] M. Zhang, "Effective safety message dissemination in V2X communications," *Auckland University of Technology*, Auckland, 2020.

[3] D. Zamouche, S. Aissani, M. Omar, and M. Mohammedi, "Highly efficient approach for discordant BSMs detection in connected vehicles environment," *Wireless Networks*, vol. 29, no. 1, pp. 189–207, 2023, doi:10.1007/s11276-022-03104-8.

[4] P. Rewal and D. Mishra, "Comparative analysis of handover authentication techniques in VANETs," *Wireless Personal Communications*, vol. 132, no. 4, pp. 2487–2506, 2023, doi:10.1007/s11277-023-10727-3.

[5] H. Che, Y. Duan, C. Li, and L. Yu, "On trust management in vehicular ad hoc networks: A comprehensive review," (in English), *Frontiers in the Internet of Things*, Review vol. 1, 2022, pp. 1–29, doi:10.3389/friot.2022.995233.

[6] A. Aziz, F. Samad, and S. Siddiqui, "Optimizing privacy preservation in wireless VANETS," in *2022 International Conference on Emerging Trends in Smart Technologies (ICETST)*, 23–24 September 2022, pp. 1–6, doi:10.1109/ICETST55735.2022.9921423.

[7] L. Zhang and J. Xu, "Blockchain-based anonymous authentication for traffic reporting in VANETs," *Connection Science*, vol. 34, no. 1, pp. 1038–1065, 2022, doi:10.1080/09540091.2022.2026888.

[8] K. Vamshi Krishna and K. Ganesh Reddy, “Classification of distributed denial of service attacks in VANET: A survey,” *Wireless Personal Communications*, vol. 132, no. 2, pp. 933–964, 2023, doi:10.1007/s11277-023-10643-6.

[9] H. Taherdoost, “Understanding cybersecurity frameworks and information security standards—a review and comprehensive overview,” *Electronics*, vol. 11, no. 14, 2022, pp. 1–20, doi: 10.3390/electronics11142181.

[10] A. Wang, A. Mohaisen, and S. Chen, “An adversary-centric behavior modeling of DDoS attacks,” *2017 IEEE 37th International Conference on Distributed Computing Systems (ICDCS)*, pp. 1126–1136, 2017.

[11] M. A. Abdelmaguid, H. S. Hassanein, and M. Zulkernine, “A VeReMi-based Dataset for predicting the effect of attacks in VANETs,” *in Proceedings of the Int’l ACM Conference on Modeling Analysis and Simulation of Wireless and Mobile Systems (MSWiM ’23)*, Association for Computing Machinery, NY, USA, pp. 175–179, 2023.

[12] A. Sangwan, A. Sangwan, and R. P. Singh, “A classification of misbehavior detection schemes for VANETs: A survey,” *Wireless Personal Communications*, vol. 129, no. 1, pp. 285–322, 2023.

[13] J. Kamel, M. Wolf, R. W. van der Hei, A. Kaiser, P. Urien, and F. Kargl, “VeReMi extension: A dataset for comparable evaluation of misbehavior detection in VANETs,” *IEEE International Conference on Communications (ICC)*, Dublin, Ireland, pp. 1–6, 2020.

[14] F. A. Ghaleb, M. A. Maarof, A. Zainal, M. A. Rassam, F. Saeed, and M. Alsaedi, “Context-aware data-centric misbehaviour detection scheme for vehicular ad hoc networks using sequential analysis of the temporal and spatial correlation of the consistency between the cooperative awareness messages,” *Vehicular Communications*, vol. 20, p. 100186, 2019.

[15] M. Zang and Y. Yan, “Machine learning-based intrusion detection system for big data analytics in VANET,” in *2021 IEEE 93rd Vehicular Technology Conference*, IEEE, Piscataway, NJ, pp. 1–5, 2021.

[16] C. Zhang, K. Chen, X. Zeng, and X. Xue, “Misbehavior detection based on support vector machine and Dempster–Shafer theory of evidence in VANETs,” *IEEE Access*, vol. 6, pp. 59860–59870, 2018.

[17] S. Sharma, and A. Kaul, “Hybrid fuzzy multi-criteria decision making based multi cluster head dolphin swarm optimized IDS for VANET,” *Vehicular Communications*, vol. 12, pp. 23–38, 2018.

[18] R. W. Van Der Heijden, T. Lukaseder, and F. Kargl, “VeReMi extension: A dataset for comparable evaluation of misbehavior detection in VANETs,” Springer, Berlin, pp. 318–337, 2018.

[19] P. Jeffrey, S. Richard, and M. Christopher, “Glove: Global vectors for word representation,” *Proceedings of the 2014 Conference on Empirical Methods in Natural Language Processing (EMNLP)*, p. 1532, 2014, doi:10.3115/v1/d14-1162.

[20] P. A. Lopez, M. Behrisch, L. B-Walz, *et al.*, “Microscopic traffic simulation using SUMO,” in *2018 21st International Conference on Intelligent*

Transportation Systems (ITSC), 4–7 November 2018, pp. 2575–2582, 2018, doi:10.1109/ITSC.2018.8569938.

[21] G. Raja, S. Anbalagan, G. Vijayaraghavan, S. Theerthagiri, S. V. Suryanarayan, and X. W. Wu, "SP-CIDS: Secure and private collaborative IDS for VANETs," *IEEE Transactions on Intelligent Transportation Systems*, vol. 22, no. 7, pp. 4385–4393, 2021, doi:10.1109/TITS.2020.3036071.

[22] A. Sharma and A. Jaekel, "Machine learning based misbehaviour detection in VANET using consecutive BSM approach," *IEEE Open Journal of Vehicular Technology*, vol. 3, pp. 1–14, 2022, doi:10.1109/OJVT.2021.3138354.

[23] P. Sharma and H. Liu, "A machine-learning-based data-centric misbehavior detection model for internet of vehicles," *IEEE Internet of Things Journal*, vol. 8, no. 6, pp. 4991–4999, 2021, doi:10.1109/JIOT.2020.3035035.

[24] F. Hawlader, A. Boualouache, S. Faye, and T. Engel, "Intelligent misbehavior detection system for detecting false position attacks in vehicular networks," in *2021 IEEE International Conference on Communications Workshops (ICC Workshops)*, 14–23 June 2021, pp. 1–6, 2021, doi:10.1109/ICCWorkshops50388.2021.9473606.

[25] S. Ercan, M. Ayaida, and N. Messai, "Misbehavior detection for position falsification attacks in VANETs using machine learning," *IEEE Access*, vol. 10, pp. 1893–1904, 2022, doi:10.1109/ACCESS.2021.3136706.

[26] G. O. Anyanwu, C. I. Nwakanma, J. M. Lee, and D.-S. Kim, "Novel hyper-tuned ensemble Random Forest algorithm for the detection of false basic safety messages in Internet of Vehicles," *ICT Express*, vol. 9, no. 1, pp. 122–129, 2023, doi: https://doi.org/10.1016/j.icte.2022.06.003.

Chapter 12
Cybersecurity-enabled federated learning approach for digital healthcare

Hina Zafar[1], *Majid Hussain*[1], *Muhammad Sheraz Arshad Malik*[2] *and Ashraf Khalil*[3]

Abstract

With the rapid integration of artificial intelligence into cybersecurity, smart and digitized systems have significantly enhanced the ability to detect and prevent security threats. However, the increasing reliance on distributed AI systems has also introduced critical challenges related to data leakage, system vulnerabilities, and computational overhead. This chapter addresses the persistent problem of securing sensitive healthcare data in federated learning environments, where centralized data aggregation is avoided. The objective is to develop a cybersecurity-enabled federated learning framework that ensures privacy-preserving, secure, and scalable intrusion detection in digital healthcare systems. The proposed framework incorporates four core modules: secure data encryption and transmission, participant authentication and authorization, privacy-preserving model aggregation using homomorphic encryption or secure multi-party computation, and anomaly detection with intrusion prevention mechanisms. Deep learning models, specifically CNNs, are employed within the federated setting to enhance detection accuracy. Key contributions include maintaining data privacy without sacrificing model performance, enabling distributed training while preserving data ownership, and integrating proactive anomaly detection. Experimental results using the CIC IDS 2017 and IoT Healthcare Security datasets show the proposed model outperforms centralized systems, achieving accuracy and precision rates above 99%. Despite its effectiveness, the model faces limitations related to communication latency and computational complexity in real-time healthcare systems. Future research will focus on optimizing resource efficiency, extending the framework to more diverse IoT healthcare datasets, and incorporating adaptive threat intelligence to respond to evolving cybersecurity risks.

[1]Department of Computer Sciences, The University of Faisalabad, Pakistan
[2]Department of Software Engineering, Government College University Faisalabad, Pakistan
[3]College of Technological Innovation, Zayed University, United Arad Emirates

12.1 Introduction

In digital healthcare, ensuring the security and privacy of sensitive patient data is paramount. One innovative approach to maintaining these standards is through the implementation of. Federated learning involves training machine learning models across decentralized devices or servers holding local data samples, without exchanging them [1]. This means that instead of sending data to a central server for processing, the processing is done locally on each device, and only aggregated model updates are sent back to the central server. This approach helps in preserving data privacy as the raw data never leaves the local device. introduce cybersecurity into this federated learning framework for digital healthcare, will essentially add an extra layer of protection against potential threats and breaches. This can involve various measures such as encryption techniques, secure communication protocols, access controls, and intrusion detection systems [2]. By combining federated learning with robust cybersecurity measures, digital healthcare systems can effectively leverage the power of machine learning for insights and decision-making while safeguarding patient privacy and ensuring data security. This approach enables healthcare providers to derive valuable insights from distributed data sources without compromising on confidentiality or integrity, thus fostering trust among patients and healthcare professionals alike.

12.1.1 Overview of the significance of digital healthcare and data security challenges

In recent years, digital healthcare has emerged as a transformative force, revolutionizing the way healthcare services are delivered and accessed. With the advent of advanced technologies, such as electronic health records (EHRs), telemedicine, wearable devices, and health monitoring apps, healthcare providers can offer more personalized care, streamline administrative processes, and improve patient outcomes [3]. However, alongside these advancements come significant challenges, particularly concerning the privacy and security of sensitive patient data.

The digitization of healthcare records and the widespread adoption of digital technologies have exponentially increased the volume and complexity of data generated and stored within healthcare systems [4]. This wealth of data, encompassing personal health information, medical histories, diagnostic records, and treatment plans, represents a valuable asset for improving medical research, diagnosis, and treatment. However, it also poses significant risks in terms of data privacy, security breaches, and unauthorized access [5].

12.1.2 Introduction to federated learning

Federated learning presents a promising solution to the challenges of training machine learning models on decentralized, sensitive data sources while preserving privacy and security [6]. Unlike traditional centralized machine learning approaches, where data is aggregated into a single repository for analysis, federated learning allows for model training to occur locally on individual devices or servers

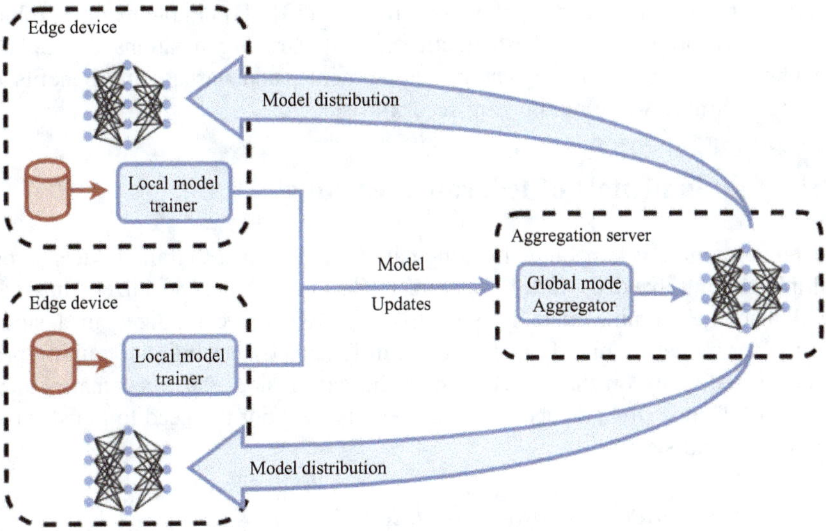

Figure 12.1 Typical framework of federated learning

without sharing raw data [7]. Instead, only model updates, typically in the form of gradients, are exchanged between the local devices and a central server.

This decentralized approach to machine learning offers several advantages, including enhanced privacy protection, reduced data transfer requirements, and improved scalability [8]. By enabling model training on distributed data sources while minimizing data exposure, federated learning facilitates collaboration and knowledge sharing across organizations without compromising individual privacy or data security (Figure 12.1) [9].

12.1.3 The need for cybersecurity measures in healthcare data handling

Given the sensitive nature of healthcare data and the increasing frequency of cyberattacks targeting healthcare organizations, robust cybersecurity measures are essential to safeguard patient privacy and ensure data security [10]. Healthcare data breaches can have severe consequences, ranging from financial losses and reputational damage to legal liabilities and compromised patient care [11].

The integration of cybersecurity measures into healthcare data handling processes is critical to mitigate risks and vulnerabilities associated with data breaches, unauthorized access, and malicious activities [12]. These measures encompass a wide range of technical, procedural, and organizational controls, including encryption, access controls, authentication mechanisms, intrusion detection systems, security audits, and employee training.

In the context of federated learning in digital healthcare, cybersecurity measures play a pivotal role in protecting sensitive patient data throughout the model development, training, and deployment phases [13]. By implementing robust cybersecurity protocols and best practices, healthcare organizations can uphold patient trust, comply with regulatory requirements, and harness the benefits of federated learning while minimizing security risks.

12.2 Fundamentals of federated learning

Federated learning is a machine learning paradigm designed to train models across multiple decentralized devices or servers while keeping data localized. In traditional machine learning, data is typically collected and centralized in a single location for model training [14]. However, in federated learning, the training process occurs directly on the devices where the data resides, such as smartphones, Internet of Things (IoT) devices, or local servers, without the need to transfer raw data to a central server.

12.2.1 Federated learning principles

The key principles of federated learning include:

Decentralization: Data remains on local devices or servers, eliminating the need for central data aggregation.

Collaborative learning: Models are trained collaboratively across multiple devices, leveraging insights from diverse data sources.

Privacy preservation: Federated learning ensures that sensitive user data remains on-device, protecting individual privacy.

Model aggregation: Model updates, typically in the form of gradients, are aggregated at a central server to generate a global model without exposing raw data.

12.2.2 Comparison with centralized learning approaches

In contrast to centralized learning approaches, where data is aggregated and processed in a centralized location, federated learning offers several distinct advantages [15]:

- **Privacy preservation**: Federated learning enables model training on decentralized data sources without exposing raw data, thus preserving user privacy.
- **Scalability**: By distributing the training process across multiple devices, federated learning can scale efficiently to accommodate large datasets and diverse data sources.
- **Data sovereignty**: Individual data owners retain control over their data, reducing concerns about data ownership and sovereignty.
- **Reduced communication overhead**: Federated learning minimizes the need for data transmission to a central server, reducing communication overhead and network bandwidth requirements (Table 12.1).

Table 12.1 Comparison of federated model with centralized model [32]

Aspect	Centralized learning	Federated learning
Privacy preservation	Data aggregated centrally, risking privacy breaches	Model training on decentralized data, preserving privacy by keeping data local
Scalability	Limited scalability due to centralized processing	Efficient scalability by distributing training across multiple devices
Data sovereignty	Data ownership centralized, raising concerns about control	Individual data owners retain control over their data, ensuring sovereignty
Communication overhead	High communication overhead for data transmission to central server	Reduced communication overhead as data remains local, minimizing network bandwidth requirements

12.2.3 Advantages and limitations of federated learning in healthcare contexts

Federated learning in healthcare offers the advantage of preserving data privacy by enabling model training directly on distributed devices, enhancing security and confidentiality. However, its effectiveness heavily relies on the quality and diversity of data across different sources, posing limitations in cases where data heterogeneity or inconsistency are prevalent.

Advantages:

- **Patient privacy protection**: Federated learning enables healthcare organizations to train predictive models on patient data while ensuring individual privacy and confidentiality.
- **Collaborative knowledge sharing**: Federated learning facilitates collaboration and knowledge sharing across healthcare institutions, allowing for collective insights without sharing sensitive data.
- **Regulatory compliance**: By minimizing data transfer and centralization, federated learning helps healthcare organizations comply with strict regulatory requirements, such as Health Insurance Portability and Accountability Act (HIPAA) in the United States or General Data Protection Regulation (GDPR) in the European Union (EU) [16].
- **Improved model generalization**: Federated learning allows models to be trained on diverse datasets, leading to improved generalization and robustness in real-world healthcare applications.

Limitations:

- **Computational complexity**: Federated learning introduces additional computational overhead due to the need to coordinate model updates across distributed devices [17].
- **Communication constraints**: Federated learning relies on communication between devices, which may be constrained by network bandwidth, latency, or connectivity issues.

- **Data heterogeneity**: Variability in data distribution and quality across decentralized devices can pose challenges for model convergence and performance.
- **Security risks**: Federated learning systems may be vulnerable to security threats, such as model poisoning attacks or data leakage through model updates.

Overall, while federated learning offers significant potential for advancing machine learning in healthcare, careful consideration of its advantages, limitations, and implementation challenges is essential for successful deployment in real-world healthcare contexts.

12.3 Security challenges in digital healthcare

Following discussion shows the unique security challenges posed by digital healthcare systems.

Digital healthcare systems present a host of unique security challenges stemming from the nature of healthcare data, the complexity of healthcare infrastructure, and the evolving threat landscape [18]. These challenges include:

1. Diverse data types: Healthcare data encompasses a wide range of sensitive information, including personal health records, medical images, genomic data, and prescription histories. Protecting these diverse data types requires comprehensive security measures tailored to each data category.
2. Interconnected systems: Modern healthcare infrastructure comprises interconnected networks, medical devices, and software applications, creating numerous entry points for cyberattacks. Vulnerabilities in one system can potentially compromise the security of the entire healthcare ecosystem [12].
3. Legacy systems: Many healthcare organizations rely on legacy systems and outdated software, which may lack essential security features and are more susceptible to exploitation by cybercriminals. Upgrading these systems to meet modern security standards can be challenging and costly.
4. Human factors: Human error and insider threats pose significant security risks in digital healthcare. Mishandling of patient data, weak password practices, and unauthorized access by healthcare employees can lead to data breaches and privacy violations.
5. Emerging technologies: The adoption of emerging technologies, such as telemedicine, wearable devices, and IoT sensors, introduces new security considerations [19]. These technologies may lack robust security controls, making them vulnerable to exploitation by malicious actors.

12.3.1 Risks associated with handling sensitive patient data

The handling of sensitive patient data in digital healthcare systems introduces various risks, including:

1. Data breaches: Unauthorized access to healthcare databases or EHRs can result in data breaches, exposing sensitive patient information to unauthorized parties. Data breaches can lead to identity theft, financial fraud, and reputational damage to healthcare organizations.
2. Data theft and ransomware: Cybercriminals may target healthcare systems to steal patient data for financial gain or deploy ransomware attacks to encrypt healthcare data and extort ransom payments. These attacks can disrupt healthcare operations and compromise patient care.
3. Medical identity theft: Stolen healthcare credentials or compromised patient records can be used for medical identity theft, where fraudsters obtain medical services, prescriptions, or insurance coverage using a victim's identity. Medical identity theft can have serious consequences for patients, including incorrect medical treatment and financial liabilities.
4. Regulatory non-compliance: Failure to comply with healthcare data protection regulations, such as the HIPAA in the United States or the GDPR in the EU, can result in severe penalties, legal liabilities, and damage to the reputation of healthcare organizations.

12.4 Regulatory requirements and compliance standards

Regulatory requirements and compliance standards play a crucial role in governing healthcare data security and ensuring patient privacy. Key regulations and standards include:

1. HIPAA: Enacted in 1996, HIPAA sets standards for the protection of sensitive patient health information (PHI) and establishes requirements for healthcare organizations to safeguard PHI's confidentiality, integrity, and availability [20]. HIPAA mandates security controls, privacy practices, and breach notification requirements for covered entities and their business associates.
2. GDPR: Implemented in 2018, GDPR regulates the processing and protection of personal data within the EU and the European Economic Area [21]. GDPR imposes strict requirements on healthcare organizations regarding the lawful processing of patient data, explicit consent for data collection, data minimization, and the appointment of data protection officers.
3. HITECH Act: The Health Information Technology for Economic and Clinical Health (HITECH) Act, enacted as part of the American Recovery and Reinvestment Act of 2009, strengthens HIPAA's privacy and security provisions by extending its requirements to business associates and imposing stricter penalties for non-compliance [22,23].

Compliance with these regulations requires healthcare organizations to implement robust security measures, conduct risk assessments, provide employee training on data security practices, and maintain comprehensive documentation of data processing activities. Non-compliance can result in significant financial penalties, legal sanctions, and damage to the reputation of healthcare providers.

Therefore, adherence to regulatory requirements is essential for protecting patient privacy and maintaining trust in digital healthcare systems.

12.5 Integrating cybersecurity with federated learning

Integrating cybersecurity with federated learning involves implementing robust measures to safeguard sensitive data during the collaborative training process. By incorporating encryption techniques and secure communication protocols, such as Secure Sockets Layer (SSL)/Transport Layer Security (TLS), the privacy and integrity of data across distributed devices can be ensured [24]. Additionally, access controls and authentication mechanisms are vital to authenticate participants and regulate their access to the federated learning environment. This integration addresses concerns regarding data security and confidentiality, fostering trust in the collaborative learning framework.

12.5.1 Exploration of cybersecurity techniques applicable to federated learning in healthcare

Cybersecurity is paramount in the context of federated learning in healthcare to ensure the confidentiality, integrity, and availability of sensitive patient data. Several cybersecurity techniques are applicable to federated learning environments:

1. Encryption methods for secure data transmission:
   Encrypting data during transmission is essential to prevent unauthorized access or interception by malicious actors. Techniques such as TLS or SSL can be employed to encrypt data exchanged between decentralized devices and the central server in federated learning setups [25].
2. Access control mechanisms to protect data privacy:
   Access control mechanisms restrict access to sensitive data and functionalities based on predefined policies or user roles. In federated learning, access controls can be implemented at both the device and server levels to ensure that only authorized personnel can access and manipulate model parameters, training data, or system configurations.
3. Secure communication protocols and authentication mechanisms:
   Secure communication protocols, such as HTTPS or MQTT (Message Queuing Telemetry Transport), ensure the authenticity and integrity of data exchanged between devices and servers. Additionally, robust authentication mechanisms, such as multi-factor authentication (MFA) [26] or digital certificates, verify the identities of users and devices participating in federated learning processes, mitigating the risk of unauthorized access or impersonation attacks.
4. Intrusion detection and prevention systems for threat mitigation:
   Intrusion detection and prevention systems (IDPS) continuously monitor network traffic, system logs, and user activities to detect and mitigate potential

security breaches or malicious activities [27]. In the context of federated learning, IDPS can identify anomalous behavior, unauthorized access attempts, or suspicious data transmissions, triggering alerts or automated responses to mitigate security risks promptly.

Integrating cybersecurity measures with federated learning in healthcare is essential to mitigate security risks, protect patient privacy, and ensure the integrity of machine learning processes. By leveraging encryption methods, access controls, secure communication protocols, and intrusion detection/prevention systems, healthcare organizations can establish a robust cybersecurity framework to safeguard sensitive data and maintain trust in federated learning systems. However, it's crucial to continuously assess and update cybersecurity measures to adapt to evolving threats and compliance requirements in the dynamic healthcare landscape.

12.6 Implementation considerations

Implementation considerations for the proposed framework encompass ensuring compatibility with existing healthcare infrastructure, addressing regulatory compliance requirements, and fostering stakeholder buy-in through effective communication and training initiatives. Additionally, prioritizing data governance and security protocols while maintaining scalability and interoperability will be paramount for successful deployment in diverse healthcare settings.

12.6.1 Practical considerations for implementing a cybersecurity-enabled federated learning system

Implementing a cybersecurity-enabled federated learning system in digital healthcare requires careful consideration of various practical factors:

1. Data privacy and compliance: Ensure compliance with regulations such as the HIPAA to protect patient privacy and maintain data security throughout the federated learning process [28].
2. Collaborative partnerships: Foster collaborations among healthcare institutions, technology providers, and cybersecurity experts to design and implement robust federated learning systems tailored to healthcare needs.
3. Resource allocation: Allocate adequate resources, including funding, personnel, and infrastructure, to support the development, deployment, and maintenance of cybersecurity-enabled federated learning systems.
4. Training and education: Provide training and education for healthcare professionals, data scientists, and IT personnel on cybersecurity best practices, data handling protocols, and federated learning methodologies to ensure effective implementation and operation.

12.6.2 Technical requirements and infrastructure considerations

Deploying a cybersecurity-enabled federated learning system in digital healthcare settings necessitates specific technical requirements and infrastructure considerations:

1. Scalable architecture: Design a scalable architecture capable of accommodating diverse healthcare data sources, varying computational resources, and fluctuating workload demands while ensuring efficient model training and inference.
2. Secure data exchange: Implement secure data exchange mechanisms, such as encrypted communication channels and secure protocols, to facilitate the transmission of model updates and ensure data privacy during federated learning processes.
3. Data standardization and interoperability: Establish data standardization protocols and interoperability frameworks to harmonize disparate healthcare data formats, facilitate data sharing across institutions, and promote seamless integration with federated learning systems.
4. Cloud infrastructure or edge computing: Choose between cloud-based infrastructure or edge computing solutions based on factors such as data sensitivity, latency requirements, scalability needs, and regulatory compliance considerations.

12.6.3 Challenges and potential solutions in deploying federated learning models securely

Deploying federated learning models securely in healthcare environments presents several challenges:

1. Data heterogeneity: Address data heterogeneity challenges arising from variations in data formats, quality, and distribution across decentralized healthcare institutions by employing data preprocessing techniques, data standardization protocols, and federated learning algorithms optimized for heterogeneous data sources.
2. Model poisoning attacks: Mitigate the risk of model poisoning attacks, wherein adversaries inject malicious data or gradients to manipulate model updates, by implementing robust anomaly detection mechanisms, model validation procedures, and cryptographic techniques to verify the integrity of federated learning processes.
3. Privacy-preserving techniques: Employ privacy-preserving techniques, such as differential privacy, secure multiparty computation (SMPC), or homomorphic encryption, to enhance data privacy and confidentiality while enabling collaborative model training across decentralized healthcare entities.
4. Regulatory compliance: Ensure compliance with regulatory requirements, such as HIPAA, GDPR, or HITECH Act, by incorporating privacy-enhancing technologies, audit trails, and data governance frameworks into federated learning systems.

By addressing these implementation considerations, technical requirements, and infrastructure challenges, healthcare organizations can deploy cybersecurity-enabled federated learning systems securely, harnessing the collective power of distributed data sources while safeguarding patient privacy and data security.

12.7 Theoretical framework

This chapter aims to leverage federated learning techniques while incorporating robust cybersecurity measures to ensure the privacy, integrity, and security of sensitive healthcare data distributed across multiple devices. Theoretical models serve as excellent foundations for understanding the emotional nuances of a topic. Based on this theoretical model, a digital healthcare system can be developed and tested to comprehend the sentiments associated with the topic effectively. Following are the main modules

1. **Data encryption and secure transmission module**:

It comprises sensitive data encryption, secure transmission and ensuring the data integrity steps.

- Encrypts sensitive healthcare data before transmission.
- Ensures secure transmission protocols (e.g., SSL/TLS) are implemented.
- Verifies data integrity upon reception.

2. **Participant authentication and authorization module:**

It involves

- Authenticates participants before allowing access to federated learning processes.
- Enforces access control policies based on participant roles and permissions.
- Utilizes techniques like cryptographic certificates and MFA for secure authentication.

3. **Secure model aggregation module:**

This module plays a very important role as it handles to perform integration of cybersecurity-enabled federated learning for healthcare data security

- Aggregates locally trained models securely without exposing raw data.
- Utilizes cryptographic techniques such as homomorphic encryption or SMPC to ensure privacy-preserving aggregation [29].

4. **Anomaly detection and intrusion prevention module:**

- Monitors federated learning processes for suspicious activities or anomalies [30].
- Implements intrusion prevention mechanisms to thwart potential cyberattacks.
- Utilizes machine learning-based anomaly detection algorithms for proactive security.

Algorithm for main modules of theoretical model

1. Data encryption and secure transmission module:

```
# Data Encryption and Secure Transmission Module Algorithm
function EncryptData(data):
    # Encrypt the sensitive healthcare data
    encryptedData = SymmetricEncryption(data)
    # or AsymmetricEncryption(data)
    return encryptedData

function SecureTransmit(encryptedData, destination):
    # Establish a secure connection and transmit encrypted data
    secureConnection = EstablishSecureConnection(destination)
    TransmitDataOverSecureConnection(secureConnection, encryptedData)
    VerifyDataIntegrity(secureConnection)

# Participant Authentication and Authorization Module Algorithm
function AuthenticateParticipant(credentials):
    # Validate participant credentials
    if ValidateCredentials(credentials):
    return true # Authentication successful
  else:
    return false # Authentication failed
```

2. Participant authentication and authorization module:

```
function AuthorizeParticipant(role):
    # Determine participant's access permissions based on role
    permissions = GetPermissionsForRole(role)
    return permissions
```

3. Secure model aggregation module:

```
# Secure Model Aggregation Module Algorithm
function SecureAggregation(localModels):
    # Securely aggregate locally trained models
    aggregatedModel=HomomorphicEncryption(localModels)
# or SecureMultiPartyComputation(localModels)
return aggregatedModel
```

4. Anomaly detection and intrusion prevention module:

```
# Anomaly Detection and Intrusion Prevention Module Algorithm
function DetectAnomaly(data):
    # Apply anomaly detection algorithms
    anomalyScore = AnomalyDetectionAlgorithm(data)
    if anomalyScore > threshold:
      AlertAnomalyDetected()
```

```
function PreventIntrusion():
    # Implement intrusion prevention mechanisms
    EnableFirewall()
    EnableIntrusionDetectionSystem()
    TakeProactiveMeasures()
```

12.8 Proposed model

Cybersecurity-enabled Federated Learning Approach for Digital Healthcare for intrusion detection systems with deep learning models, i.e. convolutional neural network (CNN) and recurrent neural network.

Experimental setup

To assess the effectiveness of our proposed method, we utilized the CIC IDS 2017 dataset, a widely available resource crafted by the Canadian Institute for Cybersecurity specifically for testing anomaly-based intrusion detection methodologies. This dataset encompasses both benign network traffic and the latest common attack patterns. We partitioned the dataset into training and testing subsets, adhering to a 70:30 ratio. Initially, a small portion of the data was allocated for training the base model, which was subsequently distributed to all participants. Additionally, the training data was further divided among the participating workers.

We employed TensorFlow to train a CNN classifier, tailored to the one-dimensional nature of the dataset. The neural network architecture comprised several layers: a 1D CNN layer, a pooling layer, a flattening layer, a dropout layer for regularization to mitigate overfitting, and two dense layers utilizing the ReLU activation function. For optimization, we utilized the Adam algorithm, a variant of stochastic gradient descent, and employed the binary cross-entropy loss function. The training process spanned 30 epochs.

12.8.1 Dataset

12.8.1.1 CIC IDS 2017 Dataset

The CICIDS2017 dataset is designed to support the development and evaluation of Intrusion Detection Systems (IDSs) and Intrusion Prevention Systems (IPSs) by addressing the limitations of previous datasets in terms of traffic diversity, attack coverage, and metadata completeness. It contains both benign traffic and modern attack scenarios, closely mimicking real-world network environments. The dataset includes raw packet captures (PCAPs) and flow-based features generated using CICFlowMeter, with labeled data encompassing timestamps, source/destination IPs and ports, protocols, and attack types. This comprehensive labeling and realistic traffic composition make CICIDS2017 a reliable benchmark for anomaly-based intrusion detection research [33].

12.8.1.2 IoT healthcare security dataset

Dataset name	Description
Number of predictor features	51
Number of target features	1

The network traffic captured is categorized into 15 distinct classes. Among these, one class represents normal traffic, while the remaining 14 classes encompass various types of attacks.

12.8.2 Comparative analysis of result

The evaluation results provided offer insights into the performance of two models, namely the centralized model and the proposed model, in the context of federated learning for intrusion detection in digital healthcare environments (Figure 12.2). These models are assessed using two distinct datasets: the CIC IDS 2017 Dataset [31] and the IoT Healthcare Security Dataset (Table 12.2).

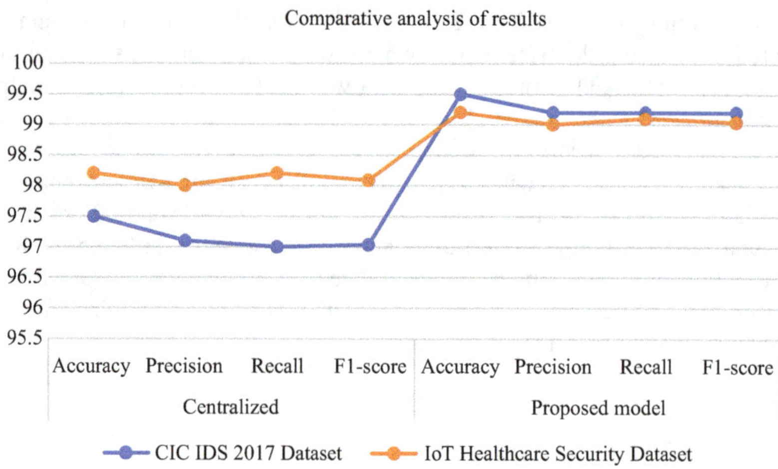

Figure 12.2 Comparative analysis of results

Table 12.2 CIC IDS 2017 Dataset

Dataset name	**Description**
Network setup	Two segments: 4 attacker machines, 10 victim machines
Data size	50 gigabytes of raw data (PCAP files)
Features	84 features (CSV files)
Duration	5 days
Instances	2,830,743
Classes	15 classes (1 normal, 14 attack types)

Table 12.3 Results

	Centralized approach				**Proposed model**			
	Accuracy	**Precision**	**Recall**	**F1-score**	**Accuracy**	**Precision**	**Recall**	**F1-score**
CIC IDS 2017 Dataset	97.5	97.1	97	97.04	99.5	99.2	99.2	99.2
IoT Health-care Security Dataset	98.2	98	98.2	98.09	99.2	99	99.1	99.04

Across both datasets, the proposed model consistently demonstrates better performance compared to the centralized model across key evaluation metrics such as accuracy, precision, recall, and F1-score. This suggests that the proposed federated learning approach yields more effective intrusion detection capabilities within the distributed healthcare data landscape (Table 12.3).

For instance, on the CIC IDS 2017 Dataset, the proposed federated learning model achieves precision and recall values ranging from 99.1% to 99.2%, indicating its ability to accurately identify intrusion patterns while minimizing false positives and negatives. Similarly, on the IoT Healthcare Security Dataset, the proposed model maintains precision and recall values within the range of 99% to 99.2%, highlighting its robustness in detecting security threats within healthcare IoT ecosystems.

These findings underscore the potential of federated learning approaches, like the proposed model, to enhance intrusion detection mechanisms in digital healthcare settings. By leveraging distributed data sources and collaborative model training, federated learning offers improved privacy, scalability, and effectiveness in safeguarding sensitive healthcare information while mitigating security risks. Thus, the results suggest that the proposed federated learning model holds promise for bolstering cybersecurity measures in digital healthcare domains, contributing to enhanced data protection and patient privacy.

12.8.3 Contribution

The theoretical framework of incorporating cybersecurity-enabled federated learning into healthcare systems contributes significantly to enhancing data privacy, security, and efficiency in healthcare settings. By integrating robust cybersecurity measures with federated learning techniques, the framework offers several key contributions:

1. Enhanced data privacy: The framework ensures the privacy of sensitive healthcare data by employing encryption techniques during data transmission and secure aggregation methods that allow model training without exposing raw patient information.
2. Improved data security: With cybersecurity measures integrated at various levels, including participant authentication, authorization, and intrusion

prevention, the framework safeguards healthcare data against unauthorized access, cyberattacks, and intrusions.

3. Efficient model training: Leveraging federated learning, the framework enables model training directly on distributed healthcare devices, eliminating the need for centralized data aggregation. This approach not only improves scalability but also reduces the risk of data breaches associated with centralized storage.
4. Empowering data owners: Individual data owners retain control over their data throughout the federated learning process, ensuring data sovereignty and addressing concerns related to data ownership and governance.
5. Proactive anomaly detection: Incorporating anomaly detection mechanisms allows for the proactive identification of suspicious activities or deviations from expected behavior within the federated learning environment, enabling timely preventive actions to mitigate potential security threats.
6. Adaptability to healthcare systems: The framework's flexibility allows for seamless integration into various healthcare settings, accommodating diverse data sources, and addressing specific privacy and security requirements unique to healthcare environments.

Overall, by addressing the critical challenges of data privacy and security while facilitating collaborative model training across distributed healthcare devices, the theoretical framework contributes to advancing the adoption of secure and privacy-preserving technologies in healthcare systems.

12.9 Future directions and implications

Future directions and implications of the proposed cybersecurity-enabled federated learning framework in healthcare systems hold significant promise for advancing patient care, data security, and research capabilities. Building upon the discussed theoretical framework, several potential directions and implications can be envisaged:

1. Enhanced healthcare data sharing: The framework sets the stage for more extensive collaboration and data sharing among healthcare institutions, researchers, and stakeholders. Future advancements may focus on streamlining interoperability standards and governance frameworks to facilitate secure data exchange while maintaining privacy and security.
2. Personalized medicine and treatment: Leveraging federated learning techniques, healthcare providers can harness insights from diverse datasets distributed across different healthcare systems to develop more personalized treatment plans and predictive models. Future research may explore novel algorithms and methodologies for improving the accuracy and robustness of predictive models tailored to individual patient needs.
3. Accelerated research and innovation: The framework fosters a collaborative research ecosystem by enabling efficient model training on decentralized data

sources. Future implications may include accelerated research breakthroughs in areas such as disease detection, drug discovery, and population health management, fueled by access to diverse and expansive datasets.

4. Ethical and regulatory considerations: As federated learning becomes more prevalent in healthcare settings, future directions should address emerging ethical and regulatory challenges surrounding data privacy, consent management, and algorithmic transparency. Efforts to develop ethical guidelines, regulatory frameworks, and privacy-preserving technologies will be crucial to ensure responsible deployment and adoption.
5. Cybersecurity resilience and threat mitigation: Continuous advancements in cybersecurity measures and threat detection capabilities are essential to safeguarding federated learning systems against evolving cyber threats and attacks. Future directions may involve integrating advanced encryption techniques, anomaly detection algorithms, and real-time threat intelligence to enhance the resilience of healthcare data ecosystems.
6. Patient empowerment and transparency: Future implications include empowering patients with greater control over their healthcare data and fostering transparency in data collection, usage, and sharing practices. Patient-centric approaches, such as blockchain-based data ownership solutions and secure patient portals, can promote trust and collaboration between patients and healthcare providers.

The future directions and implications of the proposed cybersecurity-enabled federated learning framework in healthcare systems hold immense potential for driving innovation, improving patient outcomes, and ensuring the security and privacy of healthcare data. Collaborative efforts across interdisciplinary domains will be crucial to realizing these transformative opportunities while addressing the associated ethical, regulatory, and technical challenges.

Emerging trends and advancements in cybersecurity-enabled federated learning for digital healthcare.

Potential research directions and areas for innovation.

Implications for healthcare policy, ethics, and patient care.

12.10 Conclusion

In conclusion, the integration of a cybersecurity-enabled federated learning framework into healthcare systems represents a pivotal step toward revolutionizing patient care, data security, and research capabilities. This theoretical framework offers a multifaceted approach to addressing the critical challenges of data privacy, security, and interoperability within healthcare environments. By leveraging federated learning techniques and robust cybersecurity measures, the framework enables collaborative model training on decentralized data sources while safeguarding sensitive patient information from unauthorized access and cyber threats. The implications of this framework extend beyond improved patient outcomes to encompass accelerated research innovation, enhanced data sharing, and personalized healthcare delivery. However, realizing the full potential of this framework requires concerted efforts to address ethical, regulatory, and technical considerations, alongside fostering a culture of collaboration, transparency, and trust among stakeholders. As we navigate toward a future characterized by data-driven healthcare solutions, the adoption of such innovative frameworks holds promise for shaping a more secure, efficient, and patient-centric healthcare ecosystem.

References

[1] Kateb, F., and Ragab, M. (2023). Archimedes optimization with deep learning based aerial image classification for cybersecurity enabled UAV networks. *Computer Systems Science & Engineering*, *47*(2), 2171.

[2] Newhouse, W., Keith, S., Scribner, B., and Witte, G. (2017). National initiative for cybersecurity education (NICE) cybersecurity workforce framework. *NIST Special Publication*, *800*(2017), 181.

[3] Moscato, F., and Amato, F. (2015). A model driven approach to data privacy verification in e-health systems. *Transactions on Data Privacy*, *8*(3), 273–296.

[4] Singhal, S., and Carlton, S. (2019). *The Era of Exponential Improvement in Healthcare*. New York: McKinsey & Company, pp. 1–16.

[5] El Khatib, M., Hamidi, S., Al Ameeri, I., Al Zaabi, H., and Al Marqab, R. (2022). Digital disruption and big data in healthcare-opportunities and challenges. *ClinicoEconomics and Outcomes Research*, *14*, 563–574.

[6] Mammen, P. M. (2021). Federated learning: Opportunities and challenges. *arXiv preprint arXiv:2101.05428*, https://arxiv.org/abs/2101.05428.

[7] Rieke, N., Hancox, J., Li, W., *et al.* (2020). The future of digital health with federated learning. *NPJ Digital Medicine*, *3*(1), 1–7.

[8] Xu, J., Glicksberg, B. S., Su, C., Walker, P., Bian, J., and Wang, F. (2021). Federated learning for healthcare informatics. *Journal of Healthcare Informatics Research*, *5*, 1–19.

[9] Nilsson, A., Smith, S., Ulm, G., Gustavsson, E., and Jirstrand, M. (2018). A performance evaluation of federated learning algorithms. *Paper presented at the Proceedings of the 2nd Workshop on Distributed Infrastructures for Deep Learning.*

[10] Alrowais, F., Mohamed, H. G., Al-Wesabi, F. N., Al Duhayyim, M., Hilal, A. M., and Motwakel, A. (2023). Cyber attack detection in healthcare data using cyber-physical system with optimized algorithm. *Computers and Electrical Engineering*, *108*, 108636.

[11] Süzen, A. A. (2023). Cyber attacks for data breach and possible defense strategies in Internet of Healthcare Things ecosystem. *International Journal of 3D Printing Technologies and Digital Industry*, *7*(1), 55–63.

[12] Tariq, M. U. (2024). Enhancing cybersecurity protocols in modern healthcare systems: Strategies and best practices. In *Transformative Approaches to Patient Literacy and Healthcare Innovation* (pp. 223–241): Hershey, PA: IGI Global.

[13] Kelly, B., Quinn, C., Lawlor, A., Killeen, R., and Burrell, J. (2023). Cybersecurity in healthcare. In: Sakly, H., Yeom, K., Halabi, S., Said, M., Seekins, J., and Tagina, M. (eds), *Trends of Artificial Intelligence and Big Data for E-Health* (pp. 213–231): Cham: Springer.

[14] Wang, L., Zhao, Y., Dong, J., *et al.* (2024). Federated learning with new knowledge: Fundamentals, advances, and futures. *arXiv preprint arXiv:2402.02268.*

[15] Kamei, S., and Taghipour, S. (2023). A comparison study of centralized and decentralized federated learning approaches utilizing the transformer architecture for estimating remaining useful life. *Reliability Engineering & System Safety, 233*, 109130.

[16] Odera, D. (2023). Federated learning and differential privacy in clinical health: Extensive survey. *World Journal of Advanced Engineering Technology and Sciences*, *8*(2), 305–329.

[17] Hiwale, M., Walambe, R., Potdar, V., and Kotecha, K. (2023). A systematic review of privacy-preserving methods deployed with blockchain and federated learning for the telemedicine. *Healthcare Analytics*, *3*, 100192.

[18] Elsa, J., and Ahmed, S. (2024). Data privacy and security in sustainable healthcare: Navigating legal and ethical challenges. Available at: https://easychair.org/publications/preprint/Qt42.

[19] Ahmad, I., Ahmad, I., and Harjula, E. (2024). Adaptive security in 6G for sustainable healthcare. In *Nordic Conference on Digital Health and Wireless Solutions* (pp. 38–47): Cham: Springer Nature Switzerland.

[20] Tertulino, R., Antunes, N., and Morais, H. (2024). Privacy in electronic health records: A systematic mapping study. *Journal of Public Health*, *32*(3), 435–454.

[21] Veronese, A., Silveira, A., Igreja, R. L., Lemos, A. N. L. E., and Moraes, T. G. (2023). The concept of personal data protection culture from European Union documents: A "Brussels effect" in Latin America? *UNIO–EU Law Journal*, *9*(1), 58–79.

[22] Moore, C. (2023). Health information technology. In *Chronic Illness Care: Principles and Practice* (pp. 481–495): Berlin: Springer.

[23] Vest, J. R., and Martin, E. G. (2023). Creating a 21st century health information technology infrastructure: New York's health care efficiency and affordability law for New Yorkers Capital Grant Program. In *Health Information Exchange* (pp. 505–522): Amsterdam: Elsevier.

[24] Taheri, S. I., Davoodi, M., and Ali, M. H. (2024). Mitigating cyber anomalies in virtual power plants using artificial-neural-network-based secondary control with a federated learning-trust adaptation. *Energies*, *17*(3), 619.

[25] Bhoi, S. K., Ghugar, U., Dash, S., Nayak, R., and Bagal, D. K. (2024). Exploring the security landscape: A comprehensive analysis of vulnerabilities, challenges, and findings in Internet of Things (IoT) application layer protocols. *Migration Letters*, *21*(S6), 1326–1342.

[26] Ebrahimpour, E., and Babaie, S. (2024). Authentication in Internet of Things, protocols, attacks, and open issues: A systematic literature review. *International Journal of Information Security*, *23*, 1583–1602.

[27] Jonnala, J., Asodi, P., Uppada, L. K., Chalasani, C., and Chintala, R. R. (2024). Advancing cybersecurity: A comprehensive approach to enhance threat detection, analysis, and trust in digital environments. *International Journal of Intelligent Systems and Applications in Engineering*, *12*(2), 588–593.

[28] Thummisetti, B. S. P., and Atluri, H. (2024). Advancing healthcare informatics for empowering privacy and security through federated learning paradigms. *International Journal of Sustainable Development in Computing Science*, *1*(1), 1–16.

[29] Haterd, R. (2024). Enhancing privacy and security in IoT environments through secure multiparty computation. University of Twente, Enschede.

[30] Atadoga, A., Sodiya, E. O., Umoga, U. J., and Amoo, O. O. (2024). A comprehensive review of machine learning's role in enhancing network security and threat detection. *World Journal of Advanced Research and Reviews*, *21*(2), 877–886.

[31] Tang, Z., Hu, H., and Xu, C. (2022). A federated learning method for network intrusion detection. *Concurrency and Computation: Practice and Experience*, *34*(10), e6812.

[32] Drainakis, G., Pantazopoulos, P., Katsaros, K. V., Sourlas, V., Amditis, A., and Kaklamani, D. I. (2023). From centralized to federated learning: Exploring performance and end-to-end resource consumption. *Computer Networks*, *225*, 109657.

Chapter 13
IoT guardian: explainable deep ensemble learning for reliable security in Internet of Medical Things

Hamad Naeem[1], M. Shujah Islam Sameem[1] and Danish Vasan[2]

Abstract

When it comes to smart healthcare business systems, network-based intrusion detection systems are crucial for protecting the system and its networks from malicious network assaults. To identify network-based intrusions in Internet of Medical Things (IoMT), this paper lays out an ensemble method based on deep learning that makes use of patient biometrics and characteristics of network traffic. Medical features that are complicated, non-linear, and overlapping may be learned using random forest feature significance. By feeding meta-learner (MLP) predictions from weak learners (CNN and LSTM), an enhanced deep-stacked ensemble method with explainable decisions is achieved. The suggested model demonstrated a detection accuracy of 96% on the set of networks and patient biometric characteristics that were pre-selected, and 94% on the set that were not pre-selected. Experiments conducted on various state of the art deep learning methodologies illustrate the resilience and adaptability of the proposed model. The suggested technique demonstrated superior performance compared to the current approaches across all test situations, with a notable improvement in accuracy of 1–3% on the IoMT intrusion dataset. To protect IoMT devices in addition networks from intruders in healthcare in addition medical settings, the suggested model may be used as a tool for monitoring IoMT networks.

13.1 Introduction

The healthcare sector has been significantly altered by the rapid advancement of contemporary information and communication technologies, which has facilitated

[1]Department of Computer Science, College of Computer Sciences and Information Technology (CCSIT), King Faisal University, Saudi Arabia
[2]Interdisciplinary Research Center for Intelligent Secure Systems (IRC-ISS), King Fahd University of Petroleum and Minerals, Saudi Arabia

the widespread adoption of Internet of Things (IoT) medical devices by both patients and healthcare professionals. These Internet of Medical Things (IoMT) devices, in conjunction with online services, provide substantial improvements in patient treatment. According to industry projections, the global IoMT market is expected to surpass $135 billion by 2025 [1]. Nevertheless, this expansion has also attracted the attention of cybercriminals, who have identified IoMT devices and their networks as primary targets for cyberattacks. The insufficient emphasis on security during the development phase has resulted in a significant number of these devices being vulnerable, as they lack comprehensive security measures. The healthcare and IoMT sectors were responsible for 72% of all malicious cyber traffic in 2021, with a 40% increase in healthcare cyberattacks. That year, 81% of healthcare providers acknowledged that they had at least one compromised IoMT system, which is alarming [2]. The pressing necessity for improved security measures to safeguard sensitive patient data within IoMT systems and networks is emphasized by these statistics.

The complexity, memory constraints, and heterogeneity of IoMT devices and networks are difficult for existing IT security approaches to manage. Trust-based systems, cryptographic encryption and decryption techniques, and authentication protocols were the foundation of early IoMT security methods. Nevertheless, recent research suggests that intrusion detection systems (IDS) have largely replaced cryptographic approaches, as the implementation of cryptographic solutions on memory-limited IoMT devices presents significant challenges. IDS has the capability to monitor an entire network or a single device, and it can notify administrators of any suspicious activity. Although the primary emphasis of this study is on network-based IDS, host-based systems are also briefly discussed [3]. Network-based solutions deployed at IoMT gateways are a more viable option, as host-based IDS are frequently impractical for IoMT devices due to their limited RAM. In the past, IDS relied on rule-based and anomaly-based systems to identify and categorize threats. Rule-based systems are proficient in recognizing established attack patterns; however, they encounter difficulties in identifying novel or evolving threats. Although anomaly-based systems are capable of identifying both known and unknown hazards, they frequently experience high false alarm rates.

There is an expanding body of literature that emphasizes the growing utilization of deep learning (DL) and machine learning (ML) techniques in network-based IDS for IoMT systems. These methods provide substantial benefits in the identification of both novel and known hazards, surpassing the capabilities of conventional rule-based systems. In this context, optimization-based deep neural networks (DNNs) have emerged as a promising tool for IoMT intrusion detection, obtaining a 15% improvement over previous methods when tested on the KDDCup-99 dataset [4]. Furthermore, single-model approaches have been outperformed by ensemble ML models, including those that are based on gradient boosting and transformers, in the detection of intrusions within IoMT networks [5,6]. The ToN-IoT and Endgame Malware Benchmark datasets were employed to evaluate these models, which exhibited superior performance in comparison to state-of-the-art methods.

Recurrent neural networks (RNNs) have also been suggested for IoMT intrusion detection. When tested on the NSL-KDD dataset, a benchmark derived from the 1999 Knowledge Discovery and Data Mining Tools Competition [7], they demonstrated improved performance. The versatility of ML techniques in this domain is further demonstrated by the use of swarm neural networks, active learning techniques, and random forest models. Some models have achieved accuracy rates as high as 96.44% on benchmark datasets such as CIC-IDS2017 [8,9]. Nevertheless, the datasets utilized in these studies—including KDDCup-99, ToN-IoT, NSL-KDD, and Ember—are inadequately equipped to accurately represent the intricacies of real-world IoMT environments. This is a significant limitation. As a result, these models exhibit optimistic results in controlled settings; however, their efficacy in practical IoMT applications requires further validation.

Researchers have suggested anomaly-based models as a solution to these challenges. These models utilize data from IoMT gateways, network traffic, and resource utilization metrics to identify intrusions. Although these models have demonstrated enhanced performance, the high false alarm rate that is associated with anomaly-based approaches in real-world IoMT environments continues to be a substantial challenge. Although other studies have investigated mobile agent-based IDS for IoMT, these studies also encounter constraints as a result of the datasets' inadequate representation of actual IoMT conditions [10]. More recent endeavors have concentrated on the integration of patient biometric data with network traffic data to develop a ML-based IDS that is specifically designed for IoMT environments. The divide between theoretical models and real-world applications has been bridged by the use of practical IoMT datasets, such as the Washington University in St. Louis Healthcare Monitoring Scheme (WUSTL EHMS 2020) and Edith Cowan University Internet of Health Things (ECU-IoHT) datasets.

In this investigation, we suggest a DL-based ensemble method for network-based intrusion detection in IoMT systems. Our method surpasses conventional methods in terms of precision and accuracy by incorporating features from patient biometrics and network traffic. This is accomplished by employing a random forest model to analyze intricate medical characteristics, followed by the use of weak learners—convolutional neural networks (CNN) and long short-term memory (LSTM) networks—whose predictions are aggregated by a meta-learner. The outcome is an extended deep-stacked ensemble model that substantially enhances the security of IoMT networks and reduces false positives. Additionally, the robustness and adaptability of the proposed model have been demonstrated through testing on a variety of industrial benchmark datasets.

The model's performance will be optimized through the integration of additional categories into the IoMT attack dataset and the expansion of the attack classification capabilities in future research. The accuracy of the model and the overall security of IoMT networks are anticipated to be further improved by the implementation of kernel-based feature fusion techniques in the classification layer. Although the WUSTL EHMS 2020 dataset has demonstrated superior quality in comparison to ECU-IoHT, it will be imperative to continue to enhance data preprocessing and augmentation techniques in order to preserve high detection accuracy, particularly when dealing with highly imbalanced datasets like WUSTL EHMS 2020. In this regard, cost-sensitive learning techniques may provide a more effective solution than conventional data augmentation strategies, thereby facilitating further progress in IoMT IDS. The essential elements of the suggested task are as below:

- In the IoMT environment, we suggest a DL-based method aimed at network-based IDS. Efficacy of the suggested model is assessed by considering the combined attributes of the network in addition to patient biometric sensors.
- The misclassification rate is reduced substantially by excluding less informative features using random forest-based feature importance. Random forest-based features of importance handle chaotic, overlapping, and non-linear datasets effectively and reliably.
- CNN and LSTM are utilized as weak learners in the proposed model to efficiently abstract the resilient spatial in addition time-series characteristics of patient biometrics and network traffic. The combined predictions from weak learning are subsequently input into a meta-learner known as MLP. An examination of the proposed intrusion detection model in the IoMT environment concerning previous research.

The dataset and methodologies employed in the proposed approach are detailed in Section 13.2, and the remainder of the study adheres to this structure. Section 13.3 provides a comprehensive analysis of the experimental outcomes derived from the proposed scheme, juxtaposed with those of alternative benchmark methods, to assess its performance. The analysis is concluded in Section 13.4, which explores potential future trajectories.

13.2 IoMT network intrusion detection system

The IDS is suggested in this study; it is a network observing implement and keeps tabs on the computer by the network of workstations in the IoMT setting in addition notifies the scheme administrator of any suspicious or harmful activity that occurs inside a healthcare organization. Figures 13.1 and 13.2 depict the suggested IoMT security architecture. This process comprises two primary elements: data collection and analysis. The IoMT gateway collects data regarding the network's flow and the patient's biometrics from the various medical sensors as part of the data collection phase. This data is subsequently transmitted via the router and switch to a server for visualization and analysis. Pre-processing is the subsequent stage in the data analysis procedure, during which the 29 network characteristics and 8 patient biometrics features are transmitted. To achieve a significant reduction in the misclassification rate, unimportant characteristics are omitted through the utilization of random forest-based feature significance. An approach is presented wherein deep ensemble learning is employed to detect and classify attacks within IoMT network traffic. The attributes are transmitted to the CNN and LSTM layers, both of which are weak learners; they collectively acquire knowledge of spatial and

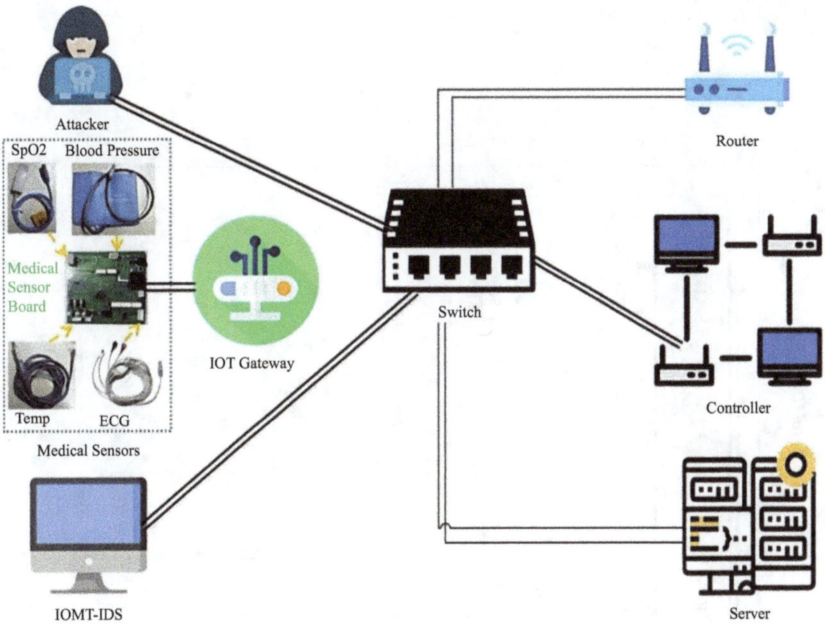

Figure 13.1 IoMT security architecture

temporal data. CNN and LSTM then combine their predictions resulting from inadequate learning. The input for an MLP meta-learner is subsequently the combined predictions. The model concludes by classifying the network traffic as malicious or benign. The IoMT-IDS that has been proposed is illustrated in Figure 13.2.

13.2.1 Explanation of IoMT network traffic dataset

Together with the IoMT real-time fitness observing testbed, [11] assistance was provided in the development of the WUSTL EHMS 2020 database. A gateway, medical sensors, a controller, and a network are all components of the testbed. Data captured by medical sensors is transmitted to servers through a gateway, which is subsequently connected to a network comprising switches and routers. The responsibility for visualizing data pertaining to patient biometrics and network traffic lies with the controller. To simulate attacks such as data injection, spoofing, and man-in-the-middle, the testbed was utilized. The ARGUS tool was employed to retrieve the attributes of the patient's biometric statistics as well as the network. The subsequent statistics are available in the WUSTL EHMS 2020 database: Total 16318, Normal 14272, and Attack 2046. Regarding WUSTL-EHMS-2020 database was produced through utilization of a real-time EHMS testbed [11]. In the absence of an all-encompassing dataset, this testbed additionally collects network traffic measurements alongside patients' biometric information. The EHMS testbed is

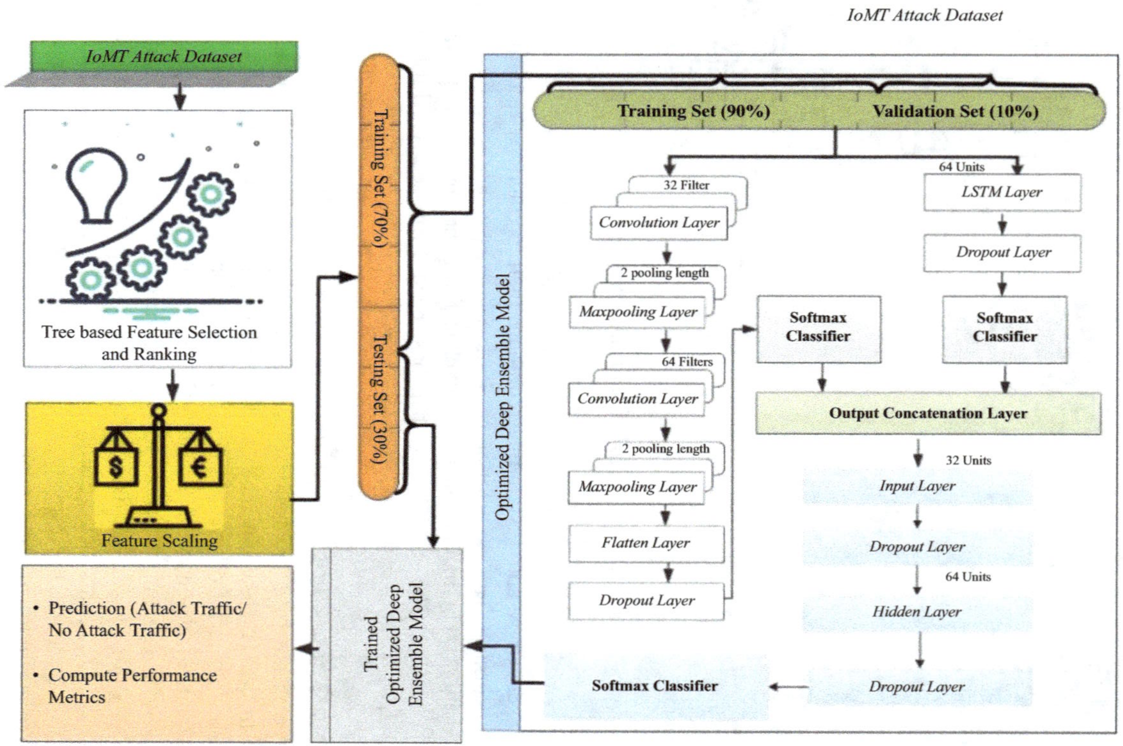

Figure 13.2 Proposed IoMT-IDS

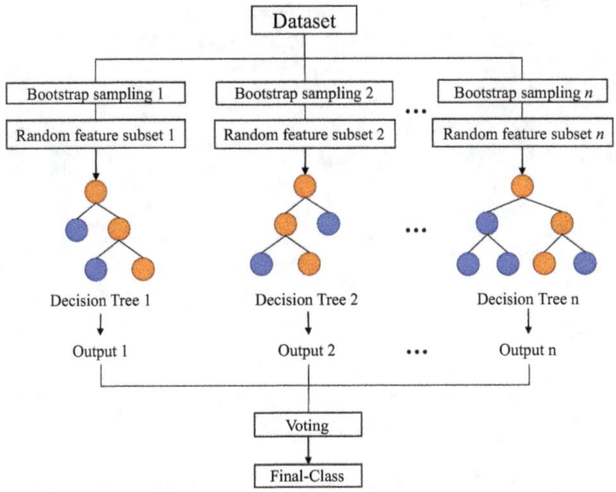

Figure 13.3 Random Forest classifier

comprised of medical sensors, a gateway, a network, and control and visualization systems [11]. Prior to reaching the gateway, data must traverse the sensors affixed to the patient's person. Following this, the data is sent from the gateway to the server for visualization via the switch and router. Before their arrival to the server, an adversary may intercept this data. The IDS records biometric information from patients as well as network traffic in real-time and looks for suspicious activity. Random Forest classifier and the details of the bootstrapping sampling are shown in Figure 13.3.

13.2.2 Tree-based feature selection and ranking

Numerous classification and regression issues are frequently addressed by random forest, an ML methodology that is constructed from a collection of decision trees [12,13]. For preventing overfitting and enhancing generalizability, random forests combine multiple decision trees with randomization. As a result, they are distinct from decision trees. An illustration of the data classification process of a random forest can be observed in Figure 13.4. Once the number of trees to be constructed has been determined, bootstrap sampling is applied to select a random subset of the data for each decision tree. Unpredictability is further compounded by the attributes employed by individual decision trees; employing random feature subsets enhances generalizability and robustness. After undergoing training, the random forest classifier may employ a voting mechanism that incorporates the predictions of each individual tree to generate a more probable prediction. Embedded feature selection represents an additional potential application of their methodology. To determine which features are most important for performance and which should be excluded, the model may compute a significant score for each individual feature. The attribute of node impurity in the decision tree constitutes the principal determinant of

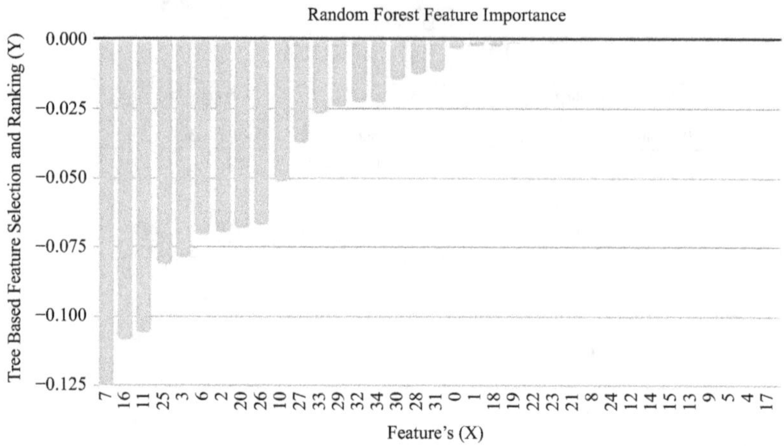

Figure 13.4 Random Forest feature importance plot

feature relevance in the random forest. Entropy or the Gini index of a node determines the priority and location of a feature when generating a node in a decision tree. Greater significance and reduced impurity are signified by a diminished Gini index or entropy. To obtain the mean feature significance score, random forests employ Algorithm 1 to ascertain the impurity of every feature within each tree.

Algorithm 1: Random Forest Feature Importance

```
T: trees in random forest {t1, t2, ..., tm}
F: features in dataset {f1, f2, ..., fn}
for i from 1 to n do
    for tree t ∈ T do
        N: nodes using feature fi in tree t {n1, n2, ..., np}
        for node n ∈ N do
            compute impurity decrease at n as a score s.
            weight the score s by number of samples.
            add up the score s to score S.
        end
    end
                                    /* get importance for feature fi */
    fi_importance = average score S over all trees t using feature fi.
end
```

The y-axis, which signifies Tree-Based Feature Selection and Ranking, is connected to the x-axis, which represents the number of features, as illustrated in the subsequent graph. −0.124468, −0.107836, and −0.10551 were the values attained by features seven, sixteen, and eleven, respectively. As evidenced by their minimum values, we are disregarding the values of lower-ranked features that are meaningless.

13.2.3 Ensemble neural networks

To achieve the objective to enhance precision, the ensemble method is constructed by combining multiple learning algorithms. Combining the outcomes of multiple classifiers boosts the efficiency of training data and reduces the likelihood of overfitting, thereby enhancing overall performance. Scholars persistently seek novel methodologies to improve intrusion classification by means of more accurate sample categorization, notwithstanding the existence of numerous ensemble classification algorithms. We present an ensemble of stacked neural networks that improves the classification performance of networks in this paper. The first step in building a reliable classifier ensemble is to reorganize the training samples by providing each sample with a base classifier. An ensemble model is constructed through the aggregation of predictions from numerous base classifiers, thereby enhancing its capacity to synthesize predictions from diverse base classifiers. The ensemble technique under consideration integrates conventional ML classifiers with a meta-learner (MLP) and weak learners (CNN+LSTM-Softmax). To effectively train a sizable multi head neural model, we employ the collective predictions generated by the combined sub-networks, which comprise CNN and LSTM architectures, each integrated with Softmax layers to serve as initial learners.

Weak learners at level 1: When it comes to handling high-dimensional data, such as photos and videos, this work presents a unique stacked ensemble architecture (Figure 13.2) that outperforms CNNs. This design makes use of a one-dimensional CNN that has a total of six layers: two for convolution, two for pooling, one for flattening, one for dropout, and one for completely connected. To extract optimal deep features, all of the filters in the convolution layer apply the selected feature set, resulting in the formation of what is referred to as a "feature map." To reduce feature sizes and spatial dimensions, the following max-pooling layer is used. Adding a flattening layer further decreases the collection of created features. A fully connected classification layer is also a part of the input layers in the proposed CNN network. To mitigate the risk of overfitting, the CNN network incorporates a layer for dropout. Classification is carried out using the Softmax activation function. Here we'll go into more detail about what makes up an initial learner's layer.

Convolutional layer: To learn the features, many kernels work together in this layer. By convolving with the neighboring input matrix, these kernels traverse the whole dataset and effectively capture spatial and temporal correlations. Equation (13.1) calculates the convolutional outcomes.

$$I_i^l = \left(\sum_j I_j^{l-1} \otimes w_{ij}^l + b_i^l \right) \tag{13.1}$$

I_i^l denotes the outcome of convolution layer, b_i^l means the bias, in addition w_{ij}^l denotes the convolutional kernel.

Maximum pooling layer: Matrix spatial dimensions may be reduced by down sampling with the use of a pooling layer. To reduce the number of parameters while preserving critical information, maximum pooling layer is used next to the convolutional layer. (13.2) yields maximum pooling layer's outcomes.

$$pl(i,t) = \max_{(j-1)W+1\leq\{a^{l(i,t)}\}} \tag{13.2}$$

a reflects the pooling layer's output and p displays the neuron's activation function values.

Dropout layer: A constant rate of weight updates may be achieved with a small number of neurons throughout training. As a result, a dropout layer may be used to train while ignoring a single random neuron.

Classification layer: It is common practice to include the Softmax activation function into the network's classification layer when handling classification jobs. The normalization function transforms the model's outcome into a likelihood distribution over the several anticipated output classes.

$$f_j(x) = \frac{e^{xj}}{\sum_{l=1}^{k} e^{xl}} \tag{13.3}$$

Here, x stands for the non-normalized parameters of the neural network that is being considered.

Long short-term memory layer: A single memory unit and three additional interaction gates—the input, forget, and output gates—make up the LSTM paradigm. The memory cell keeps the preceding state. At time t, the input gate specifies the amount of network input data that must be saved in the unit state. Data is either allowed or denied entry to the input gate at $t-1$ based on the forget gate's decision. The data for the output is defined by the output gate. The workings of the LSTM model are defined as follows:

$$\begin{aligned} i_t &= \sigma(V_{ixt} + W_i h_{t-1} + b_i) \\ f_t &= \sigma(V_{fxt} + W_f h_{t-1} + b_f) \\ \tilde{c}_t &= \tanh(V_c X_t + W_c h_{t-1} + b_c) \\ c_t &= f_t A C_{t-1} + i_t A \tilde{c}_t \\ o_t &= \sigma(V_o x_t + W_o h_{t-1} + b_o) \\ h_t &= o_t A \tanh(c_t) \end{aligned} \tag{13.4}$$

where x_t denotes the input at time t, v_*, and w_* depicts the weight matrices, b_* and h_* denote the bias and hidden states respectively. σ and tanh represent the activation functions. Input gate, forget gate, output gate, and memory cell are indicated with i_t, f_t, o_t, and c_t, respectively.

Meta learner: In this study, a neural system for meta-learning, known as a multi-layer perceptron (MLP), is employed. The MLP meta-learner uses the pooled predictions from Level 1 as input. The deep network utilized in the proposed ensemble is depicted in Figure 13.2. There is only one output layer, four hidden levels, and one input layer in this network. Since the I/O processing are handled by the first and final layers of the MLP model, respectively. Equation (13.5) provides the hidden layer Hi, with the activation function utilized to generate the final outputs.

$$H_i(x) = f(w_i^T x + b_i) \tag{13.5}$$

The symbol f denotes non-linearity. The activation function employ, namely Softmax (SM) at the output layer implies the incorporation of nonlinear elements within the neural network architecture.

13.3 Experimental results and evaluation

For this investigation, the experimental setup was used using the following software packages and computer configurations:

1. Python 3.7, the Keras Application Programming Interface (API), and the TensorFlow library, version 2.3.
2. GPU: RTX 2060 (GeForce NVIDIA)
3. CPU: Core i7 (Intel)
4. OS: Windows (64-bit)

The research utilizes data split ratio 70:30 during the training and testing phases. Ninety percent of the training dataset utilized in cross-validated experiments is also extracted from WUSTL EHMS 2020. F1-score, precision, accuracy, and recall were typical performance indicators. To evaluate these standardized KPIs, we computed the rates of TP: True Positives, FN: False Negatives, TN: True Negatives, and FP: False Positives.

- **TP**: The ratio of samples that are accurately identified as attacks.
- **TN**: The ratio of FN results found in samples of normal or natural events.
- **FP**: The ratio of samples with normal or natural events that were mistakenly marked as attack is called the FP.
- **FN**: The ratio of attack data that is misclassified as normal or natural events.

$$\begin{aligned}
\text{Precision} &= \frac{\text{TP}}{\text{TP} + \text{FP}} \\
\text{Recall} &= \frac{\text{FP}}{\text{FP} + \text{TN}} \\
\text{F1} - \text{Score} &= 2 \times \frac{\text{TP}}{\text{TP} + \text{FP} + \text{FN}} \\
\text{Accuracy} &= \frac{\text{TP} + \text{TN}}{\text{TP} + \text{TN} + \text{FP} + \text{FN}}
\end{aligned} \tag{13.6}$$

For validating the proposed methodology, empirical studies are undertaken to determine the impact of tree-based feature selection and ranking on the deep-stacked ensemble model's performance. To analyze the influence of the training or validation data on overfitting or underfitting, a graph is constructed to depict the model's accuracy and loss over the course of 100 epochs. Accuracy and loss curves for the proposed ensemble learning approach are presented in Figures 13.5 and 13.6. This distinguishes it from alternative DL models.

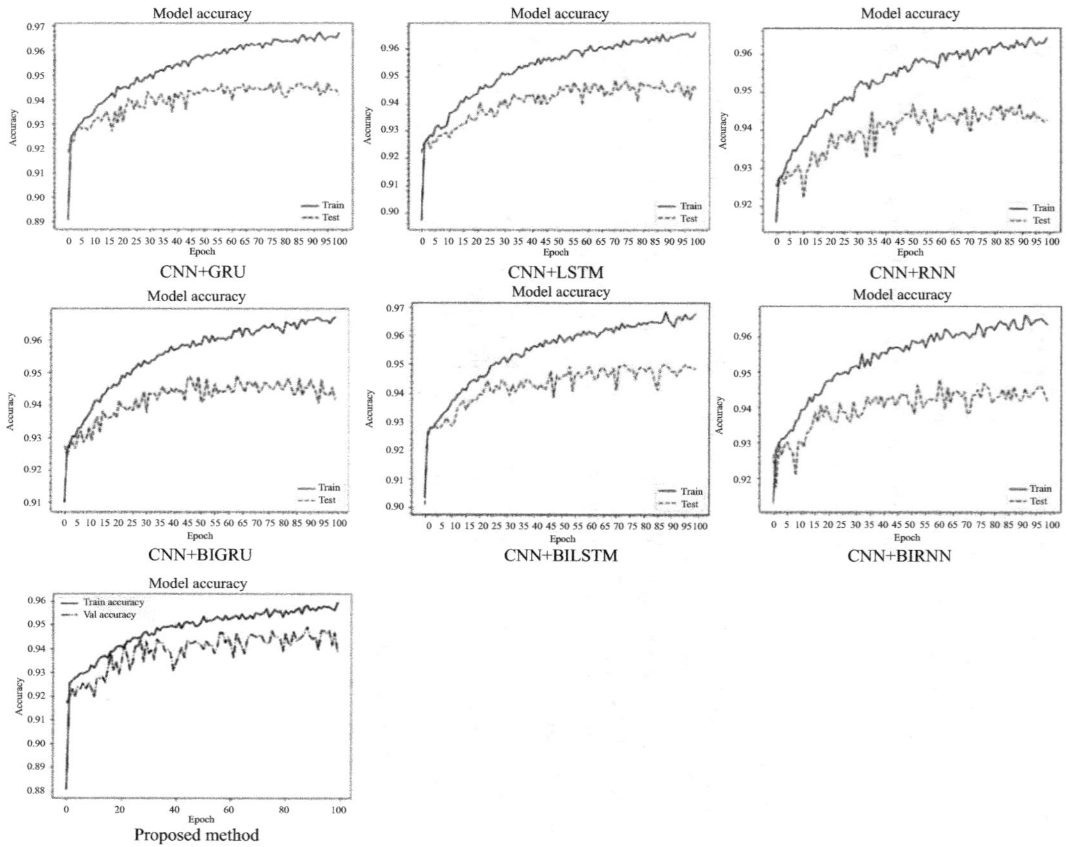

Figure 13.5 Dynamic curve graphs of training and validation accuracy

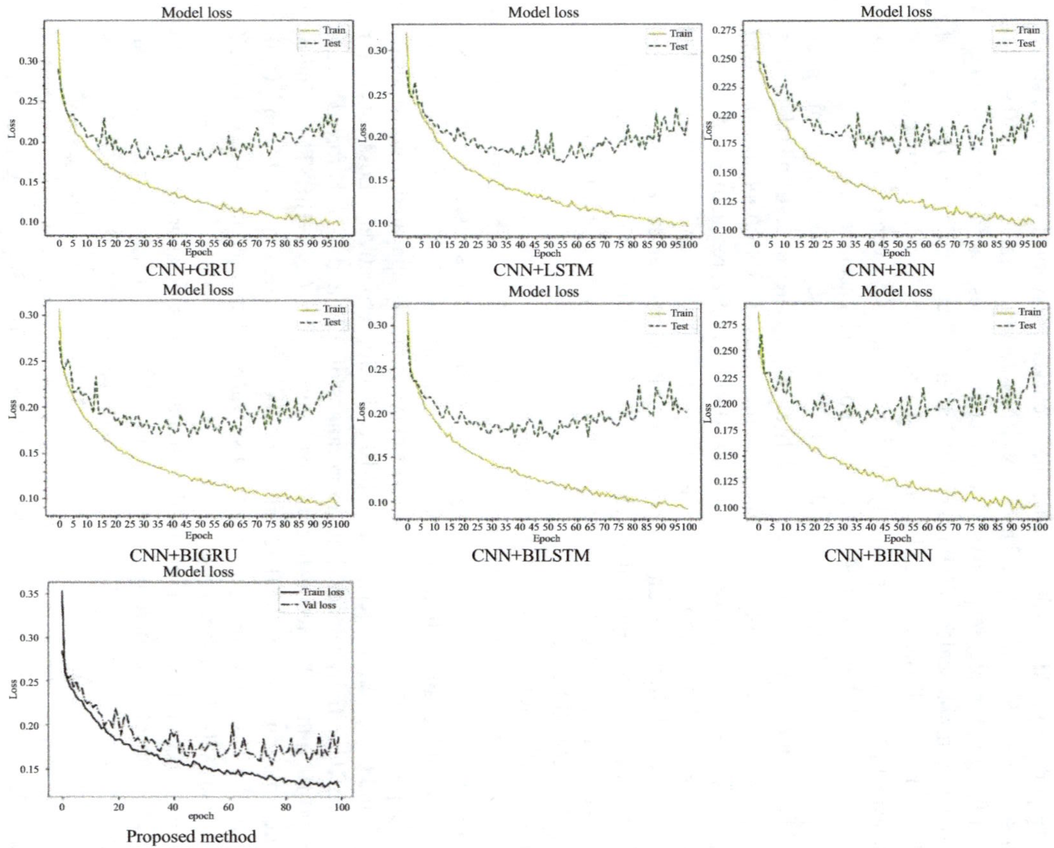

Figure 13.6 Dynamic curve graphs of training and validation loss

In contrast to alternative deep learning models that depend on tree-based feature selection and ranking, the performance of the proposed approach was found to be superior. Accuracy curves for the CNN+GRU model began with initial scales of 0.89 and 0.92, respectively, as illustrated in Figure 13.5. Over the course of 100 epochs, these curves converged concurrently to graph scales of 0.96 and 0.94. Accuracy curves for the CNN+LSTM model began with initial scales of 0.89 and 0.92, respectively. After 100 epochs, these curves converged synchronously to graph scales of 0.96 and 0.945. The CNN+RNN accuracy trajectories at 0.91 and 0.92 on the graph scale, respectively, at epoch zero. These curves converged synchronously to graph scales of 0.96 and 0.942 after 100 epochs. At the inception of epoch 0, the CNN+BiGRU model showcased accuracy curves commencing at graph scale 0.91 and 0.92, respectively. Accuracy curves converged synchronously to graph ranges of 0.96 and 0.941 after 100 epochs. The accuracy curves for CNN +BiLSTM commenced at values of 0.90 and 0.92, on the graph range, at epoch zero. These curves intersected synchronously at graph scales of 0.96 and 0.948 after 100 epochs. At the inception of epoch 0, the CNN+BiRNN model showcased accuracy curves commencing at graph range 0.91 and 0.92, respectively. Accuracy curves converged synchronously to graph scales of 0.96 and 0.941 after 100 epochs. As we shifted to evaluating the ensemble technique, the accuracy curves began at epoch zero, registering values of 0.88 and 0.92 on the graph range, respectively. Accuracy curves converged synchronously to graph ranges of 0.94 and 0.958 after 100 epochs.

Loss curves for the CNN+GRU model began with initial scales of 0.29 and 0.35, respectively, as illustrated in Figure 13.6. The graph scale of these curves had decreased to between 0.10 and 0.24 by the 100th epoch. Loss curves for the CNN+LSTM model began with initial scales of 0.29 and 0.35, respectively, before decreasing to scales of 0.10 and 0.22. Loss curves initially appeared at graph scales of 0.27 and 0.25, before decreasing to 0.10 and 0.20, respectively. Loss curves for CNN+BiGRU initially appeared at graph ranges of 0.30 and 0.27, before decreasing to 0.10 and 0.23, respectively. Loss curves for CNN+BiLSTM initially appeared at graph scales of 0.32 and 0.29, before decreasing to 0.5 and 0.20, respectively. Similarly, loss curves for CNN+BiRNN decreased from 0.25 and 0.27 to 0.10 and 0.20 at graph ranges.

Loss curves for the ensemble method initially appeared at graph scales of 0.35 and 0.28, respectively, before decreasing to 0.10 and 0.18. Generalization is an exceptionally notable benefit of neural networks; it concerns the ability of the model to predict results for new data samples by utilizing pre-existing knowledge. The generalization evaluation of the proposed ensemble was performed on the test dataset after it had been trained on the validation set. To achieve a significant level of generalizability, the IoMT dataset was divided into three discrete subsets: validation, running, and training. The outcomes of the proposed ensemble with random forest feature selection for intrusion detection are summarized in Table 13.1.

Notably, the proposed ensemble achieved validation set classification accuracies of 0.945, testing set accuracies of 0.958, and training set accuracies of 0.95. Table 13.2 displays the results of the proposed ensemble that was suggested as a

Table 13.1 Classification performance of the proposed ensemble over three data subsets (selected feature set)

	Training performance		
Families	**Precision**	**Recall**	**F1-score**
Normal traffic	90	69	78
Attack traffic	96	99	97
Average (macro)	93	84	88
Average (weighted)	95	95	95
Accuracy (training): 95.08%			
Loss (training): 0.15			
Time (training): 2.07 s			
	Validation performance		
Normal traffic	92	67	78
Attack traffic	95	99	97
Average (macro)	94	83	87
Average (weighted)	94	95	94
Accuracy (validation): 94.58%			
Loss (validation): 0.16			
Time (validation): 0.251 s			
	Testing performance		
Normal traffic	92	72	81
Attack traffic	96	99	98
Average (macro)	94	85	89
Average (weighted)	96	96	96
Accuracy (testing): 95.87%			
Loss (testing): 0.14			
Time (testing): 2.14 s			

method for intrusion detection in the absence of feature selection. Three classification accuracy values were attained by the deep-stacked ensemble that was proposed: 0.953 for the training set, 0.939 for the testing set, and 0.944 for the validation set. The proposed ensemble method possesses an exceptional capacity for generalization, which is evident from its exceptional performance on both known and unknown datasets. In addition to this, the stacked ensemble that was proposed utilized random feature selection to accomplish exceptional detection results on three subsets of the IoMT dataset. It demonstrates the effectiveness of randomly selecting features within the framework of deep ensemble learning, as suggested.

The detection outcome of the suggested ensemble, which utilizes three distinct data subsets, is depicted in Figure 13.7. The validation set, training set, and testing set all yielded detection accuracies of 94.58%, 95.87%, and 95.08%, respectively, for the stacked ensemble under consideration.

Table 13.2 Classification performance of the proposed ensemble over three data subsets (original feature set)

Training performance			
Families	**Precision**	**Recall**	**F1-score**
Normal traffic	96	66	78
Attack traffic	95	100	97
Average (macro)	96	83	88
Average (weighted)	95	95	95
Accuracy (testing): 95.87%			
Loss (testing): 0.14			
Time (testing): 2.14 s			
Validation performance			
Normal traffic	93	62	74
Attack traffic	95	99	97
Average (macro)	94	81	86
Average (weighted)	94	94	94
Accuracy (validation): 94.40%			
Loss (validation): 0.17			
Time (validation): 0.401 s			
Testing performance			
Normal traffic	91	56	69
Attack traffic	94	99	97
Average (macro)	92	78	83
Average (weighted)	94	94	93
Accuracy (testing): 93.97%			
Loss (testing): 0.18			
Time (testing): 2.091 s			

The results are displayed in Table 13.3. illustrate the efficacy of the deep stacked ensemble that was suggested for detection purposes. A comparative analysis of different DL models and deep layered ensembles is displayed in Table 13.3. The reported models were trained concurrently utilizing both a random forest feature set and an unselected feature set. When contrasted to conventional deep models, the proposed ensemble demonstrated a decreased frequency of false positive results. When compared to other DL models, it achieved the highest detection accuracy (0.958) with the lowest loss (0.14). On the other hand, the detection accuracies of the conventional CNN+RNN, CNN+LSTM, CNN+GRU, CNN +BiRNN, CNN+BiLSTM, and CNN+BiGRU models were as follows: 0.942, 0.945, 0.941, 0.941, 0.948, and 0.941, respectively. In essence, ensemble models demonstrate a higher degree of generalizability in comparison to conventional DL models. Additionally, it suggests that the proposed ensemble needs fewer training parameters and network layers for fine-tuning.

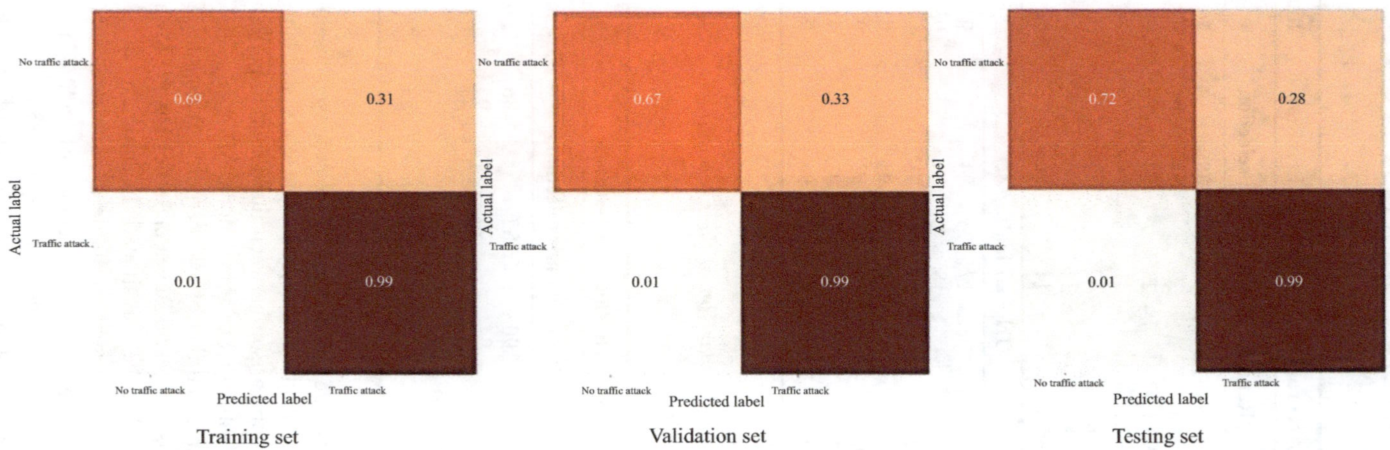

Figure 13.7 Dynamic curve graphs of training and validation accuracy

Table 13.3 Performance comparison of the proposed ensemble over deep learning methods

Methods	Accuracy	Loss	Precision	Recall	F1-score
			Random Forest feature selection		
CNN+RNN	94.26	19	85	70	76
CNN+LSTM	94.5	22	94	95	94
CNN+GRU	94.1	23	94	94	94
CNN+BiRNN	94.1	21	94	94	94
CNN+BiLSTM	94.8	20	95	95	95
CNN+BiGRU	94.1	22	94	94	94
Proposed method	**95.8**	**14**	**96**	**96**	**96**
			Original feature set		
CNN+-RNN	93.8	17	94	93	93
CNN+LSTM	93.2	18	93	93	93
CNN+GRU	93	19	93	93	93
CNN+BiRNN	93.2	17	93	93	93
CNN+BiLSTM	93.2	16	93	93	93
CNN+BiGRU	93.3	19	93	93	93
Proposed method	**93.9**	**18**	**94**	**94**	**94**

Table 13.4 Performance comparison of the proposed ensemble over machine learning methods

Methods	Precision	Recall	F1-score	Precision	Recall	F1-score
	Random Forest feature selection			**Original feature set**		
GNB	90	90	87	86	85	86
DT	94	94	94	94	93	93
RF	94	94	93	93	93	92
KNN	93	93	93	93	94	93
Proposed Method	**96**	**96**	**96**	**94**	**94**	**93**

In this study, we evaluate the outcome of the proposed ensemble in comparison to the most advanced machine classifiers presently available in the market. Table 13.4. presents a comparison between the detection performance of the suggested stacked ensemble and that of conventional ML methods. The efficacy of the suggested ensemble surpassed that of all alternatives, attaining 96% accuracy. At 90% accuracy, the Gaussian Naive Bayes classifier has the lowest rate of success among all the methods that were evaluated. In summary, in comparison to conventional classifiers, the suggested ensemble demonstrates superior performance across all metrics. The overall detection accuracy of traditional ML classifiers and deep stacked ensembles is illustrated on Figure 13.8. The suggested stacked ensemble exhibited the highest detection accuracy of any alternative, at 96%.

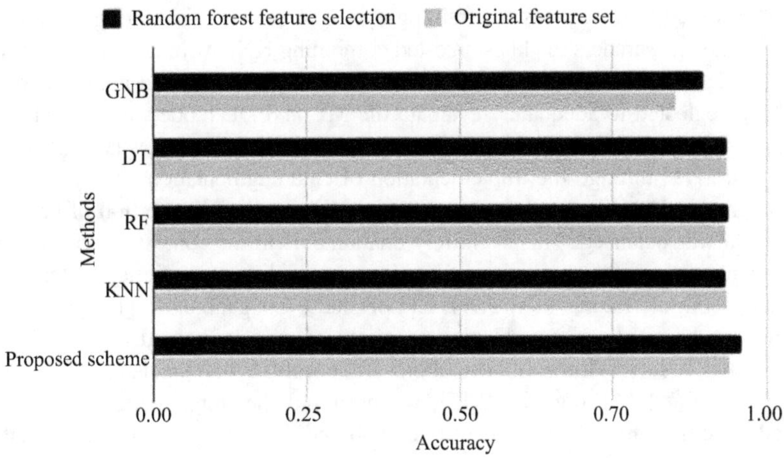

Figure 13.8 Compare deep stacked ensemble accuracy to machine learning methods

Table 13.5 Comparative analysis with previously published works

ML techniques	Accuracy	Advantages	Limitations
KNN [11]	90%	Combined the patients biometric data and network traffic	Performance can be improved.
Tree classifier [15]	93%	Performance improved compared to [15]	Data augmentation results in unrealistic dataset. The attack traffic proportion in the network is very low.
DNN [16]	94.7%	Combined the patients biometric data and network traffic	Performance can be improved.
Proposed methods	96%	Improved performance and realistic	Less resource intensive with better detection accuracy

Among all the methods, the Gaussian Naive Bayes classifier exhibits the least accurate detection at 90%. The proposed detection technique attained a maximum accuracy of 96% and 94%, respectively, for both sets of characteristics.

By integrating the attributes of patient biometrics and network traffic from the WUSTL EHMS 2020 [14], Table 13.5 compares the efficacy of the suggested methodology with existing investigations in the field of IoMT intrusion detection. When compared to prior investigations, the proposed model exhibited a 4% surge in detection accuracy, culminating in a score of 96%. Taking place, the IoMT dataset, the suggested method required 2.07 seconds for training and 2.14 seconds for testing. To identify IoMT attacks, researchers in [11] suggested combining KNN with network and patient biometric data. The authors refrained from investigating feature selection. Furthermore, the study neglected to adequately evaluate the ML and DL models utilized aimed at intrusion detection in IoMT. The performance of the IoMT IDS was improved by Gupta *et al.* [15] through the implementation of data augmentation and the tree classifier approach. By utilizing data augmentation, the datasets' proportion of normal to attack data was balanced. This is entirely unattainable in the context of real-time network attacks, where the proportion of legitimate to malicious traffic is substantial. To reduce the sum of features in WUSTL EHMS 2020, Chaganti *et al.* [16] proposed an optimization-based strategy employing a variety of models derived from DNNs and conventional ML for intrusion detection. To optimize the precision of intrusion detection in the IoMT domain [2,17], we proposed the implementation of a deep stacked ensemble model and random forest-based feature selection on the dataset features of patient biometric data and network traffic. As evidenced by the 4% improvement over the current state of the art, our accuracy was 96%.

Using the t-SNE visualization method, it is possible to ascertain whether the features contain a great deal or very little information. In addition, the t-SNE algorithm is assessed to verify the effectiveness of the suggested approach. The levels of traffic attack and normal traffic separation in the IoMT dataset, which has a perplexity value of 130, are illustrated in Figure 13.9. Figure 13.9 illustrates traffic attacks denoted by a black label and normal traffic represented by a red label. A variety of perplexity levels are utilized in the investigation, with 130 yielding the most effective visualization outcomes. During the initial test, we approached the minimum perplexity value that could be achieved to differentiate between traffic attack clusters and normal traffic clusters. t-SNE utilizes iterations to differentiate between various types of samples. To visually

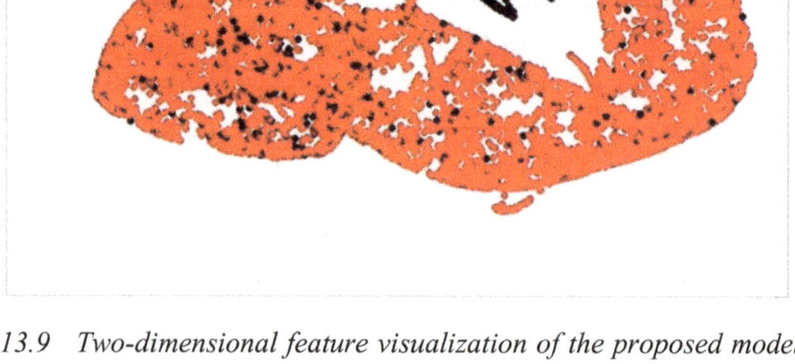

Figure 13.9 Two-dimensional feature visualization of the proposed model on the IoMT dataset

distinguish between clusters of normal traffic and assault traffic, 700 iterations are performed with varying perplexity values. The proportion of training instances in the normal traffic cluster compared to the traffic attack cluster suggests that the former contains a greater number of instances. There are numerous situations in which the hue of red closely resembles that of black. This could potentially indicate an outlier that significantly affects the aggregate findings. Notwithstanding this, most of the visualization illustrates the precise division, thereby substantiating the claim that the dataset can be effortlessly categorized yielding optimal results. The accuracy of predictions is significantly impacted by the density of the dataset. Greater density facilitates more accurate classifications by providing a greater quantity of descriptive training data. As a result of the increased separation between t-SNE clusters, classifier performance has been enhanced.

SHAP (SHapley Additive exPlanations) plot displays the SHAP values for all features and instances in selected dataset. Colors denote feature magnitude (red for high, blue for low) and each dot represents a SHAP value. A variety of SHAP values are displayed by features such as 122, 151, and 317, emphasizing the substantial influence they have. Figure 13.10 shows the impact of different feature values on predictions, providing a clear and thorough look at how the model makes decisions.

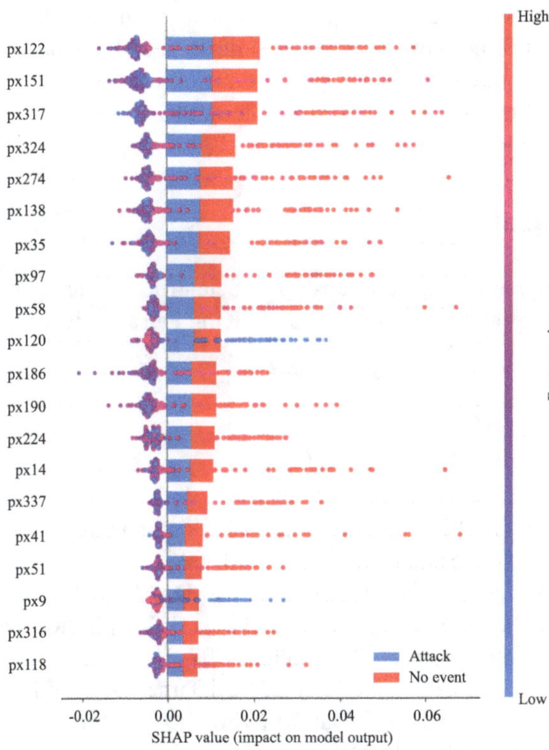

Figure 13.10 Feature effect on model decisions

13.4 Conclusion and future work

The current study proposes the DL-based method for intrusion detection for IoMT networks through the analysis of patient biometric data and network traffic characteristics. This study proposes a DL-based ensemble method for network-based intrusion detection for IoMT systems by utilizing attributes of patient biometrics and network traffic. Complicated, non-linear, and overlapping medical features can potentially be learned through the implementation of random forest feature significance. A meta-learner is fed the predictions of weak learners (CNN and LSTM) to enhance an extended deep-stacked ensemble method. Particularly noteworthy is the system's capacity to detect IoMT attacks with greater precision, which surpassed the performance of all preceding systems. This was accomplished through the combination of a DL model and a cost-sensitive learning strategy. Furthermore, when evaluated on multiple benchmark datasets constructed on networks that are industry standards, the proposed method exhibits similar performance. As a result, the proposed approach for IDS based on IoMT is sufficiently adaptable in addition vigorous to precisely perceive breaches and alert in network administrator to implement the necessary countermeasures. A multitude of attack types can be discerned, beyond those that specifically target network traffic. Further research will be conducted to assess the efficacy of the proposed model in attack categorization and to broaden the scope of the categories within the IoMT attack dataset. The characteristics of DL are structured into discrete and autonomous layers. It is advisable to incorporate kernel-based feature fusion learning methods in the classification layer. This layer type improves the model in addition to classification performance of the IoMT network.

Acknowledgments

This work was supported by the Deanship of Scientific Research, Vice Presidency for Graduate Studies and Scientific Research, King Faisal University, Saudi Arabia [Grant No. KFU250393].

References

[1] Yaacoub JPA, Noura M, Noura HN, *et al.* Securing Internet of Medical Things Systems: Limitations, Issues and Recommendations. *Future Generation Computer Systems*. 2020;105:581–606.

[2] Ghubaish A, Salman T, Zolanvari M, Unal D, Al-Ali A, and Jain R. Recent Advances in the Internet-of-Medical-Things (IoMT) Systems Security. *IEEE Internet of Things Journal*. 2020;8(11):8707–18.

[3] Rathore MM, Ahmad A, and Paul A. Real Time Intrusion Detection System for Ultra-High-Speed Big Data Environments. *The Journal of Supercomputing*. 2016;72:3489–510.

[4] RM SP, Maddikunta PKR, Koppu S, Gadekallu TR, Chowdhary CL, and Alazab M. An Effective Feature Engineering for DNN Using Hybrid PCA-GWO for Intrusion Detection in IoMT Architecture. *Computer Communications*. 2020;160:139–49.

[5] Kumar P, Gupta GP, and Tripathi R. An Ensemble Learning and Fog-Cloud Architecture-Driven Cyber-Attack Detection Framework for IoMT Networks. *Computer Communications*. 2021;166:110–24.

[6] Ghourabi. A Security Model Based on LightGBM and Transformer to Protect Healthcare Systems from Cyberattacks. *IEEE Access*. 2022;10:48890–903.

[7] Saheed YK, and Arowolo MO. Efficient Cyber Attack Detection on the Internet of Medical Things-Smart Environment Based on Deep Recurrent Neural Network and Machine Learning Algorithms. *IEEE Access*. 2021; 9:161546–54.

[8] Nandy S, Adhikari M, Khan MA, Menon VG, and Verma S. An Intrusion Detection Mechanism for Secured IoMT Framework Based on Swarm-Neural Network. *IEEE Journal of Biomedical and Health Informatics*. 2021; 26(5):1969–76.

[9] Radoglou-Grammatikis P, Sarigiannidis P, Efstathopoulos G, Lagkas T, Fragulis G, and Sarigiannidis A. A Self-Learning Approach for Detecting Intrusions in Healthcare Systems. ICC 2021 – IEEE International Conference on Communications. 2021:1–6.

[10] Thamilarasu G, Odesile A, and Hoang A. An Intrusion Detection System for Internet of Medical Things. *IEEE Access*. 2020;8:181560–76.

[11] Hady AA, Ghubaish A, Salman T, Unal D, and Jain R. Intrusion Detection System for Healthcare Systems Using Medical and Network Data: A Comparison Study. *IEEE Access*. 2020;8:106576–84.

[12] Biau G, and Scornet E. A Random Forest Guided Tour. *TEST*. 2016;25 (2):197–227.

[13] Akshay Kumaar M, Samiayya D, Vincent PMDR, Srinivasan K, Chang C-Y, and Ganesh H. A Hybrid Framework for Intrusion Detection in Healthcare Systems Using Deep Learning. *Frontiers in Public Health*. 2022;9:824898.

[14] Ravi V, Pham TD, and Alazab M. Deep Learning-Based Network Intrusion Detection System for Internet of Medical Things. *IEEE Internet of Things Magazine*. 2023;6(2):50–54.

[15] Gupta K, Sharma DK, Gupta KD, and Kumar A. A Tree Classifier Based Network Intrusion Detection Model for Internet of Medical Things. *Computers and Electrical Engineering*. 2022;102:108158.

[16] Chaganti R, Mourade A, Ravi V, Vemprala N, Dua A, and Bhushan B. A Particle Swarm Optimization and Deep Learning Approach for Intrusion Detection System in Internet of Medical Things. *Sustainability*. 2022;14 (19):12828.

[17] Hernandez-Jaimes ML, Martinez-Cruz A, Ramírez-Gutiérrez KA, and Feregrino-Uribe C. Artificial Intelligence for IoMT Security: A Review of Intrusion Detection Systems, Attacks, Datasets and Cloud-Fog-Edge Architectures. *Internet of Things*. 2023;23:100887.

Chapter 14

Artificial intelligence for next generation: social and ethical challenges

Muhammad Saeed[1], Muhammad Ibrar[1] and Muqadsa Jabeen[1]

Abstract

Artificial intelligence (AI) has rapidly evolved from rule-based systems to transformative technologies integrated into critical aspects of daily life, including healthcare, finance, and education. This chapter explores the dual nature of AI's potential—its ability to revolutionize industries and improve lives, alongside its significant ethical and societal challenges. The review begins by examining the history of AI, from its foundational moments, such as the Turing Test and the Dartmouth Conference, to its current advancements through deep learning, large language models, and generative AI. Highlighting significant trends, it discusses AI in autonomous systems and healthcare, with the latter poised to have the most tremendous potential—projected to contribute $826 billion to economic growth by 2030. This chapter addresses challenges such as workforce disruption, the digital divide, misinformation, and their impacts on individuals. It also delves into ethical issues, including bias, accountability for system misuse, privacy concerns, and the implications of autonomous systems. Case studies illustrate the risks and benefits of AI in healthcare, autonomous vehicles, criminal justice, and creative industries. The discussion emphasizes that balancing these risks demands equitable access to AI's benefits, transparency, and inclusivity. The chapter further highlights the importance of robust ethical frameworks, interdisciplinary collaboration, and proactive governance to address these challenges. It advocates for a global day of activity to foster collaboration for responsible AI development. It outlines key elements of a future where AI supports all of humanity fairly and ethically without exclusion. This work offers a comprehensive roadmap for navigating the next generation of AI's social and ethical complexities.

[1]Department of Computer Science, The University of Faisalabad, Pakistan

14.1 Introduction

Imagine a world where machines perform tasks and make decisions directly impacting our daily lives—choices about health, job opportunities, and even legal matters. According to Statista, the artificial intelligence (AI) market is expected to expand from over $184 billion in 2024 to more than $826 billion by 2030. Indeed, this is a fast-approaching reality, given the rapid strides being made in the field of AI. From virtual assistants in our homes to advanced algorithms managing financial markets, AI technologies are increasingly embedded in nearly every aspect of life [1]. This pervasive integration offers great opportunities for innovation and efficiency. However, as AI systems become more autonomous and integral to critical sectors, many ethical issues arise, including discussions on accountability, transparency, bias, and privacy; if these challenges can be addressed, AI holds great promise for serving humanity equitably and responsibly [2].

In *Artificial Intelligence for the Next Generation: Social and Ethical Challenges*, the authors highlight the dual nature of AI technologies—the opportunities they present and the significant risks they pose, such as bias, privacy violations, and job displacement. These critical challenges must be overcome for AI to truly benefit all members of society rather than exacerbate inequality. The book focuses on the development of ethical frameworks, inclusive design, and regulatory oversight as central to responsibly navigate the challenges presented by AI. By addressing such pressing issues, the work aims to foster an understanding of how the power of AI can be harnessed while maintaining ethics and ensuring that human rights are upheld in this increasingly automated world [3]. In simple terms, AI is the simulation of human intelligence in machines capable of learning, reasoning, and decision-making. From simple rule-based systems, AI has evolved into advanced autonomous technologies, revolutionizing industries and societies. However, as AI is increasingly developed for integration into critical domains, the focus must shift toward addressing social and ethical challenges such as fairness, accountability, and transparency. This will ensure that AI development aligns with human values and serves humanity responsibly.

14.2 The evolution of artificial intelligence

AI has come a long way from rule-based systems based on pre-programmed instructions to generative AI capable of creating text, images, and more with human-like creativity. In the years to come, autonomous vehicles, AI-powered healthcare, and smart cities will continue to transform daily life. However, the social implications raise fundamental questions about ethics, equity, and inclusion, making their responsible development essential [4].

14.2.1 1950s: the foundations

1950: Alan Turing established the so-called Turing Test, which evaluates the capability of a machine to mimic or demonstrate intelligence comparable to human intuition. 1956: The Dartmouth Conference coined the term "artificial intelligence", marking the official birth of AI as a field.

14.2.2 1960s–1980s: early growth

The basic development of AI algorithms includes symbolic reasoning. Examples of applications related to AI include chess-playing programs and simple problem-solving.

14.2.3 1980s: era of expert systems

AI systems are now able to simulate human expertise in particular domains; they have also gained greater popularity. Used in several applications, including medical diagnosis and financial analysis.

14.2.4 1990s: emergence of machine learning

Move from rule-based systems to data-driven machine learning. 1997: Deep Blue supercomputer of IBM defeated chess champion Garry Kasparov in chess and demonstrated AI.

14.2.5 2010s: deep learning revolution

Big data and neural networks are the keys to unlocking the future of AI. AI excels in recognizing images and processing natural language and speech. 2016-AlphaGo beat Go champion Lee Sedol, an important milestone showing massive reinforcement learning progress.

14.2.6 Transformative AI (2020–2024)

AI models, such as GPT and DALL-E, generate text and images creatively. The diffusion of AI adoption also affects every other sector, whether it be healthcare, finance, or autonomous systems.

14.3 Key developments

14.3.1 Generative AI: large language models (LLMs)

The development of LLMs like OpenAI's GPT series and Google's PaLM revolutionized natural language understanding and generation. These models demonstrated capabilities in tasks like translation, summarization, coding, and creative writing. Tools like DALL-E, MidJourney, and ChatGPT expanded creative possibilities in art, design, and content generation [5].

- Healthcare AI: AI applications, particularly in diagnostics, personalized medicine, and drug discovery, grew exponentially. AI-driven research accelerated solutions for cancer diagnostics, COVID-19 treatments, and rare diseases.
- Ethical AI: Growing concerns about AI ethics, bias, and explain-ability led to a focus on AI governance and responsible AI development.

Significant achievements

- AI systems like OpenAI Codex and GitHub Copilot made significant strides in software development by generating code from natural language.
- Autonomous vehicles, driven by AI, transitioned from testing to limited real-world deployment, as seen in Tesla's and Waymo's initiatives.
- AI is central in tackling global challenges, such as climate modeling, renewable energy optimization, and sustainable development.

14.3.2 Future-2030 and beyond

The AI market is expected to cross $826 billion by 2030. The focus would be laid upon ethical AI for better transparency and societal integration, as shown in Figure 14.1.

14.4 Application of artificial intelligence

A number of domains are using AI, and they are becoming significant and efficient industries. AI makes big entries into healthcare in diagnostics, drug discovery, and personalized treatment plans. AI impacts finance transfer as it needs mechanisms to detect fraud for algorithmic trading or risk management. Powered by AI, AI tools in education offer personalized learning, automated grading, and other similar resources. However, only if they are in the transportation domain are autonomous vehicles, traffic optimization, and route planning beneficial [6]. Retail and e-commerce use AI for inventory management, recommendation systems and chatbots. Besides that, AI is altering agriculture, manufacturing, entertainment, and conserving the environment by smart decisions, automatons and innovative solutions to the most complex problems [7,8]. Some AI Applications are below and as shown in Figure 14.2.

14.4.1 Healthcare

AI revolutionizes healthcare with applications such as robotic surgery, medical imaging, drug discovery, and epidemic forecasting. However, virtual health assistants and remote monitoring are necessary for patients, while personalized medicine depends upon the individual genetic profile.

14.4.2 Education and finance

With personalized learning platforms, automated grading, virtual tutors and adaptive assessments, AI helps businesses understand steps to streamline educational space. Built as an aid to educators, plagiarism detection and classroom analytics tool as well as our AI-based career guidance to lead students to a career they'd love to pursue. AI in finance has resulted in sentiment analysis, driving credit scoring, algorithmic trading and fraud detection. Robo advisers deliver personalized investment strategy formulations, but predictive analytics can assess the risk parameters and forecast finances.

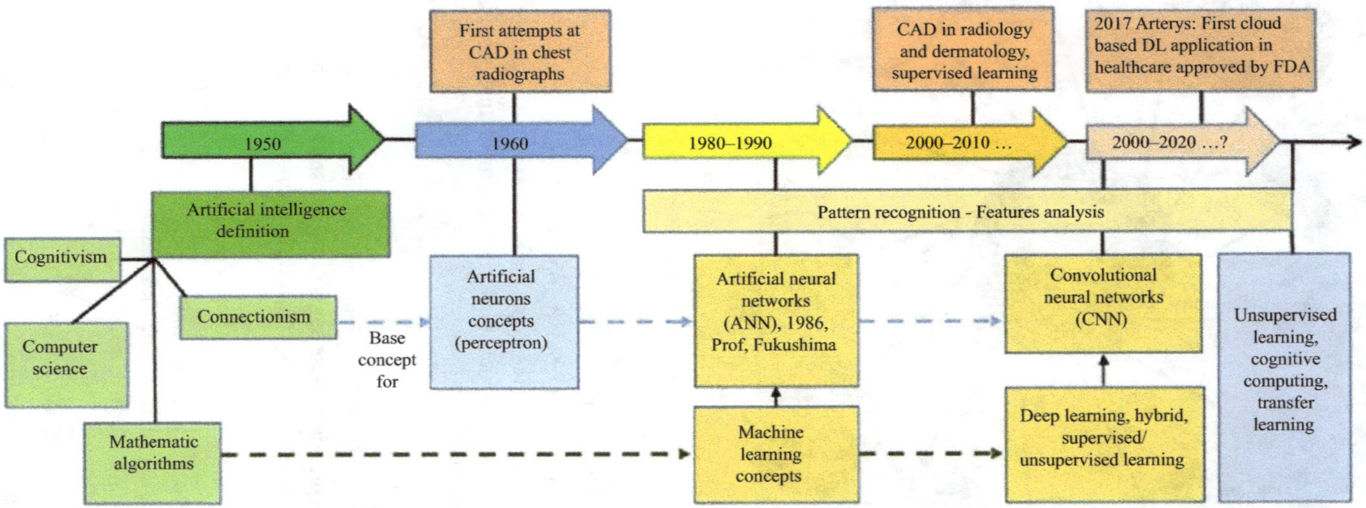

Figure 14.1 Evaluation of AI

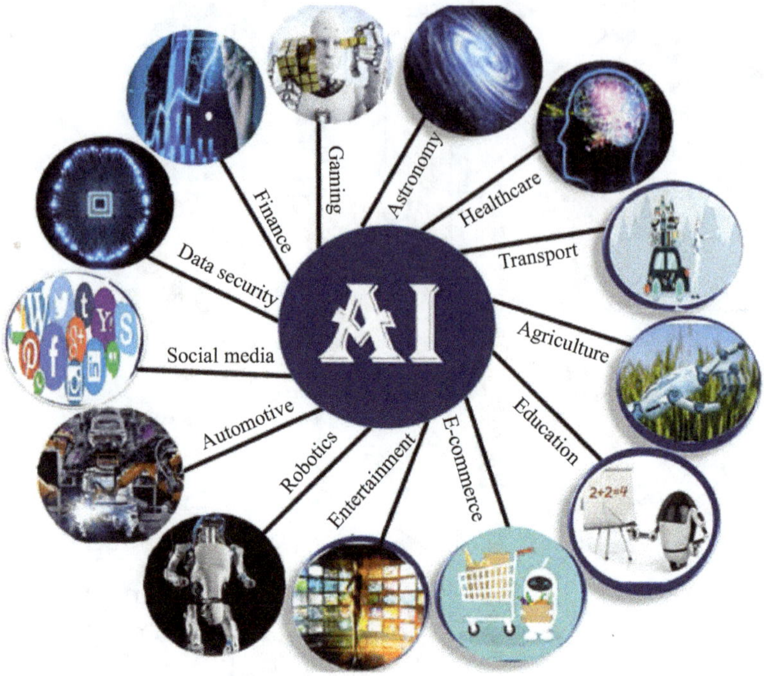

Figure 14.2 Applications of AI

14.4.3 Retail and e-commerce

AI is taking things to the next level, helping retail innovate around recommendation systems, dynamic pricing, inventory management, and Chatbot. Enhancing and securing the shopping experience, customer sentiment analysis, visual search tools, and fraud prevention tools.

14.4.4 Agriculture

AI in agriculture is also used for precision farming, crop monitoring, disease detection, and yield prediction. These consist of livestock management, AI harvesting systems and water management systems that enhance productivity and sustainability.

14.4.5 Entertainment

AI brings personalized entertainment, from entertainment recommendations to interactive storytelling to real-time translation. Video editing, emotion detection, and AI-driven gaming increase content delivery and user engagement.

14.4.6 Environment and security

By supplying climate modeling, wildlife tracking, and optimizing renewable energy, AI facilitates environmental conservation. The application of this domain is vitally important for pollution monitoring, deforestation analysis, and disaster management. AI is used in facial recognition, security with behavioral biometrics, and drones used for surveillance. AI-driven smart locks and incident response systems aid the safety of the user, and cybersecurity tools prevent and respond to the frost.

14.4.7 Marketing

The tools of AI, sentiment analyses, and predictive analytics help the marketer understand consumer behavior. The Chatbot, programmatic advertising, and customer segmentation can, in turn, improve the effectiveness and engagement of the campaigns.

14.4.8 Real estate

For property valuation, virtual property tours, and even predicting maintenance, real estate uses AI. With AI-based platforms, market trends are analyzed, and then properties are recommended to buyers and renters based on personal preferences.

14.4.9 Gaming

This has also transformed the game with adaptive gameplay, realistic NPCs, and real-time environment rendering. Gamers can learn what the player likes or does not like and improve the game development with AI-driven analytics.

14.4.10 Supply chain and logistics

AI optimize logistics, let's say, in route planning, demand forecasting, and inventory management. Beyond that, we also saw autonomous vehicles and warehouse automation cut operational costs and improve the efficiency of deliveries.

14.4.11 Insurance

Smart risk assessment of claims, more efficient claims process and more personalized policies are what AI is bringing to the insurance industry. Fraud detection chatbots reduce inefficiency and increase customer protection, whereas client chatbots increase efficiency and customer satisfaction.

14.4.12 Journalism and media

As technology improves, AI has found its way into the field of journalism, automating content creation, fact-checking, and language translation. News aggregation and sentiment analysis tools improve how we deliver and imbibe media.

14.5 Social challenges of artificial intelligence

AI has revolutionized industries but presents significant social and ethical challenges, including job displacement, the digital divide, and biases in decision-making. Ethical concerns like privacy breaches, surveillance, accountability, misuse of AI in the military, and misinformation highlight the need for responsible development. Addressing these issues requires algorithm transparency, equitable access to AI technologies, and robust global regulatory frameworks [9]. Collaboration among technologists, policymakers, and ethicists is essential to ensure AI aligns with human values, fostering inclusivity and safeguarding societal well-being while leveraging its transformative potential. Some challenges are given below.

14.5.1 Workforce disruption

AI integration has brought about great job displacement within industries, and most of such jobs involve repetitiveness, like in manufacturing and customer service. According to the World Economic Forum, by the year 2025, AI and automation will eliminate approximately 85 million jobs on the one hand while creating 97 million new ones on the other hand. This dual consequence of AI suggests that the actual impact of AI on employment is more complex: many new jobs require specialized skills, which displaced workers may not have. Need for Reskilling and Education: with the changing nature of jobs because of AI, urgent reskilling and upskilling programs are needed to prepare the workforce for emerging jobs.

14.5.2 Privacy concerns

The application of AI technologies often involves large-scale usage, which by implication, necessitates the large-scale collection of data. Often, this gives rise to serious problems related to privacy. Organizations often use personal data in the training of AI, which, in turn, sometimes results in activities amounting to surveillance at the expense of the individual's private rights. The threat of data misuse and breaches is highly critical because sensitive information can be used to the advantage of malicious actors or be mishandled by an organization. This presents a compelling case for robust data protection regulations and ethics in AI development.

14.5.3 Digital divide

The rapid rise in AI technologies has increased the gulf in the digital divide due to unequal access to these innovations, causing differences across various socio-economic strata. Those living in developed nations can benefit from this advancement in AI more than those living in developing regions. The implications are that the limited access to technology and poor infrastructure in developing nations could further stifle the uptake of AI, exacerbating inequality.

14.5.4 Ethical use in education

AI tools are increasingly being integrated into education, but concerns exist about fairness in assessment and the potential for unequal access. Students in underprivileged areas may lack access to AI-driven learning tools, widening the educational gap.

14.5.5 Impact on mental health

The rise of AI-driven social media algorithms has raised concerns about mental health. Research indicates that algorithms promoting engagement can lead to addiction, anxiety, and depression by amplifying negative or sensational content [10].

14.5.6 Security risks

AI's role in cybersecurity is double-edged. While it helps detect and mitigate threats, AI systems themselves can be targeted or manipulated by adversaries, leading to potential breaches and systemic vulnerabilities.

14.5.7 Cultural erosion

Globalized AI systems often prioritize dominant cultural norms, risking the marginalization of local languages and traditions. Efforts to preserve cultural diversity in AI development remain insufficient.

14.5.8 Ethical challenges in AI-powered surveillance

AI-based surveillance technologies, like facial recognition, raise concerns about misuse by governments and organizations. These systems can infringe on personal freedoms and promote authoritarian practices [11].

14.5.9 Misinformation and propaganda

The power of AI has been used to create and spread misinformation on an unprecedented level. Deepfakes and automated bots generate deceptive content to alter public opinion and destroy confidence in media sources. While AI can be used in identifying and mitigating the spread of misinformation, usually, its efficiency is tested by changing the tactics of the creators of fake news.

14.5.10 Human–AI interaction

Trust becomes fundamental when the dependence on AI systems starts to grow. The user would require trust that the AI system decisions are transparent and can be explained, while trying to make human life easier, increased use of AI in everyday activities appears to generate overdependence by citizens on the technology.

14.6 Ethical challenges of artificial intelligence

Things are just as challenging in that nobody understands if AI is a challenge or if it's a promising thing; everything will be based on AI sooner or later, and that means that there are really ethical challenges going forward that you have to look at really deeply, as shown in Figure 14.3 [12]. Here are some of the key areas where ethical issues come up, simple wording explained in detail below.

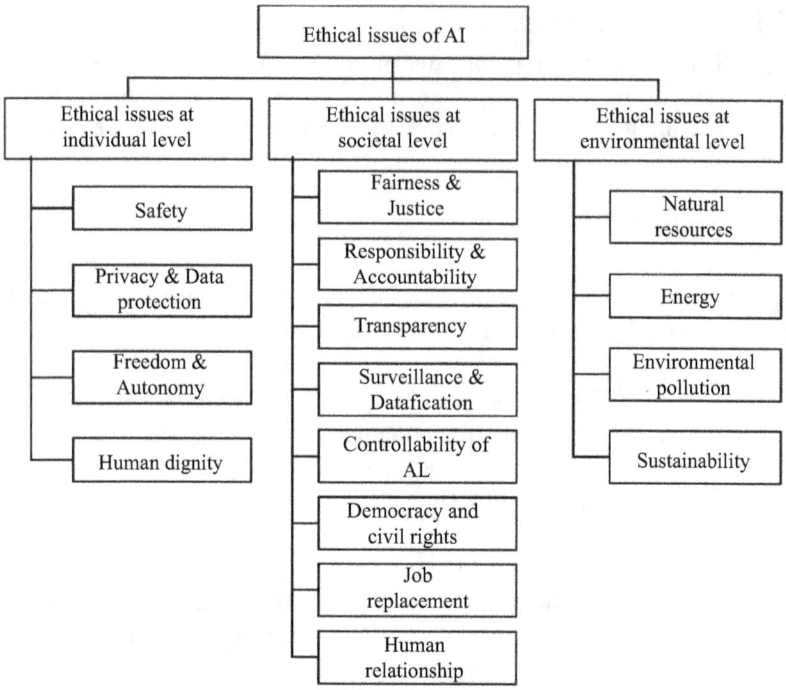

Figure 14.3 Applications of AI

14.6.1 Bias and discrimination

Suppose these values are already biased in the form of stereotypes or unbalanced representations. In that case, AI systems learn from the data they receive and match their predictions or decisions to match their biases. For instance, if you train a hiring algorithm on data that shows men tend to be taken on more often for tech jobs, it's possible that this algorithm will show a preference for men in the future. AI systems can be biased, which negatively impacts underrepresented groups such as women, minorities, and people with disabilities. Facial recognition systems are, for example, unable to recognize people with darker skin tones, leading to unfair treatment, for example, from law enforcement systems [13].

14.6.2 Accountable and responsible

Figuring out who's pulling the strings—who is responsible if an AI system misdiagnoses a patient or causes an accident—is also complex. Or maybe the developers who constructed the system, the companies that deployed it, or the users who interacted with it? Just to give you the context. AI is complicated, and it's changing quickly. It's developing so fast that governments and organizations can't keep up, and are scrambling to promulgate a set of rules to govern it. As a result, then when we don't properly regulate it, we are going to have a lot of these toxic outcomes unchecked and just accept people as victims.

14.6.3 Autonomy versus control

That's because they talk about fossil fuels, autonomous cars, and drones that rarely engage with humans. That's efficient, but it's also a safety concern. Humans need ways to take control if something goes wrong. AI could decide when to intervene and in what manner to intervene in making medical decisions that directly dictate the trajectory of someone's life. For example, if an autonomous car has to decide between protecting its passengers at all costs or choosing not to hit pedestrians—in sum, to err on the side of the pedestrians over the car—how should the vehicle make the choice? These are hardly ethical questions.

14.6.4 Ethical AI design

Ethics is if it is fair, transparent, and accountable for AI. treat every user on a pattern where they should explain to their decision and should never cause harm. Going further, for example, if some new loan applications for an AI-powered lending system, the system should be fair in this treatment: An applicant's request to lend should go through without differentially screening that fact itself because it is an application [14].

14.6.5 Privacy concerns

Extensive data requiring AI to enable facial recognition and other major use cases is very risky with regard to privacy. If such data is used illegally, it can become an instrument of the reduction of people's rights and a tool of surveillance overreach. Strong data protection policies should be implemented with the user's consent to mitigate these concerns.

14.6.6 Accountability and liability

What are the AI system actions? For example, we do not have a clear idea of whether someone is to be blamed (the manufacturer, the programmer, the user) or if, for example, the autonomous car will cause an accident. Yet, such scenarios can only be addressed with clear legal frameworks and accountability mechanisms.

14.6.7 Misuse of AI technology

In cyberattacks involving deepfakes, AI can be weaponized for evil, and so can AI-enabled weapons. The misuse of education undercuts society and threatens global security. Collaborative and international regulation and prevention of AI technology misuse take place.

14.6.8 Erosion of human autonomy

Because automation and machine decisions are necessary in societies, people tend to worry about overreliance on automation. For instance, hospitals are gutting physicians of the ability to exercise decision power in diagnosing healthcare and have turned to using AI too much. We must maintain trust and accountability to get the right balance of human oversight and AI autonomy.

14.6.9 Ethical decision-making in AI

Finally, we recapitulate the complex dilemmas raised by implementing ethical decision-making for A.I. systems, including autonomous vehicles. Here is an example: How does an AI make a decision between two bad options in unavoidable accident situations? There are definitely ethics regarding whether that should happen or if we should allow such decision-making, but they are definitely ethics around it, and so there's a collaboration of ethicists, engineers, and policymakers to decide what sort of guidelines such decision-making should be allowed.

14.7 Case study

AI is advancing rapidly all over the world. The world is only just beginning to truly understand the possibilities of AI in its ability to influence almost every domain of society tremendously, but there are complex ethical, legal, and social problems that are on the cards which AI will soon have to face. In the area of health care, AI can help to detect disease faster and to deliver individualized care best suited for a patient's specific needs. The problem with that is it also inflates biases from non-representative datasets, and it brings in privacy issues, especially in the case of sensitive medical data, but that wouldn't be all bad. While autonomous vehicles [may] be revolutionizing the way we get from point A to point B for safety and efficiency, [there's] a moral dilemma to consider if we do find ourselves in a crash situation, that is, "Can the crash be avoided?" and if so, "What do we do about that?". However, these challenges concern the bringing of moral principles into AI systems, leading to an unresolved question: Indeed, to whom should be held accountable: manufacturers or providers of basic materials, developers who altered a raw source material and put it in their systems, or those who used these systems. The risk with using AI tools in criminal justice spaces—like predictive policing or sentencing—is we're building a system that aims to increase efficiency, but at the cost of aggravating systemic biases embedded within these tools' historical data that shapes the data we get and thus harms of vulnerable populations. Since we have no clue how the algorithm works, it is hard to make any guarantees on fairness and trust on top of these applications.

Let's look at the generation of content using Generative AI. We see bleeding-edge innovation in using DALL-E and GPTs to create content at scale, coping with copyright infringement, information and misinformation through deepfakes, originality, and ideas of job replacement in creative industries. Instead, AI presents such challenges—multi-dimensional ones that not only call for forming the frameworks of strong ethics but also updating rules of the regulatory set and such cooperation among technologists, government officials, and ethicists—for AI to intervene appropriately and responsibly and equitably, and allow AI to meet its transformational promise [15].

Fast growth comes with tremendous challenges in achieving responsible use. In the case of health care or law enforcement, if flawed or incomplete data are used, there's a good chance that the AI systems themselves will perpetuate unfairness, and the resulting outcomes will be biased. Predictive policing tools are often pointed at already marginalized communities, and biased medical algorithms rarely provide equitable healthcare, for example. In addition, privacy issues aside, nearly all AI technology is based on huge amounts of personally identifiable training data that could have a privacy breach. Further, ethical dilemmas are integrated through AI into realms of autonomous vehicles, and generative AI. Aside from these moral questions—like the example of autonomous vehicles which meet and inevitably crash, what are they supposed to focus on?—there are also the accountability and liability questions: who should be blamed when the vehicle crashes? Generative AI is an enabler of creativity but also of copyright infringement, originality concerns in creative industries, and deep fakes. We need clear ethical frameworks, robust regulatory policy, and genuine engagement between governments, industries and researchers to meet these challenges.

14.8 The role of governance and policy in artificial intelligence

Governments desiring to usher in an ethical, equitable, and safe future of AI technologies are in a position to significantly affect how the future of AI will develop if such frameworks and policies to guide the development of AI are meticulously instituted. With the fast development of AI, we are facing structurally and proactively ethical, societal, and legal challenges that need to be answered. But this demands defining efficient regulations, the stimulus of international cooperation and disseminating a code of conduct for AI fair management of the complexities, as shown in Figure 14.4.

14.8.1 Regulation frameworks

Governments don't stop, though; worldwide, they have started to develop regulatory frameworks to cover AI's ethical and societal impacts. From a global perspective, we take different management directions with AI governance. Take, for example, identifying different classes of AI applications in terms of their level of risk and requiring thorough oversight of the high-risk system that deploys it in health care or law enforcement. For instance, the European Union (EU) has shown more proactive regulation through the AI Act. Instead, the United States and other countries stress sector-specific regulations while relying on voluntary guidelines to focus on innovation of issues in particular, such as data privacy and security. There is a discussion about whether current laws work, or not. While adopting data protection laws such as the EU's General Data Protection Regulation (GDPR) has helped establish norms for protecting and processing personal data inside AI, there are also missing pieces of managing algorithmic accountability and greater transparency. Existing laws were not even designed for the real intricacies of AI which explains the lag in new technologies, the measures in line with new laws in matters of AI policies to allow for ethical, equitable, and safe development of AI technologies. With AI's rapid development, ethical, societal, and legal challenges demand

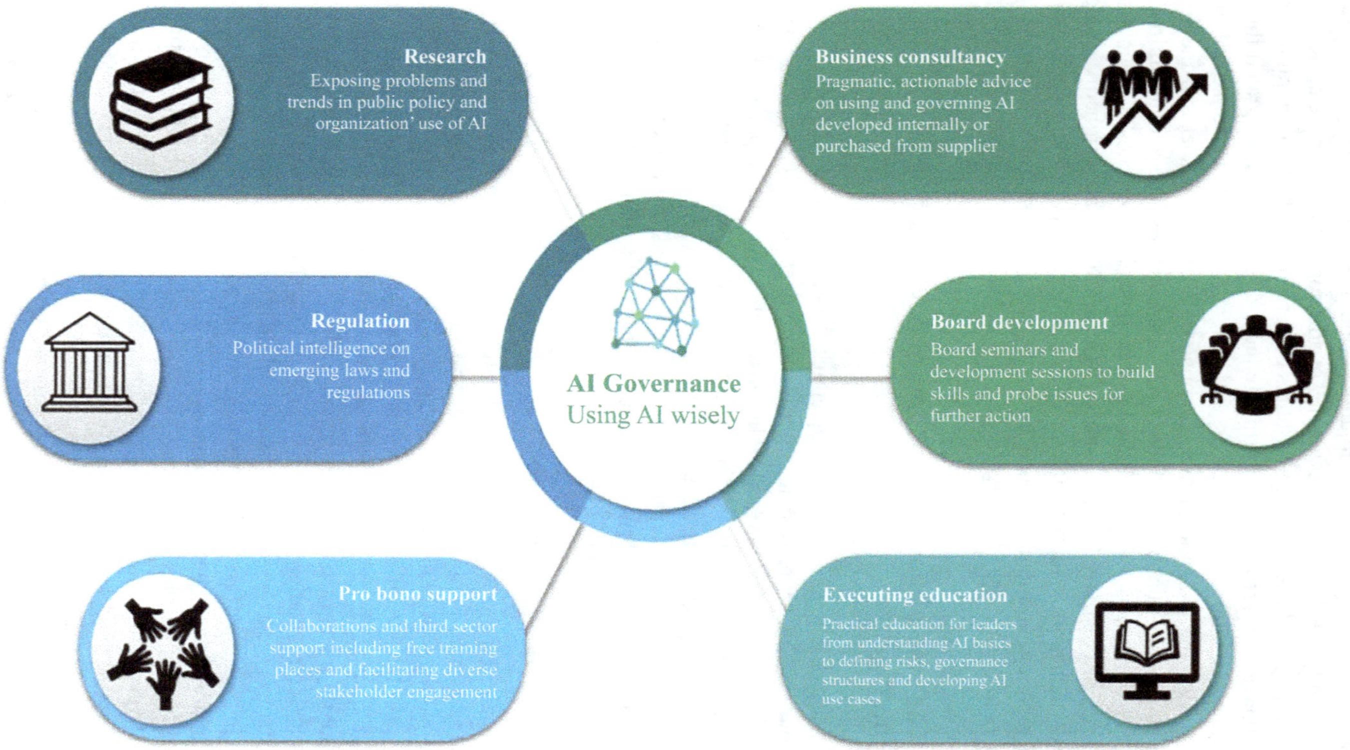

Figure 14.4 Role of governance and policy in AI

structured and proactive responses. This requires the definition of effective regulations, the promotion of international collaboration and the propagation of industry guidelines for fair management of the complexities of AI.

14.8.2 International collaboration

However, the fact that AI is a worldwide issue necessitates international cooperation to face the issues for which it has a worldwide relevance. However, the role of cross-border ethical promotion of AI development is more important for existing organizations like the United Nations (UN) and the EU. Other initiatives the UN has set are UNESCO's Recommendation on the Ethics of Artificial Intelligence for a global standard of AI governance based on human rights, inclusiveness and sustainability. It acts on the member states, much like the EU, and encourages member states to develop similar harmonized AI policies via cooperation on projects such as the Horizon Europe program. These collaborative efforts share goals for policymakers to set shared ethical standards, share knowledge, and prevent fragmented AI governance. The participants also discuss how to grapple with the transnational challenges, including how to regulate the use of AI developed for autonomous weapons, act against global misinformation and ensure that developing countries have access to AI technologies at parity. However, without such a collaboration, this could lead to uneven development and unrestrained exploitation of AI.

14.8.3 Industry guidelines

Such compliance and regulation cannot be ensured by governments alone. Still, businesses must also comply with the industrial guideline and their regulation to have some assurance of responsible AI development. Now, several tech companies have also come to accept their duty to develop ethical AI and, accordingly, have begun to roll out an internal code of ethics and frameworks in this area. For instance, Google has made its AI Principles public, pledging to "build AI in ways that are fair, effective and safe". Microsoft and IBM, however, are trying their best to bring ethical practices to work on AI research and deployment. They have also been out front of responsible AI efforts like coalescing industry leaders (coalitions like the Partnership on AI), researchers, and policymakers around what best practices should look like. These initiatives aim to proclaim transparency, independent auditing of AI systems, and ensuring that AI is built so that no one is left behind. Moreover, corporations fund research and training for their teams on understanding and mitigating performance risks.

14.9 Preparing for the future with next-generation

As AI continues to advance, preparing for its future requires a holistic approach that addresses education, ethics, governance, research, and equity. Education in AI, encompassing education, ethics, governance, research, and equity, must be seriously considered and fully practiced as AI speeds toward the future [16,17]. In struggling to make the best out of using AI and trying to encode limitations, we can have an AI future that is Good for Humanity, not dystopian [18].

14.9.1 Education and awareness

We have in education the foundation for the responsible AI ecosystem that we want. Then, we recommend including AI ethics in the teaching curricula and professional training programs that provide people with the ability to comprehend the intricate character of their relationships with AI. Instead, we introduce students to the topics of algorithmic fairness, data privacy, and ethical decision-making through interactive courses and case studies in the real world. Developers and business leaders need to be trained in ethical guidelines on professional programs that develop AI when that AI is designed and deployed with accountability in mind.

14.9.2 Building awareness on the public about AI risks and benefits

We need to build an informed society to create trust in these AI technologies [19]. Ongoing AI public awareness campaigns to inform the public about the benefits of AI healthcare and transportation, as well as AIs preventative powers (to make people aware of information, e.g., from Facebook, that might cause civic unrest), are another possibility [20]. It would be ideal for governments or organizations to run workshops and documentaries or use online resources to ensure some get the positives and challenges of AI.

14.9.3 Policymakers and leaders need to become AI literate

For policymakers and business leaders to base decisions on facts, they need to have an accurate understanding of AI. We need to teach them the technical basics of engineering, the technical basics of AI, the basics of AI ethics, and the general trends. Thus, they make sure to lead and rule in the AI development one significant need to the society.

14.9.4 Ethical AI practices

AI has an ethical impact on developers. But, they should keep up best practices—doing bias audits, using explainable AI tools, and making privacy and security part of the design. In simple, if you follow some frameworks such as Google's AI Principles1 or IEEE's "Ethically Aligned Design2", you'll have very simple rules for your responsible brewing of AI. At first sight, it's simple, it's easy, and it's primarily free. In this talk, I'm sharing how we are working to ensure we have more inclusive and diverse AI teams at Facebook and an additional talk on how we make it so that the algorithms people are building are diverse. To build bias-reducing AI systems for diverse populations, we need Inclusive teams. It's up to organizations to find underrepresented talent and actively create a place where they want to work [21]. This is good thinking for all clients in building up AI and coordinates with schools and nearby affiliations where this can be pushed for more.

14.9.5 Standards and ethics certification

Global standards and the certification of AI systems will help earn trust and accountability. And much like ISO certifications, AI systems' fairness, transparency, and safety should be examined. This, in turn, would be ethical scores for AI deployments.

14.9.6 Research and development

It should be important for anybody interested in AI safety research. We argue that this research area is being ignored, and governments, private organizations, and academic institutes need to begin rapidly investing in AI safety research at a clip comparable to their investment in AI advances. The focus areas are the axes of robustness, explainability, and human values alignment.

14.9.7 Collaboration in open source

Open-source AI, unlike other AIs out there, is about transparency and people solving problems together as a whole. As OpenAI goes to do work in the open, we can build with it despite global developers and researchers—test for risks and create ways how to solve ethical AI.

14.9.8 Strengthening governance

Governments yet, however, have to develop adaptive regulations to manage the unique challenges of AI. The data protection laws here should be covered by these frameworks, as should mechanisms of accountability if AI fails or guidelines for particularly higher-risk sectors such as finance and healthcare where the applications are high risk. These are laws intended to grow with the AI they elegantly manage.

14.9.9 Global governance

International cooperation is needed for the global implications of AI. For example, everyone should have access to AI, autonomous weapons, or something like that—the UN and the EU, one of the steps for dealing with transnational issues by creating universal ethical standards, are there. When collaborative treaties and agreements are signed these must be consistent in the governance.

14.9.10 Reskilling and upskilling programs

AI will automate the workplace and change the workforce, requiring new skills from future employers. Workers need to learn AI-specific knowledge such as data analysis and programming or digital literacy from governments and industries. These strides will guarantee that workers can find a place of work as the job market continues to change without difficulties.

14.9.11 Promoting equity in AI

Governments and organizations should work to bring AI tools and training within the financial reach of a larger constituency: potential users who do not have access to advanced AI facilities. AI4 works and pairs up with non-profits and international agencies to ensure underserved communities benefit from advancements we can provide in access to AI. Now, we've got to have our AI systems in a place where it's pretty going up against all populations because we can hardwire away societal inequalities in deploying unfair AI as long as a few of us try to honor the standards of inclusive design [22].

14.10 Future direction

A comprehensive and multi-layered approach is essential to address the social and ethical challenges posed by next-generation AI. We require a full social and ethical take on the next-generation AI challenge. They do so on a foundation of building sound ethical frameworks to promote transparency and fairness and to further accountability and inclusiveness. Overall, those policy frameworks dictate how to ensure that AI systems are constructed, deployed, and regulated (or undone so) according to the values of society and human rights protection. Yet, by creating internationally accepted ethical standards, through a collaboration of governments, industries and scientists, research will be done in line with international standards. Second, the regulatory bodies need to make policies that respond to technology because they must address the problems caused by technological development accurately and over extended periods [23].

This is because international organizations like the UN, The EU and the Organisation for Economic Co-operation and Development, are supposed to set the pace in the formulation of international treaties and guidelines. All of these frameworks must often address the immediate transnational realities of AI misuse in surveillance, of the regulation of autonomous weapons, and of the equitable deployment of AI technologies. Cross-border partnerships and knowledge-sharing platforms are promised to harmonize ethical development in AI further. This work should be global, equitable, agrarian, and driven by AI, not about AI, as we seek to ensure that the rewards of AI are not a perk of nationhood but can be rewarding to those in underserved places. This future needs to be prepared for by humans; thus, education and ways to be educated in such technology are permissible. It means including AI ethics in education curricula on all levels in order for the education system to produce a generation that is able to battle the threats of AI. Interactive case studies and real world examples teach students what algorithmic bias and data privacy might mean for society and how automation is changing the workplace. However, policymakers, business leaders, and developers all need to be trained in specialized AI to understand the extent of risks and opportunities related to technology. These knowledge gaps can be bridged with public awareness campaigns, community forums and accessible online resources to better educate people on how AI can augment the business of wider industry (healthcare, education, transportation, etc.) and reducing fears of their job displacement and exposure to misinformation.

The third and equally important pillar is investment in AI safety research. For general AI systems to attain reliability over a diverse set of conditions, research must also now address areas that make research values for the broader AI community, e.g., robustness, explainability, and alignment of (general) AI systems with (human) values. To stay abreast with the technological advancements, however, this safety research should be very close to the steps of the technological advancements, and the government, private organizations, and academic institutions should commit sufficiently to these efforts. In short, for reducing biases or making the whole thing more inclusive, there should be diversity in AI development teams. So teams that had been building AI systems by themselves had different vantage points to consider when creating AI systems for all groups of users and to check if there were cultural or social biases. This means organizations have to proactively recruit from underrepresented groups first and then build spaces where everyone can actually do their best work. Finally, working with universities, non-profits and community organizations, we can do even more to ensure that diversity is promoted and so that any development of AI is actually inclusive, representative of many perspectives and requires a broad range of human experiences and needs.

These three are becoming more common, and as they do, are becoming more and more perilous examples of the dangers of deepfakes, piss-poor misinformation, and the abuse of AI. AI carries with it many problems adjacent to it—if they don't have to be tech companies—it has to be governments or tech companies or other ways to help build detection tools and ethical standards and legal approaches to kind of throttle the growth of false information and the risk of spreading within the realm of AI. People or organizations, either a misuse of AI, can be proclaimed as new laws, which can also be used to see whether someone produces illegal media via AI-based content verification systems to detect manipulated media. This will promote the public's trust in AI technologies and decrease the harm they cause. Global monitoring bodies and artificial general intelligence (AGI) ethical guidelines can overcome most of the potential risks for AGI. Furthermore, the environmental sustainability of the proposed AI is to be stressed by suggesting green technologies and designing energy-efficient AI models. The social and ethical problems of next-generation AI can be addressed through ethical frameworks, global collaboration, education, research, diversity, and proactive governance.

14.11 Conclusion

Faster than anyone anticipated, we have come to terms with AI. Such worries as biases in the AI systems, privacy risks, displacement of jobs, and worries with respect to accountability or abuse of AI technologies must be drastically reduced by taking necessary measures. To start addressing these challenges, we need to construct strong ethical frameworks, adapt regulations, invest in AI safety research, and change who's working on AI. It will only progress in becoming a responsible, transformative change with education, international cooperation on an equal footing and public awareness. This cannot be tackled alone; it has to be done together. Global forces including the UN and the EU (government agencies) have duty to lead the world by such reasonable laws that will help the world to know that we all should cooperate in the world affairs. Their discussion and action would also have to prioritize ethical practice, self-regulation, and fair and transparent initiatives. If we're trying to make AI systems that are robust and explainable, and aligned to human values, we are getting to it. However, all are required to take part in AI responsibly and have the knowledge of its benefits and worthy morals to adhere to.

The future of AI is everyone's responsibility, governments included. Finally, governments have to make the stage ready for sound AI policies and for collaborating globally so everyone benefits from the gains from AI. Ultimately, we need to make technology available to all communities to build out the experiences we want to build out. Organizations and industries won't stay open if they are unwilling to commit to fairness, transparency and diversity. Society must be talking about the AI impact for the sake of people and demanding more of as users and advocates. When they are together, that means AI is possible for good and advancement with dignity and respect for ethical principles.

References

[1] Ibrar M, Nahom H, Mohammed A, *et al.* An explainable AI-based demand response optimization framework for smart buildings. In: *International Symposium on Distributed Computing and Artificial Intelligence*. Berlin: Springer; 2024. pp. 88–98.

[2] Illia L, Colleoni E, and Zyglidopoulos S. Ethical implications of text generation in the age of artificial intelligence. *Business Ethics, the Environment & Responsibility*. 2023;32(1):201–210.

[3] Huang C, Zhang Z, Mao B, *et al.* An overview of artificial intelligence ethics. *IEEE Transactions on Artificial Intelligence*. 2022;4(4):799–819.

[4] Ganjavi C, Eppler MB, Pekcan A, *et al.* Publishers' and journals' instructions to authors on use of generative artificial intelligence in academic and scientific publishing: Bibliometric analysis. *The BMJ*. 2024;384.

[5] Hagos DH, Battle R, and Rawat DB. Recent advances in generative AI and large language models: Current status, challenges, and perspectives. *IEEE Transactions on Artificial Intelligence*. 2024;5:5873–5893.

[6] Akbar A, Ibrar M, Jan MA, *et al.* SDN-enabled adaptive and reliable communication in IoT-fog environment using machine learning and multiobjective optimization. *IEEE Internet of Things Journal*. 2020;8(5):3057–3065.

[7] Djalilova Z. Application of artificial intelligence technologies in history education. *Prospects for Innovative Technologies in Science and Education*. 2024;1(2):5–11.

[8] Ibrar M, Wang L, Shah N, *et al.* Reliability-aware flow distribution algorithm in SDN-enabled fog computing for smart cities. *IEEE Transactions on Vehicular Technology*. 2022;72(1):573–588.

[9] Turyasingura B, Ayiga N, Byamukama W, *et al.* Application of artificial intelligence (AI) in environment and societal trends: Challenges and opportunities. *Babylonian Journal of Machine Learning*. 2024;2024:177–182.

[10] Kasula BY. AI applications in healthcare a comprehensive review of advancements and challenges. *International Journal of Management Education for Sustainable Development*. 2023;6(6).

[11] Fontes C, Hohma E, Corrigan CC, *et al.* AI-powered public surveillance systems: Why we (might) need them and how we want them. *Technology in Society*. 2022;71:102137.

[12] Reamer FG. Artificial intelligence in social work: Emerging ethical issues. *International Journal of Social Work Values and Ethics*. 2023;20(2):52–71.

[13] Floridi L. *The Ethics of Artificial Intelligence: Principles, Challenges, and Opportunities*. New York: Oxford University Press; 2023.

[14] Osasona F, Amoo OO, Atadoga A, *et al.* Reviewing the ethical implications of AI in decision making processes. *International Journal of Management & Entrepreneurship Research*. 2024;6(2):322–335.

[15] Akpan IJ, Kobara YM, Owolabi J, *et al.* Conversational and generative artificial intelligence and human–chatbot interaction in education and research. *International Transactions in Operational Research*. 2025;32(3):1251–1281.

[16] Shere L, Hill AK, Mays TJ, *et al.* The next generation of low tritium hydrogen isotope separation technologies for future fusion power plants. *International Journal of Hydrogen Energy*. 2024;55:319–338.

[17] Ahmad U, Han M, Jolfaei A, *et al.* A comprehensive survey and tutorial on smart vehicles: Emerging technologies, security issues, and solutions using machine learning. *IEEE Transactions on Intelligent Transportation Systems*. 2024;25(11):15314–15341.

[18] Ahmed A, Iqbal MM, Jabbar S, *et al.* Position-based emergency message dissemination schemes in the internet of vehicles: A review. *IEEE Transactions on Intelligent Transportation Systems*. 2023;24(12):13548–13572.

[19] Ibrar M, Wang L, Akbar A, *et al.* Adaptive capacity task offloading in multi-hop D2D-based social industrial IoT. *IEEE Transactions on Network Science and Engineering*. 2022;10(5):2843–2852.

[20] Ibrar M, Wang L, Akbar A, *et al.* 3-D-SIS: A 3-D-social identifier structure for collaborative edge computing based social IoT. *IEEE Transactions on Computational Social Systems*. 2021;9(1):313–323.

[21] Lu Q, Zhu L, Xu X, *et al.* Responsible AI pattern catalogue: A collection of best practices for AI governance and engineering. *ACM Computing Surveys*. 2024;56(7):1–35.

[22] Farahani M, and Ghasemi G. Artificial intelligence and inequality: Challenges and opportunities. *International Journal of Innovation in Education*. 2024;9:78–99.

[23] Gursoy D, and Cai R. Artificial intelligence: An overview of research trends and future directions. *International Journal of Contemporary Hospitality Management*. 2025;37(1):1–17.

Chapter 15

The ethics of artificial intelligence: issues and prospects for future generations

Zia-ur-Rehman Bathla[1], *Mohd Khalid Awang*[1] *and Muhammad Farhan*[2]

Abstract

Artificial intelligence (AI) is seeing significant growth and has numerous uses in various sectors, such as medicine, industry, and intelligent cities. With the ongoing advancement of AI, future generations will encounter a wide range of social and moral issues that require careful analysis. This book chapter examines the AI ethic, scientific, and historical background, major AI ethical problems and their reasons, fundamental reasons for ethical problems in AI, primary ethical problem handling techniques in AI, and possible solutions to AI ethical concerns. The rapid advancement of AI technology is driven by the need to protect individuals' fundamental interests and foster the community's sustainable progress. We must enhance global collaboration, implement robust laws and regulations, and support adopting ethical standards for AI and other alternatives.

15.1 Artificial intelligence

Artificial intelligence (AI) is the advancement of computing devices capable of doing activities that usually need intelligence from humans. These activities consist of a range of cognitive processes such as learning, logically solving problems, understanding, and comprehension of natural language. The primary objective of AI systems is to emulate or reproduce the cognitive capabilities of humans, hence empowering computers to do activities independently with little assistance from humans [1]. To generate benefits through data, it is essential to transform the information into practical knowledge to develop "wisdom" and predict boosts. Robust algorithmic systems are needed for this procedure. Machine learning (ML)

[1]Fakulti Informatik dan Komputeran (FIK), Universiti Sultan Zainal Abidin (UniSZA), Kampus Besut, Malaysia
[2]Department of Computer Science, COMSATS University Islamabad, Sahiwal Campus, Pakistan

techniques not only detect patterns but also additionally discover them on their own. Chris Anderson has proposed the end of theory, which argues that the information flood renders the scientific approach outdated. ML can transform it into good-quality information and draw reliable assessments if there is sufficient information. This notion has become the fundamental principle of Big Data research despite needing a solid basis [2]. Will global ML systems autonomously uncover the rules governing nature while analyzing vast amounts of scientific physics records despite relying on human skill and cognitive ability?

Despite these challenges, deep learning (DL) methods are seeing impressive results in ordinary tasks that do not need comprehension of underlying reasoning or causative interrelationships. Such algorithms may acquire any pattern or input and output relationship with sufficient duration and data. They excel in recognizing patterns in applications like listening, reading, observing, and categorizing [3]. Scientists predict that 50% of employment in the service and industrial industries will drop in the following 10–15 years. Furthermore, skills comparable to the human mind will be achieve in 5–10 years [4]. Soon, humans will require "intellectual assistants" to stay comparable to smart machines. These electronic instruments, such as Google Now, are becoming more powerful rapidly. They could eventually evolve into virtual coworkers, digital instructors, and even our superiors. In fact, robots performing as leaders have already been assessed. The Cyborgs or scientifically enhanced individuals are already available, with Neil Harbison being among the most renowned examples. Meanwhile, there has been a significant advancement in the development of machines that mimic human behavior and appearance [5].

15.1.1 AI Ethics

The use and investigation of AI systems have seen an upswing. Researchers, experts, corporations, and other individuals use AI algorithms for various purposes, such as producing predictions, generating automatic decisions, or providing decision-making assistance [6]. Enhanced AI techniques are used in several domains and typically require support or oversight from human operators [7,8]. In recent years, there has been notable media attention on the ethical aspects of AI. This attention has assisted in this field of study. However, it additionally possesses the potential to undermine it. The mass media frequently presents the problems as concerns that will arise with future technological advances, as if we already know the best ethical approaches and methods to execute them. The primary emphasis of media attention is in the areas of risk, security, and the anticipation of influence, such as its effects on job opportunities [9]. The outcome entails examining technical issues that center on strategies for attaining an expected result. An additional outcome can be observed in the ongoing debate in legislation as well as industry on image and public affairs, where the term "ethical" is essentially synonymous with the new term "green," potentially employed for "ethics cleaning." For an issue to be considered an obstacle in the context of AI ethics, it must be one where we need immediate knowledge of the correct course of action. In this context, the ethical implications of losing a job, robbery, or AI-induced death are not inherently problematic. However, their permissibility within particular circumstances becomes a significant concern. AI, being more personal than previous technology, has led to the topic of "the sciences of AI." Possible reason: AI aims to develop computers with human-like emotions, thoughts, and intelligence. AI agents primarily perform sensing, simulation, organizing, and actions, with uses in thinking, analysis of text, natural language processing, logical thinking, playing games, decision-making, data analysis, and analytics for prediction, self-driving vehicles, and robots. AI can accomplish its goals using many computing methods, such as symbolic manipulation, natural thinking, or ML via network learning. AI have both positive and negative impacts like, the positive effects include the empowerment of humans, advances in technology for the betterment of human welfare, the realization of individual and collective self-actualization, and the promotion of social harmony. The adverse effects of AI algorithms include inappropriate utilization, insufficient usage or improper application, which may lead to anxiety, ignorance, misguided worries, and exaggerated social responses [10]. Ethical AI assures society advantages and prevents these technologies' improper or incorrect application [11]. Integrating ethical principles and regulations into AI technologies enhances the fairness and accountability of AI [12,13].

15.1.2 Scientific and historical background

In the past, it is noteworthy that the word "AI" employed from about 1950 to 1975, but it lost credibility during the so-called "AI winter" from 1975 to 1995 and became more limited in scope. Consequently, fields as ML, natural language processing, and data science were typically not explicitly designated as AI. Since around the year 2010, there has been a resurgence in applying the term "AI," including a wide range of computing and technologically advanced fields. Today, it is a renowned brand, a thriving sector with substantial capital invested and on the verge of reviving excitement. The advantages of ethical AI may be delineated via the utilization, adoption, and acknowledgment of novel prospects inside a given community [11,14]. A community's adoption and use of AI algorithms are essential conditions [13]. In [15], the authors examine the possibility of a decline in autonomy control and [16] examine the confrontation between ethics and AI. The dispute at hand encompasses the domains of big data, AI independence, and the safeguarding of individual rights and autonomies. Many researchers have written about the ethical principles of AI technologies. Notable examples include the works of [17–22] research.

The ethical discussion around AI is dynamic and complex. A number of researchers have identified ethical concerns about the architecture, use, and implementation of AI structures, as well as their implications for both the corporate sector as well as society [23,24]. Some scholars debate the appropriate ethical status for machines and explore strategies for addressing the "legitimacy gap," which arises as there is no identifiable entity accountable for the activities carried out by a AI algorithm [25,26]. Some studies address the difficulties presented by the relationship between humans and machines [27,28], keeping track of privacy

[29,30] or the influence on specific domains, such as commercial operations tactics. In [31], the authors provide an example of the latter, with their research focused on data extraction and automatic projected methodologies. The increasing use of AI and revolutionary tools in society and business has led to the development of this expanding body of literary works. Although these developments and their advancements provide several advantages, they inevitably reveal the issues and doubts that may arise [32,33].

Several organizations are now engaged in proactive efforts to tackle the difficulties that are the focus of AI. Several corporations have expressed their stance and viewpoints about the potential for mitigating unexpected adverse outcomes arising from AI tools and technologies. These businesses consist of prominent technology firms such as Google [34], IBM [35], and Microsoft [36]. The European Union has undertaken research initiatives and released publications emphasizing the significance of formulating laws to tackle ethical issues arising from autonomous technology and AI. In addition, many prominent industry agencies, regulatory bodies, and academic institutions actively resolve the problem [37]. These studies offer examples to illustrate the necessity for more outstanding studies in this study area. They may provide advice for technical advancements and applications that reduce undesirable outcomes. Nevertheless, universal criteria and principles have yet to be established today.

The Institute of Electrical and Electronics Engineers (IEEE) has launched an accreditation program for ethical methods relating to automated and intelligent technologies. The program aims to prioritize transparency and accountability and minimize bias caused by algorithms. Some instances of "AI for good" concepts and requests for activity include the Montreal declaration for responsible AI development [38,39]. The High-Level Technical Committee on AI of the European Union has formulated a set of ethical guidelines that were publicly released in 2018. The previously mentioned version has been disseminated for feedback, and the ethical principles governing reliable AI were officially released in 2019 [40]. Academic research increasingly highlights the significance of credibility, transparency, and integrity in the field of information-driven and algorithm-driven platforms and the possible ramifications of applicable AI. A nascent discipline is growing that centers on Fairness, Accountability, and Transparency, sometimes referred to as FAT. The FAT framework emphasizes the application of computational methods in many contexts where extensive quantities of data, sometimes called Big Data, are applied to perform tasks such as screening, classifying, rating, recommending, personalizing, and shaping user experiences and associations.

While these systems provide advantages, they also carry inherent risks, including the encoding and strengthening of societal biases, less accountability, and intensified information imbalance between data producers and data owners [39].

15.2 Major AI ethical concerns

Currently, the legislation framework is imperfect and lacks a proper supervisory system. The advancement of AI inherently involves possible risks, including

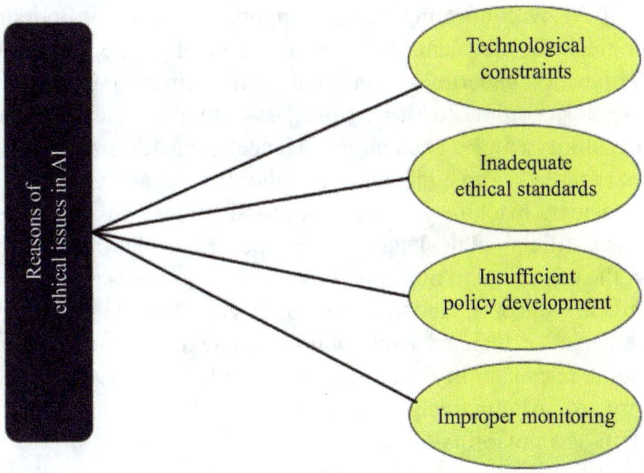

Figure 15.1 Reasons for ethical problems in AI technology

compromising individual privacy, exacerbating socioeconomic disparities, and escalating atmosphere pollution. The ethical concerns regarding human utilization of robots and AI systems, which can vary in their level of autonomy, are examined. This involves looking at the specific challenges from certain applications of these technologies, which might only exist in some scenarios. It is important to remember that innovations continually facilitate specific usage and make them more prevalent while limiting others. The ethical significance associated with technological objects' design extends beyond simple "responsible application" to encompass the concept of "responsible designing" in this domain. The emphasis on utilization does not assume the optimal ethical frameworks for addressing these concerns; it is possible that moral ethics, as opposed to deterministic or value-oriented methods, will be more suitable.

The following are the key ethical problems of AI shown in Figure 15.1.

- Moral AI ethics
- Ethics of human
- Environmental AI ethics
- Opacity
- Accountability ethics
- Bias ethics
- Malicious and exploitation usage
- Security and privacy
- Distinctiveness
- Machine ethics

15.2.1 Moral AI ethics

The maintenance of societal stability is based upon the limitations defined by the moral framework. Winfield and Jirotka [41] provide a paradigm for the ethical management of AI by connecting many components, including morality, legislation, technological advancement, and the involvement of the public. Meanwhile, our moral framework undergoes continuous transformation in conjunction with societal progress. According to Bryson [42], assessing whether AI should possess morals and capability can be challenging. Hence, evaluating AI's position within society can be regarded as an ethical matter rather than an analytical moral concern. If someone considers machine ethics about moral agents, it is possible to refer to such agents as artificial ethical agents who possess rights and responsibilities. Nevertheless, the examination of artificial creatures represents an issue with several traditional ethical concepts, and it could be highly beneficial to analyze these concepts in a detached manner, excluding the context of human beings. Will the machines assume responsibility, liability, or accountability for what they do if they take a step forward? Alternatively, should the order of threat distribution supersede deliberations on accountability?

A number of researchers employ the term artificial moral agent less strictly, drawing inspiration from the concept of "agent" in software development, where issues of accountability and responsibilities do not appear. According to researcher, four distinct categories of machine agents exist. These include ethical affect agents, such as machine jockeys; inherent moral agents, such as secure autopilot; explicit moral agents, which involve the use of formal approaches for calculating utility; as well as entirely ethical agents, which can generate explicit ethical judgments and usually able in providing reasonable justifications for them. The typical adult person can be considered a fully ethical agent. Various approaches are currently suggested to attain ethical agents that are either explicit or comprehensive. These approaches include coding the agents with functional ethics, refining the ethics directly through operational ethics, and ultimately achieving full-blown ethics with complete intelligence and awareness [43].

The conventional allocation of duty has already taken place wherein the vehicle's manufacturer assumes responsibility for ensuring the mechanical stability of the vehicle, the person who drives assumes duty for operating the vehicle, and the technician assumes responsibility for doing regular servicing. The public officials assume the duty of maintaining the technical requirements of highways, among other duties. The consequences of actions or decisions influenced by AI typically arise from many collaborations among various stakeholders, including developers, designers, consumers, software, and equipment. Spread responsibility is an effect of spreading authority. The occurrence of this division is not an issue exclusive to AI [44]. Many researchers have expressed the need for a thorough examination of the allocation of rights to existing machines. This stance predominantly depends on the critique of critics and empirical proof that machines and other objects missing human characteristics are occasionally accorded rights. In this scenario, a concept known as the "relational turn" was initially suggested. According to study, if we approach machines as if they possess rights, it may be prudent to refrain from investigating the actual existence of these rights. This inquiry pertains to the extent to which anti-realism or quasi-realism may be employed and the implications of asserting that "machines possess rights" within a human-centered framework [45,46].

15.2.2 Ethics of human

AI technology is regarded as one of the most sophisticated and technologically advanced innovations. Nevertheless, due to the disparate progress of nations and areas, individuals face inequitable chances to obtain and utilize AI. This will inevitably contribute to economic and social disparities in the coming years, exacerbating the wealth disparity and reinforcing social segregation. Human rights ethics significantly emphasize the principles of justice, liberty, and comprehensive human growth. Conversely, unfair advancement of AI technological advances constitutes a severe breach of the principles of human rights ethics.

15.2.3 Environmental AI ethics

AI research predominantly depends on tangible storage with outstanding processing capabilities, efficient logic computational methods, and extensive analysis of data capabilities. AI systems need computers that consume significant amounts of energy. In modern times, the expanding application of AI technological advances across diverse community domains requires a corresponding rise in equipment and power usage for its advancement. Consequently, society is confronted with increasing environmental and ethical concerns, which have a negative effect on the natural environment.

15.2.4 Opacity

The concepts of opacity hold significant importance within the field, commonly called “data ethics.” Data or Information ethics encompasses the ethical obligations associated with creating, distributing, administering, and using data. Currently, big data serves as the primary instrument for the advancement of AI, so inevitably exposing sensitive information to a chance of leakage. The protection of individual privacy is currently under significant threat. In the year 2018, a sequence of occurrences exemplified through the revelation of data from Facebook served to validate the concerns held by users. In the age of massive amounts of information, any entity that relies on information has the potential to become a data monarchy. The usage of big data is prominently observed in the domains of atmosphere, finance, and medical care. Nevertheless, it needs to be more logical for an educational sector to employ standardization of data examinations to evaluate student achievement, instructor performance, and institutional quality of teaching within the context of education. Automatic AI systems for decision-making and predictive analytics systems are utilized to analyze information and generate resulting choices as output. The degree of output can vary from minor to extremely important. Examples of outcomes include statements such as “this restaurant aligns with your tastes,” “the individual depicted in this X-ray imaging has achieved full bones development,” “the request for the credit card has been rejected,” “a donating organ itself will be allocated to a different patient,” “bail has been refused,” or “a concentrate on target was determined and engaged.” Analysis of data is frequently employed in the area of “predictive data analysis” in various industries such as healthcare and business. Its purpose is to anticipate upcoming advances. Since AI simplifies prediction, it is expected to become a more cost-effective resource [47]. AI platforms designed for automatic assistance in decisions are embedded within an administrative hierarchy, making it difficult for the affected individual to understand the reasoning behind the system's output. In other words, the algorithm is considered "opaque" to the concerned individual. If the method incorporates ML, it will usually be unintelligible despite to the professional, who will need to be made aware of the process or nature of identifying a particular pattern. The presence of transparency causes bias in decision structures and information sets. When there is a need to eliminate bias, the examination of transparency and bias are closely interconnected, and the political response must address both concerns simultaneously. Numerous AI uses heavily depend on ML methodologies within simulating neural systems. These networks can effectively detect correlations from a given dataset without or with the provision of "right" results. These approaches can be categorized as unsupervised, supervised or semi supervised. These strategies enable the algorithm to identify characteristics in the information and classify them in a manner that benefits the decision-making process. However, the developer needs to be aware of specific trends from the framework's data. Indeed, the programs are undergoing evolution, resulting in the modification of features employed via the learning mechanism when the latest information is received or input is provided. This implies that the result is not easily comprehensible to consumers and developers, as it needs more transparency.

Henry Kissinger, a prominent politician, highlighted an essential problem in making democratic decisions when we depend on an apparatus that is purportedly better for human beings and cannot yet provide explanations for its conclusions. In [48], Kissinger suggests that we have created an innovation that might eventually become the dominant force, but we are still looking for a leading principle. In another study, O'Neil [49] examines this topic's social and political dimension in her popular publication titled "Weapons of Math Destruction."

15.2.5 Accountability ethics

The topic of accountability problems related to the restrictions and unintentional effects of AI usage in self-driving systems is currently a subject of heated discussion in the press. A significant amount of research has started to explore ideas like algorithmic accountability and accountable AI. Caplan *et al.*'s study in data and society [50] discusses algorithmic accountability, which assigns condemn for harm caused by discriminating or incorrect judgments. It also applies to system generation accountability and its repercussions on society. If problems occur, responsible technologies should provide a compensation method [51]. Legal scholars like Hildebrand have brought up the concept of the "autonomy of objects." This refers to the notion that AI enables a higher level of continuous self-learning independence and the connection between autonomy and equality. Furthermore, according to Larsson, a socio-legal investigator, challenges undoubtedly arise concerning the autonomy of objects or the agency of software algorithms when they can analyze and acquire knowledge from extensive quantities of data, particularly in automatic decision-making procedures [52]. The ethical concern regarding accountability pertains to the intention, methods, and outcomes of thoroughly examining the conduct of the accountable individual. This study provides a comprehensive examination and investigation of ethical issues related to the relationship between liability, the assignation of responsibility, and the principles regarding accountability in modern the community [53]. The advent of AI has significantly influenced current legal frameworks, regulatory systems, and societal norms. A collision happened in an autonomous vehicle. Whoever has responsibility for the accident: the corporation liable for the creation of the product, the product holder, or the AI product? AI predominantly depends on techniques for its functioning. In contrast to conventional products, it possesses specific capacity for decision-making. Hence, the issue of responsibility arising from AI poses an important challenge to the current legal framework in the context of autonomous vehicles.

Autonomous automobiles have the potential to diminish the extensive harm caused by human drivers significantly. Each year, approximately one million lives are lost, countless others are injured, and the atmosphere suffers from pollution. Additionally, urban areas are burdened with parking lots, and roadways cover our land. The impact is far-reaching and detrimental. However, there are lingering uncertainties surrounding the behavior of self-driving cars and the allocation of liability and threats within their complex operating framework. Within this scenario, there is a certain level of discourse surrounding the concept of "trolley issues." Many challenges emerge within the renowned "trolley concerns." Imagine a scenario where a subway train is barreling down a line with its destination set to a group of five passengers. The outcome seems grim, as their lives are uncertain. However, there is a glimmer of hope—an alternate course that could save them. However, here is the catch: diverting the train on that path would mean sacrificing the life of a single individual who is also standing there. It is an ethical choice that forces us to question the value of one life versus the lives of many. Trolley issues are not meant to depict real ethical issues or be resolved by identifying a "correct" option. Instead, these scenarios are like carefully crafted chapters in a book, where the characters have limited choices and possess all the necessary information to make their decisions [54].

15.2.6 Bias ethics

Bias commonly arises when individuals form unjust judgments due to the effect of a feature unrelated to the subject matter, often stemming from a prejudiced assumption regarding those who belong to a specific community. A particular kind of bias refers to a cognition characteristic acquired by an individual, which is frequently not overtly acknowledged. The individual in question could have no awareness of their bias, and they can even genuinely and openly reject a bias that has been identified [55]. In addition to the societal effects of learned bias, the human brain structure is commonly susceptible to a range of mental biases, such as the bias toward confirmation. This bias refers to the tendency of individuals to perceive facts in a manner that aligns with their pre-existing beliefs. It is commonly believed that this particular type of bias limits success in logical judgment. However, it is worth noting that certain behavioral biases can provide an evolutionary benefit, such as the efficient utilization of tools for perceptive judgment. There is a debate on the possibility or need for AI algorithms possessing biases in cognition [56].

Another bias occurs when the information contains systematic flaws, such as "statistical bias." A dataset can only be impartial for a particular topic, creating one risk bias when utilized for an entirely separate problem. ML using this kind of information may not just fail to identify bias but may also encode and systematize it: "historical bias." In the year 2017, Amazon suspended a digital recruiting filtering method that discriminated against women, likely due to the business's record of discrimination in recruitment. The issue with such structures is bias and the need for more individual confidence. This study examines the political context of computerized systems in the United States of America. The application of predictions in "predictive enforcement" may compromise civil rights by removing control from those whose behavior can be predicted [57]. Research on detecting and eliminating bias in AI machines is still in its earliest stages [58]. Technological solutions have limitations, as they require a mathematical concept of equality that is challenging to obtain [59].

AI is predicated upon using accurate data and logical methods at its core, yet it inadvertently generates outcomes that exhibit biases. There are three possible causes of bias: firstly, the active actions of the information collector or the design technique; secondly, the inherent bias in the initial information, which therefore affects the findings of the related data-driven method; and thirdly, the deliberate layout of the method itself. Techniques have the potential to yield outcomes that are influenced by bias. The systematic pattern of bias exhibited by AI contrasts individual prejudice. The pervasive bias of AI will have far-reaching consequences, leading to unfairness and bias that will undermine the equality and equity of the community and the legal system. Enhancing the legal supervision of systems and reducing the disparity in algorithmic outcomes presents an essential challenge in the age of AI. Several research organizations have conducted studies and identified automatic ad-distribution techniques that exhibit biases based on gender, predisposing financially secure job advertisements to males rather than females [60]. Additional research indicates that widely used image databases exhibit a gender bias, consistently depicting females engaged in domestic tasks while males are involved in hunting-related activities. Consequently, this has led to the development of a self-learning program that not just repeats gender bias, but additionally magnifies it [61]. A systematic bias can occur due to the data utilized for training algorithms and the value-oriented choices of system designers and consumers. As an example, the AI Today paper examines the "legacy of prejudice." It asserts that AI lacks impartiality or fairness. "Innovations are influenced by the environment where they are developed and can bring about transformation" [62]. Our awareness of and encounters with our environment are derived from previous incidents, ideas, and anticipation of upcoming objectives. The study of cognition is a wide-ranging field that has recently started investigating how human thinking influences our relationships with and our understanding of outcomes generated by AI and self-learning computers [63].

15.2.7 Malicious and exploitation usage

Numerous scholars contend that a certain degree of obligation for the misuse and malevolent application of AI could be attributed to the developers and designers of AI systems [9]. The topic of autonomous arms and the Lethal Automatic Armaments Pledge, proposed by can be referenced [64]. Meanwhile, Bastos and Mercea [65] have suggested a dangerous situation that is less severe and does not always or directly relate to militarization. In particular, sophisticated manifestations of online attacks, like automated attacks or the remote manipulation of online and self-driven automobiles to target individuals, like deliberately directing the automobile toward densely populated areas. This encompasses socio-political and divisive actions that utilize botnets to manipulate voting or foster conflict on different issues, as shown by the recent "anti-vax" debates in the USA. Researcher's team, which is dedicated to studying the harmful applications of AI, advocates for AI developers to foster a more robust system of accountability about the utilization of their technologies. This underscores the importance of knowledge, ethical norms, and accepted standards [66]. An additional issue that requires attention is the potential for autonomous learning systems to reveal innate sociological prejudice and bias and the possibility for the software's architecture to evolve into acceptable. The issue at hand pertains to transparency, encompassing either the utilization of technologies or the underlying ideals that autonomous architecture embodies and perpetuates. This matter has been examined in connection with digital channels, specifically internet search engines and social networking sites, that have the potential not just to reproduce racial and ethnic biases and inequalities but also reinforce these systems [67].

15.2.8 Security and privacy

Privacy and security in computer science have been the subject of extensive scholarly debate [68]. This debate mainly revolves around the issue of accessing personal data and obtaining personally identifiable information. Privacy encompasses various widely acknowledged dimensions, such as the entitlement to being alone, the protection of private data, the concept of security as an integral component of individual identity, the authority to manage one's private data, and the entitlement to maintain confidentiality. Previously, privacy research has primarily concentrated on state surveillance done by secret agencies. However, contemporary research has expanded to encompass monitoring carried out by other state entities, enterprises, and even individuals. In recent years, there has been a notable transformation in science and technology, along with an almost slow response from regulatory bodies, although with the implementation of the General Data Protection Regulation in 2016 as well. Consequently, a state of chaos has emerged, wherein several influential entities use this situation overtly or covertly [69]. The scope of the digital age has significantly expanded: The entirety of information gathering and retention has transitioned into digital formats. Each of us progressively relies on electronic means, with most digital information being linked to a singular online network. Additionally, there is a growing utilization of electronic sensors, which produce data about non-digital elements of our lives. AI enhances the potential for intelligent gathering of information and data analytics. This pertains to the comprehensive monitoring of whole populations and the traditional focused monitoring. Furthermore, a significant portion of the information is exchanged among actors, typically for monetary compensation. Simultaneously, regulating data collection and accessibility becomes significantly more challenging in the digital realm compared to the analog domain, such as paper and phones. Collecting, selling, and utilizing data is filled with privacy.

Secure privacy methods that effectively cover up the identities of people or organizations have become a fundamental aspect of data science. These approaches encompass various methods like relative anonymization, control of access (including encryption), and additional algorithms that perform computations using wholly or partially secured input information. Differential confidentiality is achieved by incorporating checked distortion in encrypting the results of inquiries [70]. Although it demands additional exertion and expenses, these strategies can circumvent numerous privacy-related issues. Certain firms have also recognized improved security as a strategic benefit that could be exploited and exploited. A significant challenge lies in effectively implementing control, both on the state and personal levels, for those with a legitimate right. It is necessary to ascertain the accountable legal body, substantiate the activity, establish purpose, and locate a court that affirms its jurisdiction. Moreover, it ultimately secures the legal implementation of its ruling. The absence or difficulty in enforcing established legal protections for rights, including rights of consumers, liability for products, civil liability, and rights in intellectual property, is frequently observed with electronic items. Consequently, organizations with a solid digital foundation are accustomed to conducting customer evaluations of their products despite any concerns about legal responsibility while vigorously protecting their intellectual property ownership.

15.2.9 Distinctiveness

Some believe that current AI goals are to achieve what is known as artificial general intelligence. This concept differs from conventional AI and is considered a more general goal mechanism. It is also distinct from Searle's idea of "strong AI," which suggests that machines can understand and possess mental abilities if provided with the appropriate programs [71]. The concept of singularity posits that if the progression of AI regarding artificial general intelligence hits a point where machines possess a degree of intelligence comparable to that of humans, then these machines will have the capability to develop AI platforms that exceed the intelligence of humans, thereby becoming super intelligent. These clever AI machines will rapidly enhance themselves or create extra advanced systems [72]. The abrupt shift in circumstances following the attainment of super intelligent AI is referred to as the "singularity," which marks the point at which the advancement of AI becomes beyond human influence and is difficult to forecast. In [73], Bostrom comprehensively analyzes the potential outcomes and associated hazards for humanity at that particular point.

The apprehension regarding the potential global dominance of human-created machines has already captured the imagination of humans prior to the invention of machines. The concept was initially proposed by Irvin Good, who distinguished an ultra-intelligent computer as a system capable of surpassing the cognitive abilities of any human being, regardless of their level of intelligence. Given that robotic building is a cognitive effort, it is conceivable that a genius computer could produce robots that are even more advanced. Consequently, there would undoubtedly be an enormous increase in cognitive ability, surpassing the intellectual capacity of humans [74]. The singularity concept has faced questions from multiple perspectives. Bostrom and Kurzweil assume that intellect is a unidimensional characteristic and that the collection of intelligent individuals is systematically organized scientifically. However, it is worth noting that neither Boston nor Kurzweil extensively addresses being intelligent in their works. Overall, it might be argued that regardless of specific efforts, the basic concepts stated in the compelling argument surrounding superintelligence and uniqueness have yet to be investigated thoroughly. From the perspective of philosophy, an intriguing inquiry arises on the potential alignment of distinctiveness with the current trend of research into AI [75]. This conversation prompts an investigation as to whether or not the apprehension regarding singularity is only a narrative regarding imaginary AI rooted in human anxieties. However, regardless of whether an individual finds adverse arguments convincing and distinctiveness unlikely, there is a high chance that they could be mistaken. Therefore, examining the preeminent threat of distinctiveness seems justified, even if someone believes that the likelihood of such a singularity ever happening is extremely limited. Therefore, the initial knowledgeable computer represents the final innovation that humanity must ever create, as long as the system is sufficiently submissive to instruct us about how to maintain power over it.

The control issue refers to the challenge of humans maintaining control over an AI machine when it reaches a state of super intelligence [73]. In a broader context, the issue at hand pertains to how we can ensure that AI will yield beneficial outcomes, as seen by human beings. This concept is occasionally referred to as "value aligning." The difficulty in managing superintelligence depends on the velocity with which a super intelligent framework is initiated. A specific aspect of this issue pertains to the possibility that individuals may initially perceive a particular trait as desired, only to realize that it entails unanticipated repercussions that are sufficiently adverse to render it undesirable. The issue above pertains to king Midas, who desires all his interactions to transform into gold [76].

15.2.10 Machine ethics

The concept of machine ethics refers to the ethical principles that apply to machines, explicitly focusing on the ethical behavior of computers as individuals instead of regarding computers as mere things used by humans. The extent to which this will encompass every aspect of AI ethics or only be a component is frequently ambiguous. Occasionally, there is a questionable idea that if devices behave in ethically significant manners, then humans want a system of ethics designed explicitly for computers. A significant concept in the ethics of machines is that robots can, to a certain extent, function as ethical entities accountable for their own acts, commonly referred to as "independent ethical entities." The existence of an integrated idea of machine ethics remains to be determined, as less robust interpretations risk diminishing the idea of ethics to concepts usually regarded as inadequate, such as lacking reflection or behavior. Conversely, more robust views that progress toward AI ethics could include artificial ethical agents, which are presently absent in a comprehensive framework [43,77].

15.3 AI ethics in real world

Addressing AI ethics in real-world situations requires a comprehensive strategy harmonizing technology progress with ethical deliberations, legal structures, and social consequences. This involves the establishment of accountability and openness within AI systems, reducing the impact of biases present in algorithms and data, ensuring the security of privacy and information, the advancement of equality and fairness when performing decision-making procedures, and the examination of the broader ethical concerns associated with the implementation of AI in different industries. Establishing comprehensive rules and regulations that focus on the well-being of people and their societies when responsibly using the potentially transformative effects of AI necessitates cultivating interdisciplinary cooperation among legislators, technology professionals, ethical scholars, and interested parties. There are different applications with AI with respect to ethics, as describe in climate change [78] state researchers are responsible for explicitly informing humanity of any terrible risk and providing honest and truthful information. With the endorsement of over eleven thousand professionals from various countries, we now assert with absolute clarity and certainty that Earth is currently dealing with a climate crisis. In this context, the changing climate is an "emergency," denoting a highly significant and pressing issue. The issue is of significant concern due to its potential negative consequences, including but not limited to extreme weather events, fires, droughts, floods, and an increase in ocean levels. The significance of this issue is increased by the fact that inevitable consequences are currently observable at a temperature increase of 1.1°C compared to the preindustrial era [79].

Research on computer technology and AI suggests that AI will significantly affect the environment. Still, these studies do not evaluate the emissions from systemic impacts, such as rebound impacts [80]. The Jevons paradox is a topic of interest among experts in economics. Jevons, a British philosopher from the 19th century, contended that enhancing the efficiency of fuel utilization would not necessarily result in reduced consumption but instead increased consumption [81]. Multiple research investigations have demonstrated the existence of different forms of rebounding effects that arise from enhanced energy utilization in different domains of society. These impacts include straight rebounds, indirect rebounds, economy-wide rebounding, and integrated rebounds [82]. Consider the case of enhancing the power effectiveness of automobiles. This phenomenon has the potential to result in a rise in automobile usage (direct), subsequently leading to a rise in the need for tires (indirect). Additionally, it could contribute to an escalation in energy use within eateries and hotels frequented while traveling (economy-wide). In addition, manufacturing lower-energy vehicles requires considering power inputs, often known as integrated rebounds, and assuming that AI enhances the power effectiveness of the autos in this scenario. The given notion suggests that using AI could result in various rebound impacts. In a broader sense, the utilization of AI to enhance energy savings could lead to a rise in the need for AI applications among different sectors of the community, thus resulting in a general spike in energy use within a population. The climatic concerns associated with this form of energy are readily apparent due to its reliance on petroleum and coal [81].

It is necessary to make a specific observation regarding AI's inherent limitations (rebounds). These rebounds encompass not just the manufacturing of equipment but also other vital tools for AI, such as personal computers, information servers, wires, and the batteries for electric automobiles. Additionally, they encompass the retrieval of materials like cobalt, lithium, and other materials. Furthermore, these resources are transported to industries for manufacturing parts and subsequently transported to other companies to fabrication of the result. Ultimately, the devices are conveyed to both AI engineers and consumers. According to Bruno and Crawford [83] study, the application of energy from fossil fuels in the manufacturing process results in emissions of greenhouse gases at every stage. Consequently, it is imperative to incorporate each one of these gases into the overall emissions associated with AI.

In education, the ethical issues and risk factors associated with AI machines conflict with advertising approaches that present methods as impartial and without value equipment. Algorithmic methods fundamentally reflect the principles and beliefs of their designers, which occupy levels of authority [84]. Whenever individuals develop computational methods, they concurrently generate a collection of information reflecting past and systemic prejudices prevalent in the community. These biases subsequently manifest as algorithmic biases. Despite the absence of an express aim, the algorithmic framework inherently incorporates bias, resulting in the emergence of diverse gender and racist biases across multiple AI-based systems [85]. The application of AI in primary and secondary schooling raises significant ethical problems, particularly about the safety of both children and instructors [86,87]. Privacy breaches primarily arise when individuals divulge much private data on digital networks. Despite current laws and regulations aimed at safeguarding confidential personal information, the infringements committed by AI-based technology businesses in terms of data accessibility and safety have heightened individuals' apprehensions regarding security [88].

In order to alleviate these issues, AI systems request consumers' approval to access their private information. While permission asks are intended to serve as preventive measures and address issues related to privacy, it is observed that a significant number of users provide permission despite knowing or taking into account the full scope of data, they are providing. This includes details like the language expressed, race, personal data, and position [87]. The act of providing without proper knowledge diminishes both individual autonomy and personal security. In essence, AI systems' reduction of introspective and autonomous cognition leads to a decrease in individuals' agency [89]. In the same way, academics have raised the ethical concern of compelling learners and parents to incorporate these computer programs into their educational pursuits, even if they openly consent to surrender their private data. If public educational institutions mandate these methods, they are left with no alternative [90,91]. A further ethical issue concerning the utilization of AI in primary and secondary schools revolves around monitoring or tracking systems that collect comprehensive data regarding the behaviors and attitudes of pupils and instructors. AI systems for tracking utilize techniques and models based on ML to track behaviors and predict upcoming preferences and behaviors of consumers [86]. Another study, curriculum titled "Safety, Equity, Security, and Ethics" of AI is being developed by the researcher specifically for university students. The goal of the curriculum is to equip learners with a thorough comprehension of the scientific and ethical concerns linked to the building and implementation of AI systems. The curriculum has been constructed with a multidisciplinary strategy, incorporating principles and methodologies derived from information technology, the study of philosophy, and the law. There are four distinct components within the curriculum [92].

In medicine and various specialties, ethical and moral challenges need challenging decisions. Systems based on AI are designed to improve medical decision-making. Thus, we request AI to improve moral and ethical decisions on complex issues [93]. In April 2019, the European Commission's High-Level Expert Group on AI released the Ethics Instructions for Reliable AI to promote a safe, ethical, and resilient AI. Trustworthy AI must be legal, moral, and strong from a technological and social point of view [94].

Based on the "Human Agency and Oversee" framework, AI must protect human autonomy and decisions. This is crucial in promoting an equitable and equal community by enhancing consumer agency, safeguarding fundamental rights, and ensuring continuous human review. In order to reduce dangers arising from the existence of other agents, whether human or synthetic, that can communicate with the network detrimentally, systems built on AI must prioritize "Scientific stability and security." It is imperative to sustain the physical and psychological well-being of individuals simultaneously. The notion of "Safety and data management" states that data administration must guarantee the accuracy and reliability of the data used its relevance, accessibility procedures, and the capability to manage data while respecting security. In order to facilitate accountability, clarity, and interaction, AI must guarantee "Openness" across all fundamental elements, including information, systems, and business structures. "Diversification, equality, and justice" are other principles that AI must uphold. AI must actively promote diversity and inclusion throughout its lifespan by facilitating stakeholder involvement, ensuring equal participation by inclusive design procedures, and ensuring fair treatment for all. The sustainability and environmental responsibility assessment needs to be conducted in alignment with the idea of societal and the atmosphere wellness alongside the sustainable development goals of the United Nations [95].

Finally, AI must follow the "Accountability" theory, which demands suitable processes for maintaining accountability and responsibility for AI and its impact before and after creation, installation, and usage. How these principles need to be implemented in actual surgical treatment is unknown, but they are a significant advance. By the European Union Ethics Principles for Reliable AI, they seek professional advice on the critical ethical challenges associated with healthcare and technologies related to AI.

In AI and robots, the panelists provided insights into their respective areas of interest within AI and automation and outlined potential avenues for further study. Lionel emphasized the issues of biases in AI and proposed that future work must concentrate on monitoring and assessing AI systems. Supra employed the socio-technical perspective to analyze the AI issue and completed his analysis by emphasizing the necessity for the field of information technology to make distinctive and differentiated achievements. In light of these deliberations, we advocate for matters about the impacts of AI and robots as significant obstacles and conduct additional research on this subject [96].

15.4 Basic reasons for ethical problems in AI

There are different sources of ethical issues AI is responsible for giving reasons for ethical issues. There are four primary factors, as depicted in Figure 15.1: technological constraints, inadequate ethical standards, insufficient policy development, and improper monitoring systems.

15.4.1 Technological constraints

The development of AI technology has significantly enhanced the comfort of human existence, yet it has its limitations regarding technology. Currently, AI is significant within the field of information computation, evaluation, and decision-making processes. However, its application in the area of expressing emotions faces considerable challenges. Due to its dependence on algorithms for learning and decision-making, integrating human values and ethical principles into AI presents a significant challenge. Replicating human emotions and mental patterns is challenging and can only depend on predetermined algorithmic reasoning to take action. The restricted parameter evolution learning technique was developed by Yao to learn Bayesian system parameters using limited information. This method can be applied to automated assignment decision-making. The initial step involves the application of qualitative area information to the procedure of learning Bayesian network variables to minimize the scope of the search for parameters. This study proposes two qualitative domains of expertise using professional belief. Subsequently, an improved method is incorporated into the method, preventing the traditional learning system from becoming stagnant in a particular region. The challenge involves encoding the Bayesian network parameters in a particular manner and exploring several evolutionary techniques [97].

15.4.2 Inadequate ethical standards

The ongoing advancement of AI has led to an increasing realization of the nature of human beings, resulting in a decreasing gap between humans and robots. It is imperative to consider strategies for managing the interaction between computers and humans and establish ethical guidelines and rules for AI. Researchers suggested some changes to the Turing test to enhance the realism and appropriateness of Turing's proposition for AI exploration—a comprehensive methodology to produce intelligent assessments that effectively tackle significant ethical and practical concerns. For a competent evaluation to effectively address an issue, the mechanism of concern must be accessible rather than solely focusing on the eventual answer. Ultimately, intelligent entities must have a built-in ability for development and adaptability to discover novel methods [98].

15.4.3 Insufficient policy development

AI primarily emphasizes the technological and financial aspects at the legislative stage. The ethical and societal concerns arising from AI have attracted little interest from philosophy and social studies researchers. Nevertheless, these debates failed to reach the field of public policy and were deficient in comprehensive analysis and analysis. Consequently, the absence of pertinent laws and regulations within the community has resulted in many ethical issues. Winfield and Jirotka [41] examine the ethical management of robots and AI technologies. A suggested pathway establishes a structure for the ethical management of AI and robotics by connecting ethics, norms, legislation, responsible innovation and research, and participation from the public. Ethical administration is paramount in fostering public confidence in robots and AI. This can be summarized by presenting five fundamental practical, ethical, and good governance principles.

15.4.4 Improper monitoring

Despite the rapid advances in science and engineering today, an effective evaluation system for AI technologies must be implemented. Thus, for instance, individuals' sources of information are becoming dependent on intelligent computers, leading to the reinforcement of bias through integration and network reliance, which eventually results in enhanced bias. It is essential to build a robust monitoring structure. Researchers comprehensively analyses the social and ethical consequences of business digitization on different stakeholders, including employees and nations. The concept of business automating was clearly explained, and a new structure was created to effectively integrate the theory of stakeholders and the idea of social contracts. Integrating many conceptual frameworks, the model effectively recognizes the ethical problems associated with business automation. Additionally, it emphasizes implementing optimal practices, offers advice, and uncovers potential avenues for further study [99].

15.5 Ethical problem handling techniques in AI

There is a growing focus on the ethical considerations surrounding AI technology. Figure 15.2 shows four ways to deal with the problems of AI. These techniques are expected to effectively address the quick development of AI, protect the primary interests of individuals, and foster the sustainable progress of the community.

15.5.1 Enhance global collaboration

The fast advancement of AI technology has significant promise; however, numerous technological deficiencies and constraints persist. The primary factor is the lack of global efficient interaction and cooperation among AI methods. This results in significant differences in AI advancement across states, leading to a growing prominence of ethical concerns surrounding AI. Hence, every country across the globe must enhance their interactions and collaborations, thereby fostering the collective advancement of AI technological advances.

15.5.2 Developing effective policies for public

At the public's legislative level, regulations regarding the advancement and implementation of AI must prioritize the well-being of individuals, address their holistic growth, and encourage equitable and stable societal progress. Government agencies must establish dedicated funding to provide financial assistance to research institutions and universities in doing ethical studies on state-of-the-art technologies like AI. The governing bodies should also provide diverse individuals with a chance to acquire AI data and support information public policy deliberations over the subject within community. The primary focus of AI is to tackle significant social issues, such as alleviating inequality and poverty, facilitating the inclusion of marginalized groups in the community, and engaging in community development initiatives. Establishing an AI ethics panel composed of government agencies and business professionals is recommended to establish ethical standards for the advancement and utilization of AI. The group would be responsible for assessing AI products' ethical implications and credibility with substantial public consequences. In [100], Wasilow and Thorpe suggested the ethical evaluation approach for AI and robots. The purpose of this tool is to assist technical designers,

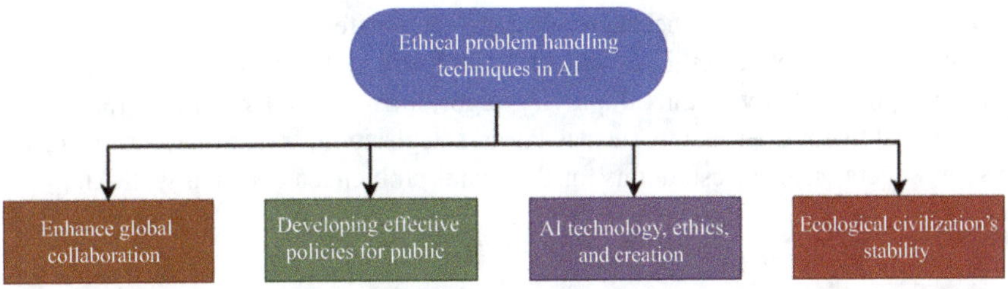

Figure 15.2 Ethical problem handling techniques

lawmakers, administrators, and other relevant parties in identifying and thoroughly examining possible military uses and ethical concerns that could emerge from the incorporation of growing AI and robots.

15.5.3 Artificial intelligence, technology, ethics, and creation

Universities, along with research organizations, engage in proactive technological and technical ethical studies at a social level, offering conceptual support for the development of appropriate standards and mechanisms. Collaboration among governments, businesses, academics, non-governmental organizations, and many stakeholders persists in encouraging AI advancement that is rooted in human capabilities. Integrating ethics into the corporate social obligation structure of AI companies is recommended. Additionally, investment firms should consider incorporating ethical considerations into the social, governance, and environmental systems to provide guidance to organizations in the responsible growth of AI products. Social groups can advance the development of ethical standards for AI by providing education, releasing papers on ethical evaluations, and summarizing exemplary situations. The White Paper of the Canadian Society of radiographers presents a detailed structure for examining the ethical and legal challenges associated with AI in healthcare imaging. The system encompasses various aspects, including patient information such as security, privacy, possession, and sharing, and methods including independence, responsibility, law, practice, optimal procedures, and the existing authorized system [100].

15.5.4 Ecological civilization's stability

The fast development of the economy, society, and civilization is obvious. The issue regarding resource deficiencies and pollution in the environment is increasingly escalating in severity. Hence, the advancement and exploration of AI must align with the principles of ecological societies, taking into account the ethics of the environment along with other issues of ethics. The integration of AI technology and environmental civilization yields significant advancements in the development of AI and the establishment of an ecological society.

15.6 Possible solutions of AI ethical concerns

There is a dire need for concentrated initiatives to offer consistent suggestions and regulations for AI-related ethical concerns. Automatic systems have taken on a crucial position in people's lives, thus improving algorithms' dependability. Therefore, it is more critical to consider factors such as fairness, legislation, and laws. Consequently, it presents several critical resolutions for the moral problems associated with AI.

15.6.1 Reducing of adverse impacts

During the use of the equipment, adverse effects can appear, particularly in cases where the programming appears to be accurate. For example, when a robot retrieves an article, it can accidentally knock into a valuable container while it is transported toward its destination. Irrespective of the robot's triumphant arrival at its destination, the damage to the container is an unacceptable adverse consequence of the robot's pursuit of its aim.

15.6.2 Recognition hacking

Recognition hacking refers to the process of optimizing the function of fitness to optimize the expected results, even if the intended goal is not achieved. For example, the primary objective of the cleaning robot is to sanitize the work environment. However, the robot's effectiveness is enhanced through the benefits that it receives for every single waste it sweeps. In that case, the robot can inadvertently increase its efficiency by creating additional things that it can clear. Robots can acquire the ability to replicate professional demonstrations, collaborate with individuals to align with their choices, or engage in incentive modeling, where a machine-learning algorithm is trained to function in line with individual priorities.

15.6.3 Secure exploration process

Secure exploration assesses the feasibility of investigating novel solutions while avoiding potentially harmful actions. It is imperative to note that the issue of secure exploration can be effectively addressed by clearly defining the goals. Throughout the training process, the agent who has received training can acquire knowledge about the workings of the target and develop the most efficient strategy to resolve the problem. As an illustration, the cleaning robot could experience a fitness penalty due to cracking a jar. In the training stage of the AI agent, it is essential to determine how to prevent the container from being broken despite the numerous actions and rewards involved.

15.6.4 Robustness

The challenge of ensuring durability to shifts in distribution lies in effectively managing the reality that arises when AI systems are deployed. They will often encounter situations that deviate from the exact one it was intended for. Accidents may occur throughout the process of engaging in new tasks. Accidents may occur within this framework when an agent's strategy leads to the execution of risky behaviors when confronted with novel circumstances. Although these exploration systems provide valuable insights into managing the distributional process, it is necessary to conduct additional benchmark studies to identify the risks associated with the certified distributional process and determine which techniques could effectively mitigate them.

15.7 Conclusion

Despite the potential restriction to the commercial development of AI solutions due to ethical concerns, numerous rules and possible remedies, exist to ensure AI systems' ethical application. This chapter has provided essential insights into the current advancements in AI ethics and emphasized the pertinent concerns. More precisely, it has been demonstrated that more research must be done, especially addressing the ethical aspects of creating AI systems. In this context, a number of essential measures for enhancing the quality of the information have been outlined. Subsequently, some significant resolutions to the ethical dilemmas posed by AI have been introduced, together with potential avenues for more investigation. The writing's insights are valuable for future investigation endeavors in this field.

References

[1] A. M. Turing, "Computing machinery and intelligence," *Mind*, vol. 59, no. 236, p. 433, 1950.

[2] C. Anderson, "The end of theory: The data deluge makes the scientific method obsolete," *Wired Magazine*, vol. 16, no. 7, pp. 16-07, 2008.

[3] J. Howard, "The wonderful and terrifying implications of computers that can learn," TEDx Brussels, 2014.

[4] T. Modis, "The singularity myth," *Technological Forecasting & Social Change*, vol. 73, no. 2, pp. 104–112, 2006.

[5] D. Helbing, *Societal, Economic, Ethical and Legal Challenges of the Digital Revolution: From Big Data to Deep Learning, Artificial Intelligence, and Manipulative Technologies*. Berlin: Springer, 2019.

[6] S. M. Carter, W. Rogers, K. T. Win, H. Frazer, B. Richards, and N. Houssami, "The ethical, legal and social implications of using artificial intelligence systems in breast cancer care," *The Breast*, vol. 49, pp. 25–32, 2020.

[7] O. I. Dolganova, "Improving customer experience with artificial intelligence by adhering to ethical principles," Бинес-инфоматика, vol. 15, no. 2 (Engl), pp. 34–46, 2021.

[8] S. Bankins and P. Formosa, "The ethical implications of artificial intelligence (AI) for meaningful work," *Journal of Business Ethics*, vol. 185, no. 4, pp. 725–740, 2023.

[9] M. Brundage, S. Avin, J. Clark, *et al.*, "The malicious use of artificial intelligence: Forecasting, prevention, and mitigation," *arXiv preprint arXiv:1802.07228*, 2018.

[10] L. Floridi and J. Cowls, "A unified framework of five principles for AI in society," *Machine Learning and the City: Applications in Architecture and Urban Design*, pp. 535–545, 2022.

[11] L. Floridi, (ed.). "Establishing the rules for building trustworthy AI," in *Ethics, Governance, and Policies in Artificial Intelligence*. Cham: Springer, pp. 41–45, 2021.

[12] J. Zhang, Y. Shu, and H. Yu, "Fairness in design: A framework for facilitating ethical artificial intelligence designs," *International Journal of Crowd Science*, vol. 7, no. 1, pp. 32–39, 2023.

[13] P. Paraman and S. Anamalah, "Ethical artificial intelligence framework for a good AI society: Principles, opportunities and perils," *AI & Society*, vol. 38, no. 2, pp. 595–611, 2023.

[14] H. Yu, Z. Shen, C. Miao, C. Leung, V. R. Lesser, and Q. Yang, "Building ethics into artificial intelligence," *arXiv preprint arXiv:1812.02953*, 2018.

[15] P. Mikalef, K. Conboy, J. E. Lundström, and A. Popovič, "Thinking responsibly about responsible AI and 'the dark side' of AI," *European Journal of Information Systems*, vol. 31, pp. 257–268, 2022.

[16] M. Mirbabaie, A. B. Brendel, and L. Hofeditz, "Ethics and AI in information systems research," *Communications of the Association for Information Systems*, vol. 50, no. 1, p. 38, 2022.

[17] A. Nguyen, H. N. Ngo, Y. Hong, B. Dang, and B.-P. T. Nguyen, "Ethical principles for artificial intelligence in education," *Education and Information Technologies*, vol. 28, no. 4, pp. 4221–4241, 2023.

[18] E. Prem, "From ethical AI frameworks to tools: A review of approaches," *AI and Ethics*, vol. 3, no. 3, pp. 699–716, 2023.

[19] M. Ryan and B. C. Stahl, "Artificial intelligence ethics guidelines for developers and users: Clarifying their content and normative implications," *Journal of Information, Communication and Ethics in Society*, vol. 19, no. 1, pp. 61–86, 2020.

[20] T. Hagendorff, "The ethics of AI ethics: An evaluation of guidelines," *Minds and Machines*, vol. 30, no. 1, pp. 99–120, 2020.

[21] D. Peters, K. Vold, D. Robinson, and R. A. Calvo, "Responsible AI—two frameworks for ethical design practice," *IEEE Transactions on Technology and Society*, vol. 1, no. 1, pp. 34–47, 2020.

[22] A. Jobin, M. Ienca, and E. Vayena, "The global landscape of AI ethics guidelines," *Nature Machine Intelligence*, vol. 1, no. 9, pp. 389–399, 2019.

[23] M. Coeckelbergh, "Time machines: Artificial intelligence, process, and narrative," *Philosophy & Technology*, vol. 34, no. 4, pp. 1623–1638, 2021.

[24] F. Tollon, *Oxford Handbook of Ethics of AI*. New York: JSTOR, 2021.

[25] V. Vakkuri, K.-K. Kemell, M. Jantunen, E. Halme, and P. Abrahamsson, "ECCOLA—a method for implementing ethically aligned AI systems," *Journal of Systems and Software*, vol. 182, p. 111067, 2021.

[26] W. Orr and J. L. Davis, "Attributions of ethical responsibility by artificial intelligence practitioners," *Information, Communication & Society*, vol. 23, no. 5, pp. 719–735, 2020.

[27] H. Losbichler and O. M. Lehner, "Limits of artificial intelligence in controlling and the ways forward: A call for future accounting research," *Journal of Applied Accounting Research*, vol. 22, no. 2, pp. 365–382, 2021.

[28] A. Miller, "The intrinsically linked future for human and artificial intelligence interaction," *Journal of Big Data*, vol. 6, no. 1, pp. 1–9, 2019.

[29] A. Guha, D. Grewal, P. K. Kopalle, *et al.*, "How artificial intelligence will affect the future of retailing," *Journal of Retailing*, vol. 97, no. 1, pp. 28–41, 2021.

[30] A. McStay, "Emotional AI, soft biometrics and the surveillance of emotional life: An unusual consensus on privacy," *Big Data & Society*, vol. 7, no. 1, p. 2053951720904386, 2020.

[31] G. A. Callanan, D. F. Perri, and S. M. Tomkowicz, "Targeting vulnerable populations: The ethical implications of data mining, automated prediction, and focused marketing," *Business and Society Review*, vol. 126, no. 2, pp. 155–167, 2021.

[32] K. Schwab, *The Fourth Industrial Revolution*. New York: Crown Currency, 2017.

[33] F. V. Giarmoleo, I. Ferrero, M. Rocchi, and M. Pellegrini, "What ethics can say on artificial intelligence: Insights from a systematic literature review," *Business and Society Review*, vol. 129, no. 2, pp. 258–292, 2024.

[34] S. Pichai. "AI at Google: Our Principles." 2018. https://blog.google/technology/ai/ai-principles/ (accessed 17/03/2024).

[35] IBM. "IBM's Principles for Trust and Transparency." 2024. https://www.ibm.com/policy/trust-transparency-new/ (accessed 17/03/2024).

[36] Microsoft. "Empowering Responsible AI Practices." 2024. https://www.microsoft.com/en-us/ai/responsible-ai (accessed 17/03/2024).

[37] European Commission. "Research and Innovation." 2024. https://commission.europa.eu/research-and-innovation_en (accessed 17/03/2024).

[38] L. Floridi, J. Cowls, M. Beltrametti, *et al.*, "AI4People—an ethical framework for a good AI society: Opportunities, risks, principles, and recommendations," *Minds and machines*, vol. 28, pp. 689–707, 2018.

[39] S. Larsson, M. Anneroth, A. Felländer, L. Felländer-Tsai, F. Heintz, and R. C. Ångström, "Sustainable AI: An inventory of the state of knowledge of ethical, social, and legal challenges related to artificial intelligence," 2019.

[40] European Commission, "Ethics guidelines for trustworthy AI," April 2019. https://digital-strategy.ec.europa.eu/en/library/ethics-guidelines-trustworthy-ai (accessed 18/3/2024)

[41] A. F. Winfield and M. Jirotka, "Ethical governance is essential to building trust in robotics and artificial intelligence systems," *Philosophical Transactions of the Royal Society A: Mathematical, Physical and Engineering Sciences*, vol. 376, no. 2133, p. 20180085, 2018.

[42] J. J. Bryson, "Patiency is not a virtue: The design of intelligent systems and systems of ethics," *Ethics and Information Technology*, vol. 20, no. 1, pp. 15–26, 2018.

[43] J. H. Moor, "The nature, importance, and difficulty of machine ethics," *IEEE Intelligent Systems*, vol. 21, no. 4, pp. 18–21, 2006.

[44] M. Taddeo and L. Floridi, "How AI can be a force for good," *Science*, vol. 361, no. 6404, pp. 751–752, 2018.

[45] J. Danaher, "Welcoming robots into the moral circle: A defence of ethical behaviourism," *Science and Engineering Ethics*, vol. 26, no. 4, pp. 2023–2049, 2020.

[46] D. J. Gunkel, "The other question: Can and should robots have rights?," *Ethics and Information Technology*, vol. 20, pp. 87–99, 2018.

[47] L. Floridi and M. Taddeo, "What is data ethics?," *Philosophical Transactions of the Royal Society A*, vol. 374, p. 20160360, 2016.
[48] H. Kissinger, "How the enlightenment ends," *The Atlantic*, 2018. Available at: https://www.theatlantic.com/magazine/archive/2018/06/henry-kissinger-ai-could-mean-the-end-of-human-history/559124/.
[49] C. O'Neil, *Weapons of Math Destruction: How Big Data Increases Inequality and Threatens Democracy*. New York: Crown, 2017.
[50] J. Donovan, R. Caplan, J. Matthews, and L. Hanson, "Algorithmic accountability: A primer," *Data & Society*, 2018. Available at: https://apo.org.au/node/142131.
[51] N. Diakopoulos, "Algorithmic accountability: Journalistic investigation of computational power structures," *Digital Journalism*, vol. 3, no. 3, pp. 398–415, 2015.
[52] M. Hildebrandt, *Smart Technologies and the End(s) of Law: Novel Entanglements of Law and Technology*. Cheltenham: Edward Elgar Publishing, 2015.
[53] H. Jonas, *The Imperative of Responsibility: In Search of an Ethics for the Technological Age*. Chicago, IL: University of Chicago Press, 1984.
[54] F. Howard-Snyder, "Doing vs. allowing harm," Edward N. Zalta (ed.), *Stanford Encyclopedia of Philosophy (Summer 2016 Edition)* 2016. http://plato.stanford.edu/archives/sum2016/entries/doing-allowing/ (accessed 06/06/2016).
[55] S. Graham and B. S. Lowery, "Priming unconscious racial stereotypes about adolescent offenders," *Law and Human Behavior*, vol. 28, pp. 483–504, 2004.
[56] D. Kahneman, *Thinking, Fast and Slow*. London: Macmillan, 2011.
[57] V. Eubanks, "Automating inequality: how high-tech tools profile, police, and punish the poor," 2018. Available at: https://www.cis.upenn.edu/~mkearns/teaching/ScienceDataEthics/files/lecture/presentations/Automating_Inequality.pdf.
[58] L. Ulbricht and K. Yeung, "Algorithmic regulation: A maturing concept for investigating regulation of and through algorithms," *Regulation & Governance*, vol. 16, no. 1, pp. 3–22, 2022.
[59] M. Whittaker, K. Crawford, R. Dobbe, *et al.*, "AI Now Report 2018," 2018. https://ainowinstitute.org/wp-content/uploads/2023/04/AI_Now_2018_Report.pdf (accessed 23/3/2024).
[60] A. Datta, M. C. Tschantz, and A. Datta, "Automated experiments on ad privacy settings: A tale of opacity, choice, and discrimination," *arXiv preprint arXiv:1408.6491*, 2014.
[61] J. Zhao, T. Wang, M. Yatskar, V. Ordonez, and K.-W. Chang, "Men also like shopping: Reducing gender bias amplification using corpus-level constraints," *arXiv preprint arXiv:1707.09457*, 2017.
[62] A. Campolo, M. R. Sanfilippo, M. Whittaker, and K. Crawford, "AI now 2017 report," 2017.
[63] T. Kliegr, Š. Bahník, and J. Fürnkranz, "A review of possible effects of cognitive biases on interpretation of rule-based machine learning models," *Artificial Intelligence*, vol. 295, p. 103458, 2021.

[64] "Lethal Autonomous Weapons Pledge," Future of light institute, 2018. Available at: https://futureoflife.org/open-letter/lethal-autonomous-weapons-pledge/. (22/3/2024).

[65] M. T. Bastos and D. Mercea, "The Brexit botnet and user-generated hyperpartisan news," *Social Science Computer Review*, vol. 37, no. 1, pp. 38–54, 2019.

[66] D. A. Broniatowski, A. M. Jamison, S. H. Qi, *et al.*, "Weaponized health communication: Twitter bots and Russian trolls amplify the vaccine debate," *American Journal of Public Health*, vol. 108, no. 10, pp. 1378–1384, 2018.

[67] S. Larsson, "Seven Shades of Transparency: On Artificial Intelligence and the Responsibility for the Social Impact of Digital Platforms," in *Platform Society: The Politics, Innovation, and Regulation of Digital Development*: London: Fores, 2018, pp. 277–313.

[68] B. Roessler, "X—privacy as a human right," in *Proceedings of the Aristotelian Society*, vol. 117, no. 2, pp. 187–206, 2017.

[69] C. J. Bennett and C. D. Raab, *The Governance of Privacy: Policy Instruments in Global Perspective*. Milton Park: Routledge, 2017.

[70] J. M. Abowd, "How will statistical agencies operate when all data are private?," *Journal of Privacy and Confidentiality*, vol. 7, no. 3, pp. 1–15, 2016.

[71] J. R. Searle, "Minds, brains, and programs," *Behavioral and Brain Sciences*, vol. 3, no. 3, pp. 417–424, 1980.

[72] D. J. Chalmers, "The singularity: A philosophical analysis," in O. U. Awret. (ed). *Science Fiction and Philosophy: From Time Travel to Superintelligence*, pp. 171–224, 2016.

[73] N. Bostrom, "Existential risk prevention as global priority," *Global Policy*, vol. 4, no. 1, pp. 15–31, 2013.

[74] I. J. Good, "Speculations concerning the first ultraintelligent machine," *Advances in Computers*, vol. 6, pp. 31–88, 1966.

[75] R. Brooks, *The Seven Deadly Sins of Predicting the Future of AI*. Rodney Brooks, 2017.

[76] S. Russell, *Human Compatible: AI and the Problem of Control*. London: Penguin, 2019.

[77] W. Wallach and P. Asaro, *Machine Ethics and Robot Ethics*. Milton Park: Routledge, 2020.

[78] W. J. Ripple, C. Wolf, T. M. Newsome, P. Barnard, and W. R. Moomaw, "World scientists' warning of a climate emergency," *BioScience*, vol. 70, no. 1, pp. 8–100, 2020.

[79] R. P. Allan, P. A. Arias, S. Berger, *et al.*, "Intergovernmental Panel on Climate Change (IPCC). Summary for Policymakers," in *Climate Change 2021: The Physical Science Basis. Contribution of Working Group I to the Sixth Assessment Report of the Intergovernmental Panel on Climate Change*: Cambridge: Cambridge University Press, 2023, pp. 3–32.

[80] P. Gailhofer, A. Herold, J. P. Schemmel, *et al.*, *The Role of Artificial Intelligence in the European Green Deal*. Luxembourg/Belgium: European Parliament, 2021.

[81] R. J. Michaels, *Energy Efficiency and Climate Policy: The Rebound Dilemma*. Washington, DC: Institute for Energy Research, 2012.

[82] P. E. Brockway, S. Sorrell, G. Semieniuk, M. K. Heun, and V. Court, "Energy efficiency and economy-wide rebound effects: A review of the evidence and its implications," *Renewable and Sustainable Energy Reviews*, vol. 141, p. 110781, 2021.

[83] D. Bruno and K. Crawford. "Atlas of AI: Power, politics, and the planetary costs of artificial intelligence," *Revista de Comunicação e Linguagens*, no. 55, Yale University Press, London, 2021.

[84] S. Hrastinski, A. D. Olofsson, C. Arkenback, *et al.*, "Critical imaginaries and reflections on artificial intelligence and robots in postdigital K-12 education," *Postdigital Science and Education*, vol. 1, pp. 427–445, 2019.

[85] B. C. Stahl and D. Wright, "Ethics and privacy in AI and big data: Implementing responsible research and innovation," *IEEE Security & Privacy*, vol. 16, no. 3, pp. 26–33, 2018.

[86] P. M. Regan and J. Jesse, "Ethical challenges of edtech, big data and personalized learning: Twenty-first century student sorting and tracking," *Ethics and Information Technology*, vol. 21, pp. 167–179, 2019.

[87] D. Remian, "Augmenting education: ethical considerations for incorporating artificial intelligence in education," *Instructional Design Capstones Collection*, vol. 52, 2019. Available at: https://scholarworks.umb.edu/instruction_capstone/52.

[88] R. F. Murphy, "Artificial intelligence applications to support K-12 teachers and teaching," *Rand Corporation*, vol. 10, pp. 1–20, 2019.

[89] L. Brownhill, S. Engel-Di Mauro, T. Giacomini, A. Isla, M. Löwy, and T. Turner, *The Routledge Handbook on Ecosocialism*. Oxon/New York: Routledge, 2022.

[90] P. Regan and V. Steeves, "Education, privacy and big data algorithms: Taking the persons out of personalized learning," *First Monday*, vol. 24, no. 11, 2019.

[91] M. Bulger, "Personalized learning: The conversations we're not having," *Data and Society*, vol. 22, no. 1, pp. 1–29, 2016.

[92] A. Alam, "Developing a curriculum for ethical and responsible AI: A university course on safety, fairness, privacy, and ethics to prepare next generation of AI professionals," *Intelligent Communication Technologies and Virtual Mobile Networks*: Singapore: Springer, 2023, pp. 879–894.

[93] D. Bertsimas, J. Dunn, G. C. Velmahos, and H. M. Kaafarani, "Surgical risk is not linear: Derivation and validation of a novel, user-friendly, and machine-learning-based predictive optimal trees in emergency surgery risk (POTTER) calculator," *Annals of Surgery*, vol. 268, no. 4, pp. 574–583, 2018.

[94] High-Level Expert Group on Artificial Intelligence. "Ethics Guidelines for Trustworthy AI," European Commission, April 2019.

[95] European Commission, "2030 Sustainable Development Goals." 2019. https://commission.europa.eu/strategy-and-policy/sustainable-development-goals_en (accessed 05/07/2025).

[96] T.-P. Liang, L. Robert, S. Sarker, *et al.*, "Artificial intelligence and robots in individuals' lives: How to align technological possibilities and ethical issues," *Internet Research*, vol. 31, no. 1, pp. 1–10, 2021.

[97] Y. You, J. Li, and L. Shen, "An effective Bayesian network parameters learning algorithm for autonomous mission decision-making under scarce data," *International Journal of Machine Learning and Cybernetics*, vol. 10, pp. 549–561, 2019.

[98] B. Srinivasan and K. Shah, "Towards a unified framework for developing ethical and practical Turing tests," *AI & Society*, vol. 34, pp. 145–152, 2019.

[99] S. A. Wright and A. E. Schultz, "The rising tide of artificial intelligence and business automation: Developing an ethical framework," *Business Horizons*, vol. 61, no. 6, pp. 823–832, 2018.

[100] S. Wasilow and J. B. Thorpe, "Artificial intelligence, robotics, ethics, and the military: A Canadian perspective," *AI Magazine*, vol. 40, no. 1, pp. 37–48, 2019.

Conclusion

Gautam Srivastava[1] *and Farhan Ullah*[2]

Explainable artificial intelligence (XAI) has the potential to transform the future of artificial intelligence by increasing transparency, trust, and accountability. As AI technologies continue to have an impact on numerous domains, XAI's ability to explain decision-making processes will be critical in reducing biases, enhancing compliance, and assuring ethical AI deployment. In cybersecurity, where the landscape is becoming increasingly complicated and dynamic, XAI can greatly increase threat detection, incident response, and resource optimization while also promoting trust and assisting with data privacy compliance. The cybersecurity sector can more effectively resolve evolving challenges and vulnerabilities by integrating XAI into cybersecurity applications. This book offers valuable insights into the use of XAI in cybersecurity, providing researchers, practitioners, and students with both practical and theoretical knowledge, ultimately contributing to the development of a safer, more transparent AI-driven future.

[1]Department of Mathematics and Computer Science, Brandon University, Canada
[2]Cybersecurity Center, Prince Mohammad Bin Fahd University, Saudi Arabia

Index

www.ingramcontent.com/pod-product-compliance
Lightning Source LLC
LaVergne TN
LVHW011835200926
848484LV00002B/358
* 9 7 8 1 8 3 7 2 4 0 3 1 9 *